"Lee Wengraf's *Extracting Profit* is at once historical and contemporary. It unpacks ongoing resource crimes by analytically exposing their historical roots and pointing to ways by which the oppressed can cut off the bonds that lock in their subjugation."

—Nnimmo Bassey, Director, Health of Mother Earth Foundation

"In recent years countries in the African continent have experienced an economic boom—but not all have benefited equally. *Extracting Profit* is a brilliant and timely analysis that explodes the myth of "Africa Rising," showing how neoliberal reforms have made the rich richer while leaving tens of millions of poor and working-class people behind. Lee Wengraf tells this story within the context of an imperial rivalry between the United States and China, two global superpowers that have expanded their economic and military presence across the continent. *Extracting Profit* is incisive, powerful, and necessary: if you read one book about the modern scramble for Africa and what it means for all of us, make it this one."

—Anand Gopal, author, *No Good Men Among the Living: America, the Taliban, and the War Through Afghan Eyes*

"*Extracting Profit* provides a great arch of scrutiny, from the earliest carve-up of the African continent through colonialism, war, and imperialism to the recent neoliberal takeover. The book demonstrates the continued importance of Marxist analysis on the continent, asserting the centrality of class and a project of revolutionary change. Wengraf provides us with a major contribution, one that highlights contemporary developments, including the role of China on the African continent, that have perplexed and baffled scholars. An indispensable volume."

—Leo Zeilig, author of *Frantz Fanon: The Militant Philosopher of Third World Revolution*

"The history of resource frontiers everywhere is always one of lethal violence, militarism, and empire amidst the house of capital accumulation. Lee Wengraf in *Extracting Profit* powerfully reveals the contours of Africa's twenty-first century version of this history. The scramble for resources, markets, and investments has congealed into a frightening militarization across the continent, creating and fueling the conditions for further political instability. Wengraf documents how expanded American, but also Chinese, presence—coupled with the War on Terror—point to both the enduring rivalry among global superpowers across the continent and a perfect storm of resource exploitation. Wengraf offers up a magisterial synopsis of the challenges confronting contemporary Africa."

—Michael Watts, University of California, Berkeley

"One of the most well-known stylized facts of Africa's recent growth experience is that it has been inequality-inducing in ways that previous growth spurts were not. Lee Wengraf, in her new book *Extracting Profit*, expertly utilizes the machinery of Marxian class analysis in making sense of this stylized fact. Along the way we learn much about Africa's historical relationship with imperialism and its contemporary manifestations. This book should be required reading for all those who care about Africa and its future."

—Grieve Chelwa, Contributing Editor, *Africa Is A Country*

"Thorough and thoughtful, Wengraf's book has a radical depth that underscores its significance. It's definitely a must-read for anyone who cherishes an advanced knowledge of the exploitation of Africa as well as the politics that undermine Africa's class freedom."

—Kunle Wizeman Ajayi, Convener, Youths Against Austerity and General Secretary of United Action for Democracy, Nigeria

"*Extracting Profit* is a very important book for understanding why the immense majority of the African population remains pauperized, despite impressive growth rates of mineral-rich countries on the continent. It continues the project of Walter Rodney's *How Europe Underdeveloped Africa*. And in several ways, it also goes beyond it, capturing the changing dynamics of global capitalism 45 years after Rodney's magnus opus.

"In this book, Lee Wengraf debunks the myth of 'Africa Rising' and the supposed expansion of an entrepreneurial middle class, revealing 'reforms' imposed by international financial institutions as mechanisms for fostering imperialism in an era of sharpening contradictions of the global capitalist economy. The adverse social, economic, political, and environmental impacts of these are elaborated on as a systemic whole, through the book's examination of the sinews of capital's expansion in the region: the extractive industries.

"But Wengraf does not stop at interrogating the underdevelopment of Africa. Her book identifies a major reason for the failures of national liberation projects: while the working masses were mobilized to fight against colonial domination, the leadership of these movements lay in the hands of aspiring capitalists and intellectuals. The urgency of the need for a strategy for workers' power internationally, she stresses correctly, cannot be overemphasized.

Reading *Extracting Profit* would be exceedingly beneficial for any change-seeking activist in the labor movement within and beyond Africa."

—Baba Aye, editor, *Socialist Worker* (Nigeria)

Extracting Profit

Imperialism, Neoliberalism, and the New Scramble for Africa

Lee Wengraf

Haymarket Books
Chicago, Illinois

Published in 2018 by
Haymarket Books
P.O. Box 180165
Chicago, IL 60618
773-583-7884
www.haymarketbooks.org
info@haymarketbooks.org

ISBN: 978-1-60846-851-5

Trade distribution:
In the US, Consortium Book Sales and Distribution, www.cbsd.com
In Canada, Publishers Group Canada, www.pgcbooks.ca
In the UK, Turnaround Publisher Services, www.turnaround-uk.com
All other countries, Ingram Publisher Services International, IPS_Intlsales@
ingramcontent.com

This book was published with the generous support of Lannan Foundation
and Wallace Action Fund.

Cover photo © 2004, Ed Kashi, shows an oil spill from an abandoned Shell
Petroleum Development Company well in Oloibiri, Niger Delta. Wellhead 14
was closed in 1977 but had been leaking for years, and in June 2004 it finally
released an oil spill of over 20,000 barrels of crude. Workers subcontracted by
Shell Oil Company clean it up.

Printed in Canada by union labor.

Library of Congress Cataloging-in-Publication data is available.

10 9 8 7 6 5 4 3 2 1

Contents

Acknowledgments

This book is the product of a decade's research and writing. Many people provided invaluable help during that time, for which I am very grateful.

Paul D'Amato and David Whitehouse worked with me from the very start to develop key ideas that became the framework for this book. *Extracting Profit* would not have been written without their input and collaboration.

Anthony Arnove at Haymarket welcomed this project from the start and offered resources and support at critical times, including nudging me across the finish line. I am very appreciative of all he's done. Nisha Bolsey gets huge thanks for shepherding the manuscript through all the necessary steps, with meticulous attention to detail and lots of encouragement throughout. Kristie Reilly did a wonderful job with copyediting—the book benefited immensely from her input. Thanks also to the team at Haymarket: Rory Fanning, Julie Fain, and Jim Plank.

Lance Selfa was my amazing editor. He gave the manuscript multiple reads and offered suggestions and key insights that made all the difference for the end result. Many, many thanks. Leo Zeilig, Annie Zirin, Andy Wynne, and Geoff Bailey also provided invaluable advice on the book draft. Again, thanks so much.

I benefited hugely from the editorial input and resources from a host of individuals and organizations. Reporting and analysis from Pambazuka News were invaluable for this book, and I'm very appreciative of the opportunity to publish my own work there as well. Many thanks also to Alan Maass and everyone at *Socialist Worker*, Paul D'Amato and team at the *International Socialist Review*, and Leo Zeilig at ROAPE.net.

Likewise, the following people provided interviews, gave feedback on articles and presentations that became sections of the book, or made critical suggestions on sources and chapter drafts: Kunle Wizeman Ajayi, Aaron Amaral, Baba Aye, Dave Bodamer, Patrick Bond, Todd Chretien, Rehad Desai, Glen Ford, Phil Gasper, Jim Nichols, Danny Katch, Sarah Knopp, Deepa Kumar, Amy Muldoon, Ahmed Shawki, Ashley Smith, Lee Sustar, Matt Swagler, Nick Turse, and Michael Watts.

Dorian Bon played a crucial role with research assistance and number crunching, especially with important data on the Chinese economy and US oil sources.

Many thanks to Aarón Martel and Khury Petersen-Smith for the original map they created for this book on current US military installations in Africa, an important record of expanded intervention on the continent.

Stewart Smith's *US Neocolonialism in Africa* (Moscow: Progress Publishers, 1974) was a treasure trove of primary sources on Africa and the Cold War era. My appreciation to Danya Abt for sharing her fascinating film *Quel Souvenir* on the Chad-Cameroon pipeline. And thanks also to Robby Karran and the *Democracy Now!* archives and library.

Thanks to Ed Kashi for his beautiful cover photo. Thanks also to Robby Karan and Claire Wengraf for the photo.

My writing comrades Megan Behrent, Danny Katch, and Amy Muldoon provided the necessary camaraderie and collaboration to making this book a reality. Big ups for everything.

This process was helped along in no small part by comrades and friends who provided input on the writing process, made sure I didn't skip meals, and just general good looking out, especially Lucy Herschel. Also: Tristin Adie, Avram Bornstein, Akua Gyamerah, Brian Jones, Donna Murch, Carole Ramsden, Jen Roesch, Lucy Smith, Sharon Smith, Keeanga-Yahmatta Taylor, Hadas Thier, Michael Ware, and Sherry Wolf.

Love and thanks to my mother, Claire Wengraf, my brother, John Wengraf, and the entire Wengraf-Simons clan: Adele Simons, Grange, and Cooper. And to my father, Richard Wengraf (1924–2005), who was with me in Cairo in 1977 the first time I was tear-gassed, whose copy of the Arusha Declaration I used for this book, and who taught me the importance of taking risks for social justice.

Chapter One

Introduction and Overview

The discovery of gold and silver in America, the extirpation, enslavement and entombment in mines of the aboriginal population, the turning of Africa into a commercial warren for the hunting of black skins signaled the rosy dawn of the era of capitalist production. These idyllic proceedings are the chief moments of primitive accumulation. On their heels treads the commercial war of the European nations, with the globe for a theatre.

—Karl Marx, *Capital*, Volume One[1]

Trade by force dating back centuries; slavery that uprooted and dispossessed around 12 million Africans; precious metals spirited away; the 19th century emergence of racist ideologies to justify colonialism; the . . . carve-up of Africa into dysfunctional territories in a Berlin negotiating room; the construction of settler-colonial and extractive-colonial systems—of which apartheid, the German occupation of Namibia, the Portuguese colonies and King Leopold's Belgian Congo were perhaps only the most blatant; . . . Cold War battlegrounds—proxies for US/USSR conflicts—filled with millions of corpses; other wars catalyzed by mineral searches and offshoot violence such as witnessed in blood diamonds and coltan; poacher-stripped swathes of East, Central and Southern Africa; . . . societies used as guinea pigs in the latest corporate pharmaceutical test; and the list could continue.

—Patrick Bond, *Looting Africa: The Economics of Exploitation*[2]

In July 2002, 600 Itsekiri women occupied Chevron's Escravos oil terminal in Nigeria's Delta State. For ten days, the occupiers held the

1

extraction site, demanding the oil corporation make good on promises for ecological and economic development: jobs, electrification of villages, and an environmental clean-up of polluted local fishing and farming communities. While billions in revenue accrued to the oil multinationals, Nigerians in oil-producing states lived under horrific conditions of oil spills and gas flares, without the most fundamental basic services.

On the heels of the Escravos action, Ijaw women took over four pipelines feeding into the terminal. Operations ground to a halt. "The rivers they are polluting is our life and death," declared Ilaje protester Bmipe Ebi. "We depend on it for everything. . . . When this situation is unbearable, we decided to come together to protest. . . . Our common enemies are the oil companies and their backers."[3]

It was a summer of struggle in the Niger Delta: thousands of women in total took over eight oil facilities owned by Chevron/Texaco and Shell Petroleum. Delta region advocate and author Sokari Ekine describes the unprecedented mobilizations:

> One of the strategies used by both the multinational oil companies and successive Nigerian governments has been to deliberately exploit existing tensions between the various ethnic nationalities in the region and to encourage antagonisms between youth and women, elders and youth, and elders and women in towns and villages. Therefore, the importance of the solidarity between women in this instance is indeed major.[4]

Protests and occupations by women from Delta communities have continued to the present day. Likewise, Chevron and its long-standing record of devastation, exploitation, and betrayal remain in the sight lines of communities of resistance: in August 2016, the Escravos site was once again targeted by activists who launched a sit-in at the company gates, demanding promised jobs. They were met by Nigerian Army troops called out to disperse them.[5]

The deeper problems of conditions in the region are not so easily dispersed. From Escravos and beyond, the Niger Delta can be viewed as embodying the contradictions of extraction on the continent. Many African economies rely heavily on natural resources and raw materials—with a relatively new rush by multinationals for oil, gold, platinum, industrial metals, and more, producing in the twenty-first century levels of economic growth and investment not seen on the continent in decades. Yet this exploitation has enriched only a tiny handful: investors, African elites, and international capital. The recent "scramble for

Africa"—its class contradictions, environmental devastation, and the resistance it has produced—is only the latest chapter.

◆

The scramble for Africa's wealth has a long and sordid history. From the era of slavery through colonialism and post-independence, the exploitation of the continent by the West has been accompanied by economic stagnation, poverty, war, and disease for millions. As Walter Rodney famously described in *How Europe Underdeveloped Africa* (1972), from its earliest days, the slave trade, colonial "encounter," industrial boom, and the rise of imperialism have combined to produce exploitation and inequality on a mass scale. "The operation of the imperialist system," Rodney wrote, "bears major responsibility for African economic retardation by draining African wealth and by making it impossible to develop more rapidly the resources of the continent."[6]

This history is by no means a distant chapter in the relationship between Africa and the West. The exploitation of Africa has continued into the recent neoliberal era. By *neoliberalism*, I mean the period of global capitalist restructuring launched by Western ruling classes as an attempt to restore corporate profitability following the economic crisis of the 1970s. Beginning under US President Ronald Reagan and British Prime Minister Margaret Thatcher, neoliberalism is marked by dismantling barriers to corporate globalization and accumulation, such as imposing free-trade agreements, austerity, and attacks on unions. Likewise, the current phase of imperialism has its roots in past eras; by *imperialism*, I mean the tendency for economic competition between nations to produce conflicts across borders—both economically, such as trade wars, as well as outright military conflict. Yet while the influences of this history continue to be felt on "Africa's economic retardation," as Rodney put it, the past likewise does not merely repeat itself. The current phase of imperialism—with critical roles played by both China and the United States—has a different dynamic than the colonial, post-independence, or Cold War eras.

The historical roots of the current period will be discussed in the pages ahead. To summarize briefly here, the division of Africa's "spoils" by colonial powers at the Berlin conference of 1885 formalized carving up virtually the entire continent. Whether through direct or indirect rule, African economies and societies were transformed to expand profits and markets for Western capitalism. These chains were finally broken three-quarters of a century after Berlin: the postwar struggles for independence saw European powers driven from the continent in revolutionary upheavals beginning in the 1950s and extending up until the 1970s. The promise of these movements and the birth of new nations in Africa brought a new generation of African rulers to power at the hands of mass movements of African workers, peasants, and students, who inspired and contributed to movements for liberation across the globe.[7]

In the immediate post-independence era, African states became weak pawns in the world economy—subject to Cold War rivalries, their path to development largely blocked by a debilitating colonial past and an unfortunate set of largely external economic circumstances. The era of neoliberalism was birthed in the global recession of the 1970s, when many so-called "Third World"[8] nations, including those in Africa, were compelled to turn to loans from Western financial institutions, such as the International Monetary Fund (IMF) and the World Bank. An onerous debt regime forced many nations to pay more in interest on debts to the World Bank and the IMF than on health care, education, infrastructure, and other vital services combined. Debt repayment was accompanied by the imposition of structural adjustment "reforms": privatization, deregulation, and the removal of trade barriers to foreign investors. Harsh austerity and deindustrialization produced a sharp decline in living conditions, while new nations were saddled with insurmountable levels of debt.

Much has been written about the past decade's so-called boom in Africa—one characterized by high primary commodity prices that have driven unprecedented growth rates in the new millennium, even (relatively speaking) during the 2008–2009 recession. Today, Western multinationals and African elites have accumulated vast profits from their investments. The value of fuel and mineral exports from Africa has reached into the hundreds of billions, exceeding the aid that flows into the continent. Surplus appropriation—that is, the value accruing to capitalists via the exploitation of labor and natural resources—reverberates across Africa, producing huge wealth while millions live in the worst poverty found on earth. The business press has championed the most recent "scramble," from oil and mining to massive land grabs for agribusiness development.

Yet there is nothing new about a scramble for Africa's natural resources. This twenty-first-century boom has appropriately been described as a "new scramble" for Africa in the media and academic accounts alike. This reference evokes the remarkably similar nineteenth-century scramble for Africa—typically understood as the period from the partitioning at Berlin to World War I—and the colonial rush at breakneck speed to claim the continent's raw materials. The so-called new scramble, over a century on, is similarly an era of competition and a drive to profit from the exploitation of Africa's valuable oil and minerals.

Case studies such as *Where Vultures Feast: Shell, Human Rights and Oil* (2003) by Ike Okonta and Oronto Douglas have documented the current plunder. Academic studies such as Padraig Carmody's *The New Scramble for Africa* (2011) and Roger Southall and Henning Melber's *A New Scramble for Africa? Imperialism, Investment and Development* (2009) provide important analyses of the resource issues in Africa today. Geographer Michael Watts has produced numerous invaluable works on the long history and dirty politics of Africa's resource wars and today's "oil insurgency," along with a damning indictment of flawed notions of a "resource curse." Journalistic accounts such as those from John Ghazvinian (2007), Nicholas Shaxson (2008), Celeste Hicks (2015), and Tom Burgis (2015) have explored similar terrain, with first-hand reporting from the frontlines of the new economy. Finally, the environmental advocacy and writings of activists like Nnimmo Bassey—as in his brilliant *To Cook a Continent: Destructive Extraction and the Climate Crisis in Africa* (2012)—elaborate on the challenges posed for the left in confronting multinational-driven devastation. Meanwhile, investigators such as Khadija Sharife and the Tax Justice Network Africa have shone a much-needed spotlight on the machinations and illegal practices that have facilitated the accumulation of profits in the extractive industries to soaring new heights.

China's key role in Africa has evolved rapidly since the turn of the millennium. The boom in China's economy has spurred a drive for new sources of energy as well as new markets, and a host of African nations have emerged as allies. Now Africa's largest trading partner, China has a footprint that can be found across large swaths of the continent. Important reports such as *African Perspectives on China in Africa* (Fahamu Books and Pambazuka Press, 2007) anticipated the growing closeness between the Chinese government and various African nations, including the major oil producers on the continent, such as Angola, and those with large deposits of valuable minerals, such as Zambia. More recent accounts, such as Howard French's *China's Second Continent: How a Million Migrants Are Building a New Empire in Africa* (2014),[9] along with writings by Deborah Brautigam,[10] have painted the picture of the transformed relationship between these regions and the dramatic changes for ordinary Africans with new Chinese immigration and investment.

China's expanded presence in Africa highlights its global rivalry with the United States and has accentuated imperial competition between the major powers. As the US Department of Defense states in a critical strategy document:

> In order to credibly deter potential adversaries and to prevent them from achieving their objectives, the United States must maintain its ability to project power in areas in which our access and freedom to operate are challenged. . . . States such as China . . . will continue to pursue asymmetric means to counter our power projection capabilities.[11]

Twenty-first century wars and military expansion thus characterize a new imperial phase of economic volatility and political instability. Heightened competition—with China, above all, but also with the European Union and "emerging" nations—over control of resources, especially oil, along with the drive for "energy security," have produced a wider global militarization that now encompasses sub-Saharan Africa. The United States has approached this environment of heightened competition with an eye toward protecting its strategic interests, deploying military might alongside aggressive economic and trade policy to do so. Former US President George W. Bush created the African military command known as AFRICOM in 2007 as means of containing its competitors and projecting US power on the continent (see chapter 7 for more on this period).

A decade later, military "involvement" on the continent shows no signs of abating. The Obama administration widened these activities to include new military outposts, drone warfare, logistics infrastructure, and a heightened "war on terror." Intrepid investigative reporting by US journalists Nick Turse, Jeremy Scahill, and the *Washington Post*'s Craig Whitlock have made key contributions to our understanding of a vastly more militarized continent in the age of AFRICOM. As Turse has written, the US military now has a presence in virtually every country on the continent.[12] By the midpoint of the 2010s, a sharp downward turn of the Chinese economy, along with a crash in commodities prices, has once again subjected African—and global—economies to the "boom and bust" vacillations of capitalism. Today's intensified militarism in Africa only raises the prospects for economic crises to take a military form, where capitalists increasingly turn to the armed power of "their" states to secure access to markets, territories, and control of natural resources, especially oil. The deep crisis in the neighboring Middle East poses dangers for imperial powers with the spread of that instability into Africa. In addition, that increased instability undermines the geostrategic "usefulness" of the African continent for the United States, in particular to project its power into the

Middle East. All told, imperial expansion and its contradictions have made Africa—and the world—a vastly more dangerous place.

Finally, militarization, neoliberal structural adjustment, and the boom in investment and extraction—accompanied by an increase in productivity and exploitation—have been met by resistance across the continent. From the explosive strikes and protests against debt crisis created by the IMF and World Bank in the 1980s to pro-democracy struggles and mobilizations against cuts to social services in urban areas and land grabs in the rural countryside, the organizing of workers and ordinary people across the continent has indicated that the new African boom will not unfold without challenges from below. As Firoze Manji and Sokari Ekine describe in *African Awakening: The Emerging Revolutions* (2011), the processes of rebellion and revolution in North Africa and the Middle East during the Arab Spring were by no means separate from the dynamics of struggle throughout the rest of Africa, and in fact were accompanied by struggle throughout the continent. And as Leo Zeilig, Trevor Ngwame, Peter Dwyer, and others have described, the long history of trade union struggle and social movements have produced critical lessons and important continuities for resistance today.

Myths and Realities of African "Underdevelopment"

Running through the history of African exploitation, from the age of slavery onward, are a host of racist theoretical and ideological explanations and justifications for the continent's subjugation. In the post-independence era, new African nations saw initial growth in the first decades, then a plunge into sharp crisis and a contraction of growth, particularly in contrast to other "emerging" regions of the world. As Thandika Mkandawire and Charles Soludo describe, "By the early 1980s, . . . African and Latin American countries were abruptly frozen out of international financial markets. . . . Explaining the African crisis has become a veritable industry."[13] The so-called "East Asian tigers," for example, experienced industrial expansion and spectacular growth rates in the 1980s and 1990s. African nations, who fell largely outside of this global economic growth, inspired a raft of explanations for these conditions and accompanying political instability, as well as distorted assumptions for the persistence of African poverty and volatility intended to "explain" development and trade policy, foreign relations, investment strategies, and even outright military intervention. In actuality, I would argue, these are mythical explanations, theorized and propagated by "development" experts, global leaders, and public officials alike—unwittingly or otherwise—in the service of maintaining and deepening inequality. These myths include the following:

- *African poverty is an inevitable, inescapable feature of African states themselves.* In this view, poverty and crisis are permanent features of African governance and policy failures. Mkandawire and Soludo have characterized this approach:

  > Championed largely by Africanists based in North American universities and immediately embraced by the World Bank as it developed its political-economic analysis of African policy-making, this view takes as its starting point the claim that the postcolonial African state, by its very nature and definition, is at the heart of the economic and governance crises pervading the continent. This state, stripped of the most basic checks and balances of the (late) colonial period, has failed signally in its developmental mission.[14]

- *Any debt owed by the West has been paid in full and must be put behind us.* More recent policy narratives on the legacy of colonialism tend to accept this assumption. Figures such as former British Prime Minister Gordon Brown have unapologetically declared that "the days of Britain having to apologize for its colonial history are over. We should celebrate much of our past rather than apologize for it."[15] In actuality, African poverty is rooted in the global relations of postcolonial states burdened by the legacy of colonialism and neoliberal policy, policies embraced today by the world's ruling classes, including African ones. The latest iterations of such "blame-the-victim" foreign policy approaches aim to paper over that stark reality.

- *Africa is "cursed" by natural resources.* In sharp contrast to "advanced," resource-rich nations—especially those replete with large oil supplies like Norway, Canada, and the United States—African nations ostensibly have not been able to escape the "resource trap" of chronic underdevelopment, corrupt rulers, and bloated extractive sectors. Paul Collier, Jeffrey Sachs, and Joseph Stieglitz are among the most prominent proponents of such analyses, which are anchored in an assumption of the supposed omnipotent power of oil and other natural resources to create societies permanently mired in corruption and theft. Michael Watts has provided valuable and extensive critiques of these approaches. In a review of Collier's widely read *The Bottom Billion* (2007), he describes how the book speaks to a wider interest taken by economists (and political scientists) in what seems like a challenge to economic orthodoxy: namely that resources wealth (as a source of comparative advantage) turns out to be a "curse": . . . whether emphasizing poor economic performance, state failure (oil breeds corruption) or [the idea that] "resource rents make democracy malfunction."[16]

Yet as Watts and others have pointed out, these ahistorical explanations overlook the structural roots and the distorting impact of the extractive industries and capitalist global relations more broadly.

- *African nations are ungovernable, dominated by failed states, and trapped by an unrelenting propensity for war and violence.* As with the "resource curse," African states are doomed to a "conflict trap" (again, see Collier's *The Bottom Billion*). This curse ostensibly produces the "democracy deficit" characteristic of authoritarian rule, inevitably spilling over into civil war. Such a view is perpetuated by decontextualized media portrayals of African war and violence as commonplace. Mahmood Mamdani has pointed out the racist assumptions in such a view, and how

  the same media that downplays the specificity of each African war is often interested in covering only war, thereby continually misrepresenting the African continent. Without regard to context, war is presented as the camera sees it, as a contest between brutes. No wonder those who rely on the media for their knowledge of Africa come to think of Africans as peculiarly given to fighting over no discernible issue.[17]

- *Ordinary Africans are merely passive victims of authoritarian African rulers or fueled by the conflicts of "age-old" ethnic divides.* Such myths of African rulers and citizens as rooted in primordial violence create a dangerous justification in an imperial context. As a result, ostensibly only "international" (i.e., Western) intervention—of the "watchdog," "humanitarian," or direct military kind—can "save" the continent from inevitable bloodshed.

- *Mass unemployment and crisis make resistance in Africa futile.* Whether due to widespread poverty and the explosion of urban slums, the weight of dictatorship, neoliberal assault on workers, or the presence of foreign labor and capital-intensive industry, these factors have rendered political organization and sustained resistance nearly impossible. These arguments have cropped up on the left from critics of corporate globalization and imperial intervention in Africa; see, for example, Mike Davis's *Planet of Slums*. Certainly these social and economic conditions do exist, and those building working-class movements in Africa have long engaged with these political questions, just as the left elsewhere across the globe must confront challenges to building movements and organization in an era dominated by assaults from ruling classes worldwide. However, a view that sees those struggles as doomed is decidedly mistaken. The long tradition of class struggle and resistance, and the radical theoretical currents in Africa, show conclusively that such a view is unfounded.

Broadly speaking, these myths lead in two directions, yet both distort the legacies of colonial and capitalist domination in Africa, not to mention the prospects for resistance. These themes will be discussed throughout the chapters ahead. Generally, these distortions produce, on the one hand, explanations that situate Africa permanently *outside* the systems of global capitalism. As mentioned above, in these ahistorical approaches—such as the "resource curse" idea—Africa is governed solely by nonmarket forces, rules of governance and warfare that lead inevitably to conflict, corruption, and poverty. On the other hand, a range of theories, including some from the left, assume that African societies are merely cogs in a global machine. Such forces vary from urbanization to trade policy and many more. For example, the well-known dependency theorists Andre Gunder Frank, Immanuel Wallerstein, and others have tended to see Africa's economies as locked in a world system, part of a "one-way" conveyer belt of unequal exchange between its centers and peripheries. These views tend to conclude African societies are subject to worldwide forces but lack the potential for resistance and change.

Confronting these myths are the actual roots of environmental devastation, crippling rates of poverty, unemployment, and war. Africa remains a continent abundant in human and natural resources, but these conditions have managed to enrich only a handful of African rulers and foreign capitalists. Still, the "stubborn reality" of long-standing traditions of struggle and resistance among ordinary Africans challenges assumptions of the futility of change.

The Marxist Approach

Debunking these mythical explanations about African "development" requires a dynamic theory that describes past and present conditions in systemic terms of capitalism, imperialism, and class. I use the insights of classical Marxism, developed over the last 150 years, to understand Africa today. This book draws on the ideas of what is called the classical Marxist tradition—namely Karl Marx, V. I. Lenin, Rosa Luxemburg, and Leon Trotsky—to argue that today's African political economy is profoundly shaped by its colonial roots as well as the contemporary forces of neoliberalism and imperialism.

Marxism is invaluable in several respects, and the chapters that follow will focus on three important elements of the theory. First, Marxism provides a framework for understanding conditions in African societies as part of a systemic whole. The historical development of capitalism is that of a global system where the growth of wealth is invested in human labor and the means of production, and where that wealth has been transformed into capital. In Africa, although the slave trade and other commodity trading were crucial engines of growth for the colonial powers, it wasn't until the late eighteenth and especially the nineteenth centuries that capitalism as a dominant economic system emerged.

The rise of these new relations as part of a world system of production and exchange—how capitalism's spread transformed social and economic relationships in totality—was best described by Marx. In a well-known passage in *The Communist Manifesto* (1848), Marx and his collaborator Friedrich Engels wrote:

> The need of a constantly expanding market for its products chases the bourgeoisie over the entire surface of the globe. It must nestle everywhere, settle everywhere, establish connections everywhere. . . . In place of the old wants, satisfied by the production of the country, we find new wants, requiring for their satisfaction the products of distant lands and climes. In place of the old local and national seclusion and self-sufficiency, we have intercourse in every direction, universal inter-dependence of nations.[18]

The chapters ahead contend that African poverty, inequality, and crisis are inextricable from the globalizing dynamic Marx and Engels describe. Past and present, the relations of capitalist production and the "need of a constantly expanding market" bind nations together in a unified system. Unlike the myths that African poverty, corruption, and war are rooted in African "causes" alone, Marxism's focus on the totality of social relations emphasizes their connections across "the entire surface of the globe." Further, Marxism's internationalism—rooted in revolutionary working-class struggle—links resistance to capitalism across the continent and worldwide.

Second, Marxists argue that this expansive and competitive system produces deep contradictions worldwide, with its tendencies toward economic crisis spilling over into military conflict and imperial war. Marx devoted significant attention to the process of class formation within the capitalist powers themselves, both the struggles between sections of old and new ruling classes over the course of industrialization, as well as the emergence of a new class of proletariat, meaning the modern working class. Because of the competitive nature of that development, the earliest powers on the scene—namely Britain—were hegemonic and could set the terms of territorial control over colonies abroad as well as the strategic advantage of access to raw materials and markets for the remaining European powers. Equally, Britain's dominance over trade solidified the development of a strong state able to back up the growth of capital through control of the new working class, the development of a military, an educational system, and so on. The growth of the British state produced a race among the other European powers also seeking to protect their "own" nation's capitalists. Thus, capitalist development produced conflicts over its further accumulation and control abroad.

While Marx did examine the workings of foreign trade as well as the connections between conquest and profit, he made no systematic theoretical treatment of the topic. The twentieth-century revolutionaries Lenin and Luxemburg built on Marx's analysis of the dynamics of capitalism to describe colonialism, imperialism, and the motor by which capitalism tends to expand beyond the confines of a single state or national borders. By the second half of the nineteenth century, European powers were in increasingly sharp competition for an ever-increasing need for markets for their goods and for capital investment. The nineteenth-century scramble for Africa grew out of the struggle with newer European powers, who grabbed what natural resources they could from Africa on the cheap to sustain the growth of industry at home. The classical Marxist theorists on imperialism of the early twentieth century—from Lenin[19] and Luxemburg,[20] along with Bukharin,[21] Hilferding,[22] and others—aimed to extend Marx's theory of the inherently competitive nature of capitalism to explain the massive expansion of the system both at home and abroad, along with growing evidence of higher levels of integration and conflict between capitalists as well as their national states. Luxemburg captured the growing imperial tensions well:

> On the international stage, then, capital must take appropriate measures. With the high development of the capitalist countries and their increasingly severe competition in acquiring non-capitalist areas, imperialism grows in lawlessness and violence, both in aggression against the non-capitalist world and in ever more serious conflicts among the competing capitalist countries.[23]

Her *Accumulation of Capital* anchors the potential for capital expansion *outside* of the boundaries of its own system into the "non-capitalist"—meaning colonized—world. Geographer David Harvey describes her approach as follows:

[Luxemburg] concludes that trade with non-capitalist social formations provides the only systematic way to stabilize the system. If those social formations or territories are reluctant to trade then they must be compelled to do so by force of arms (as happened with the opium wars in China). This is, in her view, the heart of what imperialism is about. One possible corollary of this argument (though Luxemburg does not state it directly) is that, if this system is to last any length of time, the non-capitalist territories must be kept (forcibly if necessary) in a non-capitalist state. This could account for the fiercely repressive qualities of many of the colonial regimes developed during the latter half of the nineteenth century.[24]

Yet as history was to prove, capital accumulation does not require colonies, and, in fact, largely takes place *within and between* major powers. Thus, Luxemburg's analysis of the motor for expanded reproduction was fundamentally flawed. Bukharin correctly critiqued Luxemburg for a flawed characterization of imperialism as "the political expression of the accumulation of capital in its competitive struggle for what remains *still open of the non-capitalist environment*," saying she claimed "a fight for territories that have already become capitalist is not imperialism, which is utterly wrong."[25]

Notwithstanding these conclusions, Luxemburg's polemics within the Second International of socialist organizations during World War I and her devastating portrayal of the impact of imperialist violence on colonial societies have had a profound influence on Marxist thinking on imperialism and colonialism. Her ideas have shaped Harvey's writings, such as his notion of "accumulation by dispossession," as well as those focusing on the African context. For example, Patrick Bond, Horman Chitonge, and Arndt Hopfmann's edited volume *The Accumulation of Capital in Southern Africa: Rosa Luxemburg's Contemporary Relevance* pays tribute to the ways in which her theories inform both colonial dispossession and the continued looting of today.[26]

While a close collaborator in the revolutionary socialist movement of the time, Lenin took a different approach to imperialism. For him, the in-built contradictions of capitalist reproduction spilled over national borders, leading to rivalries, conflicts, even war. Lenin writes in "Imperialism: The Highest Stage of Capitalism":

> The tremendous "boom" in colonial conquests begins [after the 1870s], and . . . the struggle for the territorial division of the world becomes extraordinarily sharp. . . . The more capitalism is developed, the more strongly the shortage of raw materials is felt, the more intense the competition and the hunt for sources of raw materials throughout the whole world, the more desperate the struggle for the acquisition of colonies.[27]

Yet these contradictions also produced a tendency for competitors to consolidate—that is, a tendency toward monopoly. Because of this capacity for "concentration," Lenin described imperialism as the "highest stage of capitalism." For him, understanding the dynamics of imperialism—including the development of colonies—had to be anchored in an analysis of the competitive relationship between *the major capitalist powers*. Those competitive tendencies he describes, I would argue, also characterize imperialism throughout the past century. As against a mythical "conflict curse," competition between today's imperial powers—chiefly the United States and China—profoundly influence conditions in African nations today. Lenin's theory on imperialism is valuable for understanding the modern era and neoliberalism, the rising African ruling class, and the "new scramble" of the present day.

Third, the chapters that follow stress the importance of the Marxist theory of combined and uneven development. As Lenin describes, "the growth of internal exchange, and, particularly, of international exchange, is a characteristic feature of capitalism. The uneven and spasmodic development of individual enterprises, individual branches of industry and individual countries is inevitable under the capitalist system."[28] Given these conditions, Lenin argued that uneven levels of economic development both within nations and across the globe produced an in-built tendency toward imperial rivalry. From his perspective, according to Richard Day and Daniel Gaido's *Discovering Imperialism*, "the fact that uneven development occurred on a global scale meant that the shifting balance of military and economic power would inevitably lead to imperialist wars to re-divide the colonial possessions."[29] In other words, the *unevenness* of capitalist relations of production led inevitably to instability and conflict.[30] In addition, the advancement of capitalism *reverses* development across sections of society, both within and between the colonizing and colonized world. For, as Lenin wrote, "both uneven development and a semistarvation level of existence of the masses are fundamental and inevitable conditions and constitute premises of this mode of production."[31]

For Trotsky, the combined and uneven nature of capitalism produced both uneven relations of production and an international class "combined" yet distributed over a very uneven landscape and centers of accumulation. Trotsky's theory rested on the assumption that this unevenness was woven into the history of capitalism:

> The extraordinary unevenness in the rate of development during the various epochs serves as the *starting point* of capitalism. Capitalism gains mastery only gradually over the inherited unevenness, breaking and altering it,

employing therein its own means and methods. In contrast to the economic systems that preceded it, capitalism inherently and constantly aims at economic expansion, at the penetration of new territories, the surmounting of economic differences, the conversion of self-sufficient provincial and national economies into a system of financial interrelationships. Capitalism, however, operates by methods of *its own*, . . . by anarchistic methods which constantly undermine its own work, set one country against another, and one branch of industry against another, developing some parts of world economy while hampering and throwing back the development of others.[32]

These processes unfolded in Africa. Historically, capitalist relations of production expanded across the continent, "combining" with and developing more "advanced" sections in some areas while undermining economic and social relations in others. This reality turns the myth of the "inevitable poverty" of African nations on its head. African political economy today expresses these contradictory dynamics: an explosion in investment and the veneer of "development," intertwined with a reversal of economic growth and widening inequality.

The Importance of Walter Rodney

The Marxist ideas outlined above are recurring themes throughout the chapters that follow and provide a means to explain the persistent "underdevelopment" on the continent. As mentioned above, the ahistorical myths often used to describe conditions in Africa fall far short of showing the roots of today's poverty, inequality, corruption, and civil war. While a number of African economies have experienced a massive boom in wealth and investment over the past decade, many ordinary Africans live in dire poverty with diminished life expectancy and high unemployment and in societies with low levels of industry. In explaining the background to these conditions of "underdevelopment," one historical account stands alone in importance: Walter Rodney's *How Europe Underdeveloped Africa* (1972).

Walter Rodney was a scholar, working-class militant, and revolutionary from Guyana. While Rodney was influenced by Marxist ideas, he is especially viewed as central to the Pan-Africanist canon for many on the left, playing a key role in the development of revolutionary currents in his own time. In *How Europe Underdeveloped Africa*, Rodney situates himself in several theoretical traditions: the writings of Caribbean revolutionary Frantz Fanon, the dependency theories of Frank and others, the Pan-Africanist tradition including George Padmore and C. L. R. James, and African socialism as popularized by national leaders such as Tanzania's Julius Nyere and Guinea's Sekou Toure.

As Horace Campbell describes, "His numerous writings on the subjects of socialism, imperialism, working-class struggles and Pan Africanism and slavery contributed to a body of knowledge that came to be known as the Dar es Salaam school of thought. Issa Shivji, Mahmood Mamdani, Claude Ake, Archie Mafeje, Yash Tandon, John Saul, Dan Nabudere, O Nnoli, Clive Thomas, and countless others participated in the debates on transformation and liberation."[33] Rodney's scholarship and leadership in the working-class movement thus had a long reach, including within the revolutionary movement in his native Guyana. He was assassinated in 1980, likely by agents of the Guyanese government. The Nigerian novelist Wole Soyinka, in noting Rodney's legacy, wrote how "Walter Rodney was no captive intellectual playing to the gallery of local or international radicalism. He was clearly one of the most solidly ideologically situated intellectuals ever to look colonialism and exploitation in the eye and where necessary, spit in it."[34]

Rodney's work has assumed a foundational place in understanding the legacies of slavery and colonialism for the underdevelopment that unfolded, over centuries, on the continent. The core of his analysis rests on the assumption that Africa—far from standing outside the world system—has been crucial to the growth of capitalism in the West. What he terms "underdevelopment" was in fact the product of centuries of slavery, exploitation, and imperialism. Rodney conclusively shows that "Europe"—that is, colonial and imperial powers—did not merely enrich its own empire but actually *reversed* economic and social development in Africa. Thus, in his extensive account of African history from the early African empires through to the modern day, Rodney shows how the West built immense industrial and colonial empires on the backs of African slave labor, devastating natural resources and African societies in the process. A key aspect of his project is breaking apart any ideological justification for the ongoing interference of these foreign powers, including claims made for expanding Western domination in the interests of African peoples. As he emphasizes throughout his book, "it would be an act of the most brazen fraud to weigh the social amenities provided during the colonial epoch against the exploitation, and to arrive at the conclusion that the good outweighed the bad."[35]

For Rodney, underdevelopment is a condition historically produced through capitalist expansion and imperialism, and very clearly *not* an intrinsic property of Africa itself. He thus situates underdevelopment within the contradictory process of capitalism, one that both creates value and wealth for the exploiters while immiserating the exploited. Rodney writes:

The peasants and workers of Europe (and eventually the inhabitants of the whole world) paid a huge price so that the capitalists could make their profit from the human labor that always lies behind the machines. . . . There was a period when the capitalist system increased the well-being of significant numbers of people as a by-product of seeking out profits for a few, but today the quest for profits comes into sharp conflict with people's demands that their material and social needs should be fulfilled.[36]

And so, argues Rodney, not only did the expansion of capitalist trade—especially the slave trade—as well as production threaten the ability to meet human need, but these relationships actually undermined development of African societies overall. In Rodney's view, Africa's level of development up through the fifteenth century was somewhat comparable to Europe's. State-building prior to the start of the slave trade was well underway, with a number of African societies transitioning from types of subsistence economies to those with some degree of class stratification.

As Rodney describes, African trade was central to Europe's growth, most importantly through the slave trade from approximately 1445 to 1870, transforming Africa into a source of human raw material for the new colonies in North America and the Caribbean. Some 275,000 slaves were brought to America and Europe between 1450 and 1600. But in the seventeenth century, in response to the expansion of sugar cane cultivation in the Caribbean, the number jumped to 1.3 million. And although Britain outlawed the slave trade in 1807, the bulk of it—80 percent—took place between 1700 and 1850. All told, a very conservative estimate puts the total number of slaves who made it to the New World at around ten million people.

The period of slavery was fraught with competition for territorial control over trade routes. African kingdoms also developed alongside of key trading areas in West Africa as they intensified their own role in the slave trade, such as the Oyo kingdom in what was called the Slave Coast—where Benin is today—and the Asante kingdom in the Gold Coast, today's Ghana. But it was to the three major powers involved in the slave trade—Britain, France, and Portugal—that massive profits accrued. Trade with Africa was closely tied up with the growth of European port cities such as England's Liverpool, with the exchange of slaves for cheap industrial goods established as the primary motor for profits of European firms. Drawing on the work of Eric Williams's classic *Capitalism and Slavery* (1944), among others, Rodney concludes that the slave trade provided England with the capital for the Industrial Revolution to take off, and by the eighteenth century, exports to European markets had exploded. Ultimately, the slave trade provided Britain with the dominant edge over its rivals.

But Rodney, crucially, not only elaborates on the vast wealth accumulated by Europe through the slave trade, but shows conclusively the thwarting of African societies in the process of capital expansion. First and foremost, for Rodney, was the lost labor potential due to the slave trade.[37] From its economic foundation in slavery, the range of exports from Africa likewise narrowed to focus on just a few commodities, while imports were typically in the form of nonproductive luxury items and weapons; neither process led to the development of productive capacity in Africa itself. The nature of trade relations meant that technological development stagnated, creating a barrier to innovation within Africa itself, even in regions not directly engaged in the slave trade, because of the distorting influence on relations overall.[38] The result, concludes Rodney, was "a loss of development *opportunity*, and this is of the greatest importance. . . . The lines of economic activity attached to foreign trade were either destructive, as slavery was, or at best purely extractive."[39]

Against this historical backdrop, the nineteenth century "race for Africa" began. Beginning in the mid- to late-1800s, European "explorers" sought trade concessions from African chiefs for access to copper, gold, cotton, palm oil, rubber, and tin, among other materials. Trade in this era ran along lines parallel to the slave trade and transformed old slave centers into new centers for goods like gold, ivory, and palm oil. But by the 1870s, recession had set in: the rate of profit had fallen in Europe, markets were depressed, and European traders—as well as African producers—were hit hard by the fall of commodities prices, while imperial rivalries intensified. Britain's technological advances were being overtaken by Germany and the United States, and Britain and the other powers looked to overseas expansion—where they could find higher rates of profit—to resolve this crisis.[40]

Overseas territory began to take on new significance for British and other European merchants, expanding into new African territory through the use of force. Thus, territorial acquisitions tripled, foreign investment skyrocketed, and profitability was eventually restored. In 1876, on the eve of the first scramble for Africa, European powers controlled only 10 percent of the continent, namely Algeria, Cape Colony, Mozambique, and Angola. The opening round of the so-called scramble was launched in western Africa in the late 1870s, over what came to be known as the Congo and areas surrounding the Niger River and present-day Nigeria. European troops conquered the inland kingdoms of Oyo, Dahomey, Asante, and Benin and many more, along with the outright theft of large swaths of land in the Congo, Tanganyika, and the Gold Coast (today's Ghana), among others, and the expansion northward from the British Cape Colony in South Africa into what came to be called Rhodesia (today's Zimbabwe).

The centrality of Africa for European capital was underscored during this period, formalized by the infamous Berlin Conference of 1885 and the partitioning of Africa—as well as new colonies in Asia—to protect "their" new investments and markets. The Berlin agreement paternalistically declared its lofty goals, in which "all the powers . . . bind themselves to watch over the preservation of the native tribes, and to care for the improvement of the conditions of their moral and material well-being." Such declarations only masked the intensified competition for colonies that lay barely beneath the surface, where Berlin established the rules for annexation and negotiated the terms of the plunder. After the imperial carve-up, as Chris Harman has described, "The number of genuinely independent states outside of Europe and the Americas could be counted on one hand—the remains of the Ottoman Empire, Thailand, Ethiopia and Afghanistan."[41]

Thus, by the turn of the century, virtually the entire African continent was partitioned, with colonies covering over 90 percent of its territory—nine million square miles and approximately a fifth of the globe carved into dozens of colonies by the five largest colonial powers. Through warfare, torture, and deception, European rulers subdivided the continent into nations whose new geographies served only their own ends and had no logic based on local language, culture, religion, or other factors. This process was facilitated in part through establishing a network of African leaders willing to collaborate with foreign rule. The subjugation of the continent through forced labor and territorial conquest, and the loss of tens of millions of lives, rendered Africa an engine of growth in the expansion of capitalism, for the consolidation of both imperial powers and rivalries, and the immense accumulation of wealth for international capitalists.

Racist ideology justified and facilitated European imperialism in Africa as a "civilizing mission" to bring Christianity and commerce to those viewed, as anthropologist Eric Wolf has described, as "a people without history."[42] Or as Rodney remarks:

> Revolutionary African thinkers such as Franz Fanon and Amilcar Cabral expressed the same sentiments somewhat differently when they spoke of colonialism having made Africans into *objects of history*. Colonised Africans, like pre-colonial African chattel slaves, were pushed around into positions which suited European interests and which were damaging to the African continent and its peoples.[43]

Accounts like the following from a leading colonial administrator rationalized expansion in terms of a timeless savagery:

> If you read the history of any part of the Negro population of Africa, you will find nothing but a dreary recurrence of tribal wars, and an absence of everything which forms a stable government, and year after year, generation after generation, century after century, these tribes go on obeying no law but that of force, and consequently never emerging from the state of barbarism in which we find them at present.[44]

Yet, as Rodney emphasizes, the reality of African economic and political history was far different. Important economic centers had emerged by the eve of colonial partition, such as the empires of the Sokota and Wassoulou (led by Samori Ture, who mounted one of the fiercest resistances to occupation, both French and British). Nyamwezi in the South led trade routes connecting the Indian and Atlantic Oceans. Such developments had reached new levels of economic integration and internal centralization, with some elements of a modern state system, infrastructure, and class stratification. As described by historian Adu Boahen, "By as late as 1880, an overwhelming majority of the states and polities of Africa were enjoying their sovereign existence. . . . Old Africa appeared to be in its dying throes, and a new, modern Africa was emerging."[45]

Africans met European expansion with great resistance. One ruler, Machemba of the Yao in East Africa, declared to the German commander, "I have listened to your words but I can find no reason why I should obey you—I would rather die first. If it is friendship that you desire, then I am ready for it . . . but to be your subject, that I cannot be." Wobogo, the king of the Mossi in West Africa—in today's Burkina Faso—told French colonialists, "I know the whites wish to kill me in order to take my country, and yet you claim that they will help me organize my country. But I find my country good just as it is. I have no need for them. I know what is necessary for me and what I want: I have my own merchants: also, consider yourself fortunate that I do not order your head to be cut off. Go away now, and above all, never come back." Menelik and the Ethiopians defeated the Italians in 1896, described by one writer as the "greatest victory of an African over a European army since the time of Hannibal."[46] Some Africans attempted diplomatic negotiations with the Europeans, agreements later shunted aside by the colonialists as it suited them. In fact, the overriding lesson of colonial occupation was of the absolute necessity of resistance. Rebellions targeted forced labor schemes and taxation, as well as oppressive laws that forbade Africans to own land outside of designated areas and later imposed forced conscription during World War I. Workers went on strike and

engaged in boycotts, and nationalist organizations—many of them illegal—
were formed from the earliest days of colonial rule.

Yet African resistance was caught between the struggles of large forces. The
European "scramble for Africa" subjected independent states to colonial rule,
transforming peasant and trading societies within a short span of time into wage
labor and cash crop systems. The increasingly intense economic competition in
European capitalism that eventually exploded into World War I likewise spilled
over into military clashes in the Sudan, South Africa, and Morocco. Staking out
territory also led to clashes with the declining Ottoman Empire, which controlled Eritrea, Somalia, and part of the Sudan. Alliances between and against
the various powers attempted to block one another's rivals, such as the fight for
control of the Congo region between France, Britain, and Belgium, and of East
Africa between Britain and Germany. France and Britain sought competing axes
of control over the continent: France aimed for a "Niger to Nile" swath, Britain
a "Cape to Cairo" one. The struggle over these axes fueled near-clashes such as
the 1898 Fashoda incident, in which French and British troops nearly went to
war over an area of the Sudan. Beneath the ideology of the "civilizing influence"
of the age of empire, imperial powers were on a collision course, not only for
sources of raw materials and markets for goods but for the strategic control of
access to major trade routes and investments worldwide—namely, the path from
Europe to India and China around the tip of South Africa and through the Suez
Canal. Control over the canal and the Nile was a key objective for the British in
dominating transportation networks and agricultural exports, as well as access
to Asian trade. The final defeat in 1898 was led by Lord Kitchener, who killed
10,000 Sudanese while losing only 48 of his own troops. A soldier at the time
wrote in his diary: "They called for water and they called for our aid, but our
officers spurned them."[47] Kitchener made the skull of the Mahdi leader into an
inkstand in an infamous display of imperial victory.

As is well known, colonial brutality was standard practice across virtually
the entire continent, with the chief aim of leveraging force to subdue resistance and extract profits. Turning Africa into a conveyor belt for raw materials and industrial goods required transportation and communication systems
and, as Rodney describes, a pacified—and minimally educated—labor force.
The major powers on the continent set up administrative apparatuses that in
some cases—mainly the British and the Germans—utilized local rulers, but,
as Rodney writes, in no instance would the colonizers accept African self-rule.
The French, on the other hand, virtually destroyed all indigenous political systems to establish their own networks of administrators, thus reversing African

state building. Infrastructure, such as roads, was built not only to facilitate the movement of commodities and machinery, but was also relied upon by the colonial armies and police to discipline the indigenous population, whether via the expulsion of people from their land or the forced cultivation of cash crops. The growth of cash crops reached such an extreme during the decades of colonialism that food had to be imported, while industrial development was thwarted in Africa itself because manufacturing and the processing of raw materials happened exclusively overseas. Africans were discriminated against in most areas of economic life, wages were kept very low, and the profits from the exploitation of African laborers went directly to European bankers and trading companies.

Colonial practice reached new heights of barbarism. Adam Hochschild's *King Leopold's Ghost* is a crucial history of the central African region, called the Congo Free State, controlled by King Leopold of Belgium: Hochschild describes the human cost of exploitation in the rubber industry, the slave labor, corporal punishment, kidnapping, and the destruction of countless villages that led to 10 million dead.[48] An international campaign exposing these horrors, including photographs of rubber workers with severed hands and feet, led by what were known as the Congo reformers, including Mark Twain and Arthur Conan Doyle, eventually forced Leopold to give up his colonial fiefdom, but the billions in profits from the Congo rubber trade merely passed into new hands. Similarly, the German decimation of 80 percent of the Herero population of South West Africa—approximately 65,000 people, many driven into the desert and the borders sealed—was yet another example of the human toll of the scramble for profit. In East Africa, German "explorer" Carl Peters left a trail of murder and wreckage in his wake in the founding of the German East Africa colony. After the destruction of Vagogo villages, he declared triumphantly, "After brief resistance, the Vagogo took flight, torches were thrown into the houses, and axes worked to destroy all that the fire did not achieve. . . . My gun had become so hot from so much firing I could hardly hold it."[49] Meanwhile, German colonialism in East Africa aimed to block any uninterrupted line of British control from the Cape to the Suez Canal, stoking further rivalries with European competitors.

The British victory over the formerly Dutch Boers in South Africa's Boer Wars in 1902 also unfolded at great expense to the region's native Africans. As Rosa Luxemburg wrote, "it was on the backs of the Negroes that the battle between the Boers and the English government . . . was fought. Both competitors had precisely the same aim: to subject, expel or destroy the colored peoples, to appropriate their land and press them into service."[50] It is in South

Africa where the super-profits and imperial contradictions were among the sharpest. As Rodney describes, "From the very beginning of the scramble for Africa, huge fortunes were made from gold and diamonds in Southern Africa by people like Cecil Rhodes. . . . In the final analysis, the shareholders of the mining companies were the ones who benefited most of all. They remained in Europe and North America and collected fabulous dividends every year from the gold, diamonds, manganese, uranium, etc., which were brought out of the sub-soil by African labor."[51] South Africa's virtual monopoly of diamond production exacerbated competition with other imperial powers, while helping to underwrite that warfare as a major source of revenue for Britain in World War II to the tune of some $300 million.

Europeans learned well the colonial lessons of divide and conquer and applied them on a wide scale to bribe sections of the indigenous people to fight alongside the colonial conquerors, as well as to sway a tiny section of African rulers to back the annexation by one power versus another. As Rodney puts it, "one of the decisive features of the colonial system was the presence of Africans serving as economic, political or cultural agents of the European colonialists . . . agents or 'compradors' already serving [their] interests in the pre-colonial period."[52] For these insights, Rodney draws on work by Caribbean revolutionary writer Frantz Fanon, known for his book *The Wretched of the Earth* (1961) and other famous works, as well as his participation in the Algerian anticolonial struggle against the French. Citing Fanon on the role of local elites, Rodney is scathing in his contempt for these "puppets" of "metropolitan" capitalism, operating at the dictates of their "masters" by "remote control," thus concluding that "the presence of a group of African sell-outs is part of the definition of underdevelopment."[53]

As during the era of slavery, the plunder and colonization of the "scramble" defined previously as ending at the World War One period—was fundamentally tied to the expansion of capitalism as a system and the massive accumulation of individual capitalists. As Rodney describes: "The colonisation of Africa and other parts of the world formed an indispensable link in a chain of events which made possible the technological transformation of the base of European capitalism."[54] Copper from the Congo, iron from West Africa, chrome from Rhodesia and South Africa, and more, took capitalist development to unprecedented heights of what Rodney calls "*investible surpluses.*" The tendency within the drive for profit toward innovation and scientific advancement built a "massive industrial complex," as Rodney described it.[55] Due to the markets provided by Africa for finished goods, as well as its export of raw materials, African trade played a vital role of stimulating European innovation and technological development, such as in shipbuilding.[56] Critically, for Rodney, African trade not only generated economic growth and profits, but created *capacity* for future growth in what he called the "metropoles"—the global centers of political and economic power located in Europe.

The colonial state apparatus played a critical role in this process, instituting taxation of Africans that paid for their own exploitation and repression. Colonial policies heightening exploitation, such as those preventing Africans from growing cash crops, drove workers into forced labor, like the building of infrastructure to facilitate extraction.[57] Thus, capital accumulation was derived at the expense of greatly weakened African states and economies, effectively reversing previous development. These two processes were dialectically related. As Rodney writes, "the wealth that was created by African labor and from African resources was grabbed by the capitalist countries of Europe; and in the second place, restrictions were placed upon African capacity to make the maximum use of its economic potential."[58] This process of underdevelopment only intensified over time; as he points out, investment and "foreign capital" in colonial Africa were derived from past exploitation and provided the historical basis for further expansion. "What was called 'profits' in one year came back as 'capital' the next. . . . What was foreign about the capital in colonial Africa was its ownership and not its initial source."[59]

As with the age of "classical imperialism," competition into the twentieth century created new contradictions as accumulation and the expansion of technology, weaponry, and production fed the rivalries between the European powers, spilling over into conflicts in Africa and paving the way for massive loss of life and productive capacity in World War II. The global depression in the 1930s and the collapse once again of the prices of raw materials intensified the pressures on colonized people, especially peasants, to rebel. This resistance gained deeper traction after the war. The invasion of Ethiopia by the fascist Italian government—the very last chapter of the "scramble for Africa"—along with the conscription of African soldiers in World War II, the increase in forced labor during wartime, and the weakened state of European powers by the war's end all deepened anticolonial currents and the nationalist forces that won independence across the African continent in the 1950s, 1960s, and 1970s.

Rodney argued that development in the so-called "periphery" was proportional to the degree of independence from the "metropolis," a central tenet of the dependency theorists. He looked to state-directed national development in the postcolonial period as a template for growth, a model later proven—in the years after Rodney's death—not to be viable. National development in Africa, as elsewhere, proved unable to overcome the legacy of colonialism and weak economies. The wake of such failures and the onset of global crisis pushed many African states into the vise grip of neoliberal structural adjustment "reforms," which brought only austerity and crushing Third World debt.

Yet these ideas had a distinctive imprint on Rodney's variant of Marxism and that of many leftists of his day. For Rodney, independence in Africa rested on "development by contradiction," by which he meant that the contradictions within African society were only resolvable by "Africans regaining their sovereignty as a people."[60] In his view, the disproportionate weight and importance of even a small African working class offered a potentially more stable base of resistance. However, he emphasizes, that possibility cannot be fully realized, as it was in the "developed" world, because production in Africa proceeded on a different path than in Europe. In the latter, the destruction of agrarian and craft economies increased productive capacity through the development of factories and a mass working class. In Africa, he argues, that process was distorted: local craft industry was destroyed, yet large-scale industry was not developed outside of agriculture and extraction, with workers restricted to the lowest-paid, most unskilled work. "Capitalism in the form of colonialism failed to perform in Africa the tasks which it had performed in Europe in changing social relations and liberating the forces of production."[61] So, concludes Rodney, the African working class is too small and too weak to play a liberatory role in the current period. Instead, somewhat reluctantly, he identifies the intelligentsia for that role:

> Altogether, the educated played a role in African independence struggles far out of proportion to their numbers, because they took it upon themselves and were called upon to articulate the interests of all Africans. They were also required to . . . focus on the main contradiction, which was between the colony and the metropole. . . . The contradiction between the educated and the colonialists was not the most profound. . . . However, while the differences lasted between the colonizers and the African educated, they were decisive.[62]

Thus, while Rodney sees the "principal divide" within capitalism as that between capitalists and workers, the revolutionary role for the *African* working class was nonetheless a task for another day. On this score, Rodney was mistaken: mass upheavals by workers across the continent have shown the capacity for struggle, from the colonial period up to the present day. Recent mass strikes in South Africa, Nigeria, and Ghana, among others, underscore workers' power on the continent.

Yet, however contradictorily, some of Rodney's conclusions on political leadership and liberation can be elaborated upon to explain the potential for resistance under today's conditions. First, as we have seen, Rodney—following Fanon—was keenly aware of the class contradictions embedded in the new African ruling classes, tensions bound to be thrust to the surface with greater clarity in the future. He writes: "Most African leaders of the intelligentsia . . . were frankly capitalist, and shared fully the ideology of their bourgeois masters. . . . As far as the mass of peasants and workers were concerned, the removal of overt foreign rule actually cleared the way towards a more fundamental appreciation of exploitation and imperialism."[63] The potential intrinsic in that dynamic, as we shall see in subsequent chapters, has only grown over time. Furthermore, Rodney implies, internationalism on a class basis lay in the historical development of capitalism and solidarity as a crucial "political" question. "European workers have paid a great price for the few material benefits which accrued to them as crumbs from the colonial table," he writes. "The capitalists misinformed and mis-educated workers in the metropoles to the point where they became allies in colonial exploitation. In accepting to be led like sheep, European workers were perpetuating their own enslavement to the capitalists."[64]

Rodney's characterization of European workers "led like sheep" may be too simplistic a description of workers' understanding of capitalism. But Rodney is correct in stressing that racist ideas undermined their own liberation. The "crumbs" Rodney describes are the products of divisions sown by ruling class ideology, and *not* of insurmountable material barriers. The prospect of actually *realizing* this (future) possibility—that of an international movement among workers of Africa and the West—has much to gain from Rodney's invaluable research and analysis.

The Book Ahead

Rodney's method and analysis of the fundamentally exploitative nature of capitalism and the distorting processes of its development are a jumping-off point for the chapters that follow. Much as Rodney asserted the interconnections of Africa and the global economy, recent history demands a similar perspective. For while, as we have seen, public officials, financiers, and economists have tended to locate Africa outside this system, the narrative of "rising Africa" would seem to turn this view on its head. How, then, to explain these developments—and the implications for change from below—becomes crucially important.

Drawing on Rodney's approach to the historical roots of continued "underdevelopment" in Africa, the remaining chapters take up the recent history of state development, trade, investment, and militarism on the continent. Running throughout the book is a reliance on key themes of classical Marxism: a unitary global system; the tendency of economic rivalries to spill over into military conflict; and the uneven nature of capitalist development across the globe. The next three chapters sketch different eras in modern African history. Chapter 2 picks up Rodney's historical narrative of the era of independence, with a particular look at the dynamics of Cold War rivalries and the contradictions of the "national development" model of newly liberated states, including much of Africa. Chapter 3 discusses the era of neoliberal austerity and debt in Africa in the context of global economic downturn. Finally, chapter 4 turns to the recent economic history of new heights of investment on the continent, a boom often described as "the new scramble for Africa" or, in the business press, "Africa rising." Together, these chapters take the legacies of the colonial era as the context for the more recent history of economic crisis and imperial rivalry on the continent. They draw on the contributions of a host of political economists, historians, and Marxists who have analyzed the contours of debt, structural adjustment, and neoliberalism in the African context—including Thandika Mkandawire, Patrick Bond, Leo Zeilig, Jean Nanga, Eric Toussaint, Peter Lawrence, Yao Graham, Alemayehu G. Mariam, James K. Boyce, Léonce Ndikumana, Roger Southall, Henning Melber, Mahmood Mamdani, Yash Tandon, Baba Aye, Biodun Olamosu, and Andy Wynne, among many others.

Chapters 5, 6, and 7 explore the dynamics surrounding the recent surge in investment on the continent—what I describe as the "extractive landscape" of the new scramble for Africa. Extractive industries—especially oil—have been the source of new narratives in Africa today, including the supposed growth of an African middle class and diminished poverty. In fact, a rising tide of oil has not lifted all boats. Heightened inequality between a growing African elite and the rest of the population—not to mention continued deindustrialization and ecological devastation—gives lie to the myths of "development" amidst the boom. And just as Lenin outlined a century ago, economic rivalry between superpowers is fueling new crises: competition between the United States and China is unfolding on the continent, threatening dizzying levels of militarization and ever-greater heights of instability and destruction.

Finally, this account attempts in Chapter 8 to offer a direction for resistance and solidarity. As Marxism argues, a unified global system to extract profit links together the workers that produce it. Combined together unevenly, across the continent and across the globe, workers in Africa at key sites of accumulation and struggle are a crucial element of social change. Far from the overwhelming weight of poverty extinguishing possibility for resistance, struggles by Africans in workplaces and communities demonstrate in no uncertain terms their centrality to challenging—and overturning—capitalism. As recent organizing has shown, the hope for change from below—suggested by Rodney, and argued for by a new generation of radicals and revolutionaries today—contains the seeds of optimism amidst the latest chapter of Africa's "scramble."

PART ONE

Chapter Two

Legacies of Colonialism

The Conference of Berlin was able to carve up a mutilated Africa among three or four European flags. Currently the issue is not whether an African region is under French or Belgian sovereignty but whether the economic zones are safeguarded. Artillery shelling and scorched earth policy have been replaced by an economic dependency.

—Frantz Fanon, *The Wretched of the Earth*[1]

The Bretton Woods institutions are like arsonists, lighting new social fires, then waiting for the NGOs and local communities to play firefighter.

—Eric Toussaint, *Your Money or Your Life: The Tyranny of Global Finance*[2]

The Past Matters: Poverty in Africa Today

US President Barack Obama made his first visit to sub-Saharan Africa as president in July, 2009, to speak in Accra, Ghana. Despite a decades-long trail of broken promises to Africa on aid and development, Obama's speech was marked by finger-wagging and reprimands and an insistence that African nations' own "mismanagement" and "lack of democracy" are to blame for their economic and social problems. Obama told the Ghanaian parliament:

> Yes, a colonial map that made little sense bred conflict, and the West has often approached Africa as a patron, rather than a partner. But the West is not responsible for the destruction of the Zimbabwean economy over the last decade, or wars in which children are enlisted as combatants. . . . No

person wants to live in a society where the rule of law gives way to the rule of brutality and bribery. That is not democracy, that is tyranny, and now is the time for it to end.[3]

Obama's speech was made at the height of the 2008–2009 global recession. Yet lest we imagine that this approach was somehow exceptional, we can note the echoes of Obama's words in an address given by International Monetary Fund head Christine Lagarde in Nigeria in early 2016. There she likewise chastised the Nigerian government on fiscal policy and corruption in the face of a major commodity price collapse, admonishing that "hard decisions will need to be taken on revenue, expenditure, debt, and investment" and prescribing a stern dose of "resolve, resilience, and restraint."[4] Tough-love talk of "responsibility" aside, then and now, US policy actually views economic crisis as an opportunity to rebuild the global economy at the expense of ordinary Africans. In 2008, then Treasury Secretary Timothy Geithner tripled the International Monetary Fund's resources from their current level of about $250 billion, with $100 billion coming from the United States. Yet while the IMF directed industrialized nations to enact stimulus plans and bank bailouts, Africa and other nations of the Global South were compelled to accept spending cuts and other harsh conditions for loans. In fact, said Jubilee USA Network at the height of the 2008–2009 global recession, "There is a significant danger that the new borrowing that has resulted from a lack of sufficient international grant support . . . will force low-income countries to prioritize debt repayment over essential social services and lead to renewed debt crises throughout the developing world."[5]

Similarly, today's economic crisis for "emerging nations" will provide an opportunity for the reimposition of global capitalism's fiscal priorities, what anti-illegitimate debt activist Eric Toussaint has described as "the tyranny of global finance." As the business presses reported in early 2016, a new round of indebtedness and austerity is now unfolding for African economies.[6] Likewise, just as during the last crisis, ordinary Africans will likely be compelled to accept punishing conditions handed down by the global financial institutions. The dynamics of the most recent crisis and its impact will be explored in greater detail in the following chapters.

Obama's comments turn the reality of African poverty and its root causes on their head. Decades of loans and structural adjustment policies from the International Monetary Fund (IMF) and World Bank—often referred to as the Bretton Woods institutions for their creation at the Bretton Woods conference in New Hampshire at the close of World War II—have placed an economic stranglehold on African and other Third World nations. US capital drove the establishment of the World Bank and the IMF.[7] Using the IMF and World Bank as a battering ram, the neoliberal policy of trade liberalization forced its way across Africa and the rest of the globe, leaving in its wake decimated social programs, a debt crisis, and low wages—that is, conditions favorable for US investment. The last few decades of neoliberal policy have spelled disaster for the vast majority of ordinary Africans. Each Ghanaian, for example, owes the equivalent of approximately $350 to international financial institutions.[8] Countless other examples of poverty and inequality could be given.

The comments from Obama and Lagarde illustrate two general kinds of explanation in the mainstream media and official circles about poverty in Africa, neither of which are mutually exclusive: the first is a scolding approach in which Western politicians, officials, and investors chide African governments on economic policy, combining stern paternalism with hand-wringing concern. Admonitory warnings from the West transform into narratives on Africa as an eternal basketcase in a blatantly hypocritical blame-the-victim rhetoric. This version emerges from certain development, global advocacy circles, which claim an antipoverty agenda but also share key assumptions with their Bretton Woods and development bank partners: that Western intervention must dictate policy as the core of any development initiative in Africa. These shared assumptions include a conviction in the inability of African governments and ordinary people to independently run their own societies. As a case in point, Bono's ONE Campaign issued a strong finger-wagging warning about the need for African governments to act more responsibly, saying the "new global development agenda has little hope of succeeding unless those same governments—together with private-sector partners and many others—also agree on an effective strategy to finance it."[9] However, this version is a vastly distorted account that elides or erases the destructive role played by foreign multinational corporations and free-market institutions. As Clark Gascoigne of Global Financial Integrity commented in 2013, "in development circles we talk a lot about how much aid is going to Africa, and there's this feeling among some in the West that after we've been giving this money for decades, it's Africa's fault if the continent's countries still haven't developed."[10]

The other narrative is a newer kind of story, found in the business presses beginning around the early to mid-2000s, championing—with scarcely contained excitement—a new surge in investment on the continent. Certainly Africa has undergone a recent boom for global corporations, asset managers, and the like, with vast returns on commodities that enabled African growth rates to bounce back faster than many other parts of the globe after the recession in 2008–2009.

In recent years, investment in other industrial sectors has also taken off, with booms in communications, technology, and the service sector. Accompanying this growth has been the excited declaration of a new African middle class and a "diversified" economy ready to weather any global downturn in prices.

In the meantime, suffice it to say that shocking levels of inequality, oppression, and poverty are no less true today than they have been since the end of colonialism. In fact, Patrick Bond, for one, has argued that Africans are poorer today than they were at independence.[11] Today, however, even sharper unevenness exists, not only between Africa and the West, but also within African nations themselves. While the dramatic narrative of "Africa rising" of the first decades of the new millennium champions the "boom" in investment and growth, poverty and underdevelopment remain dire. Crippling poverty has meant, for example, a health care crisis that has reached epidemic proportions on a continent where, according to the World Health Organization, the average life expectancy at birth is only 58 years. Almost twenty times as many people on the continent will die of HIV/AIDS than in Europe, while Africa has less than one-tenth the number of physicians per unit of population compared to Europe and the United States.[12] One billion people worldwide (14 percent) have no access to any form of sanitation facilities;[13] and 695 million of those without access live in sub-Saharan Africa.[14]

Postcolonial economic development on the continent has also resulted in combined and uneven development that has concentrated industrial growth in key centers such as Nigeria and South Africa. According to the World Bank, those two countries together have accounted for 55 percent of the industrial value in sub-Saharan Africa, while the other forty-eight countries share the remainder.[15] Africa's manufacturing exports nearly tripled from $72 billion in 2002 to $189 billion in 2012, but a mere four countries—Egypt, Morocco, South Africa, and Tunisia—accounted for a full two-thirds of these exports.[16] Class polarization has expressed itself most sharply in these centers, with enthusiastic ruling-class support for market-based neoliberal reform on the one hand and higher levels of working-class resistance on the other.

In fact, within those centers, the class contradictions are profound. In South Africa, more than 40 percent of the population languishes in extreme poverty while the top quarter of the population earns 85 percent of the country's wealth.[17] In Nigeria, 80 percent of the nation's oil wealth is concentrated in the hands of 1 percent of the population.[18] As John Ghazvinian describes in *Untapped: The Scramble for Africa's Oil*, "foreign oil companies have conducted some of the world's most sophisticated exploration and production operations

. . . but the people of the Niger Delta have seen none of the benefits."[19] The surge in commodity prices and foreign investment has replicated this inequality in other sites on the continent. As Mike Davis has written, "the boom in exports all too frequently benefited only a tiny stratum. One of the most extreme cases was Angola, a major producer of oil and diamonds. In Luanda, where in 1993 a staggering 84 percent of the population was jobless or underemployed, inequality between the highest and lowest income deciles 'increased from a factor of 10 to a factor of 37 between 1995 and 1998 alone.'"[20] This dynamic has been multiplied many times over across Africa.

The forces underlying African poverty are far from reducible to problems of "corruption" and "governance," but rather are rooted in historic relationships of exploitation of a larger capitalist system, wherein political and economic strategies on the part of the West came to the fore and were advanced at key moments. To sketch out this period here, broadly speaking, the thwarting of industrial development in conditions created under colonialism, the national-development models African ruling classes attempted after independence, the narrowing of those horizons into single-commodity export economies, and World Bank/IMF-imposed austerity have all combined to produce debt crises, collapses of infrastructure, poverty, lack of access to health care, high rates of HIV/AIDS, low wages, low literacy rates, an explosion of urban slums, and a host of other poor grades on human development "indicators."

Deep inequality, oppression, and immiseration persist despite the African boom. The dominant narrative on African poverty thus becomes, essentially: why hasn't a rising tide lifted all boats? Various explanations, many of them ahistorical, continue to grapple with these questions, from the academic "economic development" literature to the pages of the *Financial Times*, and many conclude that intrinsic characteristics of African societies and economies are at fault. Charlie Kimber has pointed out that the dogma on "good governance" has its own historicity. Particularly during the Cold War, the West actively sought alliances with African elites—some with horrific records on authoritarianism, corruption, and brutality—yet looked away from this track record when expedient. Zairean leader Mobutu Sese Seko, who managed to accumulate vast sums in the course of his rule, was a case in point. Later, however, with the neoliberal concern for breaking through obstacles to privatization, Western opposition to strong state regulation became increasingly reframed as a focus on political and government "reform" while stressing the urgency for favorable investment climates. As Kimber describes, the moment was one of "corruption regarded as rooted in the state itself and therefore the 'war against corruption' could usefully be emblazoned on the banners of the privatizers and the pro-market militias. Today governance-related conditionalities are central to aid packages."[21]

How state power and its institutions are characterized is, of course, a political question. Imperial powers have wielded the hammer of "governance" as a weapon to ensure the subservience of oppressed nations, to facilitate profits, and as a tool to maintain competitive advantage against its rivals. On the other hand, these strictures can easily be brushed under the rug when expedient. Apartheid South Africa—like Mobutu's Zaire and its close relationship with the United States—well exemplifies the hypocrisy of the selective critiques of the West. As Gavin Capps writes:

> On average as much as 7 percent of GDP per annum left South Africa as capital flight between 1970 and 1988, an equivalent of 25 percent of non-gold imports. This was entirely due to the transfer activities of the major corporations like Anglo-American and the Rembrandt Group. And their behavior was no less illicit than that of the dictators. Shifting private funds out of South Africa in the 1980s not only defied local capital controls, but broke the international sanctions regime on apartheid. As such, the neoliberal pathologization of the corrupt black African state simply does not hold. The private "white" capitalists of South Africa were busy engaging in capital flight as well.[22]

The left has reached a very different set of conclusions for understanding inequality in Africa today via a range of frameworks—from the dependency theories of Andre Gunder Frank[23] and Samir Amin[24] and Walter Rodney's "underdevelopment" thesis, to the "accumulation by dispossession" of David Harvey[25] and others such as Patrick Bond[26] and the classical Marxist approaches. Yet the common thread connecting these varied approaches is a shared assumption regarding the detrimental legacies of colonialism and neoliberalism: essentially, that imperial powers and global financial institutions such as the International Monetary Fund and the World Bank are to blame for both the historic and contemporary inequality on the continent; that African poverty is not simply a fact of nature but was *manufactured* through the historical processes of exploitation and neoliberalism, built upon and impacted by the legacies of colonialism and underdevelopment. Writers such as anti-debt activist Eric Toussaint, among many others, have made critical contributions to an understanding that Western foreign policy toward Africa does not merely produce poverty and inequality as an accidental *by-product*, but rather that Third World debt, structural adjustment, privatization, and trade liberalization are *intentional* strategies of a neoliberal agenda of widening opportunities for investment worldwide.

Marxists have situated the neoliberal era in a context of a crisis, not just of profitability in the post-1970s recession period, but also more broadly of a political and economic program to manage the contradictions of the system of capitalism—the competitive drive to continuously secure access to markets, investment opportunities, and resources. For David Harvey, the neoliberal era is the period of the post-1970s crisis to the present, marked by a host of economic policies to break down barriers to trade and investment by global capital and to facilitate the political and social conditions most favorable for capital accumulation: compliant local regimes; low wages; weak (or no) unions; overall high levels of labor exploitation; and weak "regulatory environments" (i.e., legal and environmental safeguards protecting the interests of the host country).

In post-independence Africa, Western governments and Bretton Woods institutions—through the structure of investment, aid, loans, and trade policy— extended relationships whose nature was fundamentally similar to the prior era. In other words, within the newly emerged rubric of independence, the West aimed to impose economic and political policies that largely continued— rather than overturned—structural conditions of weak states, political instability, and a lopsided structural pattern of economies inherited from colonialism. Within this historical trajectory, various strategies emerged at particular moments: Western investment and development of the 1950s and 1960s facilitated extraction and accumulation while balancing the new political realities of independent states; the devastation of structural adjustment, Third World debt, and neoliberal diktat of the 1970s to 1990s; and the explosion in private investment and the "favorable business environment" of today.

Weak States and Economic Underdevelopment

The weakness of postcolonial nations in Africa was a legacy of colonialism, where weak states had limited control over territory, and regimes relied on ethnic divisions, centralized authority, and patronage inherited from colonial rule. New national leaders were thus vulnerable to the pull of internal influence and corruption and the support of external imperial patrons, contributing to conditions in which the United States or the USSR found an opening to replace the influence of these countries' former colonial masters. Both sides weighed strategic considerations and influence in various African countries, which became contested states in early Cold War competition.

Under colonialism, the major European powers on the continent used different types of administrative apparatuses and colonial policies. Prior to the turn of the twentieth century, colonial authorities had relied on educated Africans as local administrators. But by the turn of the century, fierce imperial competition drove an expansionist push in Africa, deepening conflict between European and local populations as they tightened their overall control over the colonies altogether. Under these intensified conditions, alliances with educated Africans as local "partners" were increasingly unsustainable. European officials increasingly excluded this section of the African middle class from the state, cultivating instead colonially created "tribal" authorities for a compliant "partnership" role.[27] These processes undermined the development of a modern bourgeois class carrying political and economic weight. As Peter Dwyer and Leo Zeilig describe, "colonialism had in most cases severely hampered the growth of an indigenous bourgeoisie."[28] As a result, African national liberation movements were relatively late-forming. Upon independence, African leaders assumed power within a newly created state apparatus and a weak national identity that tended to rely upon pitting ethnic groups against each other to mobilize power. Thus, in the postcolonial era, new ruling classes were disadvantaged as they attempted to establish some degree of political and economic independence. In the case of the Congo, for example, Dwyer and Zeilig show that with "the economy already cornered by foreign corporations, . . . all that [aspiring African elites] could sell was their political power and influence in the state machinery."[29] These historical developments formed the material basis for new regimes vulnerable to the pull of patronage or "clientelism," as Ugandan scholar Mahmood Mamdani has called it.[30]

For some new rulers, adhering to the "colonial mold of the state" was a logical objective, cemented by nationalist leaders who fought to secure sovereignty for small states.[31] For those states emerging from colonialism, new ruling classes were mainly drawn from the urban middle classes, who had little accountability to weak indigenous landowners or capitalists[32] and were able to remain relatively autonomous vis-à-vis local capital while remaining under the rule of foreign investors and powers.[33] Frantz Fanon describes how these new rulers draped themselves in the nationalism and aspirations of the anticolonial revolutions so as to facilitate accumulation in which they would also be beneficiaries:

> Spoiled children of yesterday's colonialism and today's governing powers, they oversee the looting of the few national resources. Ruthless in their scheming and legal pilfering they use the poverty, now nationwide, to work their way to the top through import-export holdings, limited companies, playing the stock market, and nepotism. They insist on the doctrine of

nationalization for business transactions, i.e., reserving contracts and business deals for nationals. Their doctrine is to proclaim the absolute need for
nationalizing the theft of the nation.[34]

Governmental and legal structures bore the marks of the colonial era, an
imprint extended to the present day in some cases. "Tribalism" intersected with
political rule in the postcolonial period as district and local-level leaders continued on in appointed (unelected) roles, accountable only to the newly formed
central governments. Countries such as Kenya—the site of large-scale colonial
land seizures—maintained the legal basis for such practices, keeping laws on the
books that enshrined communal land as "government property."[35] The impact
of legal "loopholes" established in the colonial era continues to be felt today in
the open theft of commonly held land in an agricultural "land grab" by foreign
multinationals that has seized millions of hectares for corporate investment.[36]

The ideological visions for these new states were not unidimensional. A
political divide within the nationalist currents expressed competing frameworks at the top among those new layers of leaders who explicitly embraced
coordination and collaboration with the West for the coming era, and those
leaders championing independence, "Africanization," regional unity, and
a left-wing framing of state-directed national development. The radical
wing of the nationalist movements also tended to draw upon a base of trade
unions, migrant workers, and students.[37] An influential leader under the man-
tle of "African socialism," Ghanaian Prime Minister and President Kwame
Nkrumah represented the sharp contradictions of this left leadership. Taking
power in 1957, Nkrumah could correctly identify in 1963:

> In the dynamics of national revolution there are usually two local elements:
> the moderates of the professional and "aristocratic" class and the so-called
> extremists of the mass movement. . . . The moderates are prepared to leave
> the main areas of sovereignty to the colonial power, in return for a promise
> of economic aid. The so-called extremists are men who do not necessarily
> believe in violence but who demand immediate self-government and com-
> plete independence. They are men who are concerned with the interests of
> their people and who know that those interests can be served only by their
> own local leaders and not by the colonial power.[38]

Later, however, his class background would prove decisive, and Ghana became emblematic of the failure of those left-wing aspirations—the "end of an illusion," as Bob Fitch and Mary Oppenheimer would describe it: "Nkrumah was
the perfect representative of the Gold Coast petty bourgeoisie. With admirable
clarity he defined his position as one which opposed 'particular consequences'

but accepted the assumptions of the political system."[39] These divergent views as described by Nkrumah—the "moderates" and the "extremists"—both reflected variants on rule "from above," a new, postcolonial order that nonetheless retained the class divisions of a society resting on accumulation and competition, along state capitalist lines. As Mamdani has described it, in "conservative African states, the hierarchy of the local state apparatus, from chiefs to headmen, continued after independence. In the radical African states. . . . the antidote to a decentralized despotism turned out to be a centralized despotism."[40] He continues, "The day-to-day violence of the colonial system was embedded in customary Native Authorities in the local state, not in civil power at the center. Yet we must not forget that customary local authority was reinforced and backed up by central civil power. Colonial despotism was highly decentralized."[41]

As we have seen, Rodney recognizes the disproportionate weight and importance of the small African working class as a more stable base of resistance.[42] However, he thought the potential of that power would not be realized until the limits of the new African ruling classes had been laid bare. Yet despite Rodney's somewhat stageist description here of class formation in the postcolonial era, he identified an important characteristic—namely, the weak political base of these new nations, hobbled from the beginning by the inherited weaknesses of the prior period.

Lopsided Economies

The legacy of plunder and colonization has been the expansion of capitalism as a system and the massive accumulation of capitalists—and "their" nation-states—at the expense of greatly weakened states and economies in Africa. As Rodney describes, "African economies are integrated into the very structure of the developed capitalist economies; and they are integrated in a manner that is unfavorable to Africa and insures that Africa is dependent on the big capitalist countries."[43] When colonialism ended, the weak economic and political footing of new African states left them vulnerable to interference from industrialized nations and the companies based there. Several aspects of economic development under colonialism produced highly distorted and fragile economies. States' economic systems were anchored to a narrow export base with a concomitant weak industrial sector and anemic rates of growth. These states inherited an underdeveloped infrastructure geared toward exports, lacking capital, and skewed toward supplying unfinished goods to advanced countries. In essence, Frederick Cooper writes, "the development effort of late colonial regimes never did provide the basis for a strong national economy; economies remained externally oriented and the state's economic power remained concentrated at the gate between inside and outside."[44] These conditions posed severe challenges to the prospects for building self-sustaining economies diverse enough to buffer nascent industries from the turmoil of global markets. As British socialist Chris Harman has pointed out, "success in trade in the modern world is only possible if you already have a high level of investment in modern technologies. Countries which do not have that are doomed even when no barriers exist to their selling goods in advanced countries."[45] Overcoming these historic disadvantages would prove to be immensely difficult.

In 1968, 80 percent of Africa's exports consisted of raw materials such as oil, copper, cotton, coffee, and cocoa.[46] At the close of the 1960s, per capita growth was just above 1 percent.[47] This rate can be contrasted with the United Nations' goal of a 3 percent growth rate for the 1960s, the "Decade of Development" launched by President John F. Kennedy at the United Nations on the heels of his inaugural address, when he declared: "To those peoples in the huts and villages of half the globe struggling to break the bonds of mass misery, we pledge our best efforts to help them help themselves."[48] The growth of cash crops reached such an extreme during the decades of colonialism that governments had to import food, while industrial development was thwarted on the continent because manufacturing and the processing of raw materials happened exclusively overseas. Colonial authorities discriminated against Africans in most areas of economic life, depressing wages to a very low level. The vast bulk of the profits from the exploitation of African laborers went directly to European bankers and trading companies.

Economic development under colonialism was highly uneven—especially British colonialism, which created concentrations of workers in key locations, such as the mines of central Africa and at the port of Mombassa in Kenya. While this result was an unavoidable outcome of the orientation on extractive industries and its associated transportation infrastructure, these needs were necessarily balanced against colonial concerns over too much industrialization potentially producing "disruptive proletarianization"[49]—that is, class struggle and resistance. These fears were by no means unfounded: working-class and peasant struggles were a central feature of the colonial period, and this resistance—among unionized and nonunionized workers, students and agricultural laborers—formed the basis of mass anticolonial struggles.

Alongside this unevenness, colonial policy produced some institutional uniformity in methods of extracting capital from the continent. British colonial monopolies in the form of marketing boards reinforced the tendency toward single-commodity production for export by controlling most of the value of exports. These monopolies also amounted to loans in hard currency on the part of the colonies to Britain in the form of the difference between producer and market prices. This dynamic provides context to the resistance of the British Empire to the decolonization process, as these boards provided access to the currencies that enabled the import of capital to Britain itself and thus its industrial recovery in the wake of World War II.[50] As Fitch and Oppenheimer, for example, describe in their important account—written on the heels of the overthrow of Nkrumah's government—the institutional legacy of these colonial marketing boards, as well as the total refusal of banks to provide local credit,[51] were critical in the outflow of capital from Ghana and the "stunting" of the indigenous capitalist class.[52] As at least one study of French colonialism in Africa has shown, Africans themselves—and not the colonizers—far disproportionately carried the weight of colonial expenses through taxation.[53] The same study demonstrates that very minimal funds were devoted to "productive sectors," namely agriculture, which could have provided the basis for economic diversity. Meanwhile, "colonial investments focused on infrastructure supporting export/import transportation rather than focusing on transforming and improving local productive capacity."[54]

At the time of independence, staggering human and social needs confronted new nations. Contrary to colonial propaganda, in which colonizers claimed an investment in the "well-being" of the colonized, the vast bulk of funds spent went toward the military or colonial administration. Colonial policy actively suppressed education for the majority. Technical education was introduced only in rare instances. For example, the Congo had only 16 secondary school graduates at the time of independence, out of a total population of 13 million![55] Likewise, not one doctor was trained in Mozambique during 500 years of Portuguese colonialism.[56] Across the continent as a whole, only 1 percent of those in school reached the secondary school level. In 1960, there were only 50 university graduates per year, when "it is calculated that 10 times the number are needed annually—half of them for government service."[57] All told, colonialism left a wake of destruction across the continent: life expectancy plummeted, while ecological devastation spread across rural areas that suffered from minimal social services. As Rodney so succinctly puts it, "Colonialism had only one hand—it was a one-armed bandit."[58]

Democratic institutions were similarly very weak. Mamdani describes how colonial political systems actively cultivated accumulations of power in some sites over others based on the particular political interests and alliances at a given moment. In Nigeria, for example, electoral reforms pre-independence were introduced but applied selectively across the country, generating the seeds of inequality whose reverberations would be felt in the decades to come.[59]

Imperial Objectives in the Cold War Era

In this context, what were the imperial aims of the United States with regard to Africa in the new era? With the approach of the era of independence after World War II, the United States saw the emerging period as an opportunity to cement political and economic ties with the new nations of the continent: to forge alliances to curb the influence of their competitors, namely the USSR but also Western European powers, and to remake the economic order so as to best facilitate accumulation for US capital. For the United States, but also for the USSR, the end of colonialism opened a door for imperial powers to forge their own relations with the new African nations free from the domination of the European colonial system, a system that had in fact received overall US support at the time. Imperial strategy and policy toward Africa—especially that of the United States—since the end of colonialism thus provides crucial context to the roots of African inequality.

During the Cold War, superpower competition drove both the United States and the USSR to create allies and proxies in Africa as a way to extend their global reach and overcome the historical advantage of colonial powers' exclusive domination there. As Sidney Lens has pointed out, the postwar military superiority of the United States provided the opportunity for its imperial domination and the position from which to subordinate its rivals. The Cold War became an expression of this global aspiration: the US challenge to the geopolitical power of the USSR and the large areas of the world within its orbit.[60] Africa, of course, was by no means an exception within this global dynamic. As Fanon described, "every peasant revolt, every insurrection in the Third World fits into the framework of the cold war. . . . The full-scale campaign under way leads the other bloc to gauge the flaws in its sphere of influence."[61]

In the economic realm, the United States aimed to extend its influence through global financial institutions such as the World Bank and the International Monetary Fund (IMF)—founded in 1944 with heavy US support—using private and public loans to impose their financial terms on the rest of the globe and ram through protective trade barriers to open up new markets on terms favorable to the West.[62] Shrouded in the "soft" language of "aid," "modernization," and "development," the terms of these global financial institutions belied the intentions of extending the subordinate role of African economies into the new era. Africa must accept, declared World Bank president Robert McNamara in 1969, "tax measures" and "choice of projects that might be politically unpopular," while demonstrating a "willingness to accept and implement advice from outside experts."[63]

From the end of World War II until 1975, the colonial powers were compelled to "give up" state power across virtually the entire continent. The process of decolonization tended to produce relatively strong ties between the new nation and the former colonial powers when the latter were able to establish trade and political agreements on terms favorable to themselves prior to departure[64]— that is, where anticolonial resistance did not prevent the departing powers from "disengaging" on their own terms. The United States had a particular advantage of appearing as seemingly free of the colonial legacy. Ideological veneer notwithstanding, US capital was able to benefit from the political and economic relationships established under colonialism by the "older" powers, while likewise benefiting from the loosening of the monopolistic ties of the colonies to its colonial "home." In this climate, the United States was able to project its power relative to both the continent's new nations as well as those few that had remained free of colonial domination. This posture was in keeping with the so-called Truman Doctrine—an interventionist US foreign policy intended to contain the USSR and support anti-Communist regimes and movements abroad. As early as 1951, the Truman administration and the imperial Ethiopian government signed an agreement promising "to cooperate with each other in the interchange of technical knowledge and skills and related activities designed to contribute to the balanced and integrated development of the economic resources and productive capacities of Ethiopia."[65] A host of trade agreements and arms deals occasionally shifted to emphasize one set of short-term political-economic interests over the other, but the overall thrust of the US posture toward Africa remained essentially part of its broader imperial ambitions as a global superpower.

Stepping into the postcolonial gap, the US government in the 1960s took steps to facilitate investment on the part of its own corporations through covering investment risk, granting of tax credits, and so on. In that same period, the initiation of Eurafrica into the first meetings of the European Economic Community in 1958 sought to bring eighteen African nation-states into a common market with Europe. This formation became a competitive bloc relative to the United States because of the preferential trade relations it cemented, as well as a vehicle for other noncolonial powers, such as German capital, to get a leg up with regard to trade and investment.[66] Above all, however, these "free" trade agreements were disastrous for the new African regimes, which were denied protections for their own goods—and therefore denied access to badly needed foreign exchange—while thwarted in their own national development and industrialization.

Certainly these challenges and contradictions of nation-building were not lost on the anticolonial movements and new national leadership of the postwar period. For left-leaning nationalists, the dangers of the grip of the West were understood as of paramount importance. Oginga Odinga, Kenya's first vice president and later opposition figure, warned in 1967:

> The stage following on independence is the most dangerous. This is the point after which many national revolutions in Africa have suffered a setback, for there has been a slide back into complacency after the first victory over external control and pressure, and national governments have left too much in the countries unchanged, have not built for effective independence by transferring power and control to the authentic forces and support of the national revolution, and have forgotten that internal elements of exploitation are closely related to reactionary external pressures.[67]

For Nkrumah, neocolonialism threatened self-determination and unity among the new nations of Africa, which, in the Pan-Africanist view, shared a common interest in regional integration and economic development. As Nkrumah wrote in 1964, for example:

> Now that African freedom is accepted by all . . . as inescapable fact, there are efforts in certain quarters to make arrangements whereby the local populations are given token freedom while cords attaching them to the "mother country" remain as firm as ever. . . . The intention is to use the new African nations, so circumscribed, as puppets through whom influence can be extended over states which maintain an independence in keeping with their sovereignty. The creation of several weak and unstable states of this kind in Africa, it is hoped, will ensure the continued dependence on the former colonial powers for economic aid, and impede African unity. This policy of balkanization is the new imperialism, the new danger to Africa.[68]

Fanon, from a different perspective, also described the double-edged sword of the process of decolonization and the legacy left by the "departing" powers:

> The apotheosis of independence becomes the curse of independence. The sweeping powers of coercion of the colonial authorities condemn the young nation to regression. In other words, the colonial power says: "If you want independence, take it and suffer the consequences." The nationalist leaders are then left with no other choice but to turn to their people and ask them to make a gigantic effort. . . . Each state, with the pitiful resources at its

disposal, endeavors to address the mounting national hunger and the growing national poverty.[69]

In Western official circles, 1960 was dubbed the "Year of Africa" by both the former colonialists and critics of colonialism, such as influential US academic Ralph Bunche, with a shared recognition that the momentum of anticolonial struggles could not be undone. In that year, seventeen African countries won their independence. Then British Prime Minister Harold Macmillan famously declared in early 1960, "The wind of change is blowing through this continent. Whether we like it or not, this growth of national consciousness is a political fact." Yet despite this general understanding, the question of decolonization was by no means resolved. The year 1960 was also marked by the Sharpeville Massacre and repression by the South African apartheid regime. Thousands marched that year in the township of Sharpeville against the detested "pass laws," which controlled the activities and movement of nonwhites; police fired on the crowd, killing 69 people and injuring 180. The brutal violence of colonial powers, such as in South Africa and Rhodesia (later Zimbabwe), highlighted the lengths racist settler regimes were willing to travel to remake the new era on their own terms.

In anticipation of the new postcolonial era, the US Senate sponsored a trip late that year to nineteen African countries. In a report authored by Senator Frank Church upon their return, the contingent detailed ruling-class considerations for future relations: "American policies towards African causes," they cautioned, "have tended to draw down our reservoir of good will and understanding in Africa."[70] New African nations, they warned, expressed suspicions about the bulk of US investment going to South Africa, as well as persistent racial discrimination in the United States. Forging the road ahead required a thoughtful balancing act: a careful nurturing of nationalistic aspirations, while ensuring that these new nations remained within the orbit of imperial influence. Senior government advisor W. W. Rostow, the chairman of the US State Department's policy planning council, likewise conveyed the challenges for US aims, describing how

> in trying to assist in the maintenance of the independence of nations, in their modernization, and in keeping peace in the regions—the United States finds itself often in a rather complicated position. Our friends in the developing countries are, in one part of their minds, pleased to receive our help and support; but, in another part of their minds, one of the major purposes of revolutions of nationalism and modernization is to achieve a higher degree

of independence of the more advanced powers of the world and in particular a higher degree of independence of the United States.[71]

Similarly, "we have been trying to steer a careful course," reported the Church Senate document, "between harmless expressions of idle sympathy for African nationalism, and active support of independence which we fear might unduly antagonize certain of our NATO allies."[72] The objective for the United States was fundamentally about overcoming the legacies of colonialism perceived as antithetical to the interests of US capital:

> The antagonism felt by Africans toward the European colonial powers will certainly continue to plague Western efforts to assist Africa with its problems. . . . The large amounts of aid provided by European powers to their former colonial territories may decrease in size as those powers determine that considerations of their national prestige and commerce are no longer deeply engaged. There could be a net reduction of aid despite all efforts to stimulate a concerted Western approach to the economic development problem. . . . The new African governments will be turning more and more to the United States for help. Under foreseeable circumstances, this country will not be able to satisfy the full measure of such requests.[73]

For their part, the British in colonial Africa grappled with a similar balancing act. As Fitch and Oppenheimer describe, "the problem for the British in colonial Africa has been to shape a native ruling class strong enough to protect British interests, but still weak enough to be dominated."[74] A former head of the African Division of the Colonial Office described the potential threat in 1959: "Where local political forces or movements are powerful, smooth progress depends on imagination as well as firmness on the part of governments, not only on strength but on flexibility."[75] A tactic of this imperial strategy required, from very early on, political and ideological approaches that attempted to undermine the legitimacy of those new states emphasizing an independent political will. For example, the embrace by Nkrumah of a "socialist economy" was the object of derision because "Ghanaian officials have not had sufficient experience with sound financial practices," which was understood as a failure to "create a better climate for foreign private investment. . . . The United States has to some extent been made to serve as a whipping boy for the relative failure of the more militant drive toward Pan-Africanism."[76] Thus, from its earliest days, the posture of imperial powers in the postcolonial era draped foreign policy toward Africa in paternalism and facile justifications for their own intervention.

Of significance for the United States was the goal of ensuring cheap imports of raw materials, including "strategic minerals" critical for defense and the shoring up of the Cold War arms race. And although US investment in Africa was a very small proportion of total US foreign direct investment (FDI)—and smaller than the size of investments of the other major powers—the *rate* of increase of private investment by the United States was actually greater in Africa than elsewhere on the globe. Investment in Africa increased by 3.5 times during the immediate independence period, while US global FDI less than doubled in the same period (see table).[77]

US investment in Africa and South Africa, 1957-1970				
	1957	1964	1967	1970
Total	$25,394	$44,386	$59,267	$78,090
Africa	$664	$1,769	$2,277	$3,476
South Africa	$301	$467	$667	$864

The objectives of US imperialism did not unfold without opposition, and the white settler regimes were an important case in point. Yet at a time when international criticism was mounting against the South African government, a large bulk of US investment at the time continued to go to South Africa; the majority was in extractive industries or infrastructure to facilitate extraction. By the mid-1970s, US policymakers explicitly acknowledged the urgency of managing "political risk" vis-á-vis the apartheid regime so that US and South African capital retained "control of the richest and most strategically important part of Sub-Saharan Africa."[78] Despite growing condemnation of apartheid rule, at the time, the value of US investment in South Africa was approximately one-third of its total investment in Africa and increased by 300 percent from 1960 to 1975.[79] Given the importance of this economic relationship, the United States was content to sidestep opposition to apartheid, despite the knowledge that "there was little evidence that US firms deliberately adopted a socially conscious policy of avoiding support of the South African government or its apartheid policies."[80]

In the end, the priority of foreign capital on extraction was no different in South Africa than elsewhere on the continent, priorities that decisively shaped how infrastructure was deployed. For example, investment in electricity and power generation was heavily geared toward digging mines and wells. Laying railroad track, digging harbors, and laying roads were similarly oriented on moving African exports of raw materials abroad, and foreign aid was structured to support those aims. Thus, given the uneven geographical distribution of natural resources across the continent, "development" along these lines tended to be concentrated in particular areas, such as the Congo or the racist states of South Africa and Rhodesia (later renamed Zimbabwe).

For the United States, competition drove an ever-shifting network of Cold War alliances in Africa expressed through a host of tactics, from military funding to proxy and clandestine operations and the use of the CIA. Military strategy aimed at containment or rollback of the Soviet sphere of influence on the continent and entailed undermining African nationalist regimes perceived as in danger of aligning with the USSR or charting a path independent of the West, with its concomitant threat to "stability"—that is, a climate conducive to investment and capital accumulation. In Ghana, for example, Africa's first leader of the postcolonial era, Pan-Africanist president Nkrumah, was removed in a coup in 1966 later revealed to have been orchestrated by the CIA. As one US national security advisor commented at the time, "Nkrumah was doing more to undermine our interests than any other black African."[81] Despite the willingness of the Nkrumah regime to collaborate with foreign investors,[82] from the US vantage point, Ghana's example in charting the anticolonial path posed an ideological threat to US aspirations on the continent because of the inspiration the Ghanaian anticolonial movement represented for struggles across the continent, or, as Yao Graham describes it, where "the turning of the Ghanaian capital Accra into a staging point for the African anticolonial movement started almost immediately after independence and the lessons of the Ghana experience were pressed home."[83]

Militarism was inextricable from the political and economic aims of the day. The major powers deployed military bases as political leverage and the basis for outright intervention from the earliest days of this new period. Former colonial powers maintained a military presence in their former colonies, while in the 1960s the United States became increasingly interested in establishing outposts of their own, crucially making aid and loans contingent on that presence. Strategic military relationships with African nations such as Liberia as early as the World War II period established the precedent of US aid and infrastructure—geared toward US interests—in exchange for a military presence.[84] Aid in all forms expressed US strategic aims and was directed in the early years of independence disproportionately to those nations with large US investments, such as the resource-rich Congo-Kinshasa (later Zaire) and Nigeria.

Nonetheless, in the 1960s, US aid to Africa averaged less than one-tenth of the US global aid budget,[85] and other tactics to cement US preeminence dominated besides economic aid. Not coincidentally, those countries identified for their strategic importance for investment potential tended to also be on the receiving end of concerted US intervention, notably the assassination of Congolese radical nationalist leader Patrice Lumumba in 1961. As David Renton, David Seddon, and Leo Zeilig describe, Lumumba believed that "independence would not be sufficient to free Africa from its colonial past; the continent must also cease to be an economic colony of Europe."[86] In his famous "Independence Speech," Lumumba declared: "The Congo's independence is a decisive step towards the liberation of the whole African continent. . . . I call on all Congolese citizens, men, women and children, to set themselves resolutely to the task of creating a national economy and ensuring our economic independence."[87] This stance, and the ties he forged with the USSR, were received with alarm by Western powers anxious to ensure that the Congo was neither pulled into the Soviet orbit nor a beacon for revolutionary nationalism. Renton, Seddon, and Zeilig write:

> The Western powers used the threat of "Soviet Communism," arguing that the Congo and its great mineral wealth would inevitably fall to the Soviet Union if Lumumba were allowed to take power. . . . There is no question that the period was marked by vicious Cold War rivalry, which was played out to devastating effect on the continent, but in the Congo in 1960 it seems to have been more of a cover for Lumumba's immediate removal.[88]

Coups and other forms of intervention allowed the United States to deepen the vulnerability of new African states and pursue its imperial objectives. In 1966, on the heels of the Ghanaian coup, the new regime formally established ties with the International Monetary Fund, later to be the bearer of devastating structural adjustment policies.[89] All told, American fingerprints can be found on numerous assassinations and secret operations in Africa, and worldwide, throughout the Cold War.[90] The United States was joined in these murderous policies by the former colonial powers, all in the interest of creating new African states compliant with the wishes of the West. France, for example, intervened militarily in a long series of invasions throughout the 1960s, 1970s, and 1980s, from Cameroon to Gabon, Chad, Central African Republic, and Ivory Coast. No less brutal was US support for right-wing forces in Africa, such as UNITA, the Angolan insurgency led by Jonas Savimbi in their nearly three-decade-long civil war, or the Renamo organization in Mozambique. These right-wing resistance movements waged wars responsible for the deaths of hundreds of thousands.

National Development

As we have seen, the legacy of colonialism reproduced a political and economic straitjacket for the newly independent nations from the beginning. Competing economic ideologies of the post-independence societies battled over whether development would proceed along free-market or state-directed lines. As Marxist Nigel Harris describes in *The End of the Third World*:

> Poverty was not inevitable, nor could the problem of poverty safely be left to the normal working of the world market. . . . The group of poor countries, identified as "underdeveloped" in the late forties, could not afford to await the possible long-term effects of free trade. . . . There were two different conceptions of economic development. On the one hand, the orthodox economists, known as "neoclassical," envisaged a world economy in which different countries played specialized roles and were therefore economically interdependent. . . . The radicals, on the other hand, saw national economic development as a structural change in the *national* economy rather than a relationship to the world economy. . . . With a fully diversified home economy, it was thought, self-generating growth was possible on the basis of an expanding home market, regardless of what happened in the world at large. The starting-point for these preoccupations was the attempt to explain why the orthodox theory of world trade did not work for the poor countries— why for them, it apparently produced impoverishment.[91]

For advocates of national development, economic growth was only considered possible by extricating the local national economy from the capitalist system. Championed in the Arusha Declaration by Julius Nyerere's TANU Party—and lifted up by prominent left intellectuals such as Rodney—"African socialism" such as Tanzania's *ujamma* was embraced by some nationalist leaders as a model for the underdeveloped world. (*Ujamma*—Swhaili for "family" or "brotherhood"—was the concept embraced by Nyerere for his economic development model emphasizing nationalization and village-based production described in the Arusha Declaration.) But the strategic vision of national development—of rapid progress and industrial development—was, for both the African bourgeoisie and the left, inseparable from key political questions. Its adherents embraced the model of economic development and industrialization they observed in the USSR, typically the path for states emerging from colonialism in that era.[92] As Pete Binns has described, "in many cases new leaders appeared speaking the languages of 'socialism' or 'humanism'; they would harness the toiling masses behind the efforts of the state and state-planned economic growth would take place, eliminating poverty, exploitation, inequality and suffering."[93] Historian Leo Zeilig notes how, following the

Soviet Union, "independence represented a race for top-down, autonomous industrialization in scores of emergent nations. . . . [where] state capitalism offered the magic key to development."[94]

African ruling classes emphasized state investment and national development based on import-substitution industrialization—that is, diversifying domestic production in order to make economies less dependent on foreign imports to compel development of local manufacturing, sometimes described as "industrialization at the periphery." As Harris similarly describes, a diversified economy required coherent direction and coordination from above: "For such an economy to be reasonably self-sufficient at a tolerable level of income, it would have to reproduce domestically all the main sectors of a modern economy. . . . Such a strategy could only be implemented by the state; its control of external trade and financial transactions was the key to reshaping domestic activity."[95] For theorists of neocolonialism, as Roger Southall describes,

> the remedy to dependence lay in the delinking of the former colonies from metropolitan capital by revolutionary nationalist regimes. In practice, however, such few attempts as were made invariably ran aground on the shoals of Western hostility, impractical economics, lack of developmental alternatives, self-interested leadership, and the demobilization and subversion of revolutionary regimes.[96]

The heavy reliance on state intervention was a feature not only of decolonization in Africa, but of the rapid and uneven transition from predominantly peasant societies to concentrated industrial development in the formerly colonized world. Statification was the order of the day. As Binns writes: "Indeed in the post-war world, above all in the 1950s, 1960s and the early 1970s, the use of the state to centralize capital and to push development forward leapt ahead as never before—above all in the newly emerging third world nations."[97] Harris notes that, ironically, "with decolonization, the removal of a former imperial ruling order (as in much of Asia and Africa) vested unprecedented power in the hands of the new states. It is scarcely to be wondered that, as Trotsky observed in tsarist Russia, 'Capitalism seemed to be an offspring of the state.'"[98] By the end of the 1970s, public-sector investment in less developed countries made up over half of total investment. Nationalized corporations in places like Ghana and Zambia produced around 40 percent of GDP.[99] However, despite political ideology and aspirations, independent economic growth was severely challenged in Africa for a number of reasons. First, instances of economic development, acquired in the prior colonial period, were a product of a relatively high level of integration into the world system. This integration translated into hesitancy on the part of some regimes to embark on some of the hallmark tasks of the national development project, such as import substitution, nationalization of industry, and redistribution of previously colonial-held land. Agricultural production, meanwhile, was retooled to focus on exports, with a dramatically negative impact on subsistence farming and consumption by the majority.

Binns's account of revolution and state capitalism in the Third World describes this contradictory dynamic in which, conversely, weaker states could more easily *attempt* the nationalization project given their position of weaker connection to the world system. Binns provides, writing in 1984, the following example to illustrate the point:

> South Africa currently provides Zimbabwe with a quarter of its imports and trans-ships fully *one half* of all the rest of its trade. The import-substitution industries built up in 1965–79 are no exception to this situation. . . . Mugabe's government has therefore neither moved significantly against the white landowners nor attempted to do anything that might provoke South Africa into cutting Zimbabwe's life-line to the outside world. In contrast with Mozambique whose very backwardness made such a policy feasible for a few years, the relative economic strength of Zimbabwe and its greater integration into the world market has, paradoxically, been the very feature that prevented such a policy being possible there.[100]

Second, autonomous national development faltered soon after independence, when Western powers took steps to ensure African nations could not establish a basis for economic independence. Intervention aimed at undermining economic development took up a range of strategies that included extending and reinforcing unfavorable trade policy from the colonial era and limiting foreign investment to areas that would directly facilitate extraction.

Third, as Binns notes, another important factor in the weak economic footing of the newly independent nations and the tendency toward state-directed economies was changes in foreign investment patterns:

> The pattern of international investment and trade changed quite dramatically; before the war around 40 percent of world trade was in primary products—agricultural produce, fuel, raw materials—but by the end of the long boom this figure had fallen by a half. International trade became much less a matter of exchange between primary producers on one hand and manufacturers on the other, and much more a question of the mutual exchange of manufactures between relatively industrialized nations or parts of nations. This meant that international capital flowed increasingly from one industrialized part of the world economy to another; American capital, for

instance, found many more opportunities for profitable investment in advanced Europe than in . . . Africa.[101]

Import substitution—the economic strategy focused on growing local industries by limiting imports—also produced its own problems: for one, it created very high costs for domestically produced manufacturing. By the same token, low interest rates meant to encourage industrial investment tended to create not only high-priced goods, but also relatively low job creation and overcapacity, thus producing further problems despite the symbolic value of heavy industry. Industrial investment also had the effect of further exacerbating class divisions, with a shift away from production oriented to consumption toward industrial sectors. Many Third World nations, especially in Africa, were hobbled in their ability to overcome these obstacles. "Only some large countries could pursue such policies, and only for limited periods of time in given historical circumstances," Harris notes. "Sooner or later, if growth were to continue, the domestic accumulation process—whether wholly or partially in the hands of the state—would have to be reintegrated in the world process."[102]

As Harris outlines, numerous critiques of the model emerged from within different currents of the left. The Stalinist model of heavy industrialization was in competition with the approach of widening employment opportunities. This model seemed to imply that stages could be skipped in the process of development. More broadly, by the 1970s, many of the assumptions of the national development model came to be questioned. The "cures" had come to be seen as the source of the problems of underdevelopment. Theorists such as Baran, Amin, and Gunder Frank correctly argued that national planning and import substitutionism were bound to fail without revolutionary change in the class structure. Internationalists, writes Harris—including Michael Kidron and others—placed their critique within a Marxist framework by arguing that economic development required revolutionary change on a global scale, not merely within national borders: "Removing the old ruling class, nationalizing the means of production (and expropriating foreign capital), redistributing income and land, forced accumulation, would not suffice to overcome the paralysis imposed by the changed structure of world capitalism."[103] The size and scale of major industrialized powers left weaker ones unable to compete. By the close of the era of national development, Harris writes, the poorest countries

> remained trapped in producing and exporting a single raw material at low levels of productivity, lacking reserves to guard against the ravages of famine. The triumphs of world capitalism were indeed more spectacular in the

less developed countries than they had been in the more developed, but victories in the long march of capital accumulation should not be confused with the conquest of hunger.[104]

As Toussaint notes, "countries of the periphery have faced a twin difficulty: in the first place, they were pillaged; second, the only path left open to them was under the wing of the center's main powers."[105] Likewise, the bourgeoisie of newly independent nations in Africa—new arrivals on the world economic scene—faced serious obstacles in directing their own domestic growth. Even while workers' power brought down colonialism, workers, socialists, and other activists have struggled since to challenge single-party regimes and build alternatives to state-run trade unions.

New ruling classes were now called upon to manage "their own" working classes to pursue the project of national development of industry and agriculture. Yet working classes across the continent—only recently at the helm of anticolonial struggles—were unwilling to suffer these new attacks silently. In post-independence Nigeria, for example, the government's calls to unite for "national development" were unsuccessful at papering over their assaults from above or deflecting the rise of class consciousness and class divisions in the general strike of 1964. Similarly, Zambian mineworkers battled attacks by the new government that were also mounted in the name of "national development," while the years following independence in Zimbabwe saw strike waves for wage hikes and social reforms. As elsewhere, new rulers such as Zambia's Kenneth Kaunda and Zimbabwe's Robert Mugabe faced off workers' militancy with repression and co-optation.[106]

Ultimately, the contradictions of "African socialism" and the process of turning the reins of the accumulation process over to indigenous capitalists were unsustainable. The critical issue, ultimately, was not merely one of "sell-outs" and political betrayal. In the African case, the weak basis of African capitalism, as well as the pressures of the world system, compelled an accommodation with foreign capital. Attempts to establish the advantage of local capitalists ran up against the resistance of global capital, which cannot ultimately be overcome with a strategy of national development from above. As Harris writes, "the needs of accumulation limited the potential for social reform. Furthermore, an increasingly world system lays down narrower and narrower limits to the possibility of local eccentricity, including reform. In a competitive system, holding down the price of labor takes precedence over protecting it, and the domestic economy becomes increasingly a spin-off of a wider order."[107] In the end, a "development" model that replaced state ownership by colonialists with that of new African ruling classes failed to create genuine socialism from below, and thus the real potential to pose an alternative both to a world system based on profit or to the inevitable dead end of a nation-based model.

Nationalism and Its Limitations

Ultimately, state capitalist and national development models failed in Africa, both in their ability to overcome the legacies of colonialism and specifically in their inability to create nations able to grow while seeking to de-link from the world capitalist system. As Binns notes: "The third worldist 'socialist' vision of utilizing the state *against* capital and the multinationals is . . . not only a hopeless dream, but has been made dramatically more so by the sharpening competition and increasing internationalization of the world capitalist system itself."[108]

The brutal reality of these dynamics and the compulsion of the world market were borne out in the coming decades: the collapse of the USSR formalized for many regimes a shift from a state-directed model to free-market capitalism, even for those leaders in Africa previously hailed by some as "Marxist," such as those of Angola, Benin, and Ethiopia.[109] The contradictions of these political and economic legacies—the weaknesses of the new national leaders, the emergence of a new African ruling class, the newness of the postcolonial state, and above all the pressures of the international economy—thrust regimes toward abandoning the most militant or "socialist" projects. For example, Binns points out, "in the southern African revolutionary states—Angola, Zimbabwe and Mozambique— . . . revolutionary regimes, often established after a long and bitter guerrilla war, have performed a remarkable about-face and have ended up with a series of very significant accommodations with western capital."[110]

Thus, the project of building genuine revolutionary socialism from below was postponed. The combined pressures of the legacies of colonialism, the Stalinist development model, and the restrictions imposed by the Cold War imperialism proved impossible to transcend, despite their alternatives' political appeal. Nigel Harris summarizes the pull of this vision and its challenges:

> The attempt to establish an independent national economy was just as much an affirmation of self-determination as the struggle to throw out the imperialist powers. Development was no longer something to be awaited as the ultimate product of the working of an invisible hand but rather something that could be created by the intelligent action of the state. . . . It was this

element of liberation, of self-emancipation, which in part recruited the left to import-substitutionism and reconciled them to the apparently unlimited growth of state power. . . . Thus, "exploitation," supposedly for Marxists a relationship between capital and labor, came to describe the relationships between governments or countries or groups of countries. . . .

An incidental byproduct of the process was that the left, in the name of socialism, was subverted, and bent to the tasks of supporting and defending the process of national capital accumulation in the name of national libera-tion. It was a harsh process, and required radical terminology to conceal it. When elementary accumulation was complete, the ruling orders, willingly or not, returned to the global market.[111]

The requirements of the continent's new ruling classes—accentuated by the structural constraints inherited from colonialism—could by no means es-cape the competitive pressures of the broader system, particularly as it lurched into crisis. Yet running through this period is likewise the legacy of the anti-colonial struggles of the organized working classes and peasants that rid the continent of the colonial order and continued heroic and sustained movements into the independence period. Despite the contradictions of nationalism and Pan-Africanism, organizing from below also characterized this era and con-tributed a vital legacy to the worldwide upheavals and revolutionary tradi-tions in the formerly colonized world. As then, it is the mass-based workers' struggles and social movements that offer up liberatory potential for the ma-jority in Africa, as we will explore at greater length in the chapters to come.

Chapter Three

Neoliberalism: Crisis, Debt, and Structural Adjustment

[Some Africans] believe all of Africa's problems are basically rooted in Western nastiness: colonialism, slavery, debt, and the like. But my own sense is that opinion has shifted tremendously in Africa over the last ten years, that there's greater openness to accepting that African problems have roots in Africa.... One of the good legacies of colonialism [is that] there are Western nations that could have turned their backs on Africa a long time ago if they didn't have some historical, economic, and sentimental connection.... For me to suggest that we reduce rather than increase aid to Africa will sound to many like spitting in the face of a dying man, but I see it as analogous to dragging a dope addict to his feet and bringing him to a rehabilitation clinic.

—Former World Bank official Robert Calderisi[1]

Most African nations emerged from the period of independence and national development thwarted in their efforts to industrialize and develop an economic base. Despite this legacy, blame-the-victim rhetoric has become commonplace in official circles as Western investors and ideologues chide African economies as "basket cases" for having "missed the globalization boat."[2] Castigating crisis-ridden African economies for these failures, as Robert Calderisi does, distorts the historical role of global capital and international financial institutions in producing economies unable to compete on the world market. It also reveals a shameful disregard for the policies imposed on his watch: an era of massive loans with harsh conditions of austerity and privatization demanded in return. All told, this was the economic experience of the neoliberal era in Africa.

The Marxist approach to imperialism provides a valuable framework for understanding this period of the early 1980s to the turn of the century. Marxist theory argues that ever-increasing competition between global capital spills across borders, threatening conflict between capital's "own" nation-states. In this framework, imperial tensions can take many forms, from economic policy and trade wars to outright military clashes and armed conflict. During this period, Africa was the site of Cold War imperial rivalry and, after the collapse of the USSR, the emergence of a largely unipolar world with the United States at the helm. In this new order the United States was not, however, without competitors. In this chapter, I lay out how a crisis in the world economic system opened up a harsh regime of neoliberal dictates. This regime was an expression of imperial conflict first described by Marx, Lenin, and Bukharin, but in a new form: a crisis of profitability for capital driving efforts to further pry open markets and pave the way for investment. Fundamentals of the classical Marxist approach remain crucial: that states play a key role as the executive committee of their national ruling classes, which includes maintaining control over "their" working classes.

Key to the aims of global capital at this time were to subordinate foreign markets and trade to its interests. A major strategy was a reliance on the US state and international financial institutions such as the International Monetary Fund and World Bank to act as battering rams against the economies of the Global South. These institutions were, above all, instruments of US capital in the Cold War rivalry with the USSR as well as its competitors, Western Europe and Japan.

While the Marxist approach emphasizes that competitive dynamic and the interrelationship of state and capital at the heart of imperialism, many contemporary left approaches to this period focus on "globalization." Typically, such theories describe the apparent rise of multinational corporations operating with *only limited constraints* from the nation-state and its laws and borders. What is commonly termed globalization does describe obvious characteristics of multinational corporations whose markets, employees, production, and supply chains increasingly span multiple countries. But this perspective incorrectly minimizes the role of the state in this process. Such an approach was famously put forth in Michael Hardt and Antonio Negri's book *Empire* (2000), which states that power is projected in a "transnational" or even "borderless" world, with an ever-decreasing relevance of nation-states. Their ideas seemed to capture and underscore the ideas of the global justice and anti-globalization movements of the late 1990s: namely, that states were becoming increasingly irrelevant. Unfortunately, their argument proved disastrously wrong shortly after the book's release with the attacks in New York on September 11, 2001, and the advent of a new era of US intervention abroad, particularly in Afghanistan and Iraq. Their portrayal of a free-floating, unmoored empire, while seemingly esoteric before 9/11, afterward seemed out of step with reality.[3]

But the preceding period by no means lacked outbreaks of conflict and military intervention. As we have seen, superpower support for African regimes in the 1970s and 1980s aimed to shore up and stabilize weak states for their own ends, while resting on internal contradictions of a narrow ruling class base, ethnic divisions, and massive economic inequality. These contradictions, pronounced in the postcolonial period, were pushed to the breaking point under conditions of neoliberal austerity. As Abayomi Azikiwe notes, "much of the instability led to a further fracturing of the political landscape which found its expression in military coups and other forms of anti-democratic practice. These seizures of power by the armed forces and the police were often prompted by economic crises engineered by the financial institutions and multi-national corporations who were seeking to maximize their profits at the expense of the majority of workers, farmers, and youth."[4]

From the earliest days of independence, the fragility of African economies and states created vulnerability to imperial "meddling," including on the part of the CIA. As discussed earlier, Ghana's coup makers, who brought down President Kwame Nkrumah in 1966 with the assistance of the CIA, found fertile ground in the upheaval caused by reverberations from global markets. As Yao Graham has described, "by that time the crisis in the international price of cocoa had wrought considerable damage to revenue and growth projections, putting pressure on imports and consumption. The shortages and associated discontent were a perfect climate for the CIA."[5] The coup also served as the entry point for early IMF "involvement" and a template for the dictates of these global institutions. In fact, Azikiwe writes, "the hardships engendered by the IMF role in the [post-Nkrumah era] in Ghana created the social conditions which resulted in yet another military coup in January 1972. Instability continued with successive military seizures of power in 1978, 1979 and 1981."[6] From the early days of independence in Africa, intensifying economic vulnerability paved the way for heightened political instability and imperial intervention, reverberations that continued to be felt decades later. The precedent set by this dynamic in the context of economic liberalization unleashed devastating results on African nations.

The Origins of Neoliberalism and the Debt Crisis

The World Bank and the International Monetary Fund were founded after World War II to facilitate Western investment overseas and to ensure that the new era of independence configured the globe on political and economic terms favorable to the world's most powerful nations, especially the United States. During the immediate postcolonial era, the World Bank was led by Robert McNamara, who made it clear that "development" was a strategy to strengthen capital accumulation for the benefit of the West. "The World Bank," he declared in 1969, "is a body that makes investments whose objective is development. It is neither a philanthropic institution nor a social welfare agency."[7] As such, the World Bank under McNamara advocated chiefly for policies that cemented economic and political ties between the governments of the North and South. In so doing, the Bretton Woods institutions laid the groundwork for the neoliberal turn of the early 1980s and its drastic shift toward privatization and deregulation.[8]

By the mid-1970s, with the sharp collapse of worldwide commodity prices, state capitalist economies had lurched into recession. The crisis proved to be long term and deeply felt. As the UN Conference on Trade and Development (UNCTAD) has described, "There has been a long-term downward trend in real nonfuel commodity prices since 1960 . . . the commodity prices recession of the 1980s was more severe, and considerably more prolonged, than that of the Great Depression of the 1930s."[9] Bade Onimode has written of the staggering devastation caused by this collapse, which produced a foreign exchange loss of $2.2 billion from 1979 to 1981 alone.[10] Desperate for funding, many Third World nations looked to the West for credit.

Thus, beginning in the late 1970s, the dogma of "development" began to change. This shift reflected the need to spur world trade and restore profitability in the advanced capitalist countries in the context of global recession[11] and the debt crisis. These crises provided an opportunity to use the international financial institutions to remake global markets in the interest of Western capital and, as Joel Geier describes, "bind debt-burdened countries more tightly into the web of a world trade system that chiefly served the needs of US corporations and banks."[12] Reflecting the programmatic shift from an earlier Keynesian framework of stimulating demand to one of austerity, the IMF and the World Bank now relied on loans to low-income nations accompanied by harsh repayment terms. These efforts ultimately aimed to drive down national incomes, both to facilitate the repayment of massive Third World debt and to transform economies of the Global South into ones based on "export-led" strategies—those set up to best serve the market needs of global capital. This turn marked the arrival of what's now often called the neoliberal era.

Industrializing nations, according to neoliberal dogma, would grow their economies by focusing on producing commodities that could be exported to rich countries while importing the latter's finished goods. Export-oriented production compelled by global financial institutions created an economic straitjacket of single-commodity production and a shift from Third World industrialization. For Western ruling classes, the sharp decline in rates of profitability in Western capitalism offered both a crisis and an opportunity: a conjuncture where crisis-ridden nations in the "developing" world were compelled to retreat from the national development model. The moment provided the cover under which the neoliberal era could be launched to sweep away barriers to free trade and economic growth in the capitalist centers of accumulation, "barriers" that were a legacy of the national development project. Likewise, the neoliberal assault in Africa was aimed at undermining working-class resistance and potential challenges from below through attacks on unions and social spending.

With the dramatic arrival of high interest rates—launched by the interest rate hike in 1979 by the US Federal Reserve, the so-called "Volcker Shock"—and the inability of debtor nations to pay their loans, the West prescribed bitter medicine. As Toussaint describes, these changes resulted in "an increase in interest rates on short-term loans to unprecedented levels. . . . For Third World countries, this new policy meant a tripling of payments on the same levels of debt."[13] World Bank figures chart the increase in interest rates from a negative 4 percent (where the rate of inflation exceeded the stated interest rates for borrowing) in 1975 to over 10 percent in 1985.[14] As a result, these loans turned into crippling, unpayable debts to the World Bank and IMF, who required governments to slash social spending and privatize government-owned industries and services. As David Harvey has put it, "The IMF and the World Bank thereafter became centers for the propagation and enforcement of 'free market fundamentalism' and neoliberal orthodoxy. In return for debt rescheduling, indebted countries were required to implement institutional reforms, such as cuts in welfare expenditures, more flexible labor market laws, and privatization. Thus was 'structural adjustment' invented."[15] Housed in Washington, DC, the Bretton Woods institutions from their inception have been disproportionately impacted by US priorities, down to the present day: voting rights in the IMF in 2014 consisted of only two countries from sub-Saharan Africa, for a total of 4.5 percent of the vote, as compared to the United States's 16.8 percent, by far the largest share.[16] Former World Bank chief economist Joseph Stiglitz describes how, despite some "minor adjustments" since its founding, "the major developed countries run the show, with only one country, the United States, having effective veto."[17] Harvey's *A Brief History of Neoliberalism* describes the class warfare laid out by this period of crisis and the shift toward a direct confrontation with the world's working classes:

> One condition of the post-war settlement in almost all countries was that the economic power of the upper classes be restrained and that labor be accorded a much larger share of the economic pie. In the United States, for example, the share of the national income taken by the top 1 percent of income earners fell from a pre-war high of 16 percent to less than 8 percent by the end of the Second World War, and stayed close to that level for nearly three decades. While growth was strong this restraint seemed not to matter. To have a stable share of an increasing pie is one thing. But when growth collapsed in the 1970s, when real interest rates went negative and paltry dividends and profits were the norm, then upper classes everywhere felt threatened. . . . The upper classes had to move decisively if they were to protect themselves from political and economic annihilation.[18]

Neoliberalism's Arrival in Africa

Economist Bade Onimode has pointed out that the Bretton Woods institutions were not newcomers to Africa. Writing in 1989, he stated that "even though the policies of the IMF and the World Bank have become prominent in the 1980s, they date back to the colonial era. By 1953, for example, a World Bank mission had arrived in Nigeria at the invitation of the colonial government to advise on various development programmes."[19] The long history of these agencies on the continent set the stage for the imposition of harsh policies to come, as well as their cooperation with African rulers.

Respectable growth rates in Africa of 4 to 6 percent in the 1960s and increased spending on education, health care, and "development" initiatives gave way to stagnation and decline in the 1970s. As latecomers to industrialization, most African states proved unable to marshal sufficient capital resources, even with state intervention, to overcome the legacies of colonialism. As Patrick Bond has pointed out, African economies spiraled downward in a context of a global economy in marked decline over several decades: per capita GDP growth went from 3.6 percent in the 1960s to 2.1 percent in the 1970s, then 1.3 percent in the 1980s.[20] This growth, weak as it was, was highly uneven across the globe, with the bulk of it concentrated in the West and East

Asia; other parts of the world declined all the more dramatically.[21] Subsequent decades have exposed the disastrous impact of these Western global financial institutions—the IMF and World Bank—on African societies. Loans from the World Bank were the origin of Africa's debt crisis, debts incurred to create industrial sectors that could not effectively compete on the world market.

Biodun Olamosu and Andy Wynne outline the economic history of the period, describing the convergence of developments that rendered African economies vulnerable to Western strictures:

> Heads of African governments voiced their position in the 1980 Lagos Plan of Action [under the auspices of the Organisation of African Unity]. This placed most of the blame for the then dire economic performance of sub-Saharan Africa on factors beyond the control of its governments—namely, the seemingly ever-declining real commodity prices and declining overall terms of trade, world recession, rising international interest rates and debt burden, and extended periods of drought which the economically ravaged governments were less able to manage.[22]

Underlying the dogma of the "greater opportunities" of neoliberalism and unfettered free trade lay a host of constraints imposed by the unequal terms of the global economic system, vastly limiting the options of African rulers.[23] In fact, the process of neoliberalism facilitated the creation of more compliant states. Describing the Ghanaian experience of structural adjustment, Eboe Hutchful writes: "What has emerged in Accra is a parallel government controlled (if not created) by the international lender agencies . . . [while] the other side of the external appropriation of policy-making powers is the deliberate de-politicalization that has occurred under the . . . [Economic Reconstruction Programme], and the displacement of popular participation and mobilization by a narrowly based bureaucratic management."[24]

Writing in 2005, Gavin Capps pointed out another important feature of African debt: the high proportion historically of public debt as compared to other regions of the world, such as Latin America, which mainly hold private debt. The high proportion of African debt originating from "public" sources—namely Western governments, the IMF, and the World Bank—creates the potential for a high degree of subordination of African states to their creditors, namely vulnerability to imposed structural adjustment "conditionalities" and punishing neoliberal terms. In this period the West strategically oriented on regions such as Africa to stimulate their own economies, including arms and military equipment. Capps writes:

The Western powers responded to the world recession of 1974–75 with a scheme which tried to boost demand for their home industries by underwriting the export of arms and machinery to the Third World. The liability for this 'export Keynesianism' lay with the Third World states themselves. The 'export credits' were in reality tied loans that could only be used for the purchase of specified imports . . . Bilateral debt has in effect really been killing Africans twice—by underwriting the export of arms to fuel its many wars, and then by sucking out desperately scarce resources to ensure that British and other firms can keep up their lively trade in death.[25]

In Africa, as elsewhere in the Third World, the World Bank and IMF mandated a shift away from industrialization toward economies based solely on the export of raw materials and agricultural products. Loans were now to be used as leverage to impose what were called structural adjustment programs (SAPs) that mandated a reversal of initiatives implemented under a "national development" framework. Social investment and protections for nascent industries were confronted by requirements to slash social spending, eliminate price subsidies and trade tariffs, and privatize government-owned industries and services—all in order to pay down foreign debt. SAPs likewise mandated "reform" of investment and labor codes and numerous corporate incentives, such as reduced tax burdens.[26] Structural adjustment thus became a central strategy in the remaking of Africa on neoliberal terms. And as Michael Watts has described, Africa became the test case for the ability of the ideologues to roll out the strategy elsewhere: "Long before shock therapy in Eastern Europe or even the debt-driven 'adjustments' in Latin America, it was sub-Saharan Africa that was the playground of neo-liberalism's assault."[27]

From privatization, deregulation, free trade zones, and attacks on labor, neoliberalism's arrival was an economic, political, and ideological project that remade African economies and societies while sharpening class formation. Global capital and the international financial institutions (IFIs)—that is, the World Bank and the IMF—that serve it did not operate without local assistance. A feature of this class formation was the development of new ruling classes of African states that facilitated liberalization and capital accumulation through state intervention. As Peter Lawrence and Yao Graham write:

The issue of SAPs should not be separated from the social and economic context in which a new power alliance developed between finance ministries and the IFIs such that finance ministers were effectively in charge of government and were responsible to the IFIs rather than their own democratic institutions. They then presided over the dismantling and retrenching of the state, such that capital now cannot do without the state but requires a state that subsidizes rather than regulates capital.[28]

Foreign capital relied on the African state for the imposition of these "reforms," hence the later embrace of the ideological and programmatic requirements for "good governance," to become a favored rubric through which to assert conditions for African nations for loans and aid. Beneath the veneer of Western concerns for "governance" and "political instability" lies a highly hypocritical set of assumptions, since backing deregulation and privatization has "stripped the African states of what little control they had previously exercised over . . . foreign firms."[29]

African elites had played an important role under colonialism in facilitating capital accumulation. In the neoliberal era, the African bourgeoisie played a similar role, now as new national ruling classes and often enthusiastic "partners" of global elites. This process was in evidence even in South Africa, where the historic mass movement against apartheid brought national liberation movement leaders to power. Following the African National Congress's (ANC) accession to power in 1994, GDP growth shrunk to a slow crawl while unemployment grew, and the ANC broke its social-justice, redistributive promises. Peter Dwyer's account of the embrace of neoliberalism in South Africa by Nelson Mandela and his successor, Thabo Mbeki, describes how the *Financial Times* gloated as Mandela "delighted investors, businessmen, and white South Africans [with] his commitment to free-market economic and political moderation. Again and again, Mr. Mandela has stressed the need to restore business confidence and attract foreign investment."[30] As activist Trevor Ngwane of the Anti-Privatization Forum has commented, "There are no miracles in history, and this has been decisively proven in South Africa, where the miracle is turning out to be nothing but the betrayal of workers by its self-appointed liberators."[31]

Today's neoliberal African-based initiatives, like the New Partnership for Africa's Development (NEPAD) and the African Union, championed by Mbeki and former Nigerian president Olusegun Obasanjo, provide no solution to African inequality and poverty as they merely create opportunities for more African ruling-class involvement in trade policy.[32] NEPAD helps to create favorable conditions for Western investment through (African-imposed) requirements for privatization, cuts in social spending, and "good governance"—that is, subjecting African policy making to the political will of Western imperialism and its allies. These African "partnerships" highlight the tremendously uneven benefits of neoliberal policy across classes and nations. The Tax Justice Network Africa has described NEPAD as follows: "NEPAD's agenda is essentially based on the Africanised version of the Washington Consensus agenda: that Africa's fate lies intertwined with foreign investment-driven development."[33] In 2002, members of some forty African social movements, trade unions, youth and women's organizations, nongovernmental organizations (NGOs), religious groups, and others rejected NEPAD in the African Civil Society Declaration.[34]

Individual African nations "innovated" with their own neoliberal initiatives. In 1996, South Africa's embrace of the free market included the launch of the Growth Employment and Redistribution Program (GEAR). As Ashwin Desai has described, this initiative represented a break from the redistributive program of the African National Congress. "In practice," he writes, "GEAR operated as a homegrown structural adjustment program. Markets were opened, taxes to the rich were cut, state assets were privatized, services were commodified, and social spending was reduced. Small wonder that Pamela Cox, head of the South Africa division of the World Bank, enthused: 'what they [the ANC] have done to put South Africa on a right footing, is, I think, almost miraculous.'"[35] In sum, the history of structural adjustment and neoliberal "reform" of the past half-century conclusively demonstrates, whether African elites are at the table or not, the priorities for Africa are set by the needs of global capital rather than the needs of ordinary Africans.

For the continent as a whole, these policies were ultimately proven failures at their own stated goals of driving up foreign direct investment (FDI) and fueling growth in Africa. Toussaint identifies the period of structural adjustment and the debt crisis as 1983 to 1998. During that period, he writes, FDI as a percent of GNP fell by more than 50 percent. FDI in Africa fell from 25 percent of the world's total at its peak during the 1970s to less than 5 percent by the late 1990s, according to data from UNCTAD. Meanwhile, the average rate of growth in Africa in the 1970s was about 3.5 percent; by the 1980s it had fallen to 2.5 percent, and by 1998 to 2.2 percent.[36] During this same period—the closing decades of the twentieth century—African debt rose at a rate outstripping other regions of the world.

Cuts to Social Programs

Ultimately, neoliberal strategy heightened social and economic crisis exponentially. But why exactly were both growth and development reversed in Africa in this period? For one, structural adjustment programs require that debt be repaid, compelling devastating cuts to social programs to make payments with interest and sometimes penalties for late payments. As a result, IFI requirements not only failed to meet the needs of ordinary Africans, but often actually *reversed* development. For example, as James K. Boyce and Léonce Ndikumana describe, "in Sub-Saharan Africa (SSA) as a whole, debt service amounted to 3.8 percent of . . . GDP in 2000. By comparison, SSA countries spent 2.4 percent of GDP on health."[37] To add insult to injury, the requirement to repay is enforced regardless of the project's actual "success."[38] Civil society organizations have rejected these terms, demanding that governments refuse to repay loans for failed projects. A disastrous water privatization scheme in Tanzania led by the British company Biwater, for example, was strong-armed by the World Bank and the IMF.[39] The executive director of Agenda Participation 2000, Moses Kulaba, asked, "Is it necessary for the government to repay money borrowed to implement a project with the World Bank when there are no results?" Advocates called on the government to refuse to repay the $61.5 million owed for this failure.[40]

The general trend of increased debt paired with *decreased* development was borne out in country after country across Africa, and millions of people paid a high price for the immense weight of foreign debt, even under conditions where official growth was held up as a model. Capps writes:

> The social and economic cost of servicing Africa's debt has been immense. Year on year greater proportions of shrinking national budgets were diverted to repaying Western creditors at the expense of welfare or productive investment. During the 1980s debt service payments averaged 16 percent of African government expenditure compared to 12 percent on education, 10 percent on defense and 4 percent on health.[41]

For example, notes the Jubilee Debt Campaign,

> in the mid-1980s, Mozambique's government external debt was already 60 percent of GDP. Government foreign debt payments averaged 15 percent of revenue through the 1980s and 1990s, and this increased in the mid-1990s after the end of the [civil] war. . . . Between 1996 and 2011, GDP per person doubled. Yet at the same time, the number of people classed by the UN as undernourished increased from 8.1 million in 1996 to 9.6 million by 2011. The number of people living on less than $2 a day increased even more dramatically, from 15.2 million in 1996 to 19.3 million in 2009.[42]

Two studies of Africa for the period 1990 to 2005 found increased maternal mortality associated with IMF and African Development Bank (AfDB) structural adjustment loans, with one finding an additional 360 maternal deaths per 100,000 births attributable to IMF structural adjustment and approximately 231 additional maternal deaths per 100,000 births due to AfDB structural adjustment.[43]

It is hard to underestimate the full scale of the reverberations of budget cuts and the debt crisis across virtually every area of African society. On the occasion of US President Barack Obama's 2013 visit, the Jubilee Campaign summarized both the scope of the problem and its role in deepening inequality: "IMF policies . . . lead to cuts in needed social services, actions that in turn have a ripple effect on the rest of the economy and on the health and well-being of women and children. In Senegal, for instance, policy conditions on loans from the 1980s and 1990s badly harmed the civil service, which led to the collapse of both the agricultural and industrial sectors. In this process, civil servants lose their jobs and their source of income, and girls who might otherwise be in school are forced to drop out and help support their families when their parents lose their jobs. Many of Africa's greatest challenges, including food insecurity, growing urban poverty, and conflict can be traced to these policies."[44] The financial crisis of 2008–2009 drastically accelerated these trends, inflicting severe damage to the fight against AIDS, for example, among a raft of other social problems. At the time, many nations on the continent had less than one health worker for every 1,000 people, well below the World Health Organization (WHO) minimum. Yet, typically, the IMF has barred nations from hiring doctors and nurses while privatizing public health programs.[45]

Economies Geared for Export and Deindustrialization

Neoliberal policy has further stultified developing economies. The "conditionalities" that dictated the terms of the loans demanded investment be limited to a very narrow range of primary commodities geared for export, usually in the extractive sector. Rather than building diverse industries and developing a broad technological and industrial base, growth was narrowed to capital-intensive production, typically for pulling raw materials out of the ground. And because indigenous production was undermined in this way, African economies during that period also became entirely reliant upon the West for imports to meet domestic needs. Worse, these conditions exacerbated the tendency toward lopsided economies inherited from the colonial period, when economies were reliant on a handful of exports. By 2000, primary commodity exports accounted for an astounding *80 percent* of African exports, as compared to 31 percent for countries elsewhere in the developing world, and a mere 16 percent for the advanced economies.[46]

This uneven structure has left the economies of African nations more vulnerable to the volatility of the market, because if the price of one commodity falls, it sends the entire nation into recession. As Toussaint writes, "sub-Saharan Africa has seen the terms of exchange of its export products on the global market deteriorate since the 1980s. . . . The value of a basket of goods exported by Africa has lost half its value compared to products imported by the North."[47] In the context of structural adjustment and indebtedness to IFIs, this result was especially painful, since external debt must be entirely repaid in hard currency, which is drawn from export revenues. By the turn of the century, according to the World Bank, many nations were compelled to make payments on their foreign debt representing *several hundred percent* of that export income.[48]

Africa is also saddled with another burden: because their economies are narrowly tied to exports, many African nations are compelled to import oil for their own use, so higher oil prices actually hurt them. And in the name of liberalizing trade, championed above all else by the West, actual trade deals have compelled African countries to eliminate tariffs, the results of which have been shown to cut 25 percent of their income—the equivalent, for example, of Zambia's yearly budget for dealing with AIDS.[49] Free-trade agreements also force developing regions, including Africa, to import Western foods, which, according to Oxfam, destroys the "livelihood for many small producers. . . . The adverse impact on poverty [is] substantial."[50] Driven off their land, small farmers have flooded urban areas, producing the massive slums and unemployment documented in Mike Davis's *Planet of Slums*. The world's highest percentages of slum dwellers are found in the African nations of Ethiopia and Chad (99.4 percent of the urban population in each).[51] According to the British organization ActionAid International:

> Rich countries are using their muscle to secure new markets for their exports of farm produce, industrial products and services. Their aim is to push all countries, including the poorest and least developed, to sign up to new liberalization commitments in these three areas of trade and further open up their economies to international competition. Unless this push is halted now, poverty and inequality in many poor countries could deepen.[52]

The impact of these policies has been to reduce growth, and in some cases led to a reversal of trends toward industrialization. As shown by figures from the World Development Movement, in Zambia, for example, "there were 140 textile manufacturers employing 34,000 people in 1991; just eight remained by 2000. Formal manufacturing employment fell from 75,400 to 43,320 between 1991 and 1998; and paid employment in agriculture from 78,000 to 50,000 in that decade."[53] Likewise, Zimbabwe's share of manufacturing declined from 32 percent of GDP in 1992 to a mere 17 percent just six years later—results that received, tellingly, high marks on the World Bank scorecard.[54] In Nigeria in the 1980s, 250 textile factories employed half a million people; the number of such factories stands at 25 today.[55] The majority of jobs in African societies now lie in the informal sector, meaning casual labor or self-employment.[56] Manufacturing output per head in sub-Saharan Africa actually fell 14.3 percent from 1990 to 1996.[57] A 2005 Christian Aid report found that lifting trade barriers designed to protect young industries cost sub-Saharan Africa $272 billion over the previous two decades.[58] In practice, this had the effect, as under colonialism, of turning Africa into a one-way conveyor belt of raw materials. Africa today exports the bulk of its natural resources. For example, as Davis describes, "in Abidjan [Ivory Coast], one of the few tropical African cities with an important manufacturing sector and modern urban services, submission to the SAP regime punctually led to deindustrialization, the collapse of construction, and a rapid deterioration in public transit and sanitation; as a result, urban poverty in Ivory Coast—the supposed 'tiger' economy of West Africa—doubled in the year 1987–88."[59] GDP growth in Ivory Coast stood at 1.6 percent in 1990, but by 2000, its GDP had shrunk 3.3 percent; the value of its industry declined 11 percent in that same period.[60]

Another disastrous result of neoliberal policy was the transformation of formerly food self-sufficient nations into economies coerced into an export-driven framework. As Toussaint writes, citing West African and other exports as examples:

> Throughout its existence, the World Bank has contributed powerfully to intensifying agricultural production for exportation. . . . Countries with a tradition of self-sufficiency in cereals and vegetables have gradually become net importers of those products, leading to loss of food security and sovereignty. The deliberate wish of the United States to end the food security of the developing countries was crudely expressed by John Block, the US agricultural secretary, in 1986 in the Uruguay Round: "The idea that developing countries should feed themselves is an anachronism from a bygone era. They could better ensure their food security by relying on US agricultural products."[61]

Export-driven policies increased hunger across the continent. Food consumption fell 25 percent from the 1960s to the 1990s.[62]

Loss of Capital Controls

Neoliberal structural adjustment also increased instability and fragility in debtor nations because of greater flexibility and freedom of movement for capital.[63] Crucially, investment of funds by African capitalists abroad is facilitated by the dictates of global financial institutions, which require that capital controls be lifted as a condition for loans.[64] Weakening of capital controls produces several interrelated problems. For one, it heightens speculation and highly volatile movements of money in and out of the markets. For weaker economies, such as in Africa, these kinds of speculative swings wreak havoc on the value of local currencies, fueling economic and social instability.

Mohamed Sultan and Stephen Yeboah, using Africa Progress Panel data, conclude: "Africa lost US$69 billion from illicit financial flows in 2012. That's more than the total annual financing required to meet Africa's energy and climate adaptation needs: $66 billion. . . .Two-thirds of Africans—about 621 million people—lack access to electricity. . . . Unless current trends change, it will take Africa until 2080 to achieve universal access to electricity."[65] Patrick Bond has termed this process "exchange control liberalization," where the much-heralded model of greater "integration" into the global economy has heightened instability.[66] Estimates guess that vast sums have disappeared from the continent under these conditions; at least one study has documented that close to $2 trillion has disappeared from the continent through these "reforms."[67] In fact, Léonce Ndikumana writes, "the era of financial liberalization since the mid-1990s has seen an escalation of capital flight."[68] As a result, he continues, "African countries exhibit higher ratios of capital flight in relation to GDP, domestic capital accumulation, foreign direct investment and official development."[69]

Accompanying this dynamic, looser capital controls heighten the tendency for illicit capital flows as they become increasingly mobile, and volatile markets increase the incentive to move funds abroad, including into tax havens. Boyce and Ndikumana argue that the conditions created by austerity have actually *exacerbated* the tendency for African ruling classes to move capital outside their borders. A positive correlation, they write, between rising debt and increased capital flight has been demonstrated, "suggesting that capital flight was also a response to the deteriorating economic environment associated with rising debt burdens."[70] Western denunciations of poor governance and the "kleptomania" of African despots must therefore be understood as, at best, a distorted and dehistoricized explanation for a structural crisis of their own making.

Net Creditor to the World

From the birth of their "involvement" in Africa, the World Bank and IMF operated as global loan sharks. From 1970 to 2002, Africa received some $540 billion in loans, yet paid back $550 billion in principal and interest. Global downturns—including the 2008–2009 recession—only exacerbate the crisis of indebtedness. According to the Jubilee Debt Campaign, "Globally loans to low income countries have trebled since the financial crisis began, rising from $5.1 billion in 2006 to $19.9 billion in 2014 according to the World Bank."[71] Although the total dollar amount of African debt may be low compared to other regions in the world, this figure is highly deceptive, since the ratio of both debt to GNP and to export income is much higher.[72] The All-Africa Council of Churches has called Africa's debt burden "a new form of slavery, as vicious as the slave trade."[73]

Yet despite the massive weight of this debt, the ultimate irony is that Africa is actually *not* a debtor continent because of the vast sums, including interest, repaid on their debt. Salaheddine Lemaizi of the Committee for the Abolition of Illegitimate Debt documents the massive inequality and injustice of the debt burden: "In Sub-Saharan African countries indebtedness has increased 165-fold between 1970 and 2012, rising from $2 billion to $331 billion. Over the same period 30 Sub-Saharan countries have repaid the debt they owed in 1970 217-fold."[74]

Additionally, because of capital flight, as described above, with African ruling classes depositing huge sums into foreign banks, billions more have gone *into* those banks than has been lent to Africa. According to Thandika Mkandawire, sub-Saharan Africa experienced capital flight of $196 billion between 1970 and 1996—whereas these countries' combined debt in 1996 stood at $178 billion.[75] Or to put it yet another way, based on 2013 African Development Bank and Global Financial Integrity figures, "over the past three decades, Africa has functioned as a 'net creditor' to the rest of the world, the result of a cumulative outflow of nearly a trillion and a half dollars from the continent."[76] Significantly, a good portion of this money sent back to the private accounts of African rulers in Western banks originates in funds siphoned off from foreign aid. This dynamic helps explain why African ruling classes do not refuse the World Bank and IMF terms, as deadly as they are for the majority in Africa: these classes profit from foreign assistance.[77]

Relatedly, taxation "reforms" have accelerated these outflows. Structural adjustment dictates have produced such conditions for several reasons. For one, cuts to public sector employment seriously weakened civil-service sectors across Africa, nascent public sectors recently built in the independence era. As a result, systems of taxation and monitoring are overburdened and underequipped. As the Tax Justice Network Africa describes, "What is often overlooked is that African countries have lost substantially more tax revenue as a result of the difficulties in taxing the illicit flows of money out of the continent. Tax administrators face huge challenges in detecting these illicit outflows that occur through sophisticated tax avoidance schemes involving transfer pricing mechanisms and the exploitation of loopholes in the tax law, and are facilitated by the financial secrecy offered by tax havens to multi-national corporations . . . and wealthy individuals."[78]

As has been well documented by the Tax Justice Network Africa, the imposed liberalization of tax laws has undermined the stated goals of the IFIs. Citing official statistics, the group says the Organisation for Economic Co-operation and Development (OECD) "recognises that developing countries lose more to tax havens than they receive in foreign aid. It is therefore no surprise that the past 10 years of private sector-led economic growth and reliance on foreign aid have by and large failed to stimulate productive domestic enterprise, or raise sufficient revenue to meaningfully reduce poverty."[79] Their report *Tax Us If You Can* estimates that, for example, of the total taxes owed in Kenya, only 35 percent of corporate income taxes, and 56 percent of VAT taxes, are actually collected.[80] The ability to tax must be partly understood, in the African context, as a legacy of weak governmental institutions and a weak state. "During the past 25 years, tax revenues in sub-Saharan Africa have largely stagnated at levels around 15 per cent of GDP," the group reports. "This is under half the equivalent collected in the OECD countries. . . . This extraordinary lack of personnel is a product of decades of failed tax policy in Africa, where the role of tax administrations was squeezed as part of austerity programmes prescribed by the international finance institutions including the IMF."[81]

Khadija Sharife has written extensively on how practices such as "tax avoidance" operate through a range of mechanisms, such as trade mispricing and other corporate maneuvers. As exporters chiefly of primary commodities, these tactics are particularly relevant for African extractive industries, where liberalization has allowed for multinational structures to hide resource revenues and escape taxation. Broadly speaking, she and Tax Justice Network co-authors note, "phasing out trade taxes and tariffs, which comprised 30 to 50 per cent of tax revenues in many developing countries prior to trade liberalization, has greatly reduced government revenues."[82] According to Oxfam in 2016: "Almost a third of rich Africans' wealth—a total of $500 billion—is held offshore in tax havens. It's estimated that this costs African countries $14 billion a year in lost tax revenues, enough to employ enough teachers to get every African child into school."[83] Conversely, if capital flight were even partially reversed, the financial picture for African economies would change substantially. Janvier Nkurunziza has documented the potential increase in capital under conditions of modest reinvestment: "It has been estimated that if only a quarter of the stock of flight capital from Africa was repatriated to the continent and invested, Africa's ratio of domestic investment to GDP would increase from 19 percent of GDP to 35 percent of GDP. This would raise Africa's investment to GDP ratio significantly, from the lowest to one of the highest in the developing world."[84]

Poverty and Broken Promises

When we hear the head of a European nation declare with hand on heart that he must come to the aid of the unfortunate peoples of the underdeveloped world, we do not tremble with gratitude. On the contrary, we say among ourselves, "it is a just reparation we are getting." So we will not accept aid for the underdeveloped countries as "charity." Such aid must be considered the final stage of a dual consciousness—the consciousness of the colonized that *it is their due* and the consciousness of the capitalist powers that effectively *they must pay up.*

—Frantz Fanon (emphasis in original)[85]

The devastating history of neoliberal structural adjustment, the African debt crisis, and brutal austerity provides the backdrop for an urgent need for massive social spending. Yet Western aid to Africa is a long record of failed pledges, coercion, and hypocrisy. A prominent part of the mainstream debate on Africa is that assistance "doesn't work." Robert Calderisi, for example, has declared in his book *The Trouble with Africa: Why Foreign Aid Isn't Working:* "Africa is now responsible for most of its own problems and . . . outsiders can only help if they are more direct and demanding in their relations with the continent. Forty years of foreign aid have established one unsurprising fact. Around the world successful countries are those that have chosen the right policies for their own reasons."[86] In a later interview, he intones that Africa has been given generous amounts of aid "without showing very much in the way of economic or social success."[87]

Some NGOs have, unfortunately, embraced neoliberal assumptions of blaming the victim, issuing moralistic admonitions such as from the ONE Campaign, declaring that "research by ONE finds that most sub-Saharan African governments are breaking their budget promises. Only six of 43 examined countries, on average between 2010 and 2012, met their 13-year-old commitment to target 15 per cent of their national budgets toward health. This resulted in a staggering shortfall of over $54bn across those three years alone."[88] Yet such accounts sidestep the record of decades of neoliberal strictures insisting on a *disinvestment* from the very programs that governments are now being castigated for short-changing. Worse, this approach becomes a rationale for ongoing Western intervention. When influential officials such as Calderisi state that "African countries can be helped only if they are kept under political and economic supervision,"[89] this declaration only strengthens the logic of imperial intervention and control.

Claims by Calderisi and his ilk to the contrary, a strong case should be made that fundamental social change and a reversal of poverty have not been on the West's agenda. In fact, their blatant disregard for social conditions faced by the majority of ordinary people—in turning their backs on meager aid promises—has been horrifying. This betrayal is in keeping with over forty years of empty promises. In 1970, developed nations voted on a UN resolution to devote 0.7 percent of their national incomes to foreign aid. The figure of 0.7 percent of GDP (later changed to a percentage of gross national income, or GNI), became the internationally recognized benchmark for assessing success at delivering on aid promises. A small handful of European nations—Denmark, the Netherlands, Norway, Sweden, and Luxembourg—have at times exceeded this target, but no G8 country came close until Britain finally met the target in 2013, a shameful four decades on from the original UN pledge. As Claire Godfrey of Oxfam put it: "Governments first promised to deliver 0.7 per cent of their national income to support poor countries when Richard Nixon was President of America and the Beatles were topping the charts. In the 45 years since only a handful of countries have delivered on this promise."[90] Even the 0.7 percent target was diminished from its earliest formulation: in 1958, the World Council of Churches first proposed approaching the question of development aid through a targeted percentage of the incomes of the world's richest nations, suggesting 1 percent as the goal. As a concept, this notion was upheld by OECD members over the following decades, but subsequently pared down. The revised number was later recommitted to at several international conferences. The European Union, for example, pledged that the fifteen member nations in 2004 would meet this goal.[91]

Even these goals have not been met. Broadly speaking, the broken promises represent an almost incalculable price tag for the vast majority of Africans by any number of economic, social, and human development measures. The group Share the World's Resources reports:

Although rich countries have donated over $3 trillion in [official development assistance] ODA since 1970, the accumulated total shortfall in aid since 1970 . . . amounts *to over $4.37tn* [emphasis added]. . . . On current trends, donors will not collectively hit the 0.7 percent target for a further 50 years, until 2062. In stark comparison, rich countries mobilised $12tn within the space of a few months to bail out a small number of banks during the global financial crisis of 2008.[92]

In fact, in the lead-up to the 2008–2009 global recession, Oxfam warned that the failure to meet aid goals would mean that 45 million more children would die between now and 2015.[93] Its words went largely unheeded. According to CONCORD, European Union "member states still failed collectively to meet the 0.7 percent ODA/GNI target, which was recommitted to . . . despite missing the 2015 deadline originally endorsed ten years earlier. Total European Union (EU) ODA for 2015 was US$73.5 billion in 2015 or 0.47 percent of their total GNI."[94] In fact, global ODA remained essentially flat from 2004 (0.17 percent of GNI) to 2014 (0.19 percent of GNI); thus, the ONE Campaign notes, "most developed countries have thus far not lived up to their ODA commitments. . . . overall ODA/GNI stands at 0.29 percent, lower than the peak in 2010. The EU as a whole, who hold each other accountable to meeting 0.7 percent through EU processes, are short of meeting their promise."[95] In 2011, for example, donor countries *dropped* their level of aid by nearly 3 percent compared to 2010, an amount that could provide a full year of treatment for half the children infected with HIV worldwide.[96] Beyond a commitment to global aid, the European nations have also pledged to rededicate themselves to earmarking additional funds for Africa in particular. Yet in this area they also fail miserably. For example, says the ONE Campaign, "the EU has previously committed to provide half of its total ODA increases to Africa. . . . However, as of 2014, only 25.4 percent of the EU19's overall increase in development assistance has been allocated to the continent."[97]

As the world's wealthiest country and largest power, the US track record is especially egregious. All told, US aid to Africa has been cut by 40 percent since the 1990s. Today, US global aid is only 0.16 percent of gross national income, the lowest percentage among donor nations. For sub-Saharan Africa alone— the poorest region on the planet—US aid in 2014 was a mere 0.07 percent of GNI, at a grand total of $11,499.41 million.[98] While the sums spent by the United States are high, it amounts to far less in relative terms, representing in reality only a small proportion of national income.[99] Well before the economic crisis of 2008, austerity dictated by the World Bank and the International Monetary Fund left a trail of devastation across Africa, leaving the globe's highest unemployment and poverty rates in their wake. Fifteen of the twenty-one countries deemed most vulnerable to the global meltdown were in Africa. Yet while the United States responded to the global recession by dedicating possibly upwards of $4 trillion to bail out the financial system, the top world powers then known as the Group of Eight (G8) nations pledged a paltry $25 billion in annual aid to African states. This tiny sum is only a fraction of the wealth of some of the world's wealthiest individuals, such as Bill Gates. In fact, on the eve of the crisis, according to Oxfam, the world's poorest countries continued to send $100 million in debt servicing *each day* to the United States, other rich country governments, and international financial institutions.[100]

Yet aid is far from a humanitarian gesture on the part of the world's wealthiest. As with structural adjustment requirements, aid has been used to pursue a corporatization agenda: as part of the drive to open markets to free trade, aid itself is deployed as a political tool that comes with strings attached. The world's leading governments use their clout to push for greater liberalization and access to African markets, thus expanding African dependence on Western exports while continuing to protect their own markets from competition from African exports.

Patrick Bond cites the findings of British researcher Mark Curtis, who demonstrates, for example, that EU aid was clearly packaged to promote its own trade objectives, including requiring recipients to support present and future World Trade Organization agreements.[101] Jean Nanga details these mechanisms at work, namely strengthening the ability of IFIs to secure favorable contracts and trade agreements. But, as he points out, these global institutions rely on "local" partners who help extend neoliberal aims in the region:

> Since domination is most effective when it is coated with a "nationalist" varnish, the African relay of this power of international finance capital over countries is provided by the African Development Bank (AfDB), the principal regional financial institution. . . . Thus, it is almost impossible to distinguish the AfDB recommendations from those of the Bretton Woods institutions where the domination of the traditional imperialist powers, the United States in the lead, is maintained.
>
> "Public aid for development" gives an air of generosity to this system of the organized dependency of African societies, whereas the Committee for the Abolition of Illegitimate Debt poses the question: "In 2012, the repatriation of profits from the most impoverished region of the world accounted for 5 per cent of its GDP, against one per cent for public aid for development. In this context, it is worth asking: who is helping whom?"[102]

Because Western donors and their regional partners are driven by objectives that run counter to the needs of the majority of ordinary Africans, it is unsurprising the degree to which aid mechanisms are distorted. The practice of "phantom aid" underscores the shockingly pitiful amounts of aid disbursed by rich countries. Phantom aid describes the phenomenon in which donors are able to "count" a range of activities toward their pledged target, or, as ActionAid put it in a ground-breaking recalculation of *actual* aid: "The official aid figures exaggerate rich countries' generosity. . . . According to our analysis, more than 60 percent of aid flows are 'phantom'; that is they do not represent a real resource transfer to the recipient. For the worst performing G7 donors, the figure is as high as 89 percent."[103] Exacerbating global economic conditions, the trend toward packaging loans as "aid" jumped markedly after the 2008 recession.[104] "Tied aid"—that is, aid requiring concomitant purchases of goods and services from the donor—has also been folded into these numbers, an especially pernicious requirement, since industries and services in recipient nations are further thwarted. Likewise, "technical assistance" in the form of overpriced international consultants and advisors, as well as any sums reflecting debt forgiveness have all been found to artificially inflate the aid totals.[105] These dubious practices express such a blatant failure to live up to the stated goals of foreign aid that even major international bodies such as the OECD—directing policy and economic objectives for the world's wealthiest nations—have been compelled to offer reforms.[106]

Another questionable aid practice is the directing of aid allocations to companies and organizations of the *donor* nation, namely into the coffers of a host of consultancies and technical advisors. Citing the British government's "history of lending for dodgy, damaging and corrupt deals," economist Tim Jones of the Jubilee Debt Campaign stated, "British people think UK aid money should be used to reduce poverty and inequality around the world. But too often it is driven by the interests of British companies at the expense of increased poverty and inequality." The group found in 2012 that *92 percent* of British aid contracts given in the previous eighteen months went to British corporations.[107] These and similar practices became so notorious that even some of the global institutions of the rich nations were compelled to suggest some mild reforms, reforms so insufficient that campaigners could only denounce them as lip service. "Despite a global upward trend in ODA," according to Oxfam,

> figures for 2014 show that aid to Sub-Saharan Africa fell for the second consecutive year—back to levels they were a decade ago. This is happening against a background of a long history of developed countries' failure to meet the UN target for development aid of 0.7 percent of GNI, recouping on odious debt and decades of turning a blind eye to the scandal of illicit

financial flows which continue to bleed Africa of billions of dollars in much
needed development finance.[108]

High-profile aid initiatives have grabbed media attention in recent decades. The World Bank and IMF launched the Highly Indebted Poor Country
(HIPC) plan in 1996, which effected only a miniscule reduction in debt because of the high bar to qualify for relief. This program was undoubtedly a
failure on its own terms, as described by UNCTAD in 2000: "Current expectations regarding the implementation of the enhanced HIPC Initiative are
unrealistic. The scale of debt relief will prove insufficient to ensure sustainability in the medium term . . . moreover, the magnitude of debt relief, and its
manner of delivery, will not have major direct effects on poverty reduction."[109]
As Bond correctly argues, the HIPC is "debt relief smoke and mirrors" since
forgiven loans were not going to be repaid anyway due to the severity of the
debt burden.[110] Finally, these meager funds are designed to facilitate payments
to Western creditors, *not* debt forgiveness, and are implemented along with the
harsh conditionalities of neoliberal structural adjustment, thus cementing the
hold of global financial institutions over nations of the Global South. Some
have called for the outright repudiation of past loans based on the well-es-
tablished principle in international law of rejecting the obligations of "odious debt."[111] These conditions are only intensified when the global economy
goes into crisis. As Africa Action commented during the "Great Recession"
of 2008, "The situation will be exacerbated through [those] new loans by the
IMF. The loans still carry conditions that have the potential to subvert economic growth, and urgent action is needed more than ever to see that all debt
is canceled to Africa as it faces this current financial crisis."[112]

To add insult to injury, any forgiven amounts were to be deducted from
promised aid. The initiative, says the Tax Justice Network Africa,

> cancelled just US$40 billion of debt of the 41 poorest countries, of which 33
> are African. But not all countries benefited from HIPC. For example, Kenya
> and the Democratic Republic of Congo (DRC) did not meet the HIPC
> criteria. As late as 2007, a disproportionate share of the DRC's state bud-
> get—some 50 per cent—was allocated to servicing public debts incurred by
> corrupt lifetime dictator Mobutu Seso-Seko.[113]

Toussaint elaborates:

> From 1996–2000, the amount of money actually deposited into the trust
> fund used to finance debt reduction by the IMF was less than the amount
> required to pay its 2,300 employees in the year 2000 alone. . . . The total
> amount disbursed by all of the contributors to the HIPC Debt Initiative

between 1996 and 2003 is equal to or less than the cost to the US Treasury of only one month of occupation in Iraq in 2003.[114]

From the perspective of true debt relief for the forty-two target nations, the program was an abject failure.

With regard to aid, international organizations have cohered behind the collective interests of the world's major powers and so have similarly failed to provide any leadership in reversing these trends. For example, half of the OECD's Development Assistance Committee countries (consisting of the world's most powerful nations and international bodies) reduced their assistance to sub-Saharan Africa from 2013 to 2014.[115] The moral authority of the United Nations to compel holding to aid promises has proven similarly elusive. Convening a 2011 "conference on the world's poorest nations" in Istanbul, Turkey, the United Nations managed only to generate hollow reiterations of past promises alongside dictates for the economies of the recipient nations, a conclusion roundly denounced by civil society campaigners.[116]

In 2000, the United Nations launched a fifteen-year initiative called the Millennium Development Goals targeting income, child mortality, disease, and environmental sustainability, among other metrics. Given the reverberating effects of liberalization, budget cuts, and aid drop-offs, the ongoing persistence of poverty and inequality in Africa was far from surprising. In its final report on the goals' progress, the United Nations documented that 41 percent of Africans still lived on less than $1.25 a day, considered "extreme poverty" by the report's authors. For employed Africans, the extreme poverty rate drops only minimally, to 36 percent. Of the world's poorest 1 billion people, close to 60 percent were concentrated in just five countries in 2011, including Nigeria and the Democratic Republic of the Congo.[117] In keeping with past tradition, the fanfare surrounding the goals failed to push foreign aid up to the 0.7 percent benchmark in most cases; according to the OECD, even though ODA has increased by 66 percent in real terms since the goals' launch, aid to the *poorest* nations has been falling.[118]

Aid for Africa has been shortchanged across all areas, including under the most brutal crisis conditions. South Sudan in 2015 faced a dire refugee crisis, with 8 million people in urgent need of food assistance. Despite the need for $1.1 billion for a humanitarian response, months after pledges were made, a shortfall of $200 million persisted.[119] Drought in Ethiopia has similarly created conditions in which, as of mid-2017, up to 3.3 million people required emergency humanitarian assistance, according to some estimates, with the United Nations World Food Programme citing a shortfall in aid funding as a major risk for Ethiopians.[120] Another prominent example is in the area of

HIV/AIDS. At 24.7 million people, sub-Saharan Africa has the largest number of people living with HIV in the world—a full 71 percent of the world's total with HIV. A drop in AIDS-related deaths in the past decade has had a substantial impact.[121] However, the G8 had proposed 2010 as a target date for universal access to HIV/AIDS treatment. Yet several years past that target, 63 percent of Africans living with HIV or AIDS still lacked access to treatment.[122] According to the Global Fund to Fight AIDS, Tuberculosis and Malaria, the total pledged by public and private donors has fallen short by over $3.2 billion,[123] including among initiatives that have been underfunded by the United States for some years, despite high-profile declarations of support by both Presidents George W. Bush and Barack Obama. Bush was particularly notorious for methods used to link funding to conservative "faith-based" initiatives. As poet and author Mukoma Wa Ngugi has pointed out, "Instead of allocating the promised money through the Global Fund," Bush

> channels it through PEPFAR, the President's Emergency Plan for AIDS Relief which is [according to Africa Action] "often influenced by restrictive and ideologically based policy prescriptions, such as abstinence-only regulations." Bush undermines his own efforts through what most experts understand as unworkable ABC programs (Abstinence, Being Faithful and as a last resort, Condoms). Worse is the AIDS-Industrial Complex. The US under Bush opposed the loosening of patent laws which would allow countries to manufacture or import generic drugs. Donated AIDS money is therefore being spent on expensive premium drugs. The pharmaceutical companies pocket the money then lobby against the loosening of patent laws. The system is locked into a cycle of profit making at the expense of the dying.[124]

The Legacy of the G8 Gleneagles Summit

> In addition to providing raw materials, labor, and markets for finished products, Africa also cleanses the conscience of Africanist scholars, evangelists and missionaries, the rock and roll musicians who want to save Africa through orphan adoption, and philanthropists with Mother-Theresa complexes. But at the top of the pack—Western politicians. Occupy Iraq and Afghanistan but do not forget to rescue the African from the clutches of war-lords,

poverty, corruption, and disease. Africa has become the continent where the guilt-ridden come to score quick moral points.

—Mukoma Wa Ngugi[125]

Many remember the massive "Make Poverty History" demonstrations and Live 8 concerts in Britain in the summer of 2005, in the lead-up to the Gleneagles Summit in Scotland that, in the tradition of Live Aid, drew hundreds of thousands.[126] The actual record of the conference policy proceedings themselves deserve equal attention. Western rulers have shown a fondness for pledging funds and declaring a commitment to ending poverty in Africa. Former British Prime Minister Tony Blair rebranded himself as an anti-poverty campaigner for the Global South, chiefly by making a name for himself in African debt relief. The famous G8 summit in Gleneagles, Scotland, in 2005 produced a guarantee to increase aid to the world's poor countries by $50 billion. The leaders of eight of the most powerful nations of the world—the United States, Japan, Britain, France, Germany, Italy, Canada, and Russia—also made a commitment to double aid to Africa by 2010, a total increase of $25 billion annually. That figure was arrived at as a representation of 0.7 percent of the G8 countries' GNI. Yet meeting the target of Gleneagles has proved a dismal failure.

At the time of the conference, the track record on poverty alleviation on the part of the world's major powers was disastrous and had been getting worse. Despite this horrendous record, Gleneagles leaders unashamedly declared the meeting the "100 percent debt relief summit," embraced by Blair and US President George W. Bush alike. On the eve of Gleneagles, world leaders announced a "historic" breakthrough on debt forgiveness to "highly indebted poor countries" (HIPC), many of which were in Africa. But activists denounced the conditionalities required of recipients, in which the "G8's plan for saving Africa is little better than an extortion racket," according to journalist and global justice activist George Monbiot.[127]

The war in Iraq was palpably felt as the backdrop to the proceedings. In this context, the debt reductions provide another perspective on the imperial designs of the United States and the United Kingdom, who sought to diminish the economic hold of their competitors such as Germany, France, and Japan and their own national capitalists through the multilateral loans those competitors had extended. In other words, not only aid but debt forgiveness was fashioned into a tool to further ruling-class aims, and the major imperialist powers used the Gleneagles moment to press their own advantage.[128]

Given the political balancing act of the Blair regime—under fire for the war in Iraq—it is hard not to conclude that his ability to host Gleneagles played a vital public relations role for the embattled administration.[129] Yet imperial aims dominated the proceedings. As Gavin Capps pointed out: "If the G8 were serious about writing off Africa's debt they could do it at a stroke. There was, for example, no problem cancelling Iraq's $120 billion debt when it suited their interests after the invasion in 2003. At the time, Bush argued that Iraq's liabilities endangered its 'long-term prospects for political health and economic prosperity.' This is true of Africa's debt a thousand times over."[130]

Most prominently the war, but also the wider havoc unleashed by global capitalism, hung over the event. As global justice activist Walden Bello put it:

> We have not only in Bush, Sarkozy, Brown, and Fukuda a group of discredited leaders with very low ratings at the polls in their own countries. We have, as well, a G8 that is, more than ever, lacking in legitimacy, as the typhoon unleashed by the project of globalization that it has promoted is wracking the globe in the form of the simultaneous crises of skyrocketing oil prices, rising food prices, global financial collapse and worsening climate change.[131]

In the years following the conference, numerous organizations issued warnings that the Western powers were falling far behind their goals. According to Oxfam International, G8 leaders fell short of their 2005 promise to increase aid by $20 billion.[132] And as the European Network on Debt and Development notes, any debt forgiven was cut from those nations' aid packages.

The United States was, in fact, one of the worst culprits in the fall-off of aid pledges to Africa after Gleneagles. The United States spent around $100 billion a year for its occupation of Iraq, but only $0.680 billion for the entire continent of Africa in the same period. In the same year as the summit, ActionAid criticized the performance of the world's wealthiest nations once phantom aid had been subtracted, pointing out that "the G7 countries are the worst performers when it comes to real aid. On average, the world's seven largest economies give just 0.07 percent of national income in real aid."[133]

Gleneagles set the template for aid to Africa, and the follow-up G8 summits failed to break from this model. In the lead-up to the 2008 summit in Hokkaido, Japan, posturing from the world's leaders was the order of the day. "We need people who not only make promises, but write checks, for the sake of human rights and human dignity, and for the sake of peace," Bush declared at a White House press conference on the eve of his departure for Hokkaido, at which he highlighted the battle against HIV/AIDS and malaria. "Accountability is really important when it comes to our work on the continent of Africa."[134] Yet world leaders have consistently fallen short on accountability themselves, breaking their own promises time and again. Advocates and activists stressed the continued crisis in the gap of human needs unmet. Wole Olaleye, a researcher with ActionAid International, commented just days later that the dangers of the G8 backtracking on its HIV/AIDS commitments were enormous: "G8 funds have made a difference. . . . However, the need remains enormous: three-quarters of people who need HIV/AIDS treatment are still not receiving it. Almost 90 percent of HIV-positive pregnant women are still unable to get drugs that could prevent the virus being passed on to their child."[135]

At the height of the global recession, leaders at the L'Aquila Summit of 2009 touted a $20 billion aid package, but as *Pambazuka News* pointed out at the time, this sum was for three years, to be shared between *fifty-three* African countries. This total amounts to an average of about $132 million each, a drop in the bucket by any measurement.[136] Insisting that past G8 pledges—not yet delivered—could save more than three million lives, Oxfam's Emma Seery denounced these failures, saying, "The Africa discussion was relegated to an insultingly token session. How can we take the G8 seriously when all they offer Africa is broken promises and photo opportunities?" In a statement on the L'Aquila meeting, the organization predicted that Africa would lose $245 billion in revenue that year[137]—almost seven times the amount it receives in global aid—as a result of the global economic crisis, but would receive only about $5 billion in additional support. Executive bonuses paid to failed US insurance giant AIG could alone, they concluded, pay for enough teachers for seven million children in Africa.[138]

Poor countries around the world, but in Africa especially, bore the brunt of a global food crisis in which food prices rose by more than 80 percent since the G8 met in Gleneagles. According to "Africa's Development Report: Promises and Prospects," released in June 2008, 100 million people were in dire need of food worldwide, with Africa accounting for 57 percent of the victims. Compiled by the Africa Progress Panel, chaired by former UN Secretary General Kofi Annan, the report stated that G8 commitments would fall $40 billion short of their targets under current spending plans.[139] Ten years after Gleneagles, nearly 100 countries are either at risk of a new crisis, or in the midst of one.[140] Given the track record demonstrated by the Gleneagles failures, ensuring accountability to pledges of genuine aid relief requires significantly more thorough-going change than policy denunciations, as helpful as Oxfam's public declarations are in exposing the shameful failure of the global elite to live up to their obligations.

Instability and Civil War

A discussion on the history of structural adjustment, neoliberalism, and the debt crisis would be incomplete without an account of their contribution to devastating instability and civil war. Very far from being rooted in some kind of primordial hatreds, the long reach of imperial intervention, shaped by the weaknesses and ethnic and national divisions sown under colonialism, is critical for understanding the nature of the continent's civil wars years later. Despite this structural legacy, the perceived intractability of bloody wars and conflicts have opened the door for reactionary suggestions that Africa was better off while under direct European rule. *Time* magazine shamefully posed that very question in a 2008 article on the Democratic Republic of Congo entitled "Come Back, Colonialism, All Is Forgiven"[141]—which, as Bond rightly points out, is a wholesale distortion of the historical production, by Belgian colonialism and later the United States, of dictatorship and the seeds of brutal civil war.[142] What cynical accounts such as *Time*'s also paper over is that these conflicts were not a continuous feature of the African historical landscape, thus avoiding the important question of *why* a number of these civil wars emerged in a particularly virulent form at the moment they did.

With the end of the Cold War and superpower patronage at the beginning of the 1990s, Western-backed regimes lost their bulwark against the social and economic contradictions facing postcolonial states, and experienced massive crisis and collapse that brought to the surface deep inequalities between classes and also between ethnicities. Journalist Jeffrey Gettleman has described this moment:

> Africa . . . had the bad luck of gaining its independence as the cold war was at its height and the United States and Soviet Union were trying to recruit proxies; the East–West rivalry therefore shaped much of Africa's internal politics and many of its rebellions. The superpowers propped up brutal, thoroughly hated tyrants purely because they supported one side or another, and likewise co-opted rebel groups and plied them with money and guns to fight for or against communism. When the cold war abruptly ended in 1990, the superpowers' sudden disengagement from the African continent left a number of tyrants exposed and ripe for overthrow. . . . What we are seeing is the decline of the classic wars by freedom fighters and the proliferation of something else—something wilder, messier, . . . and harder to define.[143]

Thus the end of the Cold War ushered in a new era of rebellion and conflict. Combining the economic disaster of the 1980s with the withdrawal of state patronage from imperialist powers and the particular ethnic character of African state power inherited from the colonial era also provides a fuller explanation of the *way* African rebellions unfolded at the end of the Cold War. For example, as socialists Avery Wear and David Whitehouse describe in their account of the crisis in Darfur, Sudan:

> The focus on wealth extraction was universal among colonial overlords, and it produced two legacies that still fuel today's conflicts. First is a string of weak post-colonial states whose infrastructures were shaped to assist the flow of wealth to the colonial power. . . . Second, the practice of setting up colonial "centers" to serve as nodes of wealth-extraction produced outer colony boundaries that have no relation to language or ethnicity—or were drawn deliberately to split troublesome groups . . . [producing] a pattern of rebellions by peripheral minorities against discrimination by the center, backed by rulers of neighboring states who exploit their ethnic connections to disrupt their regional rivals.[144]

The imprint of these colonial divisions continued to echo decades later as global contractions deepened instability. As Vishwas Satgar has commented, the uneven economies and political weaknesses of the new states exacerbated these legacies: "African states remade racial and ethnic cleavages in the context of economic crisis. Ethnic and reactionary nationalisms came to the fore: Africa turned on itself even more. . . . Many of these conflicts were the result of failed attempts to achieve market democracies or took on the characteristics of resource wars."[145]

One of the clearest and most tragic examples of this dynamic—repeated elsewhere across Africa—was the civil war in Rwanda begun in 1990. A French-backed, Hutu-led government unleashed a genocide against the Tutsi people in 1994 in which 800,000 Tutsis were killed, along with tens of thousands of Hutus, in the span of a mere 100 days. The roots of this violence lie in the colonial-era ethnic divisions that sowed the seeds of future conflicts. Belgian colonial policy and the displacement of Africans in Rwanda and across the border in the Congo by huge land seizures of white settlers created artificial divisions and thus the basis for widespread instability between the later migrant populations.[146] As Philip Gourevitch describes, "in 1933–34, the Belgians conducted a census to issue 'ethnic' identity cards, which labeled every Rwandan as either Hutu or Tutsi. . . . The Belgians had made 'ethnicity' the defining feature of Rwandan existence."[147] And as elsewhere across Africa, the subordination of rural populations to "traditional" chiefs backed by colonial governments reinforced these divisions.[148]

The immediate backdrop to the civil war, however, was the collapse of world currency prices, including coffee, which devastated the Rwandan economy. In that context, Hutu rulers made Tutsis scapegoats for the crisis, mobilizing hatred against the Tutsi minority. The United States and France, in the meantime, backed the Tutsi forces led by Paul Kagame and the rebel Rwandan Patriotic Front (RPF), who overthrew the Hutu who had led the genocide, then turned and unleashed a war of retribution in which thousands were killed and close to a million Hutu refugees were driven across the border of neighboring Zaire (now Democratic Republic of the Congo, or DRC) and elsewhere in central Africa. Hutu extremists then allied with Mobutu, prompting Rwandan and Ugandan backing in late 1996 when an umbrella group of Congolese rebel factions launched an insurgency to oust Mobutu, with rebels eager to get their hands on the Congo's vast mineral wealth. This conflict spawned a Congolese civil war for control over the eastern region's vast natural resources, in which the national armies of Uganda, Rwanda, and the DRC, alongside Hutu and Tutsi militias who served as their proxies, decimated the region and killed approximately 5 million people from 1998 to 2003. It is the bloodiest conflict since the end of the Second World War and continues at a lower intensity to the present day, with the United States and other major powers supporting various national armies whose militia proxies continue to exploit ethnic divisions inherited from colonialism for their own ends.

The origins of the murderous conflict lay in those divisions, then accentuated by the immiseration of the Congolese people by a vaunted US ally, Mobutu. One of the first recipients in the early 1980s of a harsh structural adjustment regime, Mobutu decimated public institutions and the formal economy through privatization and liberalization, all at the behest of the World Bank and the IMF. By the time Mobutu left power in 1997, the government of the DRC (then Zaire) was in debt to international foreign institutions in the amount of $12 billion, an amount almost entirely accrued under his rule. Reports at the time to the World Bank and the IMF exposed the extent to which funds sent to the DRC were siphoned off by Mobutu, contributing to his billions in vast personal wealth. As former World Bank chief economist Joseph Stiglitz comments in *Globalization and Its Discontents*, "when the IMF and the World Bank lent money to Democratic Republic of Congo's notorious ruler Mobutu, they knew (or should have known) that most of the money would not go to help that country's poor people, but rather would be used to enrich Mobutu. It was money paid to ensure that this corrupt leader would keep his country aligned with the West."[149] Yet rather than forgiving these loans, the IMF, with the assistance of neoliberal South African president Thabo Mbeki, offered a new round of punishing loans to further cement the old obligations and accrue new ones.[150] The societal instability, deep indebtedness, and vast poverty created by these policies must be included in the balance sheet of this bloody war.

In fact, the enormous debts incurred by Mobutu are only a snapshot of a larger dynamic across the continent. As Bond lays out, modern African history is littered with the accumulation of "odious" debt, taken on by dictators, many of whom collaborated quite easily with the United States and other Western powers. The list is lengthy:

> Nigeria under the [first] Buhari and Abacha regime (1984–1998; $30 billion), South Africa under apartheid (1948–93: $22 billion), . . . Sudan under Numeiri (1969–85: $9 billion), Ethiopia under Mengistu (1974–91: $8 billion), Kenya under Moi (1978–2002: $5.8 billion), Congo under Sassou (1979–2005: $4.5 billion), Mali under Traore (1968–91: $2.5 billion), Somalia under Siad Barre (1969–1991: $2.3 billion), Malawi under Banda (1966–94: $2.2 billion), Togo under Eyadema (1967–2005: $1.4 billion), Liberia under Doe (1980–90: 1.2 billion), Rwanda under Habyarimana (1973–94:

$1 billion), Uganda under Idi Amin Dada (1971–79: $0.6 billion), and the Central African Republic under Bokassa (1966–70: $0.2 billion).[151]

Overall, as Mahmood Mamdani concludes, "Given that the nature of twentieth-century 'indirect rule' colonialism in Africa shaped the nature of administrative power along 'tribal' (or ethnic) lines, it is not surprising that the exercise of power and responses to it tend to take 'tribal' forms in newly independent states."[152] Far from being the product of "age-old" tensions, the tendencies for African civil wars to take on these aspects are rooted in its colonial history, which unfolded in the context of late twentieth-century global conditions of structural adjustment and debt crisis to disastrous results.

Finally, fueling the tendency in some parts of the continent for political conflicts to become protracted civil wars is the dramatic increase in military funding. This new development made a dramatic arrival in the first five years following September 11, 2001. For example, as Frida Berrigan describes, "Kenya, which the State Department describe[d] as a 'frontline state' in the war on terrorism, . . . received eight times more military aid than in the preceding five years."[153] The advent of heightened militarism and the birth of a new US military command in Africa will be discussed in more detail later on. Suffice it to say, the decisions on types of aid for Africa underscore the West's stark spending priorities. But above all, flooding regions with weaponry— from the Great Lakes region to the Sahel and the Horn—have only made these regions more crisis-prone and vastly more dangerous.

A Critique of the Washington Consensus Is Not Enough

In the face of sharpened inequality, some of neoliberalism's former boosters, like Stiglitz, have been forced to conclude that free-trade agreements "are not right for developing countries . . . it is not a negotiation, it is rather an imposition."[154] Stiglitz was compelled by the evidence that nations adopting structural adjustment policies actually saw their economies shrink. Mamdani, for one, has argued that Stiglitz's analysis does not adequately explain the roots of the crisis in a systemic sense. Countering Stiglitz's formulation of greater state involvement as the solution for "market failure," Mamdani offers a broader framework:

> The antidote to the market was never the state but democracy. Not the state but a democratic political order has contained the worst fallout from capitalism over the last few centuries. The real custodian of a democratic order was never the state but society. The question we are facing today is not just

that of market failure but of an all-round political failure: the financialization of capitalism is leading to the collapse of the democratic order. The problem was best defined by the Occupy Wall Street movement in the US: it is the 99 percent against the 1 percent.[155]

All told, structural adjustment and poverty in Africa in the closing decades of the twentieth century illustrate the particularly harsh discipline of Cold War rivalries and imperial competition, in both their military and economic guises. Recent class struggle and movements for social justice in Africa—including mass struggles against the structural adjustment and austerity of the global financial institutions—show the potential for a vibrant "democracy," one based on the working class and the power of Africa's "99 percent." Waves of struggles for democracy swept the African continent during this time, although many of these electoral reforms were short-lived. The "IMF rebellions" of the 1990s put resistance to globalization on the map in the context of unfolding immiseration and crisis across the Global South. As Bade Onimode has written, "Protests and criticism of SAP began in individual countries that were amongst the first to receive SAP conditionalities, such as Ghana, Zambia, and Sudan. But as IFI policy widened, protest generalized across the continent as a whole."[156] The dynamics of these movements—their hopes and challenges—will be explored in greater detail in subsequent chapters.

Chapter Four

"Rising Africa"

Investment bankers are grappling with a novel challenge, explaining to potential investors that exotic places like Abuja and Accra, the capitals of Nigeria and
Ghana, are among the new frontiers in the international capital markets. . . .
There is a glut of liquidity in the global financial system that is helping to fuel
the current enthusiasm for far-flung markets such as those in Africa.

—*Financial Times*[1]

Around the turn of the millennium, a new narrative began to appear in
the business press: that of a "rising Africa." In this mythical account,
Africa shines with investment promise and hopes of lifted fortunes for all. In a
conversation with the *Financial Times*, a US-based investment fund representative glowed with scarcely contained enthusiasm: "Look at Nigeria, Nairobi
and what's been going on—the growth in consumption, the investment opportunities are practically tangible. You just have to drive around and you
can almost touch and feel it; it's a very important part of the process."[2] Sub-
Saharan Africa, the story went, was experiencing a boom in the growth of its
middle class, which was championed for its purchasing power and the promise
of even higher rates of investment on the continent. "The number of middle
class households in eleven key sub-Saharan African countries—excluding
South Africa—are set to triple," proclaimed the *Financial Times* again, "creating a burgeoning consumer market for items such as vehicles, insurance
policies, property and health products. . . . [This] would represent a sharp
acceleration in wealth creation."[3]

Myths abound in the "rising Africa" narrative. Poverty is falling and social well-being is improving. Africa is leaving its history behind, no longer burdened by its colonial past. The economies of yesteryear, which relied solely on extracting resources, have now developed new industries and stable, diverse economies with rising employment. Booming stock markets on the continent are yet another reason for optimism.

This story has some basis in fact. Higher commodity prices worldwide, most especially oil, fueled a drive for new sources of raw materials. Many African nations saw higher levels of GDP and investment. But there's more to the picture than this rosy account. The real story is the coincidence of two factors: the neoliberal prying open of African economies and the rise of China as a huge buyer of African commodities. Privatization, structural adjustment, and deregulation have created investor-friendly environments in Africa. Meanwhile, China's liberalized economy and its cheap, "flexible" workforce produced a flood of foreign companies in China and a boom of mammoth proportions.[4] Facilitating this dizzying growth was China's "scramble" for African commodities.

China is now Africa's single-largest trading partner, and African exports of primary commodities have surged: for most of the millennium's first decade, Africa's growth rate exceeded East Asia's.[5] But China's deepening role in Africa has unfolded in the context of heightened global competition between China and the United States. The Marxist theory of imperialism describes the tendency under capitalism for economic rivalry to spill over into military competition. This theory explains the dynamics seen in Africa today: a competitive scramble for resources, accompanied by heightened militarization on the part of the major powers that has touched virtually every nation on the continent.

The result of this neoliberal boom and the surge from China falls far short of the hype. Worldwide investment in Africa, although rising from a low level in the past, remains very low in comparison to investment in the rest of the world. What investment exists is highly concentrated in South Africa, Nigeria, and a few other countries, with the vast majority in mineral and oil extraction. A 2012 UN Economic Commission for Africa report concludes: "Since independence, African growth has been driven by primary production and export and only limited economic transformation, against a backdrop of high unemployment and worsening poverty."[6] Resting on a weak footing, this boom could evaporate with the onset of a crisis. As Marx first pointed out, capitalism is an interconnected global system, and a crisis in one section reverberates elsewhere. An economic downturn in China, for example, holds the potential to drag down many of the economies in Africa. China's massive growth rests on unsustainable contradictions and has exacerbated overproduction in the system as a whole. A crash in commodity prices in 2015 burst the economic bubble in much of Africa. Whether the growth of the prior decade can be restored remains an open question. All told, Africa may have "risen" for global capital and the continent's wealthy, but for the majority, the result has been a vastly more unequal, crisis-ridden, and dangerous place.

Financing for Underdevelopment

Structural adjustment policies, as we have seen, with their emphasis on privatization and trade liberalization, facilitated a dramatic new turn toward private investment in Africa. Borrowing from Alemayehu Mariam, "financing for (under)development" is a particularly apt description of the privatized approaches of Western powers and international financial institutions (IFIs) to address underdevelopment in Africa and, significantly, to advance the political economic opportunities of the current moment. The goal, as Mariam puts it, is "to rescue Africa from underdevelopment by financing its development, that is by mobilizing international capital."[7] Henning Melber has similarly characterized this turn as toward a "trade not aid"[8] model, succinctly describing the programmatic turn of the neoliberal era.

Part of the ideological apparatus of the new investment enthusiasm is the notion that Africa has ostensibly "escaped" the need for aid. By the end of the new millennium's first decade, the amount of private investment going to Africa had exceeded foreign aid.[9] Celebratory comments began to appear with some regularity:

> An increasing number of African countries are beginning to step away from aid dependency, as the domestic private sector becomes the engine of growth across much of Africa. Currently, at least a third of African countries receive aid that is equivalent to less than 10% of their tax revenue. They include Algeria, Angola, Equatorial Guinea, Gabon and Libya. This is a significant change from years of high dependency on aid. These are countries that have made the most progress toward replacing aid with domestically mobilized resources. On average, Africa has managed to raise an estimated $441 in taxes per person per year while receiving $41 per person annually in aid."[10]

Foreign Investment: The Largest Source of Capital Flow to Africa (US billions)

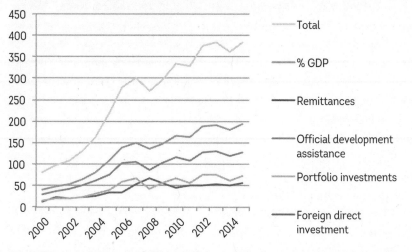

Source: EY's Attractiveness Survey Africa 2015, from African Development Bank, OECD, and UN Development Programme data.[11]

Another characteristic of the new period is that African debt owed to private creditors now exceeds that owed to "official creditors," overtaking the latter in 2010, including funds raised by record-setting sovereign bonds. This development heightened the boom while also posing additional dangers. As the *Economist* wrote in 2014:

> Africa used to borrow from official lenders: governments, the World Bank, the African Development Bank and the IMF. Today most of its borrowing is from private sources. Government loans and "assistance" are out of fashion. Instead it is private investors that are betting on Africa's future ability to pay, with bond funds, private-equity and individual investors (including African ones) buying government debt. Private debt issued by larger African companies is adding to the pile; there have been large corporate-bond issues from Ethiopia, Mozambique and Nigeria, as well as from the traditional issuer, South Africa. Corporate debt is usually dollar-denominated, making it hostage to currency fluctuations, though several governments, including those of Mozambique and Ghana, have recently had to issue bonds denominated in dollars instead of in local currencies. But the bigger worry for Africa is the nature of private lending. If governments get into trouble and need to reschedule their debts or borrow more even while they pay less, official lenders typically oblige. Private lenders are less forgiving.[12]

Any suggestion that the IMF and World Bank are "forgiving" aside, this description aptly captures an important shift. New trade agreements and convenings facilitated a strategic approach toward mobilizing capital for African investments. Several key events have marked this transition from an ostensibly aid-centered approach to an investment-focused relationship. In 2002, hundreds of heads of state, finance ministers, and others gathered at the First Global Conference on Financing for Development, where, as Mariam describes, they "issued the Monterrey Consensus which aimed at providing a new global approach to financing development. . . . The key objective in the consensus was to use financing flows for the purpose of achieving the agreed upon goals of sustainable development, not goals uniquely tailored to meet the needs of a specific country. It was [however] a one-size-fits-all development strategy."[13] In the years following Monterrey, that direction seemed to be borne out with impressive results.

The resilience of African economies, in particular, to withstand the impact of the recession of 2008–2009, only underscored the credibility of the new turn. Patrick Bond describes the strategic approach of the IFIs during the global recession and the remarkable staying power of the neoliberal model:

> The World Bank and also the International Monetary Fund, they sort of fooled us, in 2008–2009, because they seemed to shift their ideology away from a very hard-core agenda of promoting markets above everything else. And for a time it seems they were promoting government deficits and a Keynesian strategy: government should step in when the private sector fails. But now it seems like it's back to business as usual, namely export orientation and austerity. And the World Bank, led by President Robert Zoellick who had come from the Bush administration—he worked for Enron and for Goldman Sachs—this sort of leadership, and the Northern orientation and the banker mentality, means that the only way forward is to get away from these institutions, maybe to default on their debt, to kick them out of the country.[14]

So the results spoke for themselves: globally, after the recession of 2008–2009, foreign direct investment (FDI) flows made a decisive turn toward less developed economies. In 2012, for the first time ever, "developing" economies received a greater share of FDI than the so-called "developed" world. The trend continued the following year, with developing economies hitting a new high of US $778 billion, or 54 percent of global FDI.[15] Africa's trade balance in goods had experienced some dramatic fluctuations from the onset of devastating structural adjustment in 1980, as reported by the UN Economic Commission on Africa, and for the last two decades of the twentieth century, averaged around the zero mark. But around the turn of the millennium, the trade balance in primary materials began to grow, surpassing the $100 billion mark in 2008 with Africa thus becoming increasingly a net exporter of goods.[16]

African leaders enthusiastically embraced the new investment orthodoxy, seeing in financialization an opportunity to break free from the apparent stagnation of the development model. Ruling classes across the continent, as we shall see, forged new alliances and agreements in this vein, underpinned by a different political framework than the Pan-African perspectives of the post-independence generation. Business-friendly objectives dominated the ideological and political posture, for example in this account from the *New York Times*:

> M. Nathaniel Barnes, Liberia's ambassador to the United States and the country's former finance minister, says that while foreign aid is still crucial for African countries, it usually focuses on humanitarian issues like emergency food and shelter or medical supplies. In contrast, he said, foreign investment provides long-term sustainability and growth. "Instead of talking to USAID, I'd rather be talking to a company like Nike," Mr. Barnes said. "Having a partner like that means jobs and economic growth, and you just don't get that from aid."[17]

Class divisions in Africa sharpened in this period. Walter Rodney described this dynamic in a well-known passage:

> The African revolutionary Franz Fanon dealt scorchingly and at length with the question of the minority in Africa which serves as the transmission line between the metropolitan capitalists and the dependencies in Africa. The importance of this group cannot be underestimated. The presence of a group of African sell-outs is part of the definition of underdevelopment. Any diagnosis of underdevelopment in Africa will reveal not just low per capita income and protein deficiencies, but also the gentlemen who dance in Abidjan, Accra and Kinshasa when music is played in Paris, London and New York.[18]

Financing for (under)development sharpened class and social contradictions that have deepened the fragility of African societies and economies, investor and ruling-class enthusiasm to the contrary.

Trade and Economic Agreements in Neoliberal Africa

The African "boom" has been fueled and expanded by several far-reaching agreements. These "partnerships," described below, have been key prongs for economic strategy on the continent, both on the part of the West as well as the African ruling classes.

African Growth and Opportunity Act

One of the key mechanisms to expand growth has been the US-led African Growth and Opportunity Act (AGOA) of 2000, a trade agreement that helped open the door for this new boom. According to the AGOA mission, the agreement "offers tangible incentives for African countries to continue their efforts to open their economies and build free markets." It also promises that, under its program, "millions of African families find opportunities to build prosperity."[19] A hallmark of the "trade not aid" paradigm, AGOA was initially signed by then US President Bill Clinton, with further amendments later authorized and extended by Presidents George W. Bush and Barack Obama. AGOA was renewed in 2015 for another ten years.[20]

AGOA advocates claim that it provides African nations "with the most liberal access to the US market available to any country or region with which the United States does not have a Free Trade Agreement." Yet the conditions for participation are steep:

> establishment of market-based economies; development of political pluralism and the rule of law; elimination of barriers to US trade and investment; protection of intellectual property; efforts to combat corruption; policies to reduce poverty, increase availability of health care and educational opportunities; protection of human rights and worker rights, and elimination of certain practices of child labor.[21]

These requirements are so extensive that Satgar, for one, has argued that they further subordinate weak African states to IFIs and global imperialism.[22] AGOA ultimately cements unequal terms of trade, reinforcing export-based economies, heavy emphasis on primary commodities, and the import of US capital goods.[23] Michael Besha of the Organization of African Trade Union Unity has aptly described the agreement as "coercing African countries into total trade and financial liberalization."[24] The trade agreement has reproduced highly uneven economic conditions across the continent. In a 2014 report, the US labor federation, the AFL-CIO, described how "oil and gas constitute between 80% and 90% of all exports under AGOA. . . . When oil and petroleum were excluded, South Africa accounted for about 75% of all other US imports under AGOA in 2012, for goods like vehicles, chemicals and minerals." As a result, they conclude:

> To truly spark sustainable, broad growth, it is critical that African economies make the transition from raw materials into value-added and more complex production through specialization, local sourcing and regional integration. Unfortunately, AGOA has done too little to encourage policies

that build links between industry and communities, build domestic demand, enhance educational and training opportunities or build crucial infrastructure.[25]

Significantly, AGOA *excludes* agricultural products from receiving preferential status, a major blow to the ability of African agricultural producers to expand that industry. Meanwhile, employment under AGOA has been concentrated in low-wage jobs. The AFL-CIO reports:

> While AGOA is said to have created anywhere from 300,000 to 1.3 million jobs in sub-Saharan Africa, directly and indirectly, these numbers still are far below original expectations. Job growth has not necessarily meant an increase in decent work, with problems in Swaziland's garment factories being the most notable example of low-wage job growth. Additionally, AGOA has not produced dramatic economic growth.[26]

More than 50 percent of Africa's GDP still rests on the informal sector.[27]

Finally, because of the high levels of neoliberal capital mobility, investments can be relatively fleeting and short-lived, creating volatility in employment levels and economic instability more generally.[28] Under AGOA agreements, investors have made use of export processing zones with heavy use of imported inputs and much of the profits from those industries leaving Africa.[29] AGOA has further concentrated the ownership of capital based in Africa, by and large, in the hands of Western capitalists. Despite media hype about a new African millionaire and billionaire class, the *ownership* of large-scale capital by members of an African bourgeoisie remains minimal.[30]

Economic Partnership Agreements

Economic Partnership Agreements (EPAs)—such as the Cotonou Agreement, signed in Cotonou, Benin, in June 2000—are designed to open up opportunities for European capital in Africa. As with the AGOA, the European Union (EU) initiatives have been long on promises but short on delivering on economic development and reduced poverty.[31] The agreements have opened up 75 to 80 percent of African markets to European goods. Trade between Africa and the EU took off, and the EU has become the largest regional trading partner with Africa.[32] Yet the agreements also accelerated the deindustrialization set in motion by prior liberalization. Thus, as Jean Nanga has written, "through the EPAs, the EU has actually organized the suffocation of African industrial capital to the benefit of European transnational exporters."[33] The charade of these agreements was exemplified by then Senegalese President

Abdoulaye Wade, who, after protracted negotiations in 2007, refused to sign an EPA that he rightly characterized as a "straightjacket."[34]

According to a study by Christian Aid, Traidcraft, and Tearfund, under EPA agreements, "African countries would ultimately have to eliminate tariffs on 80 percent of imports from the EU. This [would] deprive African countries of vital income, where on average they rely on import taxes for 25 percent of their revenues. Zambia, for example, could lose nearly 16 million dollars, the equivalent of its yearly budget for dealing with AIDS."[35] Indeed, one advocate has predicted an EPA "could have worse consequences for Kenya" than the IMF and World Bank's structural adjustment programs of the 1980s and 1990s.[36] Citing a loss in West Africa alone of $985 million in revenue directly attributable to these new agreements,[37] Margaret Lee has concluded that EPAs are a form of "economic recolonization."[38] Britain's involvement in African investment has likewise been proactive and extensive. During the boom of the early 2000s, British capital topped all other nations in mergers and acquisitions on the continent.[39] As summed up by Nanga:

> To the delight of Business Action for Africa . . . [the UK's Department for International Development] is active in supporting British transnationals operating in Africa, such as Unilever (where former British ministers are recycled), Diageo (recently taken to court for payment of bribes in Asia), Rio Tinto (already accused of complicity in war crimes and genocide in Papua New Guinea and exposed by farmers and environmental associations in Madagascar, Mozambique, Namibia . . .), Shell (accused of complicity in the repression of the Ogonis and of falsification of information on oil pollution in Nigeria). It is no surprise that the behaviour of these British transnationals (including Lonmin, responsible for the crime of Marikana) remains marked by a certain neo-colonial spirit.[40]

New Partnership for Africa's Development

The New Partnership for Africa's Development, or NEPAD, represents a major initiative on the part of African ruling classes in leading the accumulation of capital in Africa. Launched in 2001, it began as a project of the two leaders of the continent's largest economies: presidents Thabo Mbeki of South Africa and Olusegun Obasanjo of Nigeria.[41] As with AGOA and the EPAs, NEPAD's objectives were to promote trade and investment, but under African neoliberal auspices. In some US ruling-class circles, this effort toward self-initiative was unwelcome: a council from the Office of the Director of National Intelligence dismissed the project as a feeble attempt at self-governance on the part of African rulers:

> Although it is largely ignored in the United States, NEPAD consumes a significant portion of current African discussions on development and, critically, is a substantial part of South Africa's and Nigeria's foreign policies. It is hardly exceptional for the weak to put their faith in international institutions that they will influence by fiat, or—as in the case of NEPAD—create outright, rather than in markets that will be dominated by the strong. There are obviously many obstacles before the peer review mechanism in NEPAD (the critical part) succeeds; however, Africans are likely to continue to focus on developing this continental architecture long after the West has given up on it as another failed program.[42]

However, other brokers of capital have adopted a different posture, seeing NEPAD as a useful "partner" in expanding business opportunities in Africa. NEPAD has teamed up with the World Economic Forum—one of the leading global organizations for corporate interests—on investment and privatization initiatives. NEPAD's Grow Africa project has secured billions of dollars in investor pledges for agricultural investment.[43] NEPAD has also partnered with the Bill and Melinda Gates Foundation, which has poured millions into controversial projects such as the development of genetically modified crops and impacting the "regulatory environment" for agricultural investment.[44] Thus, as Patrick Bond has described, NEPAD has proven to be nothing other than "a homegrown version of the Washington Consensus."[45] The African left has consistently opposed the plan's market-driven priorities as well as exclusion from its policies of any input from African grassroots organizations.[46] The enduring lesson of the NEPAD initiative is the arrival of an African neoliberal ruling class, aspiring to partnership with the leaders of global capital while attempting to carve out their own economic niche in the process.

"Open for Business"

By the mid-2000s, Africa was being celebrated as an investment hotspot. African leaders and the business presses alike declared "Africa rising," even during the Great Recession. Marked by a gushing enthusiasm for African business opportunities, "Africa is open for business" became a recurring theme from all quarters. At the height of the boom, Wall Street seemed like it couldn't get enough of the action. JP Morgan helped raise $300 million for Nigeria's largest bank,[47] with a banker enthusing, "there are deals we are doing today that a couple of years ago we would not even have contemplated."[48] Such clamoring for Africa was not completely unfounded: the volume of trade and levels of FDI did rise substantially over this period. While the bulk of global investment—as from the dawn of imperialism—remains between the major powers, in the twenty-first millennium, a commodity price surge and an explosion of new businesses emerging on the continent have produced growth rates well above the global average. In the first decade of the new millennium, trade between Africa and the rest of the world increased by 200 percent, with marked declines in both foreign debts (25 percent) and budget deficits (66 percent).[49] A tripling of worldwide oil prices since 2003 boosted rates of growth in GDP into the 5 to 6 percent range.[50]

All told, FDI in Africa increased *nineteen-fold* in the period up to 2013;[51] the following year it increased by another 136 percent.[52] The first decade of the twenty-first century saw higher rates of return on FDI in Africa than anywhere else on the globe, according to McKinsey, a US consultancy.[53] As late as 2015, Africa led the world in rates of growth for FDI.[54] The two largest sources of FDI into Africa are North America and Africa itself (showing the growing importance of African capital). A number of major US companies—from General Electric, Coca-Cola, and Procter & Gamble to MasterCard, Marriot, and the Blackstone Group—have led the way.[55] Some much-hyped deals of late have included an alliance between brewer SABMiller and Coca-Cola as well as the entry of giant French insurer Axa into Nigeria.[56] In 2013, FDI in sub-Saharan Africa alone captured more than 80 percent of investment for the continent as a whole for the first time, with intra-African investment practically tripling between 2003 and 2013. This development was highly significant given the continent's longstanding weak economic and infrastructural integration.[57]

Financial managers were no less impressed by Africa's ability to weather the global economic crisis, seemingly confirming hopeful declarations that robust, diverse economies in Africa had arrived.[58] "With many of its forty-eight economies rebounding from the crisis faster than the rest of the world, sub-Saharan Africa is increasingly viewed as an opportunity rather than a burden," declared the *Financial Times* in the aftermath. "It is rising rapidly up the agenda for global investment managers and is talked about as never before in almost every big financial center."[59] Emerging Capital Partners, one of the leading funds focused on Africa, concurred: "We still think the investment climate in Africa is good," said Thomas Gibian, chief executive, in 2009. "We're looking long term, and the financial crisis has not deterred us from good investments."[60] Bob Diamond, chief executive of the global equity group Carlyle, led their expansion into South Africa and Nigeria at the close of the first decade of the new millennium, describing Africa as "maybe the most exciting opportunity" worldwide.[61] Some of these funds are pension funds, including those based in the United States, such as the $180 billion New York State Common Retirement Fund and the $107 billion Washington State Investment Board.[62]

Africa likewise saw interest from private equity funds reaching record highs. Two funds raised in 2015, for example, brought in just under $1.4 billion, a new record for amounts raised for Africa in a single year,[63] surpassing a record set just that year by the Nigerian-based Helios group, who launched a $1 billion fund to much fanfare. All told, as the *Financial Times* put it, "the emergence of capital markets is hailed as a significant development."[64] As with the imperialists more than a century ago, driven to build roads and railways to move raw materials to the African coasts for export, for international capital today, infrastructure construction offers a means to more readily extract profits and capitalize on investment potential. Investors today pay lip-service to meeting economic needs while pushing for privatized development. One account captures the tone:

> For the most part, these are new markets that need everything, and there is little or no competition," said Bruce J. Wrobel, the president of Sithe Global, an energy company that is based in New York and controlled by the Blackstone Group. Sithe and the Aga Khan Group, a private international development organization, have joined to build a huge hydroelectric dam in Jinja, Uganda, which is expected to cost $860 million. . . . Projects like the dam provide a perfect example of why private investment is needed in African countries. . . . Not only do they hire people to do construction work, they also help to create hundreds of other jobs as new service businesses spring up.[65]

Other accounts in the business press concur. As a South African–based banker enthusiastically described: "We see that investors have woken up to the fact that there are projects and great opportunities in power in Africa; their horizons have changed from one of 'why' Africa to 'how' Africa. As a result, there is a wall of money poised for deployment."[66] African leaders have actively sought out funding for these projects. President Jacob Zuma of South Africa—the continent's most industrialized and advanced economy—has offered up the promise of hundreds of billions in infrastructure investment potential.[67] In reality, the infrastructure needs of ordinary Africans are enormous. The African Development Bank reports an estimated $50 billion infrastructure deficit.[68] Africans have only 31 kilometers of paved road per 1,000 square kilometers; in comparison, other developing countries have 134 kilometers, and "upper-middle-income" countries have 781 kilometers.[69] Some countries have a shockingly low household electricity access rate: in Liberia, the national average is a mere 10 percent; in Kenya, seen as a leading light for economic growth, the rate is only 23 percent, and in Nigeria, the largest economy in Africa, access just reaches the majority of the population, at 56 percent. In rural areas, the numbers are far worse, with average rates of access in the single digits for some nations.[70] As the *Financial Times* reported, "Excluding South Africa . . . the entire installed generation capacity of sub-Saharan Africa (SSA) is only 28 gigawatts, roughly equivalent to that of Argentina. . . . A recent report by the World Bank and the International Energy Agency shows that current rates of electrification in SSA are lagging well behind population growth, a direct consequence of the fact that the $11bn spent annually on boosting generating capacity in the region is merely a quarter of what is required."[71] Former US President Barack Obama launched the Power Africa electrification and energy initiative to facilitate investment. A host of deals were signed at the Global Entrepreneurship Summit during his 2015 visit to Kenya, including General Electric (doing business in Africa since 1898), which signed on to build a major wind power plant in Kenya. SkyPower Global agreed to bring solar and wind energy to the national grid,[72] and ContourGlobal, another major US-based power-generation company, has partnered with the World Bank to build a massive power plant in Senegal.[73]

Enter China: The Dynamics of Imperial Competition

The big picture for Africa today is deepening involvement of both the United States and a host of competitors in a new scramble for trade deals and investment. China and Russia, in particular, are imperial powers in their own right aiming to secure control over resources and markets and with a willingness to back up those aims with military might. China has sought to deepen African "engagement" to meet its own imperial objectives. The liberalization, privatization, and trade agreements of recent decades have opened up new opportunities for China as well as the West. These developments have fueled a fierce rivalry between the United States and China for global economic and military preeminence, with the United States moving to encircle and contain China's growing reach.

The Secretary of Defense issued a report outlining their guiding framework:

> The Department of Defense (DoD) approach to China is part of a broader US strategy for the Asia-Pacific region that is focused on ensuring and building upon a stable and diversified security order, an open and transparent economic order, and a liberal political order. Combined, these factors have contributed to the peace and prosperity of the entire region since the end of the Second World War, directly benefiting China and its neighbors. US policy toward China is based on the premise that it is in both our countries'

interests to deepen practical cooperation in areas where our countries' interests overlap, while constructively managing differences.[74]

Yet, as a Council on Foreign Relations report points out, there are inherent dangers in these underlying contradictions:

> The American effort to "integrate" China into the liberal international order has now generated new threats to US primacy in Asia—and could eventually result in a consequential challenge to American power globally—[so that] Washington needs a new grand strategy toward China that centers on balancing the rise of Chinese power rather than continuing to assist its ascendancy. . . . it must involve crucial changes to the current policy in order to limit the dangers that China's economic and military expansion pose to US interests in Asia and globally.[75]

This competition illustrates well the broad dynamics outlined by the classical Marxist theories of imperialism: the tendency under capitalism for economic competition to spill over into competition between nation-states.

China has likewise become more forceful in projecting its ambitions. As socialist Ashley Smith describes:

> The competitive drive of capitalist development has forced the Chinese ruling class to become increasingly assertive in Asia and internationally. This is not the result of ideology but of the economic compulsion for the state to secure resources, develop markets, and open sites for investment for Chinese capital. China's new imperial assertiveness is a significant departure from its traditional strategy of pursuing a "peaceful rise."
>
> Just like the rise of the United States, Japan, and Germany at the end of the nineteenth century produced conflicts with established imperial powers like Britain and France, China's rise has set it on a collision course with the United States and with regional powers in Asia. Despite their economic integration, the United States and China are at loggerheads over everything from the strength of the Chinese currency, the yuan, to violations of intellectual property rights, cyber security, and climate change, as well as over policies in Asia, the Middle East, and Africa.[76]

Some on the left reject the idea that the China–US rivalry is an expression of inter-imperial conflict. Socialists Leo Panitch and Sam Gindin argue in *Global Capitalism and American Empire* (2004) that imperial powers have a "relatively autonomous role in maintaining social order and securing the conditions of capital accumulation."[77] In this formulation, the United States serves as the global "superintendent of capitalism," transcending national allegiances, where "the US state was more than the mere agent of the particular interests of American capital; it also assumed responsibilities for the making and management of global capitalism."[78] This view echoes Karl Kautsky's idea of "ultra-imperialism" from a century ago, which envisioned the rise of imperial powers peacefully coexisting. The outbreak of World War I proved Kautsky's ideas untenable and showed that Lenin's theory of inter-imperial rivalries is a far better explanatory framework. Likewise, Panitch and Gindin's explanation fails to explain the actual intensification of the rivalry between the United States and China. Far from an informal US empire facilitating "seamless accumulation" and an end to conflict, sharp economic competition threatens to spill over into clashes between the states themselves.

For Marxist geographer David Harvey, on the other hand, capitalism has entered into a period of intractable decline. Global capital increasingly relies upon what he calls "accumulation by dispossession" to move wealth from one section of the system to another as a means of sustaining profitability. Harvey's framework elaborates on Marx's writings on primitive accumulation as a way to explain the forcible methods of accumulation and privatization today as a means to pry open the "noncapitalist" regions of the world.[79] Beyond these means, the United States and the other major powers are increasingly compelled to turn to force to shore up their weakening position.

According to Harvey, "reliance upon its unchallengeable military power indicates a high-risk approach to sustaining US domination, almost certainly through military command over global oil resources. Since this is occurring in the midst of several signs of loss of dominance in the realms of production and now (though as yet less clearly) finance, the temptation to go for exploitative domination is strong. . . . Control over oil supplies provides a convenient means to counter any power shifts—both economic and military—threatened within the global economy. . . . The capitalistic logic of power will tear the territorial logic that is now being pursued to shreds."[80] Yet this analysis has not been borne out by recent history: global capitalism, including the United States, has recovered rates of profitability. As Smith has pointed out,

> Harvey . . . downplays the expansion, however uneven, of the system over the last thirty years. While some areas of the world have stagnated and others have lurched backwards, there is no doubt that the advanced capitalist economies—and an assortment of developing countries, especially Brazil, Russia, India, and China—experienced substantial booms, achieving, in Marxist terms, "expanded reproduction."[81]

Yet despite these boom conditions, the dynamics of imperialism Marx and Lenin laid out nonetheless continue to unfold through economic and military means alike. Imperialism in Africa—as elsewhere around the globe—is not necessarily marked by the competitive death throes of *declining* powers, but rather by rivalries between the dominant powers as well as emerging ones.

These tensions have thus widened to the African stage. A report from the US military's Africa Command (AFRICOM) lays out these strategic challenges:

> Other nations continue to invest in African nations to further their own objectives. China is focused on obtaining natural resources and necessary infrastructure to support manufacturing while both China and Russia sell weapon systems and seek to establish trade and defense agreements in Africa. As China and Russia expand their influence in Africa, both countries are striving to gain "soft power" in Africa to strengthen their power in international organizations.[82]

The focus on imperial challengers like China and Russia has prompted debate on the left on their relationship to the "older" powers of the West. Sometimes grouped together as the "BRICS" nations (that is, Brazil, Russia, India, China, and South Africa), these powers play an important role in the emerging economies in Africa. Debates have emerged regarding the extent to which the BRICS are in fact imperial challengers, or whether they function as "lieutenants" in the service of the imperial project. Bond, for example, has written extensively on BRICS and Africa, arguing that the BRICS play a sub-imperial role that "lubricates" the interests of the major imperial powers in the region. His volume, *BRICS: An Anti-Capitalist Critique*, edited with Ana Garcia, explores this debate, including in the African context.[83] Not all BRICS are created equal, however, and there is great diversity across this group with regard to their economic strength and imperial reach. Other emerging powers such as Malaysia, Turkey, Mexico, and Indonesia play a similar role in the global economy. The common thread is that all aspire to be independent centers of accumulation, both as sole powers and regional blocs, able to compete on the world stage.

All told, trade between the nations of the Global South has been steadily rising. BRICS and other emerging nations have been forging alliances and pacts that may conflict with US interests. The new BRICS Bank—an institutional pillar for this new bloc—is a challenger to the hegemony of the World Bank. Likewise, especially during the African boom, economic ties with China provided opportunities to sideline the IMF. South Africa, in particular, has attempted to chart an independent economic path based on these "south-south" relationships, but other "emerging economies" in Africa, such as Nigeria and Angola, have likewise sought a similar goal. In one example, Brazil drove the revival of the decades-old South Atlantic Peace and Cooperation Zone, which involved participation by those three

African nations and has a reach that extends to the Caribbean, right in the United States' back yard.[84] Brazil has been a major player in African investment, particularly in mining and agriculture, driving massive land grabs. Similarly, bilateral India-Africa trade grew by nearly 32 percent annually between 2005 and 2011, including through the economic crisis.[85] The *African Economic Outlook* 2014 edition reports that, "in 2008, Africa's total trade with developing countries, including African countries, exceeded Africa's total trade with the EU, traditionally its major trading partner, for the first time ever, . . . part of a broader trend towards intensifying Africa-South economic relationships, particularly with large and dynamic emerging economies."[86] Overall, "south-south" deals account for 24 percent of African trade.[87]

Yet one aspiring power rises above the rest. China is undoubtedly a dominant powerhouse, of a qualitatively different order, whose interests potentially clash with those of the United States in Africa. China has not only secured mineral rights across the continent but has cemented political allegiances with African regimes through development projects such as dams, roads, and bridges. Chinese leaders very actively cultivated these relationships, with frequent high-profile visits since the start of the "boom." As the *New York Times* described at the time, then President Hu Jintao embarked on a whirlwind African tour in early 2007 "through eight nations, among them some of China's closest allies, largest trading partners and most prominent objects of Chinese investment. He left behind a multibillion-dollar trail of forgiven debts, cheap new loans, and pledges of schools and cultural centers."[88] China has attempted to reinforce its economic strategy with a political one, following up its own investment pledges with calls "for developed nations to deliver on promises of aid and market access for Africa."[89] Loans from China to poor countries, mainly in Africa, have surpassed those from the World Bank.[90] African oil-rich nations have been happy to embrace these alliances, welcoming "infrastructure for oil" deals.

Thus, the economic, social, and political relations of the Chinese projection into Africa have a different character than those of the United States and the former colonial nations. But China is no kinder, gentler imperial power: just like nineteenth-century colonialists, when the Chinese build roads and schools, the goal is to facilitate resource extraction and build allegiances. On balance, as we shall see, Chinese investment and infrastructure building has reproduced the social and economic inequality and unevenness that likewise accompany imperialism in its Western form.

"The Second Continent"

The scale of China's economic involvement in Africa has grown enormously in the twenty-first century. Chinese FDI in Africa has been massive: more than 2,200 Chinese enterprises, most of them private firms, are currently operating in sub-Saharan Africa.[91] During the crisis of 2008–2009, Chinese capital successfully sought outlets for investment overseas in the face of a failing domestic market and excess capital, while the European Union and United States floundered. "China's total outbound FDI more than doubled in 2008, even as global FDI flows fell by 15 percent, and in 2009, while global FDI plummeted, Chinese outbound FDI still managed to grow by 1 percent. Ultimately, the global financial crisis accelerated a process of outbound investment liberalization that China had initiated in the early 2000s."[92]

The United States and the former colonial powers of Britain and France together represent approximately two-thirds of total FDI in Africa, with the value for each country's stock around double that of Chinese companies.[93] The United States alone leads China in FDI; together, investments from Brazil, Russia, and India in Africa are greater than those from China.[94] However, the *rate of growth* in investment from China in Africa is outpacing that from other areas of the globe. Investment in sub-Saharan Africa from the European Union, China, Japan, and the United States grew by nearly five times in the first decade of the new millennium. But this growth was primarily driven by China, whose FDI grew at an annual rate of 53 percent, compared to 14 percent for the United States.[95] According to a 2015 World Bank report, investment from China represents 7 percent of total global flows to the continent.[96]

South Africa has received the bulk of Chinese investment, representing one-third of the investment total.[97] While other important areas for Chinese FDI include Nigeria, Sudan, and Zambia, its reach encompasses the majority of Africa. Oil and mining have captured the bulk of Chinese investment, at 30 percent of the total. But as with Western investment, there has been movement into the financial services, construction, and manufacturing sectors.[98] Close to a third of Chinese investment has been in the technology, media, and telecommunications areas.[99] Howard French, author of *China's Second Continent*, suggests that rising labor costs and ecological concerns in China are enticing some light manufacturing to look for investment in Africa.[100] Approximately a third of all Chinese overseas contracts are in Africa.[101] For contracts with Chinese and Western firms alike, African leaders and business elites aim for favorable terms on "local content"—that is, requirements that manufacturers invest locally, transfer technology, and employ local staff. However, Chinese companies have sometimes side-stepped "local content" provisions and imported Chinese labor and equipment. As a result, while light manufacturing may gain a toehold in Africa, industrial commodity production on the part of Chinese capital—that is, the production of machinery and equipment with high value—is not expected to become a major priority in the near future.[102]

From Kenya's Thika superhighway to a new $200 million African Union headquarters in Addis Ababa, Ethiopia, infrastructure has been a high-profile aspect of Chinese involvement in Africa. Indeed, *two-thirds* of Africa's infrastructure since 2007 has been funded by China.[103] At a 2007 meeting of the African Development Bank hosted in Shanghai, Chinese representatives pledged, to much fanfare, $20 billion in infrastructure and trade financing over the following few years, with the bulk intended for electricity, roads, and other infrastructure. As Miria Pigato and Wenxia Tang write, there was a "surge in Chinese financing for overseas infrastructure projects, as Chinese infrastructure financing commitments rose from US$3.5 billion in 2007 to US$5.1 billion in 2009."[104] Almost a decade later, Chinese leader Xi Jinping committed to a new round of loans and aid at the Forum on China-African Cooperation; it now totals $60 billion, with a large portion of the funds directed at South African infrastructure, Zimbabwean projects, and other initiatives. Xi also announced drought relief for the continent, prompting Zimbabwe's then President Robert Mugabe to declare, "We say he is a god-sent person."[105] All told, if Chinese pledges materialize, $1 trillion in project funding will flow into African countries by 2025, according to the Export-Import Bank of China.[106] Nonetheless, this new round of commitments still fell far short of meeting infrastructure and development needs.[107] In addition, Chinese lending actually fell sharply beginning in the 2010s compared to the prior decade.[108]

Nigeria is China's top customer when it comes to construction—$24.6 billion worth of projects since 2005—but, as elsewhere, companies typically import their materials, such as steel products, so African manufacturers have not experienced the benefits of the use of "local content" in the building boom.[109] The Nigerian case reveals some of the same underlying contradictions of the boom as a whole. As described by the *New York Times*:

> Infrastructure projects in Nigeria have been fueled by the same manic lending that has also created mountains of debt for China's economy at home. State-controlled Chinese banks have lent money at rock-bottom interest rates in deeply indebted Nigeria. A little-known Chinese government agency, Sinosure . . . insured $427 billion worth of Chinese exports and overseas construction projects around the world in 2013, the most recent year available. The Export-Import Bank of the United States, by comparison, issued just $5 billion worth of credit in each of the last two years.[110]

As Chinese investment in Africa grew, so did the volume in Sino-African trade. It has skyrocketed since the relatively tepid numbers at the turn of the century,[111] and is now nearly 2.5 times more than US trade with Africa.[112] China reportedly surpassed American trade with Africa in 2009 to become Africa's single-largest trading partner. China's booming economy and its need for energy resources was a critical factor in the global surge of commodity prices, as well as the longest period of growth in Africa since before the global downturn of the 1970s.[113] As the World Bank reports, "one-third of China's energy imports come from sub-Saharan Africa, a vital trade link, especially as energy consumption rates in China have grown by more than twice the global average over the past 10 years."[114] Angola is the third-largest supplier of oil to China in the world,[115] while China is the leading destination for African goods. The *African Economic Outlook* reports: "Over the first decade of the century, African exports to Europe doubled, exports to emerging economies quadrupled and exports to China alone increased by a factor of twelve."[116] Today, China is the destination for 27 percent of African exports; the European Union receives 23 percent, the United States 21 percent, and India 9 percent.[117]

Trade between Africa and the rest of the world has increased by 200 percent since 2000. Competition for African markets between China, EU nations, the United States, and emerging markets has sharpened over the course of the twenty-first century, except for a downturn during the global recession of 2008–2009.[118] Europe is Africa's largest regional trading partner, but its rate of increase has now been outstripped by the rate of growth for China-Africa trade. Europe's share of total trade with Africa fell by approximately one-quarter over the millennium's first decade, whereas China's share *increased* during that same period by approximately 40 percent.[119]

China has been outstripping the United States in crucial areas of economic and political engagement in Africa and has been literally elbowing it out of new business and trade deals. Yet the United States has conflicting aims and strategies with regard to China: broadly speaking, the United States has viewed China variously as competitor, potential market, and investment site, with all of these underpinned by the threat of instability within its mammoth economy.[120] Recent US strategy reflects that dual-edged relationship. As the Office of the Secretary of Defense has outlined, "the 2015 US National Security Strategy emphasizes that the United States seeks to develop a constructive relationship with China that sustains and promotes security and prosperity in Asia and around the world. At the same time, the strategy acknowledges there will be areas of competition and underscores that the United States will manage this competition with China from a position of strength while seeking ways to reduce the risk of misunderstanding or miscalculation."[121]

The US posture toward China in Africa has taken a range of sometimes contradictory approaches, including downplaying competition on the continent. President Obama declared in 2013: "I want everybody playing in Africa. The more the merrier. A lot of people are pleased that China is involved in Africa."[122] There are some elements of truth in this. When Obama spoke those words, several processes were well underway: his administration had exponentially expanded the US military footprint in Africa, providing reinforcement for its strategic political and economic aims. At the same time, a major retooling of US energy strategies—with a dramatic turn toward domestic oil production and emphasis on the "shale revolution"—created a buffer from the "China threat" in Africa. Finally, the United States has a highly interdependent relationship with China, in which the United States relies heavily on Chinese imports of American goods. These trends explain enthusiasm for African markets and China's role. The *Economist* commented, for example: "China deserves credit for engaging a continent that desperately needs investment. Millions of Africans are using roads, schools and hospitals built by Chinese companies or financed with fees from resources they extracted."[123]

Yet lying beneath the surface, tensions remain and are sometimes laid bare. China's involvement generated hypocritical hand-wringing during the boom. Western investors claimed that China's loans to Africa could pave the way for economic crisis down the road, with African nations tied to oil exports and world prices with no guarantee of sustained high levels. The IMF delivered warnings of a "new wave of African debt" led by China, but also other competitors like Brazil and India.[124] The irony of Western concerns was not lost on some in the business press; one commented that China's pattern of operation in Africa "draws comparisons with Africa's past relationship with European colonial powers, which exploited the continent's natural resources but failed to encourage more labor-intensive industry."[125] Missing from such comments are a reality check on the central role that neoliberalism and structural adjustment have themselves played in the deindustrialization process that set the stage for a renewed round of debt and crisis.

Because infrastructure development projects often go hand in hand with Chinese oil and mining deals, Western powers view with concern the potential for African states to free themselves from the punitive conditions of IMF and World Bank loans and other forms of financial dependence on Europe and the United States. As the second-largest source of oil in Africa, Angola in the mid-2000s was in a strong enough position to reject IMF loans completely.[126] As one energy consultant commented, "with all their oil revenue, they don't need the IMF or the World Bank. They can play the Chinese off the Americans."[127] Or, as another writer put it, "who needs the painful medicine of the IMF when China gives easy terms and builds roads and schools to boot?"[128]

Despite their own far longer and bloodier legacy of colonialism, Western investors and politicians engage in their own share of finger-wagging, sniffing that the Chinese "prefer" to work with undemocratic governments and ignore human rights in Africa. "Today most western institutions are preaching the values of good governance and democracy," commented the *Financial Times*. "Turning a blind eye to corruption and the abuse of political power is a recipe for political instability. It does not serve China's long-term interests, either."[129] There are also accusations of overlooking democratic norms: "China is a very aggressive and pernicious economic competitor with no morals. China is not in Africa for altruistic reasons," Assistant Secretary of State for African Affairs Johnnie Carson said in 2010 at a meeting with executives from Shell, Chevron, Exxon, Schlumberger, and the American Business Council.[130]

These tensions reached a boiling point with the targeting of the 2008 Beijing Olympics by Western politicians over Darfur, when Western politicians strong-armed China into lobbying its allies in the Sudanese government for peacekeeping forces.[131] A letter from the US House of Representatives Committee on Foreign Affairs to China's President Hu Jintao—signed by over 100 members of Congress—called the Darfur crisis "a moral challenge for us all; if China fails to do its part, it risks being forever known as the host of the 'Genocide Olympics.'"[132] The moralizing rhetoric paints underlying rivalries as strategic differences. The Council on Foreign Relations expresses this dynamic: "Despite possessing the world's second-largest economy and military budget, China has generally adopted a strategy of burden shifting, insisting that the United States and others bear the costs of providing global public goods even as China, citing its challenges as a 'developing country,' uses them to maximize its own national power."[133] Certainly the drive for profit on the part of China has helped fuel inequality in Africa alongside poor conditions for labor, the environment, and human rights. Yet the West's long record of exploitation and their own scramble for Africa—new and old—are equally problematic.

The LAPSSET Project: "Land Grabbing and Forced Destitution"[134]

We are worried, feel offended by our government. Some rich Kenyans, our leaders who have betrayed us and some foreigners, we have told them, shouted, and told them not to destroy our environment, grab our land, kill our livelihoods and culture, but we have been ignored.

—Ali Mzee, human rights activist[135]

Announced by the Government of Kenya in 2009 and formally inaugurated with Ethiopia and South Sudan in 2012, the Lamu Port-South Sudan-Ethiopia-Transport (LAPSSET) project is a massive, high-profile initiative to build transportation, communication, and pipeline corridor links across an economically critical, resource-rich area of East Africa. The Kenyan government lauded the project as one of its most important infrastructure undertakings, projected to boost its status as an East African hub for special economic zones and free trade and attract private-sector investment for power generation and numerous other development plans. Anticipated components of the project include a port at Lamu on the Manda Bay (also home to the US military's Camp Simba),[136] a standard gauge railway line to Juba in South Sudan and Addis Ababa in Ethiopia, oil pipelines to link Lamu to Lake Turkana and the South Sudan oilfields, an oil refinery in Lamu County, multiple airports and resorts, and a vast network of roads linking all three countries. The price tag for LAPSSET has been cited at $26 billion.[137]

Corporate investors have celebrated Kenya's economy as a beacon of African stability, with its supposedly well-grounded diversity of manufacturing, tourism, telecommunications, and resource-development potential. Ethiopia, to its north, also experienced strong GDP growth during the African economic boom. Meanwhile, its neighbor, South Sudan, possesses some of the highest volumes of oil on the continent. According to NEPAD, tasked with "monitoring" LAPSSET:

This project is the single largest project of its nature in Eastern Africa, and LAPSSET will become Kenya's second largest transport corridor once the project has been completed. . . . The planned investment resource is equivalent to half of Kenya's GDP. . . . The LAPSSET Corridor Project will make a tremendous contribution to Kenya's economic growth, with projections ranging between 8 percent and 10 percent of GDP.[138]

Given the vast untapped potential promised by LAPSSET, support for the project has been readily supplied by the African Development Bank and the World Bank, who pledged to build out the Kenyan power grid.

President Barack Obama's East African visit in 2015 provided the framework for concluding agreements between the LAPSSETT Corridor Development Authority and the US and Kenyan governments, committing the United States to providing backing to American firms wanting to invest. Celebrating the "private sector participation," US Department of Commerce and Treasury Department officials confirmed a raft of deals were negotiated during the trip, with an investment total of $9.5 billion in LAPSSET and an additional $7.55 billion in projected exports.[139] Engineering giant Bechtel was one of several American companies in line to receive a piece of the LAPSSET project, as was General Electric. Kenya's president Uhuru Kenyatta had been actively promoting investor-friendly measures, such as tax concessions, with explicit overtures to US multinationals, declaring that LAPSSET could eventually link the East and West coasts of Africa and spur a host of other projects and investment opportunities, from finance and technology to thermal energy and mining.[140] The DC-based Corporate Council for Africa concurred, saying "Our focus has been on infrastructure, especially the LAPSSET."[141] Obama, meanwhile, fell far short in calling attention to the gross human rights violations and repression of US-allied regimes in Ethiopia and Kenya.

With its expansive scope and proximity to strategically vital Indian Ocean shipping lanes, LAPSSET has set in motion competitive tensions between the United States and China. Obama captured this dynamic on the eve of his Kenyan visit, noting that China, "because of surplus that they've accumulated in global trade and the fact that they are not accountable to their constituencies, have been able to funnel an awful lot of money into Africa, basically in exchange for raw materials that are being extracted."[142] Along with interests in the South Sudanese oilfields, China has been involved in infrastructure in Kenya for over a decade and sponsored a major feasibility study of the Lamu port in 2010 in the hopes of gaining the upper hand with the project.[143] Ultimately, as the *Standard* (Kenya) has described,

> While the [LAPSSET] deal has unsettled the Chinese, their place in the country is far from being shaken. In the recent past, the Chinese have had the lion's share of major infrastructural projects in Kenya. The on-going 300 billion Kenyan Shilling [approximately $3 billion USD at the time] Standard Gauge Railway . . . being undertaken by the Chinese is certainly lucrative . . . no wonder the GE Africa President and CEO, Jay Ireland, in a recent press briefing said: 'We would have wanted it to be us doing it, but unfortunately we were not given [the opportunity].'[144]

In fact, even though the United States was able to sideline China in negotiations over major components of LAPSSET, the year before, Kenya's port authority had signed a contract with the China Communications Construction Company for a portion of the planned new port at Lamu.[145] In addition, Kenyan officials stated the China Exim Bank, African Development Bank, and IMF were all likely players in the oil pipeline construction from the Lake Turkana Basin to Lamu.[146]

Other major powers are likewise maneuvering for leverage in this key strategic area. Kenya issued a US$2 billion Eurobond in 2014 to raise money for its infrastructure investments.[147] The *Standard* continues:

> No sooner had the dust left by Obama's visit settled, a delegation of Japanese investors came knocking. Chief executives representing 84 conglomerates, including Toyota Tsusho and Mitsubishi, were in the country to fight for a share in the emerging opportunities in both the public and private sectors. Japan, the third largest economy in the world, was keen on grabbing part of the on-going and planned mega infrastructure projects including the [LAPSSET] project.[148]

Uganda, in addition, has launched development of an oil refinery and an "alternate" oil pipeline route terminating in Tanga, Tanzania, on the East African coast, with a target completion date of 2020. The *Daily Nation* (Kenya) reported that "Uganda intends to construct the refinery to process its crude oil estimated at 6.5 billion barrels, which border the Democratic Republic of Congo. A consortium led by Russia's

RT Global Resources won the tender to build and operate the crude oil refinery but is still carrying out a study to ascertain the quality of crude and when construction could begin."[149] Oil companies including France's Total, Uganda's main oil investor, and Britain's Tullow were heavily involved in lobbying for and bidding on the pipeline project. Compounding the investment landscape, Ethiopia then announced a rival pipeline, known as the Horn of Africa Pipeline, to Djibouti, financed and built by China,[150] along with an affiliate of US investment firm Blackstone and a South African oil and gas corporation.[151]

Underscoring the competitive tensions in the region, concerns about political stability have run through infrastructure planning and negotiations. The planned pipeline runs close to the border with the Dadaab refugee camp—the world's largest—in Somalia, where the US-supported government has been waging a civil war with al-Shabab, classified as "Islamic terrorists" by the United States. An investor guide by the consultancy Deloitte gave voice to the concerns, citing the problem as a major obstacle to investment and stating that "stabilizing the Somali border and reducing the threat of terrorism will remain major government priorities, as unsettling attacks will deter foreign visitors."[152] In the lead-up to his visit, Obama announced additional funding for Kenya's war against terrorism, declaring: "We stand united in the fight against terrorism and we will be channeling more money towards this."[153]

Caught in the multinational race to secure strategic access to this mammoth investment opportunity, conditions facing ordinary East Africans have dramatically worsened. Community groups have raised deep concerns about the social and ecological impact of LAPSSET, from the lack of adequate environmental assessment and the exclusion of the public from planning discussions to loss of livelihoods and the potential for land displacement and ecological degradation.[154] The International Work Group on Indigenous Affairs, in conducting its own assessment of LAPSSET, estimated that "more than 100 million vulnerable, mostly extremely poor and historically marginalized indigenous people, are set to be affected in the three countries."[155]

Lamu is a famed, ancient port town in northeastern Kenya, designated as a UNESCO World Heritage Site in 2001 for its ecological resources and cultural landmarks. The Save Lamu Coalition describes Lamu as "the oldest and best-preserved Swahili settlement in East Africa." A renowned archaeological site, Lamu is also home to extensive marine wildlife endangered by the planned development, such that even the government's own study "acknowledges that 30 percent of the country's existing rare mangrove trees will be lost as a consequence of building the port in Lamu."[156] Save Lamu enumerates many environmental risks as land developers and utilities encroach on ecologically fragile areas, threatening preserves, fishing areas, and pristine habitats, where the "majority of the communities still depend on nature-based livelihoods."[157]

The LAPSETT Authority claims the project is opening up 70 percent of Kenya for "economic activities."[158] Notwithstanding these claims, the area is not uninhabited, and community opposition has mounted. Mohamed Rajab of the Kililana Farmers Organisation denounced the LAPSSET Authority for grabbing 70,000 acres more than agreed upon, reporting that poor farmers were being displaced from their ancestral lands: "We are now shocked to realise that the entire Kililana area has been allocated to the LAPSSET Authority. We will not allow that."[159] Land displacement caused by LAPSSET construction has sharpened conflicts further inland as well, with development fueling clashes between pastoralists in the context of grazing land and water shortages.[160] LAPSSET-related projects have also been hit by strikes at dam- and bridge-building sites over low wages and working conditions, including repeated work stoppages against China Road and Bridge Corporation on the railway between Mombasa and Nairobi.[161]

As a step toward easing conflicts in the border regions, Kenya and Ethiopia forged an agreement in late 2015 targeting economic development and job creation.[162] Yet such attempts to secure stability in the area only belie the deeper contradictions of the new imperial scramble for investment in East Africa and the Horn, unfolding in the context of protracted conflict and civil wars. The US military's presence—under the umbrella of the US AFRICOM at Djibouti and its numerous bases and "counterterrorism" efforts—only underlines and intensifies the fraught tensions between competing powers for corporate and strategic control.

"Africa Rising" Myths and Reality

As we have seen, the supposed miracle of African growth saw the continent's economies soar in the first decades of the twenty-first century, even soldiering through the global recession of 2007–2008. In this context, champions of the African boom have made some bold claims. Africa, the story goes, has finally broken the straitjacket of extractive industries, creating vibrant, diverse economies. New light-industrial and service sectors are a celebrated phenomenon.[163] And accompanying the arrival of Africa's new middle class is a drop in extreme poverty on the world's poorest continent. The narrative embraces broad improvement in, as the consultancy EY puts it, the "strong fundamentals to encourage investment including steady democracy and macroeconomic growth; an improving business environment; a rising consumer class; abundant natural resources and infrastructure development."[164] However, behind many of these claims lies a harsh reality of deepening exploitation, inequality, and class polarization. Those celebrating "Africa rising" and its investor-friendly environment are papering over deep contradictions in the nature of the economy, weaknesses inevitably to be exposed as African nations approach a new period of downturn and crisis.

Booming Growth and "Diverse Economies"

A central claim of global capital is a surge in growth and economic diversification created by the investment boom.[165] Yet important accounts have questioned the conclusion of Africa's "strong fundamentals." Tunde Oyateru has pointed out that despite the *relative* growth of FDI into Africa, within the wider global economy, the bulk of investment flows largely *bypass* the continent altogether, remaining concentrated between advanced economies. Africa thus represents, Oyateru writes, "one percent and 3.4 percent of the total percentage of FDI by the United States and China respectively; numbers that barely constitute a skip let alone a scramble for Africa."[166] Furthermore, accompanying the rise in investment since the early 2000s has been a dramatic rise in the *consolidation* of foreign investment in Africa: all of the top 100 investing companies are from wealthy countries except for seven, and of those remaining firms, six are from China and one is from Brazil.[167]

Peter Lawrence and Yao Graham have likewise argued that investment levels remain relatively low and the neoliberal turn toward the private sector has undermined economic development. Thus, they conclude:

> The pressure for financial liberalization has not had the results predicted for
> it by the neo-liberal strategists. There are few emerging capital markets on

the continent, net capital flows into Africa have been negative, and African economies are given high risk ratings which means that returns have to be very high to justify those perceived risks of investment. The emphasis on independent central banks having the sole task of targeting inflation rather than employment and growth has been accompanied by the decline in development finance and its institutions in favor of private foreign investment.[168]

Investment flows into Africa remain inconsistent and unevenly spread across the continent, giving lie to the idea that it has developed a wider base. For example, in 2014, leading African economies such as South Africa, Nigeria, Angola, Ghana, and Kenya actually experienced a decline in FDI. The net decline of sub-Saharan Africa was only offset by an increase in investment for North Africa, especially Egypt and Morocco, to show net growth for the continent as a whole.[169] Over 3,000 companies in Africa posted more than $50 million in revenues, yet close to half of those companies were based in South Africa; a grand total of 99 firms were Nigerian-based. As the *Financial Times* commented, "that does not leave a terribly deep pool of companies in Africa's remaining 52 countries."[170] The two nations combined represent approximately three-quarters of the continent's GDP.[171]

African economies today remain highly lopsided, struggling under the mammoth weight of subsidies and tariffs that render their products uncompetitive in the West, effectively thwarting industrialization.[172] Significantly, despite the massive recent growth in investment and speculation in Africa, the continent has reversed direction. It is now *less* industrialized than it was in the 1960s and 1970s, a staggering indictment of neoliberal policy.[173] Manufacturing's share of sub-Saharan African GDP fell from 16.5 percent in 1980 to 10 percent approximately 35 years later. In industrialized South Africa and Zimbabwe, the same figure fell by 50 percent from the 1990s over the following two decades.[174] Thus, claims that the continent's narrow, extractive export–oriented economies now boast diverse industries are exaggerated at best. In reality, the median share of industrial employment is only 7 percent, and industry reflects a mere 21 percent of GDP.[175]

These conditions echo the inherited legacies of African economies structured for the export of raw materials. African economies today reflect that legacy with an extremely high proportion of natural resources making up their export revenues: Angola, Nigeria, and Equatorial Guinea all derive more than 90 percent of that revenue from oil, and copper represents more than 70 percent of Zambia's export earnings.[176] Likewise, as Emira Woods of *Foreign Policy in Focus* has commented, "Minerals and goods are put on a ship or plane and sent out of the country so the people there don't really benefit. It's hard to find good examples where foreign direct investment is leading to real concrete development."[177]

Chinese trade and investment have not altered this fundamental dynamic. According to the World Bank, in 2015, Africa mainly imported finished products from China. From 2008 to 2013, only 11 percent of exports to China were manufactured products; almost 90 percent were natural resources (83 percent) and agricultural products.[178] Despite the deeper "involvement" of China, industrialization failed to take off because, as World Bank study authors Pigato and Tang explain, of sub-Saharan Africa's "weak integration into Chinese and other international production networks" due to "the small size of many economies in SSA, the low capacity of critical public institutions, the absence of complementary private markets, bottlenecks in essential infrastructure, and the lack of regional integration, all of which can make the establishment of large economies of scale very difficult to achieve."[179]

Furthermore, even though most countries experienced appreciating exchange rates against the dollar, yuan, and euro, the close links of these economies to China's needs for basic raw materials undermined African economies' abilities to take advantage of the currency exchange. "Despite the broad diversification of Chinese investment," Pigato and Tang continue, "countries in SSA have attracted limited attention from large, export-oriented firms. Although there are exceptions—notably the Huajian shoe factory in Ethiopia and the Yuemei group in Nigeria—Chinese investment has tended to focus on activities related to extractive industries, such as the processing of mineral ores or the production of liquid natural gas."[180]

The responsibility for continued "development" failures, when recognized at all, has been directed toward African policy making in the business press. For example, according to a *New York Times* account, "Zambia and other African nations appear to have failed to benefit broadly from the commodities boom, whether by not negotiating better terms with Chinese companies, not insisting on technology transfers or not using the revenues from raw materials to diversify their economies."[181] In contrast, some on the left have correctly rooted the failures of the "African boom" in underlying structural conditions as pronounced as they were three decades ago. Lawrence and Graham, for example, note:

> While there has been greater diversification in the exports of developed countries, African exports have further concentrated in fewer products. The liberalization of world trade has not helped African agriculture as exports have declined and Africa is now a net importer of food as, despite the ideology of liberalization, developed countries' agriculture continues to

be heavily subsidized. The liberalization of trade, forced on Africa through "structural adjustment" programs, has had equally negative effects on the continent's attempts to industrialize. And despite the pressure to liberalize, this had not stopped the "tariff bias" against countries such as those of Africa which find still high barriers against exporting to developed countries compared with the tariffs between the countries.[182]

Finally, the measurements of "growth" are not straightforward. For one, when the incentives for stellar economic performance are high, the reliability of economic data is questionable. Ethiopia, for example—a close ally of the United States—reported growth rates of almost 11 percent over much of the 2000s, more than double the average for the rest of the continent. Obama once declared that "there is no better example of progress in Africa than what has been happening in Ethiopia—one of the fastest-growing economies in the world."[183] Yet even the IMF has questioned these numbers, reported by an agency with close ties to the authoritarian ruling party.[184] Reports of soaring growth are far too narrowly defined given that, according to Oxfam, "Ethiopia is one of Africa's poorest nations with half of its 77 million people currently living below the poverty line, and its level of child malnutrition is the highest in the world."[185]

In fact, growth rates are limited measures that chiefly quantify capital accumulation. Yet, as Bond has pointed out, booming rates of growth are partly a sleight of hand, and they fail to adjust for crucial "externalities" foisted on the continent by the corporate scramble. According to Bond, factoring in the depletion of natural resources actually means a *negative* rate of growth. He argues that calculations should "measure raw materials stripped from Africa's soil not just as once-off credits to GDP, but also as debits: the decline in 'natural capital' that occurs because the minerals and petroleum are non-renewable."[186] This natural depletion has a long history, but more recent forces, namely global warming, have also only accelerated this rate of decline. The Intergovernmental Panel on Climate Change, for example, estimates that Africa's crop revenue will fall by 90 percent by 2100.[187] These developments cannot be excluded from a true balance sheet of Africa's economies.

The African "Middle Class"

Given the economic weakness in the nature of African growth, the supposed explosion in the size and strength of the middle class is unsurprisingly more myth than reality. Numerically, it actually remains very small.[188] Because of the skewed nature of foreign investment toward extraction, African unemployment remains high, despite its record-breaking levels of FDI. In 2014, Africa received 17.1 percent of global FDI (but only 8.7 percent of jobs worldwide).[189] Crucially, because a large proportion of middle-class growth rests on economies based on primary commodity production, its fortunes are tied to the vicissitudes of the global market. Shockingly, as an African Development Bank report revealed, "when stripped of this 'floating class,' who are vulnerable to falling back into poverty, the proportion of middle-class Africans . . . was still only 13.4 per cent, below what it was in 1980. . . . In spite of Africa's recovery, growth remains low quality, is not accompanied by 'much needed structural transformation and diversification' and is therefore not providing the necessary jobs."[190]

The deindustrialization and weak labor protections produced by neoliberal dictates also give lie to the myth of a rising middle class. Since investment during the so-called "boom" has not been directed to labor-intensive sectors, jobs have been reduced to the more "flexible" model demanded by IFIs. As Olamosu and Wynne describe:

> It is estimated that only 16 percent of the labor force across sub-Saharan Africa works in the formal sector with 62 percent working on family farms and the remainder in the informal sector. Even in South Africa, where the informal sector is much smaller, outsourcing, labor brokers and contractors have reduced the number of permanent jobs. In mining, for example, it is estimated that one in three workers is employed by a contractor or subcontractor rather than directly by the mine owners.[191]

The benefits of a flood of imported cheap consumer goods is offset by the job-destroying impact of tariff liberalization. Undercutting local industries and job growth has been deepened by Western and Chinese capital alike. As the *Economist* reports, for example, "hundreds of textile factories across Nigeria collapsed in recent years because they could not compete with cheap Chinese garments. Many thousands of jobs were lost."[192] As a result, the number of Nigeria's textile and apparel jobs fell to just 20,000, from 600,000 in the 1990s.[193] Infrastructure weaknesses remain huge because the creation of new infrastructure requires a significant investment of technical knowledge, which has been *disinvested* historically from African nations. These structural weaknesses inevitably hold back further growth in the middle class. Thus, narrow characterizations of rising access to technology for ordinary Africans disguise deeper problems; for example, Facebook claims that the number of users increased in Africa by 20 percent between 2014 and 2015.[194] Yet such metrics cannot easily transcend the historic infrastructure gaps and the concomitant technical and political integration required to leverage such developments for stronger economies. As a South African investment manager pointed out, "Once you want to allocate capital to individual opportunities, it becomes quite tough navigating your way through the individual political regimes and political volatility. You can talk in high-level terms about 1bn consumers but you go and actually try to get exposure to that billion and it's not that straightforward."[195]

Equally problematic, in the more advanced economies on the continent, the apparent growth of the middle class is underpinned by a growth of household debt, not unlike the dynamic seen in Western industrialized nations. Bond has written:

> South African urban poverty actually increased from 1993–2008. . . . Hence economic growth during the period was illusory. If there was a factor most responsible for the 5 per cent annual GDP increases recorded during most of the 2000s, by all accounts, it was internal consumer finance, with the ratio of household debt to disposable income soaring from 50 per cent to 80 per cent from 2005–2008. But this overexposure soon became an albatross, with non-performing loans soaring.[196]

Bond has also shown how the "Africa rising" narrative plays fast and furious with the reality of what "middle class" actually represents. He recounts:

> Apparently, "one in three Africans is middle class" and as a result Africa is ready for "take off", according to African Development Bank chief economist Mthuli Ncube. . . . Ncube defines middle class as those who spend between US$2–$20 a day, a group that includes a vast number of people considered extremely poor by any reasonable definition, given the higher prices of most consumer durables in African cities.
>
> Those spending between just $2 and $4 a day constitute a fifth of all sub-Saharan Africans, even Ncube admits, while the range from $4 to $20 a day amounts to 13 percent, with 5 percent spending more than $20 a day. Below the $2 a day level, 61 percent of Africans are mired in deep poverty, a stunning reflection of ongoing underdevelopment due to imperialism, the "resource curse," and nefarious African elites.[197]

The End of Poverty?

Perhaps no other evidence summarizes the enormous gulf between the ostensible promise of a rising economic tide and the actual reality for millions of ordinary Africans than the enduring poverty in Africa. In fact, some reports have documented an *increase* in poverty in Africa over the past few decades:

a 2015 World Bank study found that an additional *100 million* Africans were living in poverty in 2012 as compared to two decades earlier.[198]

Much has been made of figures that cite a decline in poverty worldwide, as if a rising global tide has likewise lifted the African boat. But, as Bond has shown, income categories are highly suspect. Further, disaggregating the global numbers, as Marxist economist Michael Roberts has done, reveals a highly uneven picture:

> It's true that the number of people living in "extreme poverty" . . . has sharply declined over the past three decades. There are 721 million fewer people living in extreme poverty in 2010 compared to 1981 (assuming what $1.25 a day could buy in 1981 is the same as what it can buy now). That sounds better, but this reduction *is almost solely due* to a rise in living standards in the billion-plus populations of India and particularly China in the last 30 years. There has been very little reduction in extreme poverty levels (as defined) in other very poor emerging economies. While extreme poverty rates have declined in all regions, the world's 35 low-income countries . . . —26 of which are in Africa—registered 103 million more extremely poor people today than three decades ago.[199] [emphasis added]

Salaheddine Lemaizi of the Committee for the Abolition of Illegitimate Debt has also argued that superficial indices of a fall in poverty must be examined critically:

> Certainly, the percentage of Africans in poverty has dropped from 56% in 1990 to 43% in 2012. Adult literacy has gained 4% and gender differences are reduced. Life expectancy has risen by six years and the prevalence of chronic malnutrition of children under five years old has diminished by 6% to around 39%. Should these improvements in the living conditions in Africa be applauded?
>
> To think that the struggle against poverty in Africa is gaining ground is illusionary. The rate of poverty eradication on the African continent and in its three subregions remains very slow. The failure to achieve the Millennium Development Goals can be largely explained by the shortcomings in reaching the goals set for Sub-Saharan Africa. A joint report by the UN Development Programme, the African Development Bank, the Economic Commission for Africa, and the African Union confirms that "Africa's progress in reducing poverty has been slow compared to that of developing regions as a whole."[200]

The Millennium Development Goals initiative, launched in 2000, is an often-used yardstick to assess the results of poverty-reduction efforts as well as measure a host of other metrics on hunger, health, and the environment. However, only a few countries actually achieved the goals: citing *Foreign*

Policy in Focus numbers, one report describes how "out of 153 countries, only seven were able to accomplish the goal of eradicating extreme poverty. Only Botswana and Equatorial Guinea were able to achieve the goal in Africa. . . . Other African economies would have to grow at an astonishing rate of 7 percent between the years 2000 and 2015 in order to halve the number of people living in poverty."[201] Compared to the rest of the globe, other human development indicators in Africa continue to lag far behind. Significantly, because of structural adjustment programs that required African governments to slash social spending, the institutional resources and systems to mitigate these conditions remain sorely underfunded. A study on access to health care in Africa found, for example:

> Life expectancies have improved in sub-Saharan Africa, but without the same gains in personal income and health systems that accompanied longevity in wealthier countries. The median GDP per capita in OECD countries was $4,376 when they achieved a median life expectancy of 60 years in 1947. Sub-Saharan African nations just reached that life expectancy in 2011 and their median GDP per capita was $1,658. The health systems in most sub-Saharan African countries are still built for acute care, not chronic or preventative care. Health spending has increased in recent years, but remains low relative to high-income countries. All the governments in sub-Saharan Africa together spend roughly as much on health annually ($33 billion) as the government of Poland ($31 billion).[202]

The overall trends of persistent poverty and poor social conditions are replicated in country after country across the continent. For example, the percentage of Ethiopians in "severe poverty" (living on less than US $1 a day) is 72.3 percent.[203] The ONE Campaign reports that in Nigeria,

> the proportion of children enrolled in primary school has actually decreased since 2010. A quarter of all child deaths across the entire sub-Saharan region occur in Nigeria (the country accounts for 19% of the region's population). Tanzania's economic growth has averaged 7% over the past decade. Around 89% of Tanzanians collect water for their daily needs from public sources, taking an hour or more to do so.[204]

Finally, as Sungu Oyoo has concluded:

> The idea of Africa rising and its consequent economic growth has mainly been of benefit to multi-national corporations and local bourgeois classes. We must differentiate between economic growth and economic development. Economic development is wholesome, and its growth accompanied by advancements in healthcare, education, working conditions and living standards among other areas that directly impact and improve human

welfare across the board. Some practices across the continent continue to stifle wholesome growth that would result in social and economic transformation for the populace. These practices include, but are not limited to, gross human rights violations, exploitative deals surrounding oil and mineral extraction, land grabs, inhumane working conditions, insecurity, just to mention but a few.[205]

This narrow "boom" rests on a fragile base: a surge due to China's rapid growth that could evaporate if the Chinese economy takes a downturn. The *Financial Times* describes the dangers of an economic contraction threatening conditions for the majority of ordinary Africans:

> The more than halving of the number of people living in extreme poverty in recent decades has been fueled above all else by rapid growth in places like China and Brazil. And that growth is unlikely to be replicated over the next 15 years. . . . Even repeating the economic performance of the past 15 years between now and 2030 would still leave 6–7 per cent of the global population living in extreme poverty, admits Jim Yong Kim, the World Bank's president. . . . The reality is that many of the people who have risen out of poverty in recent years remain vulnerable to slipping back into it. But almost 90 per cent of people still survive on $5 a day or less. More daunting perhaps for those looking to eliminate poverty is the fact that 400m of the global poor now live in conflict-torn or fragile states like Somalia or the Democratic Republic of Congo, a number that has changed very little over the past 25 years.[206]

Poverty, cuts to social programs, and a large, "flexible" workforce in Africa, as elsewhere, are hallmarks of the neoliberal regime. The top 10 percent of the population now captures 30 to 40 percent of total income, with the bottom 20 percent earning a mere 5 to 10 percent of the total.[207] African millionaires and billionaires now find a comfortable home in the rosters of the world's wealthy. As Lemaizi aptly describes, "Only the share of added-value grabbed by Capital increased, while that distributed among labor has not changed."[208]

The African Boom

The brutal reality of the "booming" African economy is that Africa's poor have not seen a "rise" in their fortunes, as African elites and ruling classes have. Rather, the investment frenzy of "rising Africa" not only failed the mission of wider development, but rendered economies so fragile and lopsided that social conditions are all the more vulnerable to crisis. The much-touted rising "consumer class" is no match for the larger forces of falling commodity prices and a possible Chinese downturn, nor the shallowness of a commodity-based boom. As Marxist theory has outlined, capitalism is fundamentally an interconnected global system: when one section falls into crisis, the downturn threatens to drag other sections along with it. Under such conditions, as Lenin pointed out, the tendency for capital to increasingly consolidate exacerbates unevenness and instability across the system as a whole.

Levels of investment began to fall in 2015, with a looming crisis threatening yet more pain for African economies. According to UN figures, in 2015, global FDI increased by 36 percent, but African FDI *fell* by 38 percent. Nigeria and South Africa saw sharp declines in FDI of 27 percent and 74 percent, respectively.[209] A global collapse in commodity prices produced a crisis in African economies heavily geared toward exports. The *New York Times* reported on the African slowdown:

> As the slumping economies have underscored the continent's growing vulnerability to changes in China, they have quieted much of the heady talk of "Africa rising," a catchphrase that symbolized the continent's fortunes. Growing consumer demand and an emerging middle class, while real in many African nations, are insufficient to offset a fall in the continent's main driver of growth, which remains commodities. . . .
>
> Even Nigeria, which remains dependent on oil, has experienced growth in other sectors in the past decade. A rising middle class has led to the emergence of Western-style shopping malls. A booming entertainment industry helped Nigeria overtake South Africa as the continent's biggest economy in 2014. Still, experts say, most nations failed to take advantage of the boom years to carry out long-term changes to their economies. They failed to deal with some of the biggest obstacles to sustained growth—like the severe lack of electricity across the continent—and spur industries that would create jobs. In South Africa, where a chronic shortage of power has constrained the economy, the unemployment rate hovers around 25 percent.[210]

In early 2016, China announced that imports from Africa had fallen by a full 40 percent in the previous year, while currencies in the two largest economies—Nigeria and South Africa—plummeted to their lowest levels ever. These currency crashes will create a new round of crises for African nations needing to repay Chinese infrastructure loans.[211] A World Bank report cited a sharp contraction in sub-Saharan African GDP to 1.3 percent.[212] They project GDP to rise to 2.6 percent in 2017, to 3.2 percent in 2018, and 3.5 percent in 2019, but GDP on a per capita basis remains very bleak, with an expectation that it will *contract further by 0.1 percent in 2017*, and rise by less than 1.0 percent in both 2018 and 2019.[213] This picture is a shameful indictment of the so-called African "boom."

And, as we have seen, the highly globalized nature of the world's economies means that this crisis exists at the systemic level. Properly understood, as Abayomi Azikwe points out, today's "financial crisis emanates from Wall Street and other centers of borrowing throughout capitalist states."[214] A new African debt crisis looms, where "the availability of credit to African states will be far more limited during the second decade of the 21st century than what prevailed in the 1980s, 1990s and the 2000s."[215]

Without fundamental change in African economies and societies to expand employment, industrialization, and infrastructure, the ability of "the consumer" or "good governance" to overcome larger forces tending toward crisis must always be severely curtailed, both in their current iteration and in a more general sense. While a number of commentators in the business press are inclined to attribute vulnerabilities to policy failures, African nations are hardpressed to reverse policies rooted in the forces and the legacies inherited from prior eras of "underdevelopment," as Walter Rodney called it. In this context, the African left faces monumental challenges: the Third World Network Africa and the International Trade Union Confederation (Africa) gathered in July 2015 in Accra, Ghana, to grapple with these "inter-related challenges of creating jobs, transforming [the continent's] . . . primary commodity export-dependent political economy and generating social and economic development which fulfilled the needs and aspirations of Africa's working peoples."[216] The urgency of such a project remains vital. Today's collapse has been brought on by the most recent round of overproduction and commodity-based crisis. As Marxists argue, at a systemic level, the tendencies of global capitalism toward cycles of boom, overproduction, and slump cannot be resolved within the contradictory framework of the logic of capitalism itself.

PART TWO

Chapter Five

The New Scramble for Africa

Interest in African oil is nothing new. From the colonial period to the present, extraction of Africa's natural resources has dominated its economies. As Exxon boasts proudly, the company has been in Africa for over a century, since the inauguration of its first kerosene site on the continent. As far back as 1889—as part of the original "scramble for Africa"—Britain established the first concession rights to Nigerian oil. By the second decade of the twentieth century, oil exploration had begun in Algeria, Egypt, and Nigeria.[1] Developments in Africa fit a global trend: by the early twentieth century, more than 50 percent of Western foreign direct investment (FDI) was invested in extractive industries in developing countries.[2] The colonial "scramble for Africa"—the fiercely competitive drive for Africa's natural resources—and the partition of the continent between the "great" powers were essentially complete by the start of World War I. But that colonial history has decisively shaped the Western plunder in Africa up to the present day.

Following World War II, oil production centered on northern Africa, primarily in Algeria and Libya. But the discovery of oil in Nigeria in 1956 expanded the horizons for oil multinationals. A wave of nationalizations swept the continent in the post-independence period: according to the World Bank, this transition brought 41.5 percent of mineral production under state control and established another 40.5 percent as state-sector partnerships with multinational corporations. New contracts provided opportunities for imposing regulation of operations on the part of the new states, part of a broader nation-building project of the postcolonial era. Yet the new independence period was also marked by the continued influence of former colonial powers, who "held sway" over concessions in "their" former colonies. The United States, for its part, entered the post-independence era having been, as Cyril Obi describes, "disadvantaged in the first oil rush of the early to mid-twentieth century, recognizing the need to compete against European counterparts such as Shell, Total, BP, Statoil, and ENI-Agip."[3] In the scramble to secure access to resources and outbid their competitors, Africa became a Cold War battleground over key commodities. In critical areas such as Angola, such tensions spilled over into hot wars.

Nonetheless, the nationalization current continued. Roger Southall and Alex Comninos write, "expropriation of the subsidiaries of foreign companies increased from the 1960s through to the mid-1970s, and indigenization programs became popular. Whilst politically wary of African capitalist classes, states commonly attempted to create more favorable conditions for local capital by, for instance, barring foreign capital from various . . . sectors, maintaining or strengthening certain trade barriers or demanding sale of equity to local investors."[4] Yet efforts in this period ran aground in the face of broader shifts: mineral production decreased markedly in this period due to an overall drop in investment in global exploration and operations, and the sub-Saharan African share of developing-country mineral production fell disproportionately, from 31.5 percent in 1970 to 10 percent in 1987.[5]

The global recession of the 1970s and its accompanying political crisis posed new challenges to US strategic interests, in particular with regard to control over a key resource: Middle Eastern oil. These developments marked a critical shift, as Nigerian environmentalist Nnimmo Bassey describes:

> For some time, the North could be said to have everything under its control. That happened with regard to crude oil as a major energy source and driver of economic development. The United States, for instance, was self-sufficient in oil. The stuff was cheap, and there was little thought given to the possibility of change in the equation. In fact, in the early 1960s crude oil cost less than $2 per barrel and the United States was able to meet up to 70 percent of its needs from domestic production. However, things began to change from 1970 when US oil production began to dip. The Organization of Petroleum Exporting Countries . . . had come into existence and in 1973 deliberately began engineering oil supplies and pricing, driving up oil prices by about 70 per cent, hitting the unprecedented level of more than $5 per barrel. By 1981 oil prices were close to $40 per barrel, setting off alarm bells to the North. This upsurge in oil prices pushed the North to embark on serious investment in alternative energy sources."[6]

In sum, the politics of oil of the period introduced new aspects of vulnerability and instability into global imperial relations. Liberalization and privatization in Africa in the 1980s and 1990s coincided with a recovery in commodity prices, particularly in the last decade of the twentieth century. By the beginning of the new millennium, a new boom had reached Africa, and its share of global mining spending began to rise dramatically.[7] In the 1980s, oil production in Africa averaged 5.5 million barrels per day (bpd). But by the following decade, production had increased to 7.3 million bpd, with another jump to 9.4 million bpd in the 2000s. The first half of the 2010s showed another increase in the average production totals at 9.6 million bpd; 2010 marked the high point for the entire period, with 10.7 million barrels produced on average that year. All told, the decade-on-decade increase in African oil from the 1980s to the 2010s stands at 74 percent, a huge jump in a relatively short period. Comparatively, world oil production increased by only 47 percent over the same time period.[8]

Today it is estimated that Africa possesses about 10 percent of global oil reserves, a level of supply the International Energy Agency first anticipated as far back as 1973;[9] in comparison, the Middle East has approximately half of the world's supplies. The explosion in Western involvement in African oil got under way in the early 1990s, but really took off in the 2000s. Signaling the new excitement in the continent's potential, the World Petroleum Congress held its first global meeting in Africa in its seventy-two-year history, convening in Johannesburg, South Africa, in 2005.[10] Between 1999 and 2014, US direct investment in the extractive industries in Africa (including oil, mining, and other sectors) increased by close to 500 percent.[11]

The scramble for Africa's resources has, of course, always included much more than the hunt for oil. As Walter Rodney describes, the extraction of iron, uranium, diamonds, gold, and rubber, among other precious commodities, fueled the industrialization and expansion of capitalism in the West at the expense of African economic development. Mining in Africa also underwent major changes in the twentieth century. Bassey reports, "by 1931 minerals made up less than 5 percent of domestic exports. This rose dramatically to 43 percent in 1950 and 86.7 percent in 1961. At that time diamonds accounted for 60 percent of mineral exports and 43 percent of all exports."[12] Companies such as Ghana's Ashanti Goldfields Company—now AngloGold Ashanti—began gold mining in 1897, and by the mid-1990s, 45 percent of export revenue derived from that commodity alone. Privatization and deregulation led to a massive infusion of foreign direct investment in the closing years of the last millennium, with a fourfold increase in gold output by 2002.[13] Amazingly, as Yao Graham reports, "between 2002 and 2006 average net profits of the biggest mining firms increased by more than *1,400 percent.*"[14]

Alongside the parallels with the past, important divergences mark the new era. As Tom Burgis rightly points out, the historical dynamics of exploitation on the continent do not merely duplicate those of the colonial period: the "looting machine has been modernized. Where once treaties signed at gunpoint dispossessed Africa's inhabitants of their land, gold, and diamonds, today phalanxes of lawyers representing oil and mineral companies with annual revenues in the hundreds of billions of dollars impose miserly terms on African governments and employ tax dodges to bleed profit from destitute nations. In the place of old empires are hidden networks of multinationals, middlemen, and African potentates."[15] Whereas the original scramble for Africa was driven by the search for raw materials such as rubber, gold, ivory, and palm oil, today metals and minerals are major targets for Western investment. Africa arguably holds some of the greatest of the earth's wealth in terms of natural resources and leads global production in diamonds and gold, but it's also a key source of metals such as aluminum and platinum as well as coltan, a key ingredient for cell phones. South Africa's mineral wealth, for example, is estimated at $2.5 trillion.[16] In 2010, oil and mineral exports from Africa were worth $333 billion, dwarfing, by over seven times, the amount of aid that flowed *into* the country.[17] Thirty-nine out of 55 countries are considered "natural-resource rich" and are reliant on these resources for their income.[18] Unique features of today's extraction "boom" and its competitive dynamics are discussed in the following section.

Despite these new characteristics, however, a central element of continuity runs through the dynamics of capitalist competition for resources in Africa past and present. Today, as valuable commodities cover the continent, as in the "original" scramble for Africa, the pursuit of profit and hegemony continues to fuel a rush to mine and extract at whatever cost to livelihoods and the environment. Just as a century ago, the contrast between the wealth in African soil and water and the living conditions of ordinary people could not be sharper: from Guinea, ground zero for the Ebola outbreak of 2014, with the world's largest supply of bauxite (aluminum ore) to the massive copper reserves in Zambia alongside deep unemployment, to the Niger River Delta, home to immense oil wealth yet one of the most polluted spots on earth, and many other examples, the gap between the potential and reality to meet human and social needs could not be more stark.

Global Boom and Africa's Allure

The corporate "allure" of Africa has much to do with its natural resources and the opportunity to exploit some of the world's most valuable commodities. In 2013, for example, of the world's ten biggest oil discoveries, six were in Africa.[19] For the greater part of the 2000s, the new scramble for Africa centered chiefly on oil, the world's most important strategic resource. At the turn of the millennium, demand was rising while dependence on oil, particularly from developing nations, was sharpening, fueling competition between major powers. ExxonMobil, the world's biggest oil company, invested 22 percent of its capital expenditures in Africa and received 30 percent of its oil from Africa during this period.[20]

Oil imports from Africa surged: imports to the United States from its six top suppliers in sub-Saharan Africa (Angola, Cameroon, Chad, Gabon, Nigeria, and the Democratic Republic of the Congo) increased by 40 percent from 2001 to 2010; total US oil imports increased by only 16 percent at that time.[21] US oil imports from Africa *surpassed* those from the Middle East for the first time in 2009. Africa's established oil-producing states are now being joined, with the advent of deep-water drilling, by important new ones. The West African nations of Liberia, Sierra Leone, and Ivory Coast, for example, have made substantial discoveries. The capacity of Ghana's Jubilee Field find was expected, at the time of discovery, to rival that of Nigeria and Angola;[22] however, by 2017, Ghana's output still remained a fraction of Africa's leading producers, according to the US Energy Information Administration.[23] With a predicted capacity of several billion barrels, smaller oil companies like Ireland's Tullow and the American company Anadarko have secured drilling rights; Texas's Kosmos Energy Company took bids for shares from oil majors such as Chevron, ExxonMobil, Shell, and China National Offshore Oil.[24]

Nigeria has been a standout leader in oil production and a major exploration site for decades. Likewise, one could argue that nowhere on the continent has seen the most heightened expression of the contradictions of oil extraction and exploitation: billions have been invested in the extraction of resources at massive social and environmental cost, especially in the Niger Delta region, where the Niger River pours into the Gulf of Guinea. The inequality and devastation produced by an almost unfathomable drive for investment and extraction has likewise fueled a deep social crisis and resistance; from the perspective of the US ruling class, instability has inextricably followed in the wake of the drive for oil profits. The Niger Delta case, these contradictions, and the accompanying crisis will be explored in detail near the end of this chapter.

Angola, dubbed an "oil industry darling" by the business press, received massive investment funds to secure the rights to drill offshore by Chinese and European oil exploration companies alike.[25] By the end of 2009, Angola had grown its production to 1.8 million barrels per day, even overtaking Nigeria for a time. By the mid-2000s, Angola was seen as having one of the world's fastest-growing economies, with rates of GDP growth surging to the double digits. Today, Angola is Africa's second-largest oil producer.[26] Its economy is extremely reliant on oil for its export earnings, consisting of a full *95 percent* of export-derived revenue[27] and three-quarters of government revenue.

East Africa is a major focus for new oil exploration and "has emerged as a 'new frontier' for oil and gas in the past half-decade . . . newly discovered oil reserves in Uganda and Kenya have the potential of coming on-stream by the end of the decade," noted the World Bank in 2015.[28] In 2013, the industry consultancy Deloitte described finds as a "bonanza," stating that more hydrocarbons had been discovered in East Africa in the previous two years than anywhere else in the world.[29] The Great Lakes region, especially the Lake Albert area in Uganda, is among the target areas. In 2014, Uganda signed a memorandum of understanding between the government and the China National Offshore Oil Corporation, Total, and Tullow, with estimates of $50 billion to be invested over twenty years, while Tullow is also drilling in the Lake Turkana region in neighboring Kenya.[30] Meanwhile, Tanzania has discovered trillions of cubic feet of natural gas reserves offshore and had surpassed 50 trillion cubic feet by 2017,[31] with ExxonMobil, BG Group, and Norway's Statoil contracting with the Tanzanian Petroleum Development Corp on exploration and production.[32] Mozambique likewise is anticipated to become a major liquid natural gas exporter as well as one of the world's top ten coal producers.[33] However, a host of challenges and competition face investment in exportation pipelines for both countries, such as the political and logistical challenges we saw in the discussion on the East African LAPSSET and related projects in the previous chapter. Beyond exploration and production, massive amounts of infrastructure—such as refineries and transportation—are required for multinationals and host countries to fully realize the oil potential, in Africa as a whole, but in the newer discovery regions of East Africa in particular.

To the north, crisis-wracked Somalia—the site of civil war for several decades—has also experienced new oil exploration in recent years.

Interest in Somali oil is not a new development; companies such as Conoco-Phillips, Chevron, and Total held concessions there before civil war broke out in 1991.[34] Somalia may seem an unlikely prospect for investors seeking untapped oil and gas fields, but new discoveries have claimed major finds, both onshore and off. According to the Mogadishu-based research organization Heritage Institute for Policy Studies: "While exploration in this latest and, in many respects, most extreme hydrocarbon frontier region remains in the fledging stages, estimates put the country's oil reserves as high as 110 billion barrels, placing it at eye-level with Kuwait. Moreover, it is expected that Somalia's offshore territory also contains vast natural gas fields."[35] Furthermore, Somalia's prime location on the Gulf of Aden—near the Suez Canal, Arabian Sea, and Indian Ocean—provide it with access to major shipping lanes. In this light, then Somali president Hassan Sheikh Mohamud has declared that Somalia is "open for business."[36]

Somalia faces the infrastructure challenges seen in oilfields further south, but on a different order of magnitude due to decades-long civil wars. As Mogadishu's Heritage Institute points out, for "security reasons," most of the exploration has taken place in the north, in the Republic of Somaliland (which declared independence in 1991 but has not yet been internationally recognized) and the semi-autonomous Puntland region. A range of companies from Australia, India, China, Norway, and the United Arab Emirates, among others, have signed exploration agreements with the Somaliland and Somali governments. Yet the process in Somalia is, unsurprisingly, very complex and unstable, with control over regions—some of which have signed agreements directly with oil companies—highly disputed and likely to intensify if exploration expands. Within this fractured situation, the al-Qaeda–linked al-Shabaab continues its fight against the Somali government, although significantly reduced from its height. Despite this high level of fragility and a weak state apparatus, major imperial powers continue to press their advantage in the region, with the United States in 2013, for example, tying its official recognition to the "Somali government recognizing the rights of US oil companies that had declared *force majeure* when the regime of Siyad Barre crumbled [in 1991]."[37]

While oil is undoubtedly the most critical natural resource, others play an important geopolitical role. Niger, the world's largest producer of uranium, is strategically vital for several major powers who rely heavily on uranium as a power source; France, for example, consumes the most uranium after the United States and relies on the mineral for a full three-quarters of its electrical production.[38] Under a shroud of "opaque deals," France began exploiting uranium in Niger in 1970s as a strategic response to the Organization of Petroleum Exporting Countries (OPEC) oil blockade of 1973.[39]

Rising Demand in an Unstable World

Africa has attracted huge investments in oil and other extractive resources for several reasons, chiefly rising global demand and concerns of political stability in oil-producing states, or what's sometimes described as "energy security." Rapidly expanding global energy needs, especially in the so-called "emerging economies" of Asia and Latin America, has been a major engine of growth for African commodities. Citing Brookings Institute research,[40] oil giant Exxon optimistically declared that growing economies meant a growing "middle class," and hence an explosion in energy demand:

> The global middle class is expected to climb from about 2 billion in 2010 to almost 5 billion people by 2030, representing more than half of the world's population. . . . As projected, that middle class expansion—largely in India and China—will be the largest in history and will have a profound impact on energy demand. Along with income gains, on-going societal changes such as expanded infrastructure, electrification and urbanization will contribute to greater energy use. . . . Non-OECD countries will represent 70 percent of global energy demand by 2040.[41]

Above all, China's industrial growth is heavily implicated in the new scramble for Africa as it seeks out reliable sources for oil for its own growing domestic needs. China has experienced average annual growth rates of 10.2 percent over the last two decades, and is responsible for 40 percent of the world's economic growth.[42] Burgis reports that "between the early 1990s and 2010, China's share of world consumption of refined metals went from 5 percent to 45 percent, and oil consumption increased fivefold over the same period to a level second only to the United States. China's economy was eight times bigger in 2012 than it was in 2000, and demand for commodities rapidly outstripped China's own resources."[43] China, for example, uses approximately one-third of the world's steel, 40 percent of its cement,[44] and 40 percent of the entire world supply of copper,[45] and is expected to be the world's largest oil importer by 2020.[46]

Part of China's strategic approach is to establish hegemony in African regions where Western companies have been unwilling to assume economic and political risk, or to get a foothold in exploration and outbid competitors. Obi writes, "[China's] multi-pronged strategy for winning oil in Africa includes investing in countries in which Western companies have lost ground or have been forced to withdraw as a result of domestic pressure and the policies of their home governments."[47] As an early example, Obi describes conditions in Sudan during the 1992 withdrawal of Chevron and other Western companies due to the civil war and pressure from human rights groups: these conditions opened the door for the Chinese National Petroleum Company to purchase a 40 percent share of the Greater Nile Petroleum Operating Company,[48] originally granted to Chevron as a concession in 1975. The move provided China with a strategic advantage that it still holds in the Horn.

Howard French, in *China's Second Continent: How a Million Migrants Are Building a New Empire in Africa*, makes a similar point:

> Africa, more than any other place, has been . . . the focus of extraordinary Chinese energy as a rising great power casts its gaze far and wide for opportunity, like never before in its history. Sensing that Africa has been cast aside by the West in the wake of the Cold War, Beijing saw the continent as a perfect proving ground for some Chinese companies to cut their teeth in international business. It certainly did not hurt that Africa was also the repository of an immense share of global resources—raw materials that were vital both for China's extraordinary ongoing industrial expansion and for its across-the-board push for national reconstruction.[49]

China's approach to "resource diplomacy" has a different character than relations with Western institutions and corporations, sometimes characterized as "flexigemony," where Chinese negotiations tend to navigate political and economic relations in a heterogeneous fashion.[50] As we have seen, China has been adept at offering an alternative path to the conditionality-laden terms of the Bretton Woods institutions, and also at negotiating highly favorable "oil-for-infrastructure" deals. And such exchanges are not restricted to oil alone: as Khadija Sharife has written,

> Ghanaian cocoa, Gabonese iron, and Congolese oil have been swapped for construction of dams (Bui, Poubara, and River Dam), allowing Chinese corporations such as Sinohydro to capture the bulk of Africa's hydropower market. The "barter system" thus enables China to export goods and labor, facilitating for China the opportunity to "import" their recycled project capital in addition to African resources.[51]

Markers of these developments are the presence of Chinese-built infrastructure and transportation, facilitating extraction across much of the continent. According to the African Development Bank, Africa's paved road network grew by 7,500 kilometers a year for the decade up to 2016.[52] Further, Sharife writes, most Chinese companies are state-owned and "most—if not all—Chinese equity is intertwined with [state] capital."[53] With this strategic focus, China has been able to secure a decisive edge in "exploration hotspots" such as South Sudan; China was also the first nation to obtain a license to produce Ugandan oil.[54] Carmody similarly attributes to China "first-mover advantages" in "frontier markets" such as Zambia, providing China critical access to resources in new areas.[55]

Other growing economies have been entering the African extraction arena for some years now. Brazil and Malaysia, for example, have oil exploration projects under way in West Africa and Sudan; India is also a contender on the continent. But it is Chinese demand that drives expansion on the continent, and despite strategic and tactical differences between "hegemonic" and "flexigemonic" postures, it is the US–China competitive drive that serves as the central axis of imperial conflict, both in Africa and globally. China's Export-Import Bank, for example, gave an astronomical $62.7 billion in loans to African nations in the first decade of the millennium, laying the foundation for the "investment opportunities" required to meet its soaring needs.[56]

Globally, rising demand has intensified competition for control of oil and gas production and supply. At the dawn of the African boom in the 2000s, along with soaring demand from Chinese industrial growth, the United States and Mexico had slowed their own oil production.[57] Meanwhile, worldwide, a new generation of mainly state-owned companies, such as China's National Petroleum Company, Saudi Arabia's Aramco, Russia's Gazprom, Venezuela's PDVSA, and Iran's NIOC controlled one-third of the world's oil and gas reserves and production, while the major Western companies—ExxonMobil, Chevron, BP, and Royal Dutch Shell—controlled just one-tenth of production and only 3 percent of reserves.[58] The United States alone consumed a quarter of the world's oil.[59] As the *Financial Times* noted at the time: "90 per cent of new supplies will come from developing countries in the next 40 years. That marks a big shift from the past 30 years, when 40 per cent of new production came from industrialized nations."[60] Thus the new scramble for Africa took shape as a struggle between competing powers for control of new energy sources and profits at a time when the West controlled fewer resources themselves.

The global competitive dynamic remains more important given that conflicts and tensions in other energy-rich areas—such as Iraq, Iran, and Venezuela—have loosened the West's grip: hence the impetus for new strategies, particularly on the part of the United States. The contradictions of the US imperial drive in the Middle East, in particular, have produced occupations and ongoing wars in Iraq and Afghanistan that have seriously compromised American geopolitical objectives—namely, ensuring regional stability in the Middle East, cementing compliant regimes, securing access to the region's oil, and dictating access to those resources by rivals and allies.[61] Meanwhile, at the turn of the millennium, Africa was viewed as more politically stable than the war-torn areas of Central Asia and the Arab world: as Nick Turse describes in *Tomorrow's Battlefield: US Proxy Wars and Secret Ops in Africa*, no African organizations had yet received the US designation of "terrorist."[62] Of course that was to change by the middle of the 2000s. But in the first years after 9/11, Africa seemed to offer a quieter, less risky environment for the oil industry, both for the oil "majors" with ready capital to invest in new exploration, as well as the wildcat operators willing to take a gamble on the "new scramble for Africa." As John Ghazvinian comments in *Untapped: The Scramble for Africa's Oil*, "Some of the more evangelical proponents of African oil have argued that here, at last, is the longed-for 'clean break'—the chance to detach the fortunes of America once and for all from Middle East crude."[63]

As we shall soon see, US interest in African oil has since made a strategic shift toward domestic supplies and the so-called "shale revolution." The Obama administration led a dramatic shift to domestic oil sources and the US fracking boom. We shall return to these newest developments. In the meantime, it is important to underscore that both the turn to African oil, and now to domestic supplies, are driven by shared underlying forces: strategic attempts on the part of US imperialism to minimize the risks and instability concomitant with access to foreign oil supplies. These developments, however, by no means erase the competitive dynamic between the United States and its imperial power rivals—especially China—for *control over* those critical supplies.

Features of Africa's "New Scramble"

Increased global demand for oil and raw materials pushed commodity prices skyward and foreign investment in extractive industries soared, especially from Western and Chinese capital, notably China's industrialization boom. One out of every seven barrels of oil imported by China comes from Angola alone.[64] The growth in China, as well as India and other emerging markets, returned the commodities boom to earlier peaks after the 2008 global recession. Over the previous quarter of a century, the price of oil quadrupled.[65] Brent crude prices rose at an average rate of 22 percent per year, then plunged in mid-2008 before recovering at the end of the decade. These factors and others contributed to rising demand and shrinking supply, and thus the boom in prices. Other commodities besides oil also saw a massive boom in recent years. The price of platinum tripled from the 1990s to 2008; copper's price increased by 2.5 times.[66] Not surprisingly, the boom in commodities prices led to an increase in African GDP. Through the 2000s—the lead-up to the global financial crisis of 2008 and in the aftermath—compared to other regions in the world, Africa demonstrated stronger-than-average growth rates: average rates of 5.7 percent for 2000–2010, and an average of close to 4.3 percent for 2011–2015.[67] By comparison, world GDP averaged 4 percent and 3.6 percent during those same periods, respectively.[68]

What are some of the unique characteristics of this new boom in Africa, and what has the explosion in extraction—and accompanying GDP growth—meant for African economies and societies? Several important aspects characterize the new boom such as deepening tensions between China and the West, but also sharpening unevenness with regard to development and intensified ecological destruction.

Capital-Intensive Extraction

Africa hardly makes anything. For too many countries, the economic model continues to be to dig stuff out of the ground and sell it to foreign companies.

—*Financial Times*[69]

Much as the colonial scramble for Africa fueled a boom in road building and railway construction to facilitate the extraction of the continent's resources, today's scramble for resources has likewise fueled an explosion in dams, roads, telecommunications, and power sources to further oil and mining investment opportunities. Yet, as we have seen, the investment boom in Africa has failed to translate into broader industrialization and diverse economies with a more stable economic base, including job creation, because of the terms and constraints under which that "development" has unfolded. Building on the narrow economic base of extractive industries ties economies to the highly volatile and cyclical nature of the oil and mining industries, where profits—and livelihoods—are especially vulnerable to the boom-and-bust nature of capitalism.

Often business presses have asserted conditions of uneven African development as a simple statement of fact, the "natural order" of the global economy within which African nations, inexplicably, fail to develop their industrial capacity. Poor decision making is the only explanation provided. As the *Financial Times* wrote, as oil prices were booming in 2008:

> The effect of increased corporate interest has not always translated to economic well-being for African countries. Soaring oil prices have threatened to wipe out recent economic gains on what is both the world's poorest continent and its fastest-growing oil and gas exploration zone of the past decade. According to the International Energy Agency, the increase in the cost of oil in 13 non-producing countries, including stable economies such as South Africa, Senegal and Ghana has since 2004 been equivalent to 3 per cent of their combined gross domestic product. This is more than the debt relief and foreign aid received during the same period. Even in some of Africa's biggest producers, where high oil prices have driven rapid economic growth, poor governance in the use of oil funds as well as high fuel prices brought about by a lack of refining capacity and heavy import bills have added to social woes.[70]

These explanations fail to describe the underlying conditions under which the extractive industries in Africa became extremely capital intensive, weak in labor force development, and unable to generate more diverse economies. Yet these historical and structural factors are highly significant in understanding the particular character of economic unevenness in the extractive industries today.

The extent to which African nations became dependent on resource extraction for revenue was a transition begun in the early post-independence period. The need to jump-start the economies of new nations compelled a disproportionate reliance on primary commodity exports, and between 1965 and 1975 alone, petroleum production went from making up 5 percent of government revenues to 80 percent.[71] Yao Graham has described, for example, a foreign direct investment–driven "mining revival strategy" as a global response and an attempt to restore profitability in the face of the economic crisis of the 1970s and 1980s and commodity price slump.[72] According to an IMF report—running contrary to its ideas of "sound macroeconomic policy"—at least twenty African nations, or more than one-third, rely on oil or mining for at least 25 percent of their revenue.[73] For some nations, the percentage is much higher. Guinea, for example, relies on mining for 85 percent of its export revenue.[74] Nigeria receives more than 80 percent of government revenues and 95 percent of foreign exchange income from oil.[75] Timber is also a substantial source of revenues for some countries, especially in Cameroon, Ghana, Ivory Coast, and both Congos.[76]

The current dynamics of the production process for African extractive industries intensifies this historic lopsidedness: oil and mining are highly capital intensive, meaning they rely on a large investment in capital and machinery, while using a comparatively low level of labor. The UN Economic Commission on Africa reports that manufacturing FDI is 17.5 times more labor-intensive than mining FDI, for example.[77] And because foreign multinationals tend to refuse or ignore substantial "local content" contract provisions, development of locally based related industries—and additional employment opportunities—is further thwarted. In fact, the extent to which these industries are *not* labor-intensive is striking; for example, in 2014 the Tullow Oil Company employed a grand total of only 281 people in Ghana, 86 percent of whom were Ghanaian.[78] Extraction in fact provides a relatively greater boost to *indirect* economic activities, but typically in less skilled and lower-paid support services and retail that might accompany oil exploration and production. Even very large projects have not typically translated into significant job growth. The immense Chad-Cameroon pipeline, for example, led to only a small amount of job creation, with other sectors left undeveloped and, as journalist Celeste Hicks notes, "very little knock-on benefit to the wider economy."[79]

As we have discussed, trade policy for Africa under structural adjustment auspices and neoliberalism disadvantaged and even undermined any base of nascent indigenous manufacturing and industrialization. The heavy focus on extraction reinforced tendencies toward one-sided economies overly geared toward export, while creating very few jobs. Privatization of extractive industries was a common feature of the neoliberal era, with a highly negative impact on African workforces. For example, when the Zambian Consolidated Copper Mines were broken up and privatized, employment dropped by over 65 percent.[80] Further, neoliberal policy has disinvested in African education and thus the potential to build skilled, local workforces. Where mining employment has increased, the tendency has been toward casual or contract-based (i.e., "flexible") African labor, or to pay skilled Westerners. Additionally, trade policy imposed in the neoliberal era created such unfavorable terms of trade for African economies that local capital production has been uncompetitive, to say the least, with highly detrimental results. In fact, Graham argues, "if non-oil exporters in Africa had not suffered from continued terms of trade losses the per capita income would have been 50% higher in 2000."[81] And as we have seen, where income did rise, because of neoliberal policy, the poor and working class did not benefit.

Globally, dramatic technological innovations have marked the current era of exploration and extraction, and Africa has been no exception. Such innovations may appear to hold out hope for producers that notions of "peak oil" are a concern of the past. For example, Exxon, in a 2014 statement, gleefully promised: "Technologies that unlock new unconventional oil and gas supplies will help enable oil and natural gas to meet about 65 percent of global energy demand growth."[82] Today, an explosion in technological developments has widened the horizons in Africa for possible new wealth to be found both onshore and off. Deepwater or "ultra-deep" exploration has opened up vast new frontiers for untapped sources; as Michael Watts has put it, "Deepwater exploration is the new mantra."[83] Major finds off the Gulf of Guinea in West Africa such as the Jubilee Field off Ghana highlight the new potential. In August 2015, the Italian firm Eni claimed a deep-water natural gas discovery equivalent to 5.5 billion barrels of oil off the coast of Egypt, cited as the largest find in the Mediterranean to date.[84]

Furthermore, the deepwater wells that have dominated some of the recent African oil finds have held out promises of easy money by sidestepping some "energy security" concerns. As Ghazvinian writes, "even if a civil war or violent insurrection breaks out onshore . . . , the oil companies can continue to pump out oil with little likelihood of sabotage, banditry, or nationalist fervor getting in the way. Given the hundreds of thousands of barrels of Nigerian crude that are lost every year as a result of fighting, community protests, and organized crime, this is something the industry gets rather excited about."[85] Hopes for newfound offshore wealth ran aground in the Gulf of Guinea, for one, where insurgents innovated new techniques of their own to breach deepwater platforms. Nonetheless, these technologies seemed to offer solutions for oil corporations to political challenges to extraction.

Yet the massive investment in these technologies, and the vast gap between the development of this highly advanced technology and broader economic development and social equality, highlights the problems with extraction-based industries in Africa. Despite the introduction of cutting-edge equipment, the "technology transfer" that would enable wider development has not taken place on either the "backward" or "forward" ends of the process—meaning the research and development and capital production that precede extraction, nor the refining processes that follow. African economies' involvement in the production process remains limited to the actual extraction itself, without the capacity- or expertise-building that would accompany developing the means of production in Africa itself. In fact, the bulk of the oil, gas, and other equipment required for extraction is imported, mainly from the United States. Padraig Carmody has described this relationship as the outcome of "distance" from markets in a social and historical sense, rather than one of physical geography, that has created "a severe problem of a lack of value addition in Africa."[86] This dynamic is a question not of "natural" geographic features—as Carmody points out, for example, Collier's notion of the "proximity trap"—but one of politics, economics, and inequality.[87]

On the "downstream" side, a significant feature of this dynamic is the minimal amount of the crucial secondary refining and "beneficiation" that takes place in Africa itself, meaning a dire shortage of the processing that provides the "value-add" for local economies.[88] East Africa, for example, has only one oil refinery, located in Kenya.[89] Oil refineries are primarily located outside of Africa, which explains why major oil-producing nations such as Nigeria are also oil *importers*: they lack the infrastructural development to support minimally required refining. Parallel examples exist in the mining industry: diamond cutting, for example, is a highly skilled practice that typically takes place elsewhere, such as in Europe or in Mumbai, India. Because developing local manufacturing has been consistently thwarted, building the "linkages" to a manufacturing base of finished products relying upon locally produced natural resources as inputs has been virtually nonexistent. All told, exports beyond natural resources remain very limited.

In addition to manufacturing, the distorting impact on the agricultural sector by the over-focus on extraction has been pronounced. As Nigeria's oil boom got underway in the late 1960s and early 1970s, for example, a marked decline in agricultural production set in, with a decrease in cultivated land by 60 percent from 1975 to 1978.[90] The much smaller oil-producing nation, Gabon, has experienced a similar devastation to its agricultural sector, and its manufacturing exports are very minimal.[91] Watts has been sharply critical of the failures to develop industry in Nigeria. Citing the rebellions in the main oil-producing region, the Niger Delta, he writes:

> Any long-term resolution of the problems driving these insurgencies and the politics of fuel prices can only be resolved if Nigeria drastically restructures economic and social policies. Boosted by oil and gas prices, the economy currently grows at about seven per cent per annum. But this figure masks deep stagnation within the agricultural, manufacturing, and small-scale industrial sectors. Industrial employment alone has shrunk by 90 per cent over the last decade. Despite the fact that just over 50 per cent of the population lives in rural areas, Nigeria can no longer feed itself. This means at least a billion dollars' worth of rice must be imported annually.[92]

As Grieve Chelwa argues, breaking the economic stranglehold of single-commodity exports is critical for sustainable growth: "Africa needs to industrialize if it's going to meaningfully rise. That's the lesson from history.

Countries on the continent need to move away from the colonial legacy of depending on primary commodities (cocoa, copper, oil, et cetera)."[93] The recognition of the need for broader industrialization has been given lip service by institutions representing capital interests in both Africa and the West: the African Union, for example, launched Agenda 2063 as a fifty-year development plan to widen Africa's economic base and promote regional integration.[94] Thus the question of how extractive industries might be used for broader economic development, and who dictates this process, is fundamentally a political question. Graham describes this dynamic within the context of the decolonization struggle, where mining, transportation, and infrastructure projects were "pioneer sites" in the creation of an industrial working class and trade unions, "which became important in anti-colonial struggles and post-colonial politics (e.g., Ghana, Zambia, DR Congo, Guinea, South Africa, Mauritania)," along with the "global assertiveness of ex-colonies" and the centrality of nationalization of resources as a "key feature of post colonial policies."[95] Surmounting the structural constraints of neoliberalized economies is also a critical question. In this context, the extent to which development goals are pursued in the interest of labor, the broader working classes, and the poor in Africa is by no means assured: pursuing a bottom-up strategy for industrial growth and wider employment, where the terms are framed around a democratic and redistributive agenda aiming to reverse inequality, is a key political question facing unions and the left in Africa today. These prospects and challenges will be returned to in the final chapter.

A Weak Regulatory Environment

Historically, weak state structures and administrative capacity in African nations have tended to produce similarly weak governance and regulatory structures that result in highly favorable deal making and investment terms for international oil companies with, unsurprisingly, less competition from national oil companies.[96] In fact, securing favorable investment environments for extractive industries has historically been a common fixture of structural adjustment programs.[97]

Weaker regulation translates into weaker contract terms that can have a highly negative impact on revenue collection for the state. As Graham points out, the procurement and contracting process in Africa tends to be characterized by "weak negotiating capacity to stipulate linkage, capacity, . . . [and a w]eak capacity to audit."[98] Typically, production-sharing agreements with African governments enable foreign oil companies to secure an exploration license up front, with no revenue obligations until their initial investment has been covered.[99] Yet because of weak enforcement capabilities and a relative lack of legal resources, African nations can often come up short when multinationals flout deadlines and other agreements. Burgis recounts the protracted legal battles waged by mining giants Rio Tinto and Vale over Guinea's Simandou iron ore mines. While negotiations were in flux, "all the while Guinea's most valuable national asset remained stuck under a mountain, with the railway to carry the ore across the country unlaid and the port to ship it off to the steel mills of the world unbuilt. As billions of dollars changed hands among the titans of the mining industry, Guinea (annual budget: $1.5 billion) had nothing to show for being the place where the ore actually lay."[100]

That is not to say that African states are simply powerless in the face of contract negotiations with foreign multinationals. Resource nationalism has certainly shaped negotiations between the various parties. A country such as Niger—whose uranium production is unmatched virtually anywhere on the globe—can exert some degree of leverage, such as the resistance by President Mahamadou Issoufou in the face of the French company Areva's withholding of royalty payments.[101] Nicholas Shaxson's *Poisoned Wells* argues that access to oil supplies have given African producers crucial advantages.[102] And Hicks, for one, cites examples of resource nationalism as a way of explaining the supposed "failure" of African states to deliver on "good governance" promises, rejecting as simplistic the idea that poor countries like Chad and Niger have little ability to stand up to major powers such as China.[103]

Certainly a number of contract negotiation examples would seem to reinforce the potential advantages. For instance, the newer areas of offshore exploration and production have seemingly opened up some procurement opportunities. *Bloomberg* reported that "African governments' profit share from deepwater oil projects off the continent ranges from 91.1 percent in Libya to about 60.7 percent in Gambia, according to data from Wood Mackenzie. That's higher than elsewhere in the world, with the continent's average onshore take of 66.1 percent being 8.5 percentage points above the global one."[104] Other examples include moves by the major oil-producing nations to renegotiate terms, such as attempts to increase the Nigerian share of ownership of and participation in oil companies' operations, to "increase local content in the industry"—a strategy intended to benefit local elites—and collect on contractually owed payments by corporations.[105] At the same time, the price boom provided greater leverage for national governments to demand higher royalties and other contract requirements, such as increased value-added processing or refining, and some countries have taken steps to revise legislation or renegotiate contracts. Tanzania, for example, passed a bill in 2013 requiring the top mining companies to procure at least 80 percent of their goods and services locally by 2015, a change that will impact major firms such as AngloGold Ashanti, Barrick Gold, and China National Gold. Gabon and Kenya made similar moves in a "resource nationalist" direction.[106] The *Economist* reported on the trend in 2012: "Zambia, which is Africa's biggest copper producer, recently doubled its royalties on the metal, to 6 percent. Guinea, home to the world's largest bauxite reserves as well as one of the world's biggest iron-ore deposits, is helping itself to a 15 percent stake in all mining projects and an option to buy a further 20 percent. Namibia has decided to transfer all new mining and exploration to a state-owned company."[107]

Unsurprisingly, some firms reacted with horror to such moves. The *Economist* continues:

> In the past year resource nationalism has jumped to the top of the list of things that worry the 30 biggest global miners. . . . A rapid rebound after commodity prices collapsed in the aftermath of the financial crisis in 2009 convinced cash-strapped governments that large multinationals were easy targets. In Africa mining companies are often especially vulnerable—they are usually the biggest corporate beasts around.[108]

The tensions inherent in resource control are rooted in historical factors of the dynamics of capitalist development and the state in modern Africa. As Obi notes:

> Ownership of oil reserves and their control by African states are not altogether synonymous. In spite of ownership by African national oil companies, lack of sophisticated technology, limited knowledge about global oil markets and the secrets of oil technology and contracting, coupled with support from the governments of [multinational corporations] . . . all combine to ensure that they control oil production without owning the reserves. What has changed is the increased bargaining power of petro-states to demand more in exchange for access to their oil reserves.[109]

Yet neoliberal disciplining has placed severe limits on resource nationalism, and generalization from individual examples lends itself to a too-narrow reading of history, namely the context in which highly uneven procurement terms were secured in the first place: amidst the devastation of deregulation and liberalization wrought by the neoliberal era. Sharife has provided a fuller account of these dynamics and the broader context that accrues benefits to Western and Chinese multinationals alike. She notes, for example, the China Export-Import Bank's "mining-specific development" contracts, which require a *minimum* of 50 percent of the total value to be allocated to Chinese inputs, both labor and materials, an extraordinarily high figure.[110] And the recent boom in prices has fueled more aggressive and riskier corporate investment practices, which include taking even greater advantage of weak regulatory environments.[111] Relatedly, as Henning Melber has noted, the drive for resource control also has the potential to strengthen the position of African elites and class divisions, including shoring up repression and authoritarianism.[112]

The most extreme example of the gap between resource potential and state capacity can be seen in weak states such as Somalia. There, the extremely fragile central administration and contestations for power between federal and regional authorities mean that the regulatory environment is unclear, to say the least.[113] Western oil companies, while striving to balance concerns about "risk," seek to take advantage of lucrative opportunities, and, as we have seen, a plethora of multinational corporations are positioning themselves for investment on the continent.

NGO-advocated "best practices" attempt to balance this weak regulatory environment with approaches such as "free, prior, and informed consent," known as FPIC. According to Oxfam, civil society organizations and regional institutions alike have advocated for such demands; however, they state, African nations have not necessarily legislated such approaches, providing instead for "less robust" mechanisms such as "public participation" and environmental impact assessments for extraction processes.[114] Widespread support for FPIC provisions has emerged among organizations from the World Bank to oil and mining multinationals, as well as the African Union, which adopted the Africa Mining Vision framework that included FPIC goals. Major companies operating in Africa, such as Newmont Mining, DeBeers, and Rio Tinto, among others, have all adopted such provisions.[115] Yet despite the growing popularity of "corporate social responsibility" measures such as FPIC, they cannot substitute for or overcome the historic weaknesses of an underresourced African state with comparatively fewer procurement and enforcement capabilities. The proliferation of corporate social responsibility measures notwithstanding, such tools signal a neoliberal preference for multinationals to regulate their own practices—in other words, another avenue of the privatization of state services. The widespread embrace of these corporate social responsibility measures is related to a "transparency" approach, rooted in assumptions about African corruption and "rent-seeking behavior." These debates will be returned to below.

Environmental Hazards

African ecosystems are already being affected by climate change, and future impacts are expected to be substantial. . . . Africa as a whole is one of the most vulnerable continents due to its high exposure and low adaptive capacity.

—Intergovernmental Panel on Climate Change[116]

As we have seen, highly advanced technologies and sophisticated extraction expertise characterize industries in Africa as well as worldwide. Yet despite this level of technology, oil and mining in Africa have been marked by low wages, deplorable working and living conditions, and environmental devastation from one country to the next. Adam Hochschild's *King Leopold's Ghost* paints the picture of the horrific conditions of forced labor on rubber plantations in colonial Belgian Congo. Echoing the vile practices of the prior era, corporations today—in conjunction with armed force from the state—have actively participated in the destruction of communities and the outright murder of workers. As Bassey describes in *To Cook a Continent: Destructive Extraction and Climate Crisis in Africa* (2012), drilling and mining have created not only unspeakable pollution but barbaric conditions in some of the most dangerous industries on the planet, from Sutton Resources of Canada's burial of fifty-two Tanzanian miners alive to the 2012 massacre of thirty-four striking workers at Lonmin's platinum mines at Marikana in South Africa.[117]

The scramble of new exploration in East Africa and the Great Lakes region, for example, promises widespread displacement and environmental degradation. Land expropriation in the Hoima district of the Albertine Basin will negatively impact 7,000 people, who were given the "choice" of either cash or resettlement from an expected $2.5 billion refinery construction. Because the region is customary land, a host of problems face the residents seeking to claim legal ownership to these resource-rich lands; one man was offered a mere $350 for his home.[118] On the lake's shores, Murchison Falls National Park sits on top of an oil exploration block co-owned by Total and Tullow, introducing serious concerns about the contamination of Lake Albert and other possible ecological damage from gas flaring—the burning off of natural gas in the course of oil production—and other pollutants.[119] When Tullow began exploration in the lake itself, residents were prevented from fishing, essentially undermining their ability to feed their communities.[120] Similarly, the Lake Turkana region in Kenya, near the Ethiopian border, has more than 500,000 inhabitants of the Lower Omo and Lake Turkana Basins who are at risk from the exploration.[121] Activists from the environmental justice organization Friends of Lake Turkana are mobilizing to counter the threats to their livelihoods and the ecology, rejecting the notion that the small number of jobs created will compensate in the medium and long term for the dangers facing ordinary people in the area.[122] Chinese firms have also been cited for atrocious environmental and safety conditions. As the *Economist* has described, "Sinopec, an oil firm, has explored in a Gabonese national park. Another state oil company has created lakes of spilled crude in Sudan. At Chinese-run mines in Zambia's copper belt they must work for two years before they get safety helmets. . . . Miners in Sinazongwe, a town in southern Zambia, protested against poor conditions. Two Chinese managers fired shotguns at a crowd, injuring at least a dozen."[123] Workers at a mine in Collum were working for $4 a day with no time off. "We do not have support timbers everywhere they need to be, and we have no masks to protect us from the coal dust," said mining employee Boston Sikalamba.[124] Trade union agreements are frequently disregarded by the company.[125]

One region in particular stands out as an extreme expression of the contradictions of abundant natural wealth and a bloody war for resources that has left a wake of millions dead and displaced in an ongoing conflict down to the present day. As we have seen, the Democratic Republic of Congo, or DRC (formerly Zaire) is arguably the most brutal example of the violence and devastation produced by wars for natural resources. And perhaps nowhere else on earth is the gap between the value of its natural resources and the poverty of ordinary people so huge. The DRC is known famously for its mining wealth, from tin, copper, and gold to columbite-tantalite, also known as coltan, a key component for microelectronics. In the first decade of the twenty-first century, coltan prices skyrocketed. Yet during the same period, the Congolese were ranked the poorest people in the world: from 2000 to 2010, GDP per capita was less than a dollar a day.[126] In a bitterly ironic example cited by Burgis, a hospital serving 160,000 in the war-torn South Kivu province—a region rich in tantalum—had no cell phone reception.[127] Of the $41 billion in mining revenue produced from just 2007 to 2012, only 2.5 percent went into the national budget.[128] Competing local groups and guerrilla armies have laid claim to the mines of the resource-rich regions of the DRC's east and south, extracting vast sums via both "legal" and "illegal" trade circuits, as Bassey describes:

> At the height of the conflicts in the Congo axis there were up to nine armies in the fray. The diamond market that thrived in Kigali, even though Rwanda does not have any diamonds, highlighted the plunder of the DRC's resources. A United Nations report issued in 2001 accused Uganda and Rwanda of plundering diamonds, copper, cobalt, gold and coltan from DRC.[129]

Since the war began, the number of refugees (the "internally displaced") in the DRC have fluctuated between one million and 3.5 million at any given time.[130] The drive for resources—with the active support of the local African states in providing armed support as necessary—has subjected ordinary people and communities to extremely hazardous conditions, with the pursuit of profit subjugating livelihoods and environments to some of the most brutal terms of exploitation.

Some economists have attempted to take stock of the impact of this devastation on growth and development. Patrick Bond argues that despite the insistence of boosters of the "African rising" narrative, understanding actual social and economic development requires a broader understanding of the "externalities" of extraction—that is, factors not typically accounted for when measuring economic well-being, such as permanent losses to society and the environment. He writes:

> African economies suffer extreme distortions caused by the export of irreplaceable minerals, petroleum and hard-wood timber. . . . GDP calculates such exports as a solely positive process (a credit), without a corresponding debit on the books of a country's natural capital. Seeking a less-biased wealth accounting—i.e., by factoring in society and the environment so as to calculate a country's "genuine savings" from year to year—we find that Africa gets progressively poorer.[131]

The Tax Justice Network Africa has made a similar point about the costs to African people and societies for this ecological devastation:

> In Africa the ecosystem also directly bears the burden of taxation in the form of natural resource depletion, and ecosystem services are diminished as a result of reduced forest coverage, while cyanide residues pollute agricultural areas close to gold mining areas. Oil and gas exploitation causes tremendous ecological harm in terms of destruction of mangrove fisheries and associated gas flaring. People dependent on the environment therefore also bear the indirect effects.[132]

The critical importance of weighing ecological and economic impact together is highlighted in the contradictory experiences of those living and working under these conditions. For example, Areva, the French uranium producer, is Niger's largest private-sector employer, with 2,000 mine workers whose incomes support approximately 200,000 people. Yet, according to a Reuters report, "Areva's mines pay no export duties on uranium, no taxes on materials and equipment used in mining operations, and a royalty of just 5.5 percent on the uranium they produce."[133] And as Carmody describes, extractive development in Niger is unfolding in a context of ecological destruction. Boutali Tchiwerin, a Tuareg spokesperson, declared:

> The exploitation of uranium by Areva and its subsidiaries has contributed to the impoverishment of the area by accelerating the phenomenon of turning the area into more of a desert by plundering of the natural resources and the draining of the fossil deposits. It is undoubtedly an ecological catastrophe and a continuing human rights tragedy which threatens the existence of one of the oldest civilizations of the Sahara.[134]

The challenges posed to African economies due to extraction are only accelerating in the context of climate change. Coping with such changes puts a disproportionately severe burden on nations least able to manage them. Intergovernmental Panel on Climate Change data estimates that adaptation could cost approximately 5 to 10 percent of gross domestic product.[135] With temperatures rising and the amount of arable land and agricultural production shrinking, Africa's share of arid and semi-arid lands is expected to rise by 5 to 8 percent. By 2020, between 75 and 250 million people could face climate-change–induced water shortages.[136]

The Niger Delta: "Their Oil and Ours"

Home to the most extensive oil exploration on the continent, Nigeria shows most starkly how the drive for extraction has destroyed the lives of ordinary people in Africa. The eleventh-largest producer and the eighth-largest exporter of crude oil in the world, Nigeria typically produces over 2.4 million bpd of oil and natural gas. Yet Nigeria's immense resources exist alongside extreme inequality and corruption. Approximately two-thirds of the population lives on less than $1.25 per day. The electrical grid operates far below the needs for a nation of its size, producing about half the power of North Korea.[137]

The Niger River Delta is the base of Nigerian oil production and has an international commercial history that extends back in time for six centuries—including the slave trade on the Delta's Bonny Island, where approximately 2.5 million slaves passed through the Bights of Benin and Biafra.[138] Now the site of highly valued sweet crude, palm oil extraction in the Niger Delta began in the 1830s, thereby launching what G. Ugo Nwokeji has described as "the long march to petro-development."[139] Oloibiri is the site of the first oil well in Nigeria, tapped in 1956; today in Oloibiri, like many other sites in the Niger Delta, deep poverty prevails, with no running water at the very location where the world's most precious resource was originally tapped. Yet with the Oloibiri tapping was born, as Ogoni activist Ken Saro-Wiwa—executed along with eight other activists by the Nigerian government in 1995—put it, the "slick alliance" of the oil industry and African elites, a collaboration that has created and sustained the widespread immiseration of the majority in the Niger Delta.

The first oil exports left Port Harcourt in 1958, shortly before independence in 1960. At that time, Nigeria was largely indepen-dent with regard to food, and agriculture represented nearly 100 percent of exports. Yet a decade later, the picture was dramatically transformed, and oil had become responsible for the vast bulk of the nation's wealth. What can be viewed as Nigeria's first oil boom took place between 1964 and 1965, and by mid-1965, Nigeria was the thirteenth-largest oil producer in the world. In 1969, Nigeria's Petroleum Act put control of all foreign oil revenues into the hands of the federal government, as well as control over the oil-rich Niger Delta region, which established the structure governing how oil was transferred into the national coffers and distributed throughout the federal system. At a time of soaring oil prices—due to the OPEC oil embargo and Israel's Yom Kippur War of 1973—Nigeria's oil pro-duction also increased dramatically, from 150,000 barrels per day in 1968 to 2 million in 1973. Biafra's ultimately failed secession efforts and the three-year civil war of 1967–1970 accelerated the exploita-tion of the Delta. Consequently, as environmentalists Ike Okonta and Oronto Douglas have put it, the "Niger Delta has been treated as conquered territory ever since."[140] Or as *Black Agenda Report* de-scribed a decade ago:

> Where once there were poor but self-sufficient people with rich farmland and fisheries, there is now an unfolding ecological col-lapse of horrifying dimensions in which the land, air and water are increasingly unable to sustain human life, but the region's people have no place else to go. . . . Twenty percent of Nigerian children die before the age of 5, according to the World Bank. Hundreds of billions of dollars' worth of oil have been extracted

from the Niger Delta, according to Amnesty International. . . . [who describe its inhabitants as] "among the most deprived oil communities in the world."[141]

Home to some of the largest oil producers on the globe—from ExxonMobil and Chevron to Shell and Eni—the Niger Delta today is a horrific example of the societal and environmental devastation inflicted by the oil industry. It is the site of some of the worst pollution on the globe, from oil spills to gas flares. Notwithstanding the government's ban on flaring, at over 200 flow stations across the region, continuous gas flares poison the environment with approximately 400 million tons of carbon dioxide per year, along with methane and other greenhouse gasses, second only to the gas flaring records set by Russia, and the greatest cause of global warming in Africa.[142] The region has also been devastated by over 1.5 million tons of spilled oil, according to Amnesty International. Only 50 percent of the population has potable water or access to the electrical grid, and only 20 percent of housing is habitable. The United Nations Environment Programme concluded in a 2011 study of the Ongoniland region of the Delta, home to Saro-Wiwa, that drinking water contained levels of carcinogens that seriously threatened public safety, with required clean up taking a minimum of 25 years.[143]

As local activists have long pointed out, corporate complicity in this devastation is undeniable. In 2008–2009, two major oil spills by Shell contaminated the Goi fishing community in the Bodo Creek area in Rivers State. Shell claimed that only 4,144 barrels were spilled; however, over 600,000 were actually documented. Through the pressure of an international campaign, Shell was compelled to pay £55 million (N15.7 billion) to 15,600 fishermen, which at £3,500 each reflects a paltry amount relative to both the size of the corporation and the scale of the devastation; as Bassey noted, this sum "can hardly purchase a good fishing boat and equipment necessary to return to the fishing business that the people know best."[144] The ecosystem is also threatened by disruption due to the production process. For example, "the water in these riverain communities is too polluted to drink, as canals dug by Chevron have caused the salt water of the Atlantic Ocean to invade the freshwater of Ilajeland. Villagers also complain that the canals which the oil company contends facilitate local commerce have led to severe erosion causing whole communities to up and move."[145]

In the face of opposition and protest, oil corporations have invoked pledges to "corporate social responsibility" and offered up thin promises for community development and environmental remediation. Yet failing to address the underlying causes of the destruction, these promises have fallen far short, leaving communities to shoulder these burdens themselves. Bassey's essay "Oil Fever" describes how "one consequence of the unfettered and reckless exploration and exploitation of oil in the Delta is that the poor people continue to subsidize the costs of crude oil through the losses they suffer in environmental services, quality of life, and extreme environmental degradation. . . . Meetings, programs, projects, and commissions, multiply—yet the many-headed hydra that is mass poverty in the Delta simply grows more appendages."[146] The price for these broken promises has been high. As Sabella Ogbobode Abidde has described,

> there is nothing to show for the billions of dollars the region has given to Nigeria. In effect, there is no social, political or economic development. Nothing good is being done for the Ijaw. Whatever was done has been ornamental, provisional and superficial. Instead of development, we have air and waterborne diseases, social tension, social dislocation and high unemployment.[147]

Yet Saro-Wiwa's "slick alliance"—the coalition of global oil corporations and local elites—has undoubtedly reaped the benefits of extraction costs borne by the people of the Niger Delta. The Nigerian ruling class, in fact, does very well. As Watts has written, 85 percent "of oil revenues accrue to one percent of the population and a huge proportion of the country's wealth—perhaps 40 percent or more—has been stolen" through capital flight or corruption.[148] The Nigerian ruling class has long enjoyed a close relationship with US administrators, records of authoritarianism and military rule notwithstanding. As Ike Okonta, author of *When Citizens Revolt: Nigerian Elites, Big Oil, and the Ogoni Struggle for Self-Determination*, describes:

> The United States and the European Union backed the Obasanjo government in 1999 and again in 2003 even though there was abundant evidence that those elections had been marked by rigging and violence. . . . He was seen as a competent general who

could be counted on to rein in the youth activists in the Delta region and ensure that Western oil companies continue to extract oil undisturbed. Local democracy and corporate social responsibility were thus sacrificed for cheap oil.[149]

Despite these horrific records of human rights abuses, oil companies have happily collaborated with Nigerian regimes and militaries to facilitate extraction and the accumulation of profit while relying on them for security—namely, for repression against community protest. The massive exploitation and poverty has sparked rebellions and community mobilizations throughout the Delta. Activists have organized against the oil companies directly, for example, when residents from Ondo state took action against Chevron for the poisoning of their water and food supplies. Yet they were compelled to face off against the intense militarization of the region, as explained by Jean Nanga: Chevron's "maritime and air navigation equipment was placed in the 1990s at the disposal of the Nigerian Army for its murderous expeditions against the Ijaw and Ogoni peoples who were demanding social justice in the Niger oil delta."[150] In 1998, over 100 activists from forty Delta communities boarded Chevron's Parabe platform, demanding a forum to discuss a number of grievances. After protesters occupied the platform and barge for several days, they were teargassed and fired upon by soldiers who were flown in by Chevron itself.[151] Two activists, Jola Ogungbeje and Aroleka Irwaninu, were killed.

Threaded to the workings of the highest levels of state and corporate power, such struggles are understood by these activists within this broader framework. As Chima Ubani, former political prisoner and working-class leader in the Civil Liberties Organization and the United Action for Democracy described, the oil multinationals and the Nigerian government "are simply continuing what the TransAtlantic slave trade and British colonialism did to us in the past. . . . And the struggles of our people today to rid ourselves of these agencies is merely an extension of our struggle for national independence. And our independence is not yet won until we send these exploitative forces packing from our soil."[152]

Yet the level of repression and devastation have posed immense challenges to that organizing. As a result, insurgency in the Delta has also taken the form of direct attacks on oil facilities themselves, forcing Nigerian operators to shut in large sections of production, costing an estimated tens of billions in lost revenues. Hundreds of foreign workers have been kidnapped in the Niger Delta region, along with ongoing oil theft—known as "bunkering." In the first decade of the new millennium, armed insurgency peaked, chiefly from a range of forces operating under the umbrella grouping of the Movement for the Emancipation of the Niger Delta (MEND). As Okonta has pointed out, academics and development specialists have tended to view organizations like MEND as a natural outgrowth of a resource-dominated society and social relations that inevitably lead to authoritarianism at the top and bottom of society. Yet, Okonta argues, such an ahistorical analysis would be misplaced. The character of the Delta insurgency can in fact be traced to

> the legacy of colonial conquest, and the undemocratic institutions of governance put in place by the British to exploit the wealth of the country undisturbed by the local people, subsequently handed over to carefully chosen political leaders who would go on to protect their interests after the colonial rulers quit in 1960. . . . The metamorphosis of political activism in the delta region from non-violent advocacy to armed insurrection is partly explained by the deliberate infiltration of their ranks by government agents, thereby restricting the civic options of those who refused to be co-opted. . . . MEND, properly understood, is the violent child of the deliberate and long-running constriction of the public space in the Niger Delta in which ordinary citizens, now reduced to penurious subjects, can exercise their civil and political rights in the legitimate pursuit of material and social wellbeing. Behind the mask of the MEND militant is a political subject forced to pick up an AK47 to restore his rights as a citizen.[153]

Anna Zalik and Michael Watts similarly describe dynamics of struggle in the Delta, what Watts elsewhere has called petro-nationalism:

> The failure of peaceful movements led to rising discontent and militancy, particularly among unemployed youth marginalized from the oil wealth in their midst. Local communities have mobilized to make demands on both companies and the Nigerian state for a greater share of profits. The strategies employed have been various—demonstrations and blockades against oil facilities, occupations of oil installations, workers' strikes, and legal proceedings by communities against the companies for ecological compensation. The occupation of the Warri area Chevron

oil facilities in 2002 by Ijaw, Itsekiri and Ilaje women demanding company investments and jobs for indigenes reflected the tip of social dissatisfaction with the resource distribution. More contentious have been hostage takings, sabotage of pipelines—and . . . theft (from hot-tapping fuel lines to large-scale removal of crude from flow stations).[154]

An amnesty brokered with former Nigerian President Goodluck Jonathan in 2009 slowed the intensity of the Delta insurgency. Jonathan focused primarily on paying MEND resistance leaders to stop oil sabotage; Carmody reports that exploration licenses were even granted to militant-run companies.[155] Yet since underlying conditions went unaddressed, the reemergence of struggle in the Niger Delta was likely. Nigeria's new president Muhammadu Buhari has upended the amnesty by cancelling the "security contracts" with the militants. A new wave of resistance is emerging, led by a group called the Red Avengers, whose pipeline attacks have managed to bring oil output to a twenty-year low; a Bloomberg analyst commented that "the Niger Delta Avengers have certainly been busy, forcing Shell's Forcados terminal to shut in about 250,000 barrels of daily exports; and breaching an offshore Chevron facility in the 160,000 barrels per day Escravos system."[156]

In this context, urgent political questions about the control over Nigeria's natural resources and its communities arise. Ukoha Ukiwo, for one, poses the question of harnessing these resources: "Perhaps the city-states [of Nigeria] would rise once more from the ashes of colonial neglect. . . . Could black gold—the fuel of modern capitalism—hold the key to the future prosperity of the Niger Delta?"[157] Yet the benefits of Nigeria's "resource nationalism" are largely concentrated in the hands of the minority—SaroWiwa's "slick alliance," including former militants, now Delta business people. A truly redistributive framework would pose a sharp challenge to the class divisions within Nigerian society itself—both on the regional and the national scale—and their relationship to the broader system of capitalism.

Bassey argues a different approach, namely for an immediate moratorium on the issuance of any new contracts for oil exploration. As he succinctly puts it, "we must simply leave the oil in the soil, the coal in the hole and the tar sands in the land."[158] Until extraction is halted, corporations and African elites will continue to benefit from the externalized costs of pollution and environmental destruction, and without any compulsion to sustain communities or working conditions at a humane level, the costs of exploitation will continue to be pushed onto workers and residents themselves.

In part, the potential for social change in the Delta and elsewhere in Nigeria lies in the linkages and solidarity between the social movements and working-class resistance at the point of production, that is, within the extractive industries and beyond. The Delta resistance and the Nigerian working-class struggle have a long history and have posed a serious challenge to capital.[159] Yet the challenges facing the Nigerian left are also high. As socialist Baba Aye reminds us, our sights must be set wider and not limited to policy reforms that have proven incapable of reversing inequality:

> In resource rich, but economically backward countries like Nigeria, cronyism as a strategy for intra-class distribution of the wealth being appropriated is central, displacing production in the face of a poor level of industrialization. . . . The economic problem in Nigeria is reduced to one of the "correct" policy. . . . Reality is however far more complicated. What we have at hand is more of a structural problem than merely one of "policies." The international character of capitalist development and the concomitant stranglehold of imperialism on the Nigerian economy make it near impossible, particularly for a capitalist government, to get away with such "Keynesian welfare nation state" schema at this period in history.[160]

The systemic nature of the conditions posed by extraction in the Delta, and the potential linkages between movements for fundamental environmental and social change, are thus sharply posed.

Likewise, the question of imperialism is a critical one as US collaboration with the Nigerian regime sustains only exploitation and brutality in the Delta. As human rights lawyer Gani Fawehinmi has commented, "If America imposes oil sanctions today and it is supported by the EU countries, this government would be brought down to its knees in less than two to three months."[161] US imperialism in Nigeria has been profoundly concerned with the instability and risks to "energy security" posed by the insurgency: the military has devised a range of military tactics to that end, including developing war game scenarios for the Niger Delta. A glimpse, as *Black Agenda*

Report's Bruce Dixon puts it, "of American plans for African people and resources in the new century [could] be seen in Eastern Nigeria. US and multinational oil companies like Shell, BP, and Chevron, which once named a tanker after its board member Condoleezza Rice, have ruthlessly plundered the Niger Delta for a generation."[162] In 2009, then Secretary of State Hillary Clinton, when questioned about "security" risks in the Niger Delta, replied: "We have a very good working relationship between our two militaries. . . . We will, through our joint efforts . . . , determine what Nigeria would want from us for help, because we know this is an internal matter, we know this is up to the Nigerian people and their government to resolve, and then look to see how we would offer that assistance."[163]

The dangers of oil wars escalating militarization in Africa will be explored further below. The drive for extraction has only created vast social and environmental problems in the Delta, and the threat of military intervention at the behest of oil companies and African leaders exacerbates the level of crisis for Delta communities. Dixon continues, "Africans are demanding respect and a share in what is after all, their oil. They are now routinely, viciously suppressed in eastern Nigeria, in Equatorial Guinea and elsewhere, by African troops trained and equipped with American tax dollars. When resistance continues, as it certainly will, America is preparing to up the ante with more American equipment, with military and civilian advisers, with bombs, bullets and if need be, with American bodies."[164] The shape of that resistance continues to unfold, as urgent as it has been since the discovery at Oloibiri over a half-century ago.

Extraction in Africa

As the dynamics of the new scramble for Africa show, the extractive landscape of Africa has been "combined" with the wider capitalist system, but in highly uneven ways. Trotsky's analysis of this characteristic of global capitalist development explains how sections of the system can be "advanced," while throwing others in reverse. This dialectical relationship is a fundamental characteristic of the system itself. Walter Rodney's idea of "underdevelopment" likewise rests on the assumption that colonialism produced unevenness in Africa to build up European powers. Importantly, as Rodney shows, economic underdevelopment was facilitated through political means—the policies and divisions of the colonial project that centralized control over African economies.[165] Then as now, capitalism ties aspects of the entire system together, however contradictorily. Extraction in Africa inextricably links capital expansion with weak, commodity-based economies, poverty, and environmental exploitation. The ties of "underdevelopment" will only be broken when capitalism can no longer subjugate some parts of the system to the interests of a global capitalist class that requires this "unevenness" to survive.

Chapter Six

Resource Curse or Resource Wars?

The much-vaunted rise [of Africa] seems to have stalled.

—John Ashbourne, Capital Economics[1]

Commodity Crash and Crisis

By late 2014, storm clouds began to appear on the rosy glow of the African boom. Two related global factors drove this development. First, a crisis of overcapacity and slowdown in China's economy pushed down the demand for raw materials that drive industrial growth, from iron to copper to oil, all imported from Africa. Economists reported that "structural shifts in the economy, favoring expansion of the services sector rather than heavy industry (both steel and cement production are likely to have peaked in 2014), mean that 85% less energy is required to generate each unit of future economic growth than was the case in the past 25 years."[2] For the first quarter of 2016, China's growth fell to 6.7 percent, a rate only achieved through a large infusion of lending.[3] As demand fell in this powerhouse economy, primary commodity prices collapsed worldwide, with only a partial recovery since.

Second, exacerbating this crisis has been a glut in world oil production. The United States made a critical strategic shift toward the end of the first decade of the 2000s to dramatically reduce reliance on imported oil, with a turn to fracking and the "shale revolution." US domestic oil production doubled between 2009 and 2014, while shale extraction increased *eight-fold*.[4] The explosion in exploration, discovery, and extraction in the United States dramatically transformed the face of the oil industry. Imports dropped so steadily that by 2014, only about a quarter of the petroleum consumed by the United States was imported, the lowest level since 1985.[5] In response, Saudi Arabian oil producers and OPEC heads unrolled a drastic strategy of letting prices fall to the floor to drive their competitors out of business. By mid-2016, the price of oil had dropped by about 60 percent over the previous two years.[6]

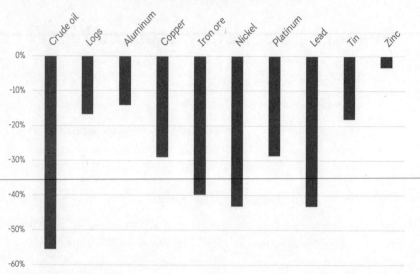

Commodity Price Declines 2014-2016

Source: World Bank[7]

Socialist Hadas Thier described the systemic dynamics behind the crisis:

> Because of the dynamics of short-term competition, this happens unevenly, in an unplanned way, and is susceptible to any number of barriers in both production and exchange, which can easily disrupt the process and throw the whole system into chaos. The example of oil is instructive because it plays such a central role in production, and therefore in the overall health of the economy. At its peak between 2012 and 2014, the price of oil rose to above $100 per barrel. In part driven by rising prices, and in part by the potential of new technologies (hydraulic fracturing, aka "fracking," and horizontal drilling) to break through the all-important international oil market, oil production shot up, particularly in the United States. During these peak years, in what is known as the "shale revolution," the United States was pumping out about a million barrels a day. But these production levels . . . were unsustainable, and in the end created such a global glut of oil that prices plummeted to below $30 a barrel. For some countries, like Venezuela or Algeria, whose economies are almost wholly dependent on oil exports,

this has had immediate and devastating effects. But stronger, more powerful countries like the United States, China, Russia and Saudi Arabia have also felt the financial health of their systems falter as well.

The oversupply of goods in one or more key industries can become generalized throughout the economy, and we end up with what Marx calls a "crisis of overproduction" . . . until capitalists can use the rock bottom prices left behind by bankrupt companies to begin expansion again. This cycle plays out over and over again.[8]

These fundamental problems are rooted in the highly anarchic nature of production itself, creating new crises as they unfold. The world is literally floating on a sea of excess oil. As described by the *New York Times* in early 2016,

the oil glut—the unsold crude that is piling up around the world—is a quandary and a source of investor anxiety. . . . As prices have dropped, the amount of excess production has been cut in half over the last six months. About one million barrels of extra oil is now being dumped on the markets each day. But that means the glut is still continuing to grow, and it could take years to work through the crude that is being warehoused, poured into petroleum depots or loaded onto supertankers for storage at sea. The shakeout will be painful, taking an even bigger toll on companies, countries and investors.[9]

Global extractive industries grappled with the crisis by selling off sections of production deemed as yielding below expectations or undesirable because of political or economic instability. The *New York Times* continues:

Major oil companies have dropped their rig count, and dozens of small businesses have gone bankrupt. But the industry cannot simply flip the switch on big projects, like deepwater production projects in the Gulf of Mexico, that require companies to keep pumping to cover their costs. Smaller companies have to keep producing from shale fields, even at a loss, to keep paying their lenders.[10]

These global developments have brought a new crisis to Africa. African GDP growth slid toward a seventeen-year low, translating into sub-Saharan Africa falling *below* the rest of the world for the first time since 2000. Accounting for population growth, GDP rates will actually be close to zero.[11] Falling oil prices will hurt not only established oil economies such as Nigeria and Angola, but also newly emerging oil producers such as Kenya and Ghana, including those that have yet to recoup investments made in developing production infrastructure. As the *Financial Times* described:

Mines are being mothballed, projects delayed and jobs shed. And countries across the continent have seen their currencies tumble against the US dollar.

"In the short term, this is the perfect storm," says Miguel Azevedo, head of investment banking for Africa at Citigroup. "It's really hitting hard in terms of demand for extractive industries—it's hitting local companies, it's hitting the budgets, and it's hitting the currencies and the forex availability. Through that, it's affecting everybody."[12]

The slowdown in China has dramatically impacted investment. Ugandan journalist Angelo Izama writes:

> In East Africa big projects benchmarked on investments in oil, gas or minerals will only suffer serious damage with the hemorrhaging of government-backed Chinese money. It's these sovereign wealth funds dispensed by the Export-Import Bank of China that have breathed life into the comatose body of the East African community, the regional economic grouping. Its leaders are speaking like Nkrumah awakened—about a common market with roads, railways, dams and jobs—for Africans paid for by China.[13]

Along with shrinking foreign direct investment (FDI), trade has fallen drastically; one study predicted a 40 percent drop in African imports to China.[14] The crisis of falling commodity prices has forced down the value of African currencies, threatening new problems. "In the past, foreign exchange weakness in Africa was largely shrugged off. Economies adapted and found a way to cope with it," says Razia Khan, chief economist for Africa at Standard Chartered. "Now, when currencies depreciate, external risks are magnified, public debt ratios rise, and perceptions of sovereign creditworthiness alter quite dramatically."[15]

The shift of the US economy to domestic oil has drastically curbed interest in African sources. As late as 2010, the United States was importing approximately 14 percent of its oil from Nigeria and Angola combined; after that year, African oil imports fell markedly,[16] and by 2014, African oil imports to the United States were virtually zero.[17] Imports from Nigeria—the leader for sub-Saharan Africa—reached a high in 2007 of over 41 million barrels per month. By 2015, that number had fallen to 627,000 barrels per month. Angola likewise reached 22 million barrels per month in 2007, but by early 2017 had declined to a mere 1.8 million.[18]

In the face of this crisis, Wall Street analysts issued warnings. Moody's scolded that "countries that didn't build up sufficient fiscal reserves, such as Angola and Nigeria, face the double threat of deteriorating external and domestic conditions, and are likely to face greater aversion from foreign investors."[19] In fact, "blame the victim" rhetoric has experienced a revival in critiques of African leaders who failed to "shore up" their economies during the boom times. "Countries that did not prepare in the good times by diversifying or building strong economic buffers are now likely to suffer a Chinese hang-over," the *Financial Times* predicted.[20] As Paul Collier bluntly put it, "this was the biggest opportunity Africa ever had, [and] it's broadly been a missed op-portunity."[21] Such tactics are only the latest guise of a longstanding approach, echoing Walter Rodney's description of a past era: "To ease their guilty con-sciences, Europeans try to throw the major responsibility for the slave trade on to the Africans . . . . [But] it was European capitalism which set slavery and the Atlantic slave trade in motion."[22] African states, for their part, have employed a number of strategies to mitigate this crisis, such as instituting sovereign wealth funds ("rainy day" funds to guard against sudden drops in demand), although some in the business presses contend that African nations missed a key window to benefit from such funds by waiting to establish them *after* the fall from peak production and prices of the 2000s.[23] Nigeria's fund is less than 1 percent of GDP. The *Financial Times* commented: "For now, many African economies are mired in a worst-case scenario. Oil production is down, oil prices have taken a hit, economies are slowing, and sub-Saharan Africa's oil producers have nothing to show for it. Having failed to plan for the future until the last second, these economies are in for a new, harsher, nor-mal."[24] Capital controls are another means of coping with the crisis, yet have created new problems for businesses relying on imports.

Revenue shortfalls have also led to cuts in oil-producing nations. Following the downturn, Nigeria forced through layoffs and cuts in the face of the weakest GDP growth—2.8 percent—since 1999.[25] Angola likewise cut its budget for 2016 by approximately $15 billion, prompting job cuts and post-poning of government projects.[26] Further, steps to lift oil subsidies had a dev-astating impact on ordinary Africans facing a jump in the price of fuel.

Angola was compelled to seek a bailout from the International Monetary Fund in 2016 totaling $8 billion, or 9 percent of GDP.[27] But Angola was not alone: "Many of Africa's once-golden economies may need to go back to the IMF for emergency financing," warned the *Wall Street Journal* in 2016.[28] Ghana received a $1 billion bailout in 2015, with $290 million for Mozambique.[29] World Bank President Jim Yong Kim commented that the bank's response to the African crisis was "our highest lending in a non-crisis period ever."[30] The depth of the crisis threatens a return to the painful medicine of structural ad-justment. Nigeria, IMF head Christine Lagarde warned, is "a country that is facing, like many other oil-producing countries, a real hardship and a necessity to very promptly redesign its business model and realign its interests with a completely new reality which is here for longer than many think."[31] The legacy of structural adjustment and harsh austerity in Africa has left the IMF highly unpopular. The nongovernmental organizations Results and the Centre for Economic Governance and AIDS in Africa, for example, attribute a 20 percent rise in poverty in Zambia to an IMF bailout program, a criticism rejected by the IMF.[32] And as even World Bank chief economist Kaushik Basu has confided: "I have to admit [the fall in prices] has gone on longer than I or we anticipated."[33]

The Resource Curse and Democracy Deficit

Despite ample evidence of this crisis of overproduction, other theories abound to "explain" the propensity for crisis and the failures of development. Among policymakers, think tanks, and community development advocates, a dominant explanation for the relationship between poverty and natural resources is a theory called the "resource curse." The "resource curse" intends to describe the phenomenon wherein a massive inflow of foreign currency due to natural resources creates a distorting impact on other sectors of a nation's economy and, more broadly, social conditions as a whole. The economic mechanism explaining this distortion is sometimes referred to as the "Dutch disease"—coined by the *Economist* magazine in 1977 and defined by the *Financial Times* as "the negative impact on an economy of anything that gives rise to a sharp inflow of foreign currency, such as the discovery of large oil reserves. The currency inflows lead to currency appreciation making the country's other products less price competitive on the export market."[34] Nigeria's currency, for example, rose dramatically from the early 1970s to the mid-1980s in the context of a jump in oil prices.[35]

The "resource curse" theory is often associated with the works of development economists and policymakers (such as Paul Collier, Michael Ross, Macartan Humphreys, Jeffrey Sachs, and Joseph Stiglitz) to explain low overall levels of industrialization and development, alongside persistent poverty, in nations with high levels of natural resources. But it tends toward an ahistorical explanation for "underdevelopment" and the role of natural resource extraction. Ultimately, this approach mistakenly attributes "causality" to mythical characteristics of natural resources themselves, rather than the legacies of colonialism and neoliberalism.

Nicholas Shaxson, writing in 2009, outlines the idea's origins:

> The so-called "resource curse" thesis is relatively new: the notion that mineral resources, like oil, can actually harm countries that produce them (or, at the very least, contribute to their failure to reach their apparent potential)

only started to emerge into mainstream academic forums in the mid-1990s, and into the popular mainstream about five years later. Early landmark studies such as *Natural Resource Abundance and Economic Growth*, a paper by Jeffrey Sachs and Andrew Warner, or Terry Lynn Karl's *The Paradox of Plenty*, emerged in 1995 and 1997 respectively; Global Witness' December 1999 report *A Crude Awakening*, focusing on Angola, was also a landmark in terms of popularizing the problem, although specialist publications such as *Africa Confidential* had been pursuing these issues for some time.[36]

The concept is common in literature on oil and Africa, corresponding to a boom in the "good governance" and "transparency" efforts, despite much evidence questioning their efficacy (see Ghazvinian 2007[37]; Shaxson 2008[38]; Hicks 2015[39]). In African economies in the post-independence period, as Southall and Comninos write, "The emergent bourgeoisie, managerial rather than capitalist, was therefore from this perspective pursuing rent rather than profit, so the key intercontinental relationships were not just those of aid and trade, but even more between multinational corporations and politicians and bureaucrats."[40] According to the "resource curse" theory, a key characteristic of these lopsided economies are states that disproportionately rely on "rents"—that is, revenues accruing through licensing of drilling and mining rights. This dynamic ostensibly produces what Shaxson has described as "misplaced lines of accountability,"[41] meaning the state is overly reliant on a centralized source of income from extractive and related industries rather than its own citizenry or workers. Tom Burgis similarly describes a "resource industry . . . hardwired for corruption."[42] Humphreys, Sachs, and Stiglitz attribute this corruption to the supposed "enclave" characteristics of natural resources: because extraction requires minimal labor participation, the need for political consensus is vastly diminished, or so the argument goes: "When a country's wealth arises from an endowment of natural resources . . . investment in a skilled workforce is not necessary for the realization of current income."[43] Thus, there are few limits to "rent-seeking behavior," meaning the hijacking of the political process by corrupt elites.[44] Yet Humphreys, Sachs, and Stiglitz are mistaken to attribute "enclaves" to political behavior alone because weak states in reality are a product, as we have seen, of their uneven integration into the global capitalist system as a whole.

Padraig Carmody argues that the notion of a "curse," however "counterintuitive" such a concept may be, has some material basis in reality. He writes, "studies suggest that real GDP and the population's standard of living nearly always decline where oil is discovered. Between 1970 and 1993, for example, countries without oil saw their economies grow four times faster than those of countries with oil."[45] Thus, the idea of the resource curse's "paradox of plenty," according to Carmody, can be generalized from growth rates and conditions seen in African nations who brought oil finds online.

Advocates of the resource curse explanation cite national budgets disproportionately allocated to the military at the expense of social spending, along with other indicators of "poor governance": corruption, authoritarianism, rigged elections, and resource-based violence and conflicts. According to this theory, overreliance on natural resources not only produces weaker-than-expected economic development but also contributes to what is sometimes termed a "democracy deficit." According to the resource curse literature, at its most extreme, the resource curse and democracy deficits engender "failed states," where many functions of governance and civil society have been dwarfed by the disproportionate role of the rentier system, so that other sectors cease to adequately function. Humphreys, Sachs, and Stiglitz, for example, argue that "the resource curse results not only in militarization but also in civil war."[46] Collier uses a term called the "survival of the fattest" to describe how resources thwart democratic functioning: that states based on resource rents will inevitably facilitate patronage politics and the undermining of democratic "checks and balances" or "restraints," in Collier's terminology. In a nutshell, "voters are bribed with public money."[47] For Collier, natural resources are one of several "traps," along with conflict and geography, that function to limit economic growth and democratic participation. Advocates of this narrow perspective cite correlations such as World Bank figures on West Africa stating that the region experiences 70 percent of the continent's military coups.[48]

The distortions in these accounts are stunning. The West, as we have seen, has a long record of supporting authoritarian rulers, in Africa and elsewhere, to advance its own interests. What's called a "conflict trap" is not produced by natural resources but rather by the historical legacies of colonial powers that pitted African societies against one another, followed by downturns in the world economic system that threw weak, newly independent nations into crisis. Civil wars in Africa, past and present, are funded by imperial powers in support of their local "proxies," armed by multinational weapons dealers. The militarization of the African continent has been imposed on African states compelled to accept arms and bases in return for "development" aid. Attributing poverty, war, and underdevelopment to "poor governance" turns historical reality on its head.

Other critiques of the "resource curse" show that underlying economic structures produce inequality, *not* resource-linked behavior. The Tax Justice Network Africa correctly argues:

Though some say a resource curse is innate to Africa, this is simply false. The continent's creativity and adaptability are not doomed to be "cursed"; the root cause is elsewhere, in structures of "maldevelopment." . . . Maldevelopment has been packaged as behavioral, rooted in the abuse of political power chiefly located at the state level in developing countries rich in resources.[49]

Carmody also shows that economic conditions cannot be explained in behavioral terms. He writes:

Colonialism opened markets around the world enabling economies of scale to be realized in the colonizing countries. Can (under)developing countries now compete, particularly under a liberal economic regime which institutionalizes the advantages of first movers over late comers . . . ? The implication is that they can, but the reason they have not done so to date is because these countries have poor politics and policies. . . . But this neglects the fact that most of the countries of the "bottom billion" (Collier 2007) have been implementing the policies of unmediated integration promoted by the Washington-based international financial institutions for the last few decades.[50]

The resource curse approach is plagued by what Marx termed commodity fetishism—that is, ascribing oil and other natural resources innate attributes rather than economic and historical relationships. Shaxson's account, for example, claims that "oil and gas companies are different. Oil provides rents, . . . money not earned by innovation and hard work but that comes out of the ground as if a gift from God."[51] Geographer Michael Watts, who has written extensively on Nigeria and "petro-states," has offered a sustained critique of the "resource curse" thesis:

Oil comes to mark a particular epoch (like the age of coal or steam) and to this extent is not only a bearer of particular relations of production but is equally a source of enormous political and economic power and therefore it carries a set of ideological and cultural valences as is implied in the moniker of "black gold" or "petro-dollars" (it is both a commodity and a commodity fetish). In this account oil (and other key resources) has causal powers: it is a purveyor of corruption, it undermines democracy, promotes civil and inter-state wars ("blood for oil"), is the mother of forms of corporate power ("Big Oil") and condemns oil-rich states to devastating economic, political and social pathologies (oil is the "devil's excrement" as a former head of OPEC once put it).[52]

In his review of Collier's widely read *The Bottom Billions*, Watts shows how this approach papers over the roots of conflict and inequality. "The language of curse invokes a merciless force for adversity, a sort of commodity determinism vesting oil with capabilities it can neither possess nor dispense. The danger is that the curse substitutes the commodity for the larger truths of capitalism, markets, and politics."[53] He continues:

> In this account oil has been invested with almost Olympian transformative powers. Oil distorts the organic, natural course of development. Oil wealth ushers in an economy of hyper-consumption and spectacular excess. Others like Michael Ross (1999, 2003, 2004) argue that "oil hinders democracy" (as if copper might promote constitutionalism) and hampers gender equality; oil revenues permit low taxes and encourage patronage (thereby dampening pressures for democracy); it endorses despotic rule through bloated militaries, and it creates a class of state dependents employed in modern industrial and service sectors who are less likely to push for democracy.[54]

As Cyril Obi has shown, the resource curse thesis fails because wars and conflicts are not characteristics of resource-rich nations alone; the historical roots of scarcity and inequality are systemic.[55] Historian Kairn Klieman likewise argues that resource curse theory concludes "corruption" is the purview of Africans alone. In fact, her research on the historical relationship between US oil firms and the Nigerian oil economy reveals corruption's highly "non-public" nature in the conjuncture of the 1960s oil boom with the heightened competition between African elites that exploded in the Nigerian civil war of 1967–1970. Corruption was in evidence on all sides, and "opacity was a characteristic of both Nigerian and independent oil company practices, shaping the way they interacted over time."[56] Much of the focus on governance, however, severely distorts the actual impact of structural adjustment on extraction in Africa and the bloated corporate contracts with signing bonuses and provisions that allow multinationals to escape even minimal social accountability. As Nigerian environmentalist Nnimmo Bassey has put it:

> The so-called resource curse can be traced not only to the corrupt, despicable dictators, whose spirited-abroad wealth often exceeded their countries' national external debt, but also to neo-colonial relations. Blaming a resource curse purely on dictators, as do some Western politicians, is a refusal to admit that the colonial pillage of Africa continues, driven on the same tracks that were set in those dark days by transnational corporations, trade rules, bilateral and multilateral arrangements, and powerful international agencies such as the World Bank and the International Monetary Fund.[57]

The narrative renders the resource wars created by global capitalism into "curses" for which African economies and policymakers are solely responsible.

Overcoming the "Resource Curse"?
The Chad-Cameroon Pipeline

Several high-profile development initiatives have attempted to reverse the "resource curse" in Africa by building moderate redistributive reforms and "transparency" requirements into individual projects. In a well-known example, the World Bank collaborated with local government in establishing development requirements for Exxon's massive Chad-Cameroon pipeline, officially called the Chad-Cameroon Petroleum Development Project (CCDP). Launched in 2001 by a consortium of partners of ExxonMobil (whose parent company, Esso, was the primary partner), plus Chevron and Malaysia's Petronas—and under World Bank auspices—the plan was championed as a major experiment in corporate social responsibility, one that ultimately ended in dismal failure for ordinary people in the region.

Totaling approximately $4.2 billion, the project was, as Simon Massey and Roy May write, "hailed by . . . the World Bank as a pioneering model for responsible private investment in Africa and the developing world."[58] The oversight committee allocated project revenue to social welfare and health care; however, despite the formalized plan, the Chadian government successfully undermined the terms by renegotiating the consortium with the multinational oil companies, granting a much larger percentage to the consortium, with more indirect revenue accruing to the Chadian government.[59]

Celeste Hicks has done extensive research in Chad on the politics and economics of the pipeline. As she notes, the program design appeared to be a means of ensuring compliance with social development goals to, ideally, wrest Chad from the resource curse. The terms required the "public-sector to fund the construction of the oil-field infrastructure, but with a set of special guarantees that all the payments made by the oil companies involved in the project would be made transparently, and that most of what Chad earned would be put towards development. But it did not go to plan," she writes.[60] Specifically, CCDP terms established an escrow account for revenue collection targets as well as targets for government spending and environmental controls.[61] Yet in many ways, the project was doomed from the start. As Anna Zalik and Michael Watts point out, "The Chad-Cameroon pipeline aimed to avoid this curse by requiring that 80 percent of the profits from the project be invested in social development—a rather unlikely feat in the context of Chad's dictatorship."[62]

Chad at this time was deeply embroiled in a civil war that created the conditions for the undoing of this "social experiment": Chadian president Idris Deby made a unilateral move in 2005, rewriting law so as to bypass the contract terms and divert funds into an unmonitored government fund. From there, Chad moved both to set up a national oil company, Société des Hydrocarbures du Tchad, and enter into direct negotiations with the Chinese National Petroleum Company. These changes had a dramatic impact on both the civil war and the pipeline project overall. For one, the Chadian rebels were effectively routed, Hicks writes, as a "direct consequence of . . . Deby's rearmament with oil money."[63] Deby set the pattern for this oil-to-arms pipeline from the project's inception, when almost one-fifth of the $25 million signing bonus from Chevron went straight into the military budget.[64]

Another major repercussion was the exit of the World Bank from the project, and with it a lost public relations opportunity to restore the bank's tarnished image from unfettered structural adjustment austerity. In the 1990s, the World Bank under the leadership of James Wolfensohn embraced projects like the CCDP as an expression of an ostensibly innovative "public-private" development project model to address weak governance and economic infrastructure.[65] But Deby's maneuver was a "red line" for the World Bank and produced a head-on collision with new bank head (and former senior adviser in the George W. Bush administration) Paul Wolfowitz in January 2006.[66]

Deby was able to force the World Bank to back down by withholding oil, compelling the organization to renegotiate terms and release suspended funds into Deby's hands.[67] Resource nationalism became a prominent factor in the imperial dynamics; as Simon

Massey and Roy May describe, "The issue of sovereignty, down-played during the original negotiations, was shuffled to the top of the agenda."[68]

Severe problems from the project plague residents. The pipeline is fully operational, yet villagers, as Brendan Schwartz and Valéry Nodem describe, "were promised fair compensation for the loss of land expropriated by Exxon, employment with the oil companies for the life of the project, and 5% of oil revenues to be invested in their villages. According to local residents, these promises were empty."[69] In fact, said Nodem, "almost 10 years after oil from Doba in Chad was pumped and transported to hungry international markets, thousands of poor farmers and families in Chad and Cameroon [were] still waiting to receive a compensation for losses they endured from the pipeline crossing their homes, farms and other livelihoods."[70] Approximately 22,500 farmers near Esso production areas in Doba filed a complaint with the International Finance Corporation, the finance arm of the World Bank, stating that their livelihoods and water supply had been destroyed.[71] In 2013, over a decade after the project's start, UN Human Development Indicators on social, health, and education indices placed Chad near the bottom of the list globally.[72]

Several factors explain the disaster of the CCDP. The project conception was deeply flawed from the start, based on terms considerably less favorable to Chad in comparison to deals with other African countries, where Chad was to receive only 28 percent of the project's revenues. A comparable agreement in Nigeria would net approximately 90 percent for the government. Other contract terms reinforced the balance of power in favor of oil corporations, with immunization from future Chadian laws that might attempt to regulate operations.[73] Further, the agreement was structured so that Chad committed large funds based on future earnings, with no reserves to balance price volatility. As a result, when oil prices fell in 2009, Chad was compelled to approach the IMF for a loan a mere three years after its debts to the World Bank had been paid off.[74]

The social justice lessons from the CCDP are multiple. For one, as we have seen here, the "resource curse" is no phantasmagorical force, but rather is shaped by historical and political factors—in this case, the highly unequal terrain in which the world's largest corporations sat down at the negotiating table with one of world's poorest countries. In this context, "transparency" regulations have very little efficacy. As Hicks concludes, "the experience has clearly demonstrated that it takes much more than a good set of written laws to guarantee that the money earned is spent on effective domestic investment that really does lead to development. . . . Good laws need political will to back them up." Yet her solution of "strong and accountable parliaments and democratic reforms"[75] seems to lead us back down the slippery slope of the development economists, who place blame at the feet of individual policymakers rather than in the disproportionate power structure encompassing major multinationals and their supportive institutions, such as the World Bank.

Ultimately, the World Bank's imprimatur was insufficient in overcoming the deficiencies of, as Nicholas Jackson describes, Chadian "governing institutions. . . . Thus, petroleum corporations did not have adequate incentives to assume the political risk required for investing in Chadian petroleum production."[76] In reality, however, global financial institutions like the World Bank do not work to *mitigate* the disproportionate accumulation of corporate wealth and capital, in the extractive sector or elsewhere. Rather, these institutions have provided the policy infrastructure and political means for colossal development projects in the service of these corporate multinationals.

On balance, the resource curse's ahistorical explanation rests on the premise that Africans are more susceptible to corruption, thereby removing accountability for multinational companies and global financial institutions alike.

Transparency and "Good Governance"

The African networks of civil society which promote "publish what you pay" and other gambits for transparency, participation and human rights should finally come to the realization that this system of looting is not going to be reformed under the prevailing balance of power, and that much more forceful resistance to extraction is required—and is underway.

—Patrick Bond[77]

From Western elected officials to nongovernmental organizations, anxieties about social instability and the siphoning of oil wealth produce incessant hand-wringing about government graft. Human Rights Watch, for example, launched an extensive campaign demanding the Angolan government in 2011 provide an explanation for $32 billion suspected of "missing" from the state oil company, Sonangol.[78] Certainly, government spending on the Angolan people has been dismal: its 2013 budget allocated 1.4 times more to defense than to health and schools combined, as compared to the United Kingdom, which spends four times more on those services than on the military.[79] Yet such campaigns can fall far short of a systemic analysis that can facilitate more deep-rooted change.

The narrowing of horizons is apparent in the organizational and policy solutions of the developmentalist approach. Collier, for example, offers a host of "solutions," such as reforming the tax system and building institutional capacity to manage state administration and "good governance."[80] But under what conditions are such solutions viable? Historical forces have undermined the ability of African states to build that "capacity." For example, as a number of writers have described, a range of practices and manipulations—illicit and otherwise—have facilitated the theft of tax revenues and outward capital flows. At a basic level, African states historically—as a legacy of colonial-era development patterns—have a very low level of integration, and are therefore in a weak position to implement and enforce policy. Amazingly, some tax codes have been directly inherited from the colonial period: as reported by Grieve Chelwa of the online publication *Africa Is a Country*,

> Malawi has a 60 year old colonial-era tax treaty with the U.K. that makes it easy for U.K. companies to limit their tax obligations in Malawi. The treaty was "negotiated" in 1955 when Malawi was not even Malawi yet. Malawi (or Nyasaland, as it was known then) was represented in the negotiations, not by a Malawian, but by Geoffrey Francis Taylor Colby, a U.K. appointed Governor of Nyasaland.[81]

Other historical examples include the case of US oil companies as described by Klieman, whose "antitax campaign contributed to the regional and ethnic tensions that led to the outbreak of [civil] war" in Nigeria.[82]

Nicholas Shaxson argues that 1996 marked a "turning point" inside the World Bank, when then president James Wolfensohn put the issue of corruption on the "development agenda."[83] Major organizations such as Global Witness established the framework, with early reports on human rights and blood diamonds as well as the oil industry. In 2002, Global Witness joined with George Soros to launch Publish What You Pay, a program to establish legislation in Western nations compelling oil companies to disclose payments to host governments. Since that time, there has been an evolving understanding in official circles that "corruption" must be more broadly understood and the "guilty" parties more broadly defined. A 2016 UN report on governance and corruption in Africa argues:

> Accounting for the external and transnational dimension of corruption in Africa facilitates strategic decision-making that is holistic and helps to tackle the problem of corruption at its root. Foreign multinational corporations often capitalize on weak institutional mechanisms in order to bribe State officials and gain unwarranted advantage to pay little or no taxes, exploit unfair sharing of rents, and to secure political privileges in State policies.[84]

The report continues:

> Anti-corruption projects and initiatives all focus on cleaning up corruption in the public sector, which is often regarded as incompetent, inefficient and corrupt, while the private sector is portrayed as efficient, reliable and less corrupt. This view has been influenced by neo-liberal economic perspectives, which argue that the private sector is the main engine of economic growth and perceive governments as being obtrusive."[85]

In fact, the high level of corruption and criminality by Western and other non-African firms is staggering, and a number of high-profile cases have implicated household names from the corporate world. The oil-services company Halliburton was convicted by a Nigerian court of corruption carried out while none other than former US Vice President Dick Cheney was at the helm.[86] In a report on "cross-border corruption in Africa" between 1995 and 2014, virtually all (99.5 percent) involved non-African firms.[87] Certainly an analysis of the impact of multinational capital is critical. But the economic and historical weight of these "weak institutional mechanisms"—the product of the privatization and disinvestment of state power—is also extraordinarily high. For one, states are highly underfunded through imposed budget cuts and privatization; many lack the means to adequately collect and enforce tax policy. As the Tax Justice Network Africa writes:

> The Kenyan Revenue Authority . . . employs approximately 3,000 tax and customs officers, to serve a population of 32 million. Meanwhile Nigeria, with its 5,000 tax officials, cannot engage in a meaningful tax dialogue with its 140 million citizens. The Netherlands, as an example of an OECD country, employs 30,000 tax and customs officials for a population of 10 million. . . . This extraordinary lack of personnel is a product of decades of failed tax

policy in Africa, where the role of tax administrations was squeezed as part of austerity programs prescribed by the international finance institutions including the IMF.[88]

Khadija Sharife has reported on the range of tactics employed by multi-nationals—from tax loopholes and tax holidays built into extraction contracts as incentives to attract FDI, to tax dodges and what's called "trade mispricing" (i.e., the manipulation of prices to avoid payment of taxes). She describes how in Africa's largest copper producer, Zambia, the

> copper industry is largely privatized, previously hosting one of the world's lowest royalty rates (0.6 per cent) with a corporate tax rate of "effectively zero" according to the World Bank . . . (once deferments etc. were factored in). Despite Zambia since increasing copper royalty rates to 3 per cent, after missing out on the five-year commodity boom, Zambian president Rupiah Banda has ruled out windfall taxes and generally opposed measures designed to prevent mispricing and other forms of revenue leakages.[89]

Charles Abugre writes that approximately 65 to 70 percent of the upwards of $1 trillion that has exited the continent in illicit capital flows is due to trade mispricing and other "commercial activities."[90] As the Tax Justice Network Africa has also outlined, structural adjustment policies have required dramatic changes to African tax codes to facilitate corporate accumulation, easing of tax rates for the export of primary commodities, and favorable tax rates for African elites.[91] As a result, they point out, the average tax revenues in African states, at approximately 15 percent of GDP, are significantly lower than in OECD countries (average 35 percent) and the European Union in particular (39 percent of GDP).[92] Meanwhile, the United States and other Western governments embrace a posture that condemns the corruption and "lack of transparency" of African regimes, a posture that merely facilitates greater regulatory and financial control benefiting foreign multinationals. In keeping with US tradition, Barack Obama deployed a finger-waving approach in his 2015 visit to Kenya and Ethiopia, declaring, "The corruption and cronyism and tribalism that sometimes confront young nations—that's recent history."[93] Yet the corruption decried by the West becomes the rationale for international policies that create the *appearance* of regulation but only camouflage ongoing exploitation and systemic inequality.

Multinational corporations operating in Africa have been able, as we have seen, to benefit from the weak regulatory infrastructure inherited from colonialism and neoliberalism alike. In this context, corporations seek out "corporate social responsibility" measures that enable them to navigate the political landscape and secure what Carmody has called a "social license to operate": sufficient consensus to pursue the extraction of profit while managing the "social" costs.[94] Carmody cites a telling account of these tensions in an interview with Shell Africa's Chairman Chris Finlayson:

> To what extent should an international oil company make the decisions about development aid for the government? This isn't simply saying, "It's not our fault" and standing away from it. But there is a genuine moral dilemma there. Should we set ourselves in the position of saying we know better or we have more democratic right than the government does to decide who gets development aid? . . . Rather than saying, "We'll up our costs so we can give more money out directly," we're saying, "No, our duty is to minimize costs, meet our social obligations to the community, pay the maximum tax to the government under the terms of the treaty, and then it is up to the elected representatives of the people to decide how to spend the money."[95]

The business presses may write off such conditions as a projected "risk," merely the cost of doing business in a weakly regulated environment. Yet those same publications offer up hypocritical characterizations of China's supposed flexible approach to problems of corruption. "The Chinese may seek to reassure their new partners that economic development is compatible with authoritarianism. . . . Today most western institutions are preaching the values of good governance and democracy," the *Financial Times* claims. "Turning a blind eye to corruption and the abuse of political power is a recipe for political instability. It does not serve China's long-term interests, either."[96] Or, as the paper wrote elsewhere, "China is not sniffy about dealing with despots."[97] In fact, the situation is far more complex than Finlayson, Shell, and others may want to concede. Corporations benefit from "official" channels that facilitate accumulation, from very weak tax provisions to outright flaunting of "social obligations," however those may be defined. "Unofficial" or illegal practices are likewise major features of the landscape, from trade mispricing and tax avoidance to outright bribery.

As Andy Wynne points out, "the Chinese economy has clearly expanded massively in recent years without good governance in the Western sense."[98] Historically, the conditions of the "middle class" have been *undermined* by structural adjustment policies that required a shrinking of the state and lay-offs of public-sector workers. "The real value of public servants' salaries reduced significantly in the 1980s across many African countries," Wynne adds, "leading to increased corruption and a deterioration in governance."[99] The hypocrisy of Western leaders is stunning with regard to the narrowness by which the problem of "corruption" is typically defined. As Sharife and her co-authors describe in *Tax Us If You Can*:

Business concerns tend to dominate thinking about corruption. For example, Transparency International's Corruption Perceptions index (CPI) draws heavily on opinion within the international business community, who first raised the alarm about the perils of corruption. While the CPI provides an invaluable ranking for investors trying to assess country risk, it is of little use to the citizens of oil-rich states such as Chad, Equatorial Guinea or Angola to know their country ranks low.[100]

Likewise, Burgis's excellent account of the "the looting machine" exposes the outright corruption by "blue-chip multinationals" such as KBR, Shell, and Willbros, who attempted to gain leverage in the Nigerian oil industry through multimillion-dollar bribes.[101] While "good governance" regulations are notoriously weak in their enforcement capabilities, they may in fact smooth over any reputational problems for multinational corporations. For example, in 2008 the Ugandan government approved the National Oil and Gas Policy outlining objectives on environmental regulation and investment of revenue derived from extraction. Yet, as Jason Hickel points out in *Foreign Policy in Focus*:

> The National Oil and Gas Policy is dangerously vague and absolutely toothless. The framework does not bear the authority of law, and includes no mechanisms that would make its proposed regulations mandatory. Even if the framework's proposals were to end up as actual legislation, it includes nothing that oil companies would not ordinarily promote in their attempts to erect a façade of legitimacy and burnish the image of an industry beleaguered by PR nightmares. In fact, the framework pays far more attention to creating a favorable investment climate for foreign companies than it does to ensuring the welfare of Ugandans. . . . For Ugandans to reap the benefits of oil production, the country must actually receive the revenues it deserves. As it stands, the framework fails to protect Uganda from being plundered by the multinational corporations that will soon come to dominate the economy.[102]

African neoliberal leaders have also embraced this approach. The New Partnership for Africa's Development (NEPAD) has a new peer review mechanism that focuses on "governance" and the implementation of "priorities"—including, among other practices, "handling of misuse of resources" and enforcement of a commitment among public officials to "codes of conduct that negate corruption."[103] Ironically, some studies have found an *inverse* relationship between governance measures and FDI.[104] Others have pointed out that there is no consistent relationship between such measures and actual growth. As described by Chelwa,

The Harvard economist Dani Rodrik, in a highly insightful essay titled "An African Growth Miracle?", points out that the relationship between standard measures of good policies (macroeconomic stability, reduced price distortions, etc. . . .) and economic growth tends to be weak. At best, good policies make economic crises less prevalent but cannot sustain and drive growth on their own. . . . Rodrik points out that Latin America has experienced positive institutional changes within the last 20 years with a small payoff in growth. On the other hand, impressive growth in South Korea (until the 1990s) and China (today) has occurred alongside rampant cronyism and corruption.[105]

In fact, Chelwa adds, much more debate and disagreement exists between experts as to the relationship between such policies and economic growth, claims by the "corporate social responsibility" boosters to the contrary.[106] As stressed by *Africa Is a Country*, the notion of "African corruption" persists despite the reality of widespread and established practices of illicit activity in the West.[107]

Quantifying Corruption

As much as former President Obama and other public officials may prefer to locate the origins of supposed corruption in "cronyism" and "tribalism," we can in fact identify more precise structural conditions, namely those produced by trade liberalization and deregulation of the tax codes. One common tactic is that of "transfer mispricing": when large corporations manipulate prices through buying and selling between their own subsidiaries to avoid taxation, a practice that amounts to outright theft of what's due on the extraction. Such processes have created a veritable crisis in lost revenues for African nations: the continent as a whole loses approximately $148 billion per year in capital flight, where 60 percent of the total is attributable to corporate mispricing of resources.[108] Zambia, for example, received only 2.4 percent, and the Democratic Republic of Congo a mere 2.5 percent, for revenues on raw materials exported *during the boom in commodity prices*. The IMF has cited a rate of 45 to 65 percent as the "global average effective tax rate in mining," according to Burgis.[109]

Development experts have proffered a host of policy solutions to address this issue through "good governance" and transparency initiatives such as Paul Collier's Natural Resource Charter[110] or the Extractive Industry Transparency Initiative (EITI), launched by Tony Blair in 2002 as a voluntary and incentive-based alternative to Publish What You Pay. Twenty-one African nations have participated in the process, but to date only three have

been validated as meeting EITI requirements.[111] The EITI, for example, cer-
tifies compliance by individual nations on a host of measures related to tax
reporting, payments, and contracts, and is overseen by a board composed of
government and trade officials along with corporate executives, including
representatives from ExxonMobil, Total, Statoil, Chevron, and Rio Tinto.[112]
Collier's charter views itself as improving on the EITI by building in greater
transparency of financial risk and contract awards.

George Soros, for one, has championed as a solution "better understanding" on the part of the people, "where the remedy is greater transparency
and accountability."[113] But many writers have critiqued this framework from
the left, questioning how improved transparency can facilitate major change
to a relationship based on competition and exploitation. Sharife has noted
that at its heart, EITI measurements are extremely limited in assessing only
the gap between corporate-reported figures and funds actually received by
the host governments, as opposed to what *should have* been paid; worse, their
very structure and focus ignore the actual illicit mechanisms that enable
tax avoidance.[114] And programs like EITI contribute to an overall climate
that creates a general *appearance* of compliance, with little change to the en-
trenched operations.[115] But despite these mammoth weaknesses and biases
and the ease with which corporations and industry bodies are able to sidestep these reforms, no efforts are spared in challenging even these minimal
reporting requirements, citing, as the American Petroleum Institute did,
"the potential for competitive harm."[116] EITI can only go so far in changing a range of corporate thievery and exploitation of natural resources.
Generally, transparency measures such as Transparency International's
Corruption Perceptions Index are fraught with methodological problems,
since, as noted above, these rankings are actually based on "perceptions" of
corruption among a narrow section of so-called experts, business executives,
and elites. Such problems in quantifying "corruption" have led the United
Nations Economic Commission for Africa to question the entire basis of the
"perceptions-based" methodology.

As Hickel correctly points out, "the EITI cannot prevent mispricing, and
nor can it expose the common practice whereby companies launder money
internally in order to report lower taxable profits."[117] Neither can EITI prevent the use of tax havens and related manipulations, which as described by
Shaxson in his study on the EITI in Nigeria, are "without doubt one of the
greatest sources of oil industry profits worldwide—causing a massive ongoing
transfer of wealth from Nigeria and other oil-producing countries to owners

of capital in the West."[118] Furthermore, Shaxson found that implementing the U.K.-based EITI can smack of a double standard imposed on African nations:

> Some interviewees were cynical about Britain's apparently hypocritical role in all of this: chiding Nigerians for corruption and encouraging the EITI process, on the one hand, then refusing to cooperate on tracking cross-border financial flows in order to protect the secrecy space and the dirty money that it harbors in the City of London and its satellites in the Crown Dependencies (e.g., Jersey) and overseas territories (e.g., the Caymans) in particular. Britain—almost certainly the largest recipient of stolen Nigerian assets—was singled out as being remarkably uncooperative.[119]

Other problems abound with EITI. Under its rules, the burden of transparency shifts from international oil companies to the "host" governments, who are tasked with the onerous burden of a raft of reporting requirements.[120] African governments' participation in EITI actually undermines their ability to identify corporate theft because of its complex and obfuscating methodology; as Sharife puts it, "catching revenue leakage through EITI —off the mark by billions—is impossible because it . . . never investigates the means through which corporations were able to circumvent taxation."[121] Tying foreign aid to adopting such "transparency" measures can rightly be viewed as a form of imperial control.

At the end of the day, Shaxson concludes, "The companies love EITI—it takes all the pressure off them and puts it onto African governments to disclose."[122] EITI enables corporations to shield themselves behind a cloak of "social responsibility," facilitating their ability to dodge accusations of corruption or skirt contract terms. Chevron, for example, one of the world's largest oil companies, has a notorious reputation for repression and ecological devastation in Nigeria's oil-producing Niger Delta region. Chevron admitted later that its approach was "inadequate, expensive, and divisive."[123] Social "responsibility" measures and weakly enforced compliance regimes allow corporations like Chevron to offer up toothless "solutions" while reaping the benefits for their thin apologies.

The Kimberley Process and Dodd-Frank

As with other natural resources, reformers have turned their attention to certification processes in an attempt to create "conflict-free" sources of minerals. The conflict minerals provision in the Dodd-Frank Act of 2010, for example, outlined stricter reporting requirements on extractive industry supply chains. Specifically, as Mark Taylor describes:

The act, passed into law in the summer of 2010, requires companies whose products rely on certain minerals—tantalum, tin, tungsten (the three Ts) and gold—to file disclosures of country of origin in their annual reporting to the . . . [Securities and Exchange Commission]. Where the origin of those minerals is not known, or where those minerals originate from DRC or certain neighboring countries, the company would then be required to file an additional report—a "Conflict Minerals Report"—explaining what due diligence it has exercised on its supply chain."[124]

But as Burgis points out, many certification projects such as Dodd-Frank and others failed on their own terms: "The legislation was drafted in Congress, not Congo. It backfired. . . . When the Dodd-Frank Act passed, many buyers of Congolese minerals simply took their business elsewhere."[125] Alternatively, the transparency requirements merely spawned illegal mining activities and process documentation of dubious reliability.[126] The American Petroleum Institute has also taken legal steps to block US attempts to impose transparency regulations on oil and mining companies.[127]

The Kimberley Process Certification Scheme is a system to classify diamonds as "conflict free"; eighteen African nations are in compliance, and the United Nations claims that the scheme "has helped to reduce conflicts and civil wars and improve revenue in diamond-rich African countries."[128] Sharife and John Grobler describe the illicit activities of a Belgian diamond company in which they

> would purchase diamonds of questionable origin for little to no money in Angola, the Democratic Republic of Congo, and Zimbabwe. They would then ship the diamonds to Dubai, where they would be given certificates of mixed origin—legal under the Kimberley Process definition—and subsequently over-value the worth of those diamonds. . . . A three-month investigation into the efficiency of the international agreement designed initially to combat blood diamonds, known as the Kimberley Process Certification Scheme (KPCS), reveals that one of the most effective tactics enabling the continued looting of Africa's mineral resources is the practice of under-invoicing the value of diamonds through subsidiary companies, based in jurisdictions providing legal and financial secrecy, like Dubai. This maneuver alone has managed to subvert and cleanse several billion dollars' worth of African diamonds of questionable origin.[129]

As Sharife and Grobler point out, the inherent flaw in the Kimberley scheme is a too-narrow definition of what constitutes a "conflict" diamond. They note: "Various forms of violence, from physical to economic and social, fall outside of the Kimberley definition, including acts perpetrated by those who control the state and their corporate partners."[130] The Kimberley certification process has raised so many red flags with regard to fairness and transparency that civil society organizations have issued strenuous objections, and some high-profile advocacy organizations, such as Global Witness, have withdrawn as participants in the process altogether.[131]

Widening Instability

"Transparency" and "resource-curse" approaches provide only distorted solutions and false explanations for inequality and "development" in Africa. Not only are weak states—with neoliberal "conditionalities" imposed upon them—hamstrung in regulating corporate extraction, but the class polarization within African societies makes policy reforms driven from above increasingly bleak. African societies are not "cursed" by natural resources, but rather by imperialism, neoliberalism, and wars produced by the drive for extraction and profit.

Social justice movements and class struggle upend such upside-down terms. Resistance to labor and environmental abuses is growing. Patrick Bond writes:

> Anti-extraction campaigns by (un)civil society are the only hope for a reversal of these neocolonial relations. . . . The only encouraging signs are the myriad of challenges to extractive industries by activists who often put their bodies on the line in sites of sustained state and corporate violence like the eastern Democratic Republic of Congo, where human rights watchdogs struggle to document the murder of approximately 5 million people, Zimbabwe's Marange diamond mines, South Africa's Limpopo and Northwest Province platinum fields and the Eastern Cape's titanium-rich Xolobeni beaches, the Niger Delta's oil-soaked creeks and Chad's oilfields, Firestone's Liberian rubber plantations, Lesotho's dams supplying Johannesburg's hedonistic water consumers, and other dam displacement zones including Gibe in Ethiopia, Mphanda Nkuwa in Mozambique and Bujagali in Uganda, to name just a few.[132]

In the coming period, the heightened contradictions of the capitalist crisis of overproduction will continue to cause supply gluts, price volatility, and unemployment. As global corporations and African ruling classes attempt to resolve their crisis of profitability at the expense of the majority, working people and the poor will face deeper austerity and harsher conditions across all spheres of society. As Marxist theory shows, crisis reverberates throughout the global capitalist economy. It will be felt across Africa, as well as elsewhere, underscoring the urgency for challenges from below.

As the contradictions of this period unfold, a deepening militarization of Western imperial nations in Africa also looms on the horizon. As discussed, the natural resources "conflict trap" is in reality an expression of imperial tensions rooted in economic competition. As instability widens, so too will the imperial web of military intervention widen as well. These resource wars, driven by competition, have fueled a recent surge of military involvement in Africa by the world's largest powers, especially the United States. It is to the contours of this new militarization that we now turn.

Chapter Seven

Militarism and the Rise of AFRICOM

[Our] comprehensive strategy on Sub-Saharan Africa is based on four pillars: first, to promote opportunity and development; second, to spur economic growth, trade, and investment; third, to advance peace and security; and fourth, to strengthen democratic institutions. . . . We're also working with resource-rich nations to help make sure that their mineral and energy wealth actually improves the lives of their citizens. The days of having outsiders come and extract the wealth of Africa for themselves leaving nothing or very little behind should be over in the 21st century.

—Secretary of State Hillary Rodham Clinton, Dakar, Senegal, 2012[1]

Marxism and Imperialism

The past decade and a half has seen a dramatic rise in the level of militarization of the African continent. Much of this heightened military presence has been driven by the United States and its drive to expand imperial influence, particularly in areas surrounding the strategically critical Middle East. China and the former European colonial powers have also sought to project imperial power in Africa. The present rivalry between these major powers and the unfolding tensions on the continent are best explained by Marxist theories on imperialism.

Lenin and the other classical Marxist writers—writing mainly at the turn of the twentieth century—aimed to explain the massive arming of states, colonization, and, finally, World War I, the highest level of carnage the world had yet seen. Their goal was both to understand these dynamics in theoretical terms as well as to arm revolutionaries and the working-class movement to oppose the war. The core of the "classical" theories were shaped through debates within the Second International, the grouping of socialist organizations from the late nineteenth century up until 1914. The crux of these arguments revolved around the fundamental nature of imperialism itself: was imperial conflict transitory, or was it systemic? At the heart of these debates lay questions of the nature of the relationship between state and capital. As World War I drew closer, these arguments took on greater resonance: for those on either side of the debate, the question was far from an abstract one. At its heart lay the possibility, on the one hand, of global powers evolving into permanent peace, or, on the other, the impossibility of an end to imperialism under capitalism.

The German socialist Karl Kautsky, representing a reformist wing of the socialist movement, held the view that imperial conflicts could be overcome through disarmament, free trade, and parliamentary and diplomatic means. He argued that substituting the working class into already existing structures of power would suffice to end the growing conflicts, writing that "the proletariat" should gain "power to determine the policy of the state, to overthrow the *policy* of imperialism and substitute the policy of socialism."[2] While "deeply as we sympathise" with "the native uprisings to throw off foreign domination," Kautsky concluded that gradual change was the only hope.[3] Imperial policy was merely a passing phase on the road to peaceful coexistence among the great powers, what Kautsky would later term ultra-imperialism.

The left wing of the movement rejected this approach, insisting that imperialism was a product of the competitive nature of capitalism. Rosa Luxemburg argued that capitalism had a terminal flaw in that surplus value could only be realized outside the capitalist world—that is, through colonization, without which capitalist growth was impossible. She believed this would lead inevitably to a "string of political and social disasters and convulsions,"[4] for which socialist revolution or barbarism were the only solutions. At a conference of the Second International in 1900, she denounced "the colonial policy of the bourgeoisie [who] has no other goal than to increase profits of the capitalist class and maintain the capitalist system, squandering the blood and the product of the proletariat's labour, perpetuating countless crimes and cruelties towards the natives of the colonies conquered by armed force."[5] The debates between the left and right wings of the Second International continued up to the outbreak of World War I, when the right wing threw its support behind national rulers and the International collapsed, no longer able to sustain such contradictory positions within its ranks.

While siding with the left wing in this debate, Lenin would develop a different analysis of imperialism than Luxemburg. For Lenin—as well as his comrade Nikolai Bukharin—imperialism was not a stage of terminal collapse but rather an uneven and contradictory stage in capitalism's development. Lenin described imperialism as the "highest stage of capitalism," with tendencies toward centralization and monopoly as well as closer links between different sections of capital. Export capital was growing in importance, driving a search for investment and markets, thus heightening competition and the tendency for expanded reproduction to spill over national borders. For Lenin, these developments strengthened the role of the state in protecting "their" national capitals and the likelihood for trade wars or outright military conflict to emerge. As Lenin described, "the monopolies, which have grown out of free competition, do not eliminate the latter, but exist over and alongside, and thereby give rise to a number of very acute, intense antagonisms, frictions and conflicts."[6]

From the era of the "original" scramble for Africa of the late nineteenth and early twentieth centuries, these imperial "antagonisms" have spilled over onto the continent through colonial competition for territory and natural resources. Following World War II, superpower rivalry between the United States and the USSR developed into a struggle for political rivalries and economic advantage that frequently resulted in the arming by both sides of a host of regimes and insurgent forces. And not unlike the period of classical imperialism, the scramble for Africa today is anchored in a sharp rivalry between the United States and China.[7] The US ruling class has made it clear in no uncertain terms that this relationship threatens its interests. A Department of Defense statement from 2012 highlighted the stakes:

> In order to credibly deter potential adversaries and to prevent them from achieving their objectives, the United States must maintain its ability to project power in areas in which our access and freedom to operate are challenged. In these areas, sophisticated adversaries will use asymmetric capabilities . . . to complicate our operational calculus. States such as China . . . will continue to pursue asymmetric means to counter our power projection capabilities.[8]

This dynamic has accentuated the race to control access to resources and markets, heightening the potential for armed conflict.

In the post-9/11 era, the "war on terror" has become the umbrella under which the United States has massively expanded its military presence across Africa, most notably with the launch, in 2007, of its new US military command, AFRICOM. The United States has also advocated for a heightened multilateral presence: by the mid-2010s, over 100,000 "peacekeepers" were deployed across the continent serving on a range of missions, with Africa hosting nearly 80 percent of all UN troops.[9] The rapid build-up of this infrastructure—and the widening of the wars in the neighboring Middle East and the Gulf—has deepened imperial involvement and instability, rendering Africa a more dangerous place overall.

Cold War Imperialism in Africa

The history of US military intervention in modern Africa extends back through the twentieth century, when former colonial empires and Cold War superpowers waged proxy warfare in constantly shifting alliances and competition. Today's civil wars are the direct descendants of colonial powers, and later the United States and USSR, creating and fueling conflict through the divisions and boundaries they carved out and the rulers they supported. During the Cold War, both superpowers armed different sides of conflicts for their own ends, funneling millions to various regimes and insurgencies to cement alliances and realms of imperial influence. Meanwhile, civil wars and counterinsurgencies produced devastation on a massive scale, with deaths in the millions over this period from violence, famines, and displacement. As we have seen, far from being explained by reductionistic theories such as Paul Collier's resource-based "conflict curse," the roots of wars today lie in the historical competition between imperial powers over strategic resources and political allegiances.

In the era of independence, the world's ruling classes were compelled, by national liberation struggles in Africa and elsewhere around the globe, to grant at least a token degree of legitimacy to the new states. Thus, in the postcolonial period, imperial justifications evolved over time. Political scientist Lance Selfa has written: "As more former colonies won their independence, the ideological target shifted. Denunciations of newly independent states as 'pro-Soviet,' corrupt, [and] ungovernable and descriptions of leading nationalists as a succession of 'new Hitlers' (from Nasser to Saddam Hussein) replaced futile attempts to defend colonialism."[10] The changed landscape of imperial power likewise ushered in tactical shifts in military terms. Yet underlying the postcolonial transformations lay a marked drive for global hegemony on the part of American imperialism and a growing willingness to deploy military might to shore up its interests in Africa.

In the mid-1960s, close to half of the thirty-six states in the Organization of African Unity (founded in 1963) had formal military agreements with former imperial powers. France, for example, used outposts and infrastructure to project itself militarily in former colonies such as Mali (1960) and Congo-Brazzaville (1963). Likewise, Britain maintained military relations with new nations such as Sierra Leone, Kenya, and Nigeria. Belgium's support for the secession, under the leadership of Moise Tshombe, of the mineral-rich Katanga province in the Congo shortly after independence in 1960 ended up drawing the United States into the conflict behind the façade of the United Nations. A US State Department official highlighted that approach in Congressional testimony shortly after the murder of Patrice Lumumba in 1961, saying, "If you throw the Belgians out tomorrow . . . there just wouldn't be anything underneath . . . the problem is to find a way of substituting U.N. strength for the Belgian strength that has been in there before."[11]

In the face of a growing radicalization and mobilization against the new government, however, concerns of inter-imperial rivalry were put aside. Tshombe was mobilized to help repress the uprising: with the support of the racist regimes of South Africa and then-Rhodesia, and supported by US bombers and Belgian mercenaries, Tshombe unleashed a campaign of horror and bloodshed in late 1964. The devastation prompted an outcry of protest from many of the new national leaders across Africa, as well as leading civil rights figures in the United States, including Martin Luther King Jr.[12] General Mobutu Sese Seko took power at this time, facilitating the transition to US preeminence in the Congo, thus displacing the Belgians and ushering in a widening military presence. US intervention in the Congo became an early test case for intervention in the national liberation movements on the continent, demonstrating the potential for strategic military "involvement" to achieve defined political ends.[13]

Thus, while the Congolese example was decisive, by the early 1970s, the United States had widened its area of influence to include agreements with a number of sub-Saharan states such as Ethiopia, Liberia, South Africa, then-Dahomey (now part of Benin), Guinea, Mali, and Senegal.[14] The United States sought, in particular, to supplant the hegemony of former imperial powers in important regional centers such as Ethiopia—with its vital geopolitical position near the Middle East and the Horn of Africa—as well as Zaire. The Organization of African Unity, in response to the posture assumed by imperial nations, sought to mitigate the presence of the former colonial powers and their potentially disproportionate influence over sections of the new African ruling classes by adopting a resolution in 1963 encouraging member states to reject foreign military pacts and bases on African soil. This post-independence political context compelled a shift in the tactics of US military involvement, producing a more indirect political presence but a distinct influence nonetheless.[15] US operations took a host of forms, from training to base building to advisory support, along with clandestine activities.

Through the 1970s, the United States attempted a balancing act of containing Soviet influence with maintaining a covert military presence, building support for African moderate leaders while closing off political space for the emergence of a genuine political alternative from below. Part of this strategy included varying degrees of military and economic support for the racist regimes of Rhodesia and South Africa, while recognizing a trajectory toward their overthrow.[16] US military aid to Africa continued to rise through the Cold War era into the mid-1980s, as shown in the table below.

US Foreign Aid to Africa, 1950–1990 (in US$ thousands)[17]			
	Economic	Military	Total
1950–1955	147.0	5.7	152.7
1956–1965	2,272.0	160.2	2,432.2
1966–1975	3,610.0	384.5	3,994.5
1976–1985	11,074.0	2,317.2	13,391.2
1986–1990	19,378.0	817.2	20,195.2

During the 1980s, US President Ronald Reagan actively supported military aid for right-wing regimes and rebel groups across the continent, with Africa becoming yet another battleground for Cold War competition with the USSR. Reagan declared: "US policy will seek to limit and destabilize activities of Soviet Third World allies and clients."[18] In Angola, for example, the United States funneled aid to the National Union for the Total Independence of Angola (UNITA), rebel forces—led by Jonas Savimbi—denounced by no less than the European Parliament as a terrorist organization. UNITA was engaged in a long-running insurgency against the leftist Movimento Popular de Libertação de Angola (MPLA) government, and the United States promoted, through its support of UNITA, sabotage of the Angolan state and infrastructure.[19] The toll of imperialism in Africa under Reagan was immense. As Noam Chomsky described:

> During the Reagan years, there was a policy called constructive engagement. There was very strong opposition to apartheid. Congress even passed legislation banning aid and support for South Africa. The Reaganites had to find devious ways to get around the congressional legislation in order to in fact increase their trade with South Africa. And the reason was that

South Africa was defending itself against what was identified [in] 1988, as one of the "more notorious terrorist groups" in the world, namely Nelson Mandela's African National Congress. During those eight years, US-backed South Africa, British-backed as well, killed an estimated million and a half people just in the surrounding countries, Angola and Mozambique, putting aside what was going on in South Africa.[20]

North Africa, with its strategic importance in terms of oil resources, was, not surprisingly, an important focus for the United States and drove a sense of urgency in curtailing the independence of nations such as Libya and Egypt. A jump in military expenditures in the region took place in the context of the instability accompanying the OPEC oil price hike in the 1970s—at a time when, as David Harvey has described, "More profitable opportunities had to be sought abroad. . . . The New York investment banks looked to the US imperial tradition both to prise open new investment opportunities and to protect their foreign operations."[21] Or, as Andrew Bacevich comments, "The strategic reorientation that Reagan orchestrated encouraged the belief that military power could extend indefinitely America's profligate expenditure of energy. Simply put, the United States would rely on military might to keep order in the Gulf and maintain the flow of oil, thereby mitigating the implications of American energy dependence."[22] The reverberations of imperial policy continued to echo down through the years. The roots laid in the Cold War period in Chad, for example, had a profound effect on the civil wars in Sudan and the region more broadly. Mahmood Mamdani describes the implications of this battleground fueled by imperial rivalries, where

> the spillover from the civil war in Chad in the mid-1980s militarised Darfur. This was a direct effect of Ronald Reagan's presidency, which led to an expansion of the Cold War into this part of Africa. The expanded Cold War focused on Chad as the United States, France and Israel supported one side and Libya and the Soviet Union the other. If one side was in power in Chad the opposition crossed the border into Darfur. The direct consequence was the militarization of Darfur—Darfur was without water in the 1980s, but it was awash with AK-47s.[23]

We return to the issue of Darfur immediately below, but here it underscores the historical roots of what are often described as "local conflicts" in broader global dynamics and competition.

"Humanitarian Intervention"

The geopolitics of imperial "energy security" continued to sharpen US foreign policy after the collapse of the Soviet Union and the confirmed preeminence of US military might on the world stage. A core part of the ideological apparatus that facilitated this tactical shift was an embrace of the rhetoric of "humanitarian intervention." Without the foil of curtailing Soviet expansionism, the United States could selectively embrace this approach as a means of rehabilitating the legitimacy of Washington's military might in the wake of the Cold War and, significantly, overcoming the so-called "Vietnam Syndrome"—that is, the limits on the United States imposed by its defeat in Southeast Asia. Crises in Africa, for one, provided opportunities for the United States to intervene, albeit on a smaller scale, and thus contribute to this rehabilitation. Selfa, writing in 2002, describes this shift:

> Today US officials speak openly and unapologetically about intervening in countries around the world. This is quite a shift from the early 1970s, when the US defeat in Vietnam made politicians and generals reluctant to commit US forces to military adventures around the world. Hawks in the US military establishment mounted a decades-long drive to rehabilitate militarism and to overcome the Vietnam syndrome. During the Cold War, the traditional rationale of fighting "communism" in Nicaragua or Afghanistan justified US intervention. As the Cold War ended, another rationale emerged—policing the "New World Order" against so-called "rogue states." The Gulf War against Iraq in 1991 provided the proving ground for this new imperialist ideology. But perhaps no rationale for imperialist intervention has been more successful than the ideology of "humanitarian intervention." The rise of "humanitarian intervention" coincided with the end of the Cold War, when unparalleled US military power was seeking new justifications for its use.[24]

US intervention in Rwanda under President Bill Clinton was a critical case in point. The horrors of the Rwandan civil war of 1990–1993 between the Rwandan Armed Forces (FAR) and the Rwandan Patriotic Front (RPF) were followed by the 1994 genocide of Hutus against Tutsis. The United States, along with the United Kingdom, backed the RPF and its US-trained leader, Paul Kagame. In fact, external economic and military support from the major powers—including through proxies such as Uganda—sustained the war, even when the RPF had been significantly weakened. As Alex Gourevitch describes:

> The split external backing reflected a certain degree of great power rivalry. The old regime had been a staunch French ally in Francophone Africa. France had traditionally seen Francophone Africa as its natural reserve, had staked its position as a great power partially on its control of this region,

and the US had granted France the mission of monitoring Francophone Africa, including former Belgian colonies like Zaire, Rwanda and Burundi, against Soviet influence during the Cold War. At the end of the Cold War, there was a renegotiation of spheres of influence in Africa, and the French became pre-occupied with the "anglo-saxon conspiracy." They feared they would lose ground to the US and the UK via an expansion of Anglophone control. To a degree, events of the mid-1990s bore this out as they saw anti-French, pro-"Anglo" candidates, parties or movements emerge in nearly every Francophone country.[25]

The famine and humanitarian crisis in the aftermath of the civil war and mass refugee crisis provided the opportunity for the United States to intervene under the cover of military-established "aid" stations in the capital of Kigali. As the *New York Times* reported in 1994:

> Under the plan, several thousand troops from the United States and other countries would unload supplies and equipment at Kigali and transport them throughout the country to encourage some two million refugees to return home. "It's an excellent idea, but it's a complex idea," [Defense Secretary William] Secretary Perry told reporters. . . . "There's just an obvious advantage to being there in terms of a location and proximity to the areas where the relief is needed."[26]

That humanitarian cover allowed for the advancement of several strategic regional and tactical aims of the United States, centered around its support for Rwandan dictator Paul Kagame and particularly with regard to mineral-rich Zaire, soon to be renamed the Democratic Republic of Congo. Edward S. Herman has described the US role in no uncertain terms:

> The aim of the United States was to support Kagame's takeover, and if vast numbers of people were killed, it was a cost that we were prepared to accept. But it doesn't look good, so we have to say that we failed to intervene; we failed to stop it. Well, in fact, we not only failed to stop it, we actually supported the mass killing. . . . The United States has been the superpower that has dominated what has happened in this area in the Congo and in Rwanda.[27]

Rehabilitating the use of military power was not the only objective in Rwanda: the United States also saw an opportunity to contain its imperial rivals in Africa—in this case, France. As historian Matt Swagler writes:

> After the 1994 Rwandan genocide and civil war, the US backed the new Tutsi-led regime . . . to undermine longstanding French political and economic influence in the region. (The French had backed the previous Hutu-led regime in Rwanda.) This is why the US supported Rwandan forces when they invaded Eastern Congo and slaughtered hundreds of thousands

of Hutu refugees—some armed, but most not—in the name of protecting Tutsi survivors. Forging Rwandan allegiance, political and corporate, was far more important to the US than the lives of ordinary Hutus.[28]

Thus humanitarian intervention provided the programmatic and rhetorical means to extend and transition core aims of US imperialism from the post–Cold War era to the current "war on terror." Deployed early on in parts of Africa, as well as in Haiti, over the next few decades this approach came to typify a new form of contemporary imperialism, later deployed in the Balkans and (once again) in Haiti. For Africa, "humanitarian intervention" became a useful bridge for intervention in the post-9/11 era of war on terror.

Crisis in Darfur, Sudan, became an imperial flashpoint as a highly influential prowar movement mobilized and the US government clamored for intervention in response to civil war between Darfuri rebels and the Sudanese government. Ashley Smith writes that the pro-intervention Save Darfur Coalition (SDC), founded in 2004,

claimed that the Arab and Muslim government was intent on genocide against Blacks and Christians in Darfur. Infamously, SDC inflated the numbers of those killed in Darfur, claiming that the Sudanese government and its allied militias had killed 400,000 people in Darfur between 2003 and 2005. SDC's claim of genocide simply does not hold water. The [US] Government Accountability Office called their claims into question. The most credible study by an affiliate of the World Health Organization found only 131,000 excess deaths, most as a result of disease and malnutrition.[29]

In response to SDC lobbying and the competitive pressures of circumscribing the reach of China and its ally, Sudan, the George W. Bush administration actively intervened via the United Nations. Under the guise of humanitarian intervention, Bush pushed strenuously for UN military operations alongside troops from the African Union as well as a no-fly zone over Sudan.[30] One of the most important critiques of the strategic framework of humanitarian intervention is Mahmood Mamdani's *Saviors and Survivors: Darfur, Politics, and the War on Terror* (2009). Mamdani contends that the influential Save Darfur movement, with its loud echoes in public policy, aimed to deploy a framework of "genocide" in Darfur to facilitate the widening of intervention in Africa, "where the language of genocide has been turned into an instrument. It is where genocide has become ideological."[31] Disputing claims of the Save Darfur Coalition that the violence is "racially motivated," Mamdani argues instead that the civil war and violence emerged out of local conflicts over land as well as attempts by the national government to suppress insurgency.

Mamdani and others have described both the long history of imperial intervention in the region as well as the highly politicized nature of the turn against the Sudanese regime. Richard Seymour writes:

> The rebellion in Darfur is animated by the same issues that caused the Sudan People's Liberation Army to rise up in the south. The elite that has dominated Sudan since it was under British colonial tutelage has persistently centralised power and economic resources in the hands of a narrow Nile Valley ruling class. Darfur, when it was added to Sudan in 1916, was especially singled out for marginalisation—only the sons of chiefs were allowed to be educated, so as to prevent challenges to colonial authority. . . . By the 1970s, under the pro-US dictator Ja'far Nimeiry, the wealth of the north came to depend increasingly on redirecting oil resources from the south, especially to finance the army and repay enormous debts. To build up a support base, the regime began to make calls for sharia law, but the United States didn't care provided Chevron was allowed to drill for oil. The US did not support struggles in the south or Darfur until Hasan al-Turabi and the National Islamic Front took control of the government in 1989. Then Western attitudes changed, in large part because the new government refused to support the war on Iraq.[32]

Mamdani, for one, advocated for the use of African Union forces as an alternative to UN or NATO forces, arguing that their regional composition renders them more accountable to African interests.[33] But as socialists Avery Wear and David Whitehouse have written, the problematic nature of US influence on the character and aims of the African Union are evident: "The new . . . [African Union, or AU] charter authorized armed force against member states that violate 'democratic principles,' and the United States stepped in to offer itself as the supplier and trainer of AU forces. It has also forged closer ties with Nigeria and South Africa, the countries with the most clout in the AU—and thus the ones to determine where the AU puts its troops."[34] Not to be outdone in its widening rivalry with the United States in Africa, China pledged $100 million to fund a rapid-deployment military force under African Union auspices.[35]

The United Kingdom's Prime Minister Tony Blair forged a close alliance with the Clinton administration, while British imperialism under "New Labour"—as Zaya Yeebo points out—embraced an ideological framework of humanitarian intervention in Africa under the rubric of food and development aid.[36] Britain's military intervention into the decade-long civil war in mineral-rich Sierra Leone posed this formulation more sharply in the country's efforts to impose stability in a conflict that began, in 1991, as a "spillover" from neighboring Liberia's civil war, according to Tunde Zack-Williams.[37] In 1997, in a precursor to Blair's direct intervention in 2000 against Revolutionary United Front rebels, the British private military company Sandline International—with its connections to both the British and Sierra Leonean governments—brought in weapons and training to support ousted President Ahmed Tejan Kabbah's bid to return to power in exchange for diamond mine concessions.[38] Blair also suspended Sierra Leone from the Commonwealth of Nations—formerly the British Commonwealth, an association of mostly former colonies of Britain—and the UN-imposed sanctions in 1997. Three years later, as Niels Hahn describes,

> When the Kabbah administration faced new problems in 2000, after the . . . [Revolutionary United Front, or RUF] had taken several hundred UN military personnel as hostages in the diamond-rich Eastern province, Britain deployed around 1,000 soldiers who were directly involved in counterinsurgency activities, and the capture of RUF leader Foday Sankoh. This intervention took place shortly after Tony Blair had introduced his "Doctrine of the International Community" in relation to the bombardment of Kosovo in 1999, which seeks to justify military intervention in the name of human rights, democracy and free trade. As in the case of Kosovo, the intervention in Sierra Leone was described as a "humanitarian intervention", and the notion of "blood diamonds" became a powerful instrument to denounce the atrocities committed by the opposition to Kabbah's administration.[39]

Michael Kargbo notes approvingly:

> British peacebuilding activities in Sierra Leone have been considered a model for peacebuilding activities elsewhere. Sierra Leone could be referred to as a policy lab for the testing of the new thinking in Whitehall's international development and conflict management strategies. . . . On balance British policy objectives have broadly helped consolidate peace and democracy in Sierra Leone.[40]

However, as Jimmy Kandeh points out in the same volume, "the international community, especially international financial institutions like the IMF who prioritize the correction of macroeconomic imbalances over social policy, may be unwittingly contributing to recreating the conditions that led to armed conflict in Sierra Leone."[41] The 1991–2002 civil war resulted in 70,000 deaths and 2.6 million people displaced.[42]

"Humanitarian" military intervention in Somalia, the Democratic Republic of Congo, Darfur, and beyond contributed to tempering left-wing opposition by building traction around the idea that military force could be deployed for good. As a result, the unconditional anti-imperialism that characterized the left of the Vietnam War era was effectively disarmed in the years prior to 9/11, in advance of the more "robust" imperialism of the major wars in Afghanistan and Iraq of the twenty-first century. Recruiting liberal support for such projects has been central to rehabilitating imperialism in a range of guises—an end that furthers neither the interests of ordinary Africans nor the potential for international solidarity and broad anti-imperialism. As Wear and Whitehouse conclude:

> The exploited and oppressed of Africa don't need an American movement built on illusions in the charitable intentions of US power. They need anti-imperial allies. They need us to hold back the US and give them a breathing space to identify and defeat their oppressors at home. That's what's missing from the liberal case—the idea that the downtrodden might be able to liberate themselves.[43]

Somalia and Operation Restore Hope[44]

To give food aid to a country just because they are starving is a pretty weak reason.[45]

—Secretary of State Henry Kissinger (1974)

The invasion of Somalia in 1992 became a template for the potential for US forces to be deployed for humanitarian ends. Continuing US President George Bush Sr.'s "Operation Restore Hope," President Bill Clinton declared US military engagement in Somalia could alleviate famine and uproot warlordism. Indeed, Operation Restore Hope in Somalia was intended to bury for good the Vietnam War syndrome. One commentator captured the US policy perspective at the time, saying: "Certainly, Somalia—a 'poor,' 'backward' country at the edge of Africa—would seem an excellent place to practice this new form of aggressive intervention. The situation in Somalia offers an entire country in which to practice drawing the lines of new world order."[46] The goal of refurbishing the US global image came at the expense of millions of ordinary Somalis, who were killed or displaced in a decades-long civil war in one of the most war-torn regions in the world.

The roots of the 1992 invasion stretch back to the Cold War era. Somalia was a longtime recipient of US aid, especially military funding, during the 1970s and the 1980s. In the early years of the Cold War, Somalia had been a client state of the USSR, while the United States supported the regime of King Haile Selassie in rival Ethiopia. Following Selassie's overthrow in 1974, the superpowers switched sides, and the United States shifted its backing to Somalia's dictator Siad Barre. The United States had clear strategic objectives in positioning itself in this Cold War battleground. Despite American support for Barre, Ethiopia was the key prize of the region, driving US–USSR hostilities in the Horn of Africa.

The global military competition between the United States and the USSR led to a period of escalating tensions between the superpowers, with one flashpoint being the Somali invasion of eastern Ethiopia in 1977 to gain control of the Somali-speaking Ogaden region. In response, the Soviet Union airlifted 20,000 Cuban troops to Ethiopia to fend off the attack, providing an opportunity for the United States to tilt toward Somalia and shore up a new client in the region. On the heels of the crisis, President Jimmy Carter withdrew the Strategic Arms Limitation Talks (SALT II) treaty from consideration in Congress. "SALT lies buried in the sands of the Ogaden," his National Security Advisor Zbigniew Brzezinski commented, signaling the end of detente and the return of Cold War.[47] Despite Barre's horrific human rights record, by 1980, Carter—the heralded human rights president—had signed an agreement with Somalia that gave the US military bases and access to the port of Berbera on the Gulf of Aden in return for millions in military aid to the Somali government. The United States was "eager for a strategic outpost near the Arabian oil fields," wrote *Time* magazine. "For the next 10 years, the US poured hundreds of millions of dollars into arming the country."[48] Beyond the geostrategic importance of Somalia's location along the Gulf of Aden—in proximity to the Red Sea and Suez Canal—US priorities were driven by oil interests. Exploration in Somalia began in the 1980s, with oil corporations such as the US-owned Conoco securing contracts under Barre worth potentially billions of dollars.[49]

Somalia was food self-sufficient until the late 1970s despite drought conditions, but global financial policy forced down wages and hiked costs for farmers, helping to pave the way for civil war in 1988.[50] Beginning in 1977, the IMF had demanded stringent neoliberal measures in Somalia—in return for loans, the government forced through privatization and slashed government spending and wage subsidies. In a period of five years, per capita gross national product dropped from an already low $250 annually to $170.[51] A decade of military aid and structural adjustment programs sowed the seeds for desperate crisis. Arms money and IMF policies severely weakened Somalia's economy—and, combined with drought conditions, laid the basis for civil war.

By 1991, Somalia was in the grips of a devastating famine that had taken 300,000 lives. By late 1991, UN officials estimated that 4.5 million Somalis—approximately 60 percent of the population—faced starvation.[52] Up to 25 percent of Somalia's children under five had died, according to Doctors Without Borders.[53] Meanwhile, the United States had begun to withdraw aid from Barre, who was eventually overthrown in 1991. With the break-up of the USSR that same year, precipitating a collapse in Soviet aid to Ethiopia, the United States saw an opportunity to cement a client relationship with the chief power in the Horn of Africa. Amid the crisis in Somalia, the United States cynically cast about for an ally that would better serve its interests.

In the wake of Barre's ouster, the United States donned the cloak of humanitarianism, citing the famine as justification for military intervention. Significantly, the most severe period of the famine had passed several months before the United States declared its commitment to ending hunger in Somalia. In 1992—on the eve of the invasion—the death rate had fallen by 90 percent.[54] The senior George Bush set the stage for the invasion by claiming that donated food supplies were being stolen by "warlords" and that Somalis needed US military protection to make sure food was distributed. In late 1992, the UN Security Council passed a resolution authorizing a US-led coalition of troops, known as UNITAF, to provide "humanitarian relief." Troops landed in Somalia early the following year in the intervention called "Operation Restore Hope."

Operation Restore Hope was, to say the very least, a misnomer. As Rakiya Omaar and Alex de Waal wrote in 1993: "If we turned back the clock a few weeks, we would see a Somalia lit up with many signs of hope. Throughout the country, ordinary Somalis were taking the initiative to bring the future of their country under control. . . . A series of local agreements were making it possible for emergency relief to be delivered in a way unprecedented in the last year."[55]

But positive developments in Somalia went by the wayside once US boots hit the ground. "Fighting the warlords" became the new call to action. The victor over Barre, General Mohamed Ali Farah Aidid, wasn't willing to make deals with the United States. Soon after the invasion, food distribution was undermined by US determination to rout Aidid by boosting forces, such as the self-declared President Ali Mahdi Muhammad, loyal to the West. As Stephen Zunes described:

> Their role escalated to attempts at disarming warlords, including armed assaults in crowded urban neighborhoods. This "mission creep" resulted in American casualties, creating growing dissent at home in what had originally been a widely supported foreign policy initiative. The thousands of M-16 rifles sent, courtesy of the American taxpayer, to Barre's armed forces were now in the hands of rival militiamen, who had not only used them to kill fellow countrymen and to disrupt the distribution of relief supplies, but were now using them against American troops.[56]

Soldiers were heard repeating the slogan "The only good Somali is a dead Somali." It had become apparent that the United States had badly underestimated the resistance. The United States was the leading force in the UN deployment, and it carried out increasingly aggressive assaults, culminating in the battle in the Somali capital of Mogadishu in October 1993 depicted in the film *Black Hawk Down*. Eighteen American soldiers were killed— and approximately 1,000 Somalis, though that fact escaped the attention of the US media, which devoted endless airtime to images of an American soldier's body being dragged through the city streets.

Three months earlier, a missile attack by US helicopters had killed fifty to seventy clan elders and intellectuals, many of them moderates attempting to broker a settlement to end the war. According to the *New York Times*, US officials estimated casualties of 6,000 to 10,000 Somalis—two-thirds of them women and children—in the summer of 1993 alone. In fact, unarmed men, women, and children became open targets for American troops. Richard Dowden, in Britain's *Independent* newspaper, described how "in one incident, Rangers took a family hostage. When one of the women started screaming at the Americans, she was shot dead. In another incident, a Somali prisoner was allegedly shot dead when he refused to stop praying outside. Another was clubbed into silence."[57] After the so-called Battle of Mogadishu concluded, Canada, Belgium, and Italy all investigated charges of torture and murder committed by their troops, but the United States never issued a reprimand or even an inquiry. The trials in Belgium uncovered horrific evidence of abuse, including a sergeant accused of force-feeding a Muslim Somali child with pork and salted water until he vomited and a sergeant major photographed urinating on the apparently dead body of a young man.[58]

In the end, as Mitchel Cohen writes,

> of the $1.5 billion earmarked by the United Nations for Somalia in 1993, only ten percent of that amount was allocated for "humanitarian" work. More than 28,000 troops occupied Somalia. The US/U.N. deployment included over 100 tanks and armored vehicles, attack helicopters, airborne gunships and an aircraft carrier. General Colin Powell approvingly called Operation Restore Hope "a paid political advertisement" for maintaining the Bush/Clinton $1.4 trillion four-year military budget.[59]

President Clinton eventually withdrew all troops by March 1994, and remaining UN peacekeeping forces were pulled out the next year.

Yet despite the widely perceived failure of the invasion, so-called humanitarian intervention was successfully deployed to justify ramped-up defense spending and military preparedness for expanded incursions in different parts of the globe. Despite the trajectory of the uses of militarized humanitarianism, important liberal figures failed to denounce the invasion in Somalia. For example, TransAfrica Executive Director Randall Robinson, US Representative John Lewis, and several Black Democratic officials called "for US military forces to maintain order in the famine-stricken African country until an effective government can be established."[60] Accompanying this embrace was a new expansion of government contracts for "humanitarian relief" agencies. As Somalia expert de Waal put it, "Somalia is a striking manifestation of a new doctrine in international affairs, which we might call 'humanitarian impunity.' . . . Aid-givers and peacekeepers, not local civilians, are becoming the beneficiaries of international law."[61] All told, approximately forty "peacekeeping" operations in the 1990s alone followed the Somalia intervention.

That intervention left the country decidedly worse off. Somalia consistently ranks near or at the bottom of virtually all human development measurements, from life expectancy to infant mortality. Since 1991, the country has been wracked by civil war, fueled by US support for various sides in the conflict. In 2006, when neighboring Ethiopia launched a brutal invasion of Somalia, US backing and funding for Ethiopian forces was a barely concealed secret.[62] Despite the depths of humanitarian crisis in Somalia today, the chief contribution on offer from the United States continues to be military aid for the Somali government's "war on terror" against the al-Shabab organization. As Somali author Nuruddin Farah wrote in 2002, as the so-called US war on global terror began to pick up speed, "The United States and its allies, having long remained impervious to the ruin of Somalia, must think hard now about firing a missile or mounting an invasion, and so bringing more pain to a land that has not enjoyed peace for . . . decades."[63] The cloak of the US military intervention of 1992–1993 soon proved there is no humanity in "humanitarian" interventions.

Opposite: Map of US military bases and installations in Africa[64]

Key bases for US military operations in Africa

Major Hubs for US Personnel & Operations

★ **US-AFRICOM HQ / KELLEY BARRACKS**
Stutgart, Germany

Ⓐ **US-ARAF HQ / CAMP EDERLE**
Vicenza, Italy

Ⓑ **CAMP LEMONNIER**
Djibouti-Ambouli International Airport, Djibouti

Bases for Surveillance &/or Attack Drones

① **NAVAL AIR STATION SIGONELLA**
Sicily, Italy

② **KASSERINE DRONE BASE**
Kasserine, Tunisia

③ **CHABELLEY AIRFIELD**
Chabelley, Djibouti

④ **OUAGADOUGOU AIRPORT**
Ouagadougou, Burkina Faso

⑤ **BASE AÉRIENNE 101 NIAMEY**
Diori Hamani International Airport, Niamey, Niger

⑥ **BASE AÉRIENNE 201**
Manu Dayak Airport, Agadez, Niger

⑦ **CAMP TASSONE**
N'Djamena International Airport, N'Djamena, Chad

⑧ **GAROUA INTERNATIONAL AIRPORT**
Garoua, Cameroon

⑨ **ASCENSION AUXILIARY AIRFIELD**
St. Helena, Ascension & Tristan da Cunha (UK)

⑩ **SEYCHELLES DRONE BASE**
Seychelles International Airport, Seychelles

⑪ **BALEDOGLE AIRFIELD**
Baledogle, Somalia

⑫ **KISMAYO AIRPORT**
Kismayo, Somalia

⑬ **CAMP SIMBA**
Manda Bay, Kenya

Other US Outposts / Presence

⑭ **ATAR AIR BASE (INACTIVE DRONE BASE)**
Nouakchott, Mauritania

⑮ **DAKAR OUTPOST**
Dakar, Senegal

⑯ **ARMED FORCES TRAINING CENTER**
Hastings, Sierra Leone

⑰ **BARCLAY TRAINING CENTER**
Monrovia, Liberia

⑱ **BANGUI**
Bangui, Central African Republic

⑲ **DJEMA**
Djema, Central African Republic

⑳ **NZARA AIRFIELD**
Nzara, South Sudan

㉑ **CAMP DUNGU**
Dungu, Democratic Republic of the Congo

㉒ **ARBA MINCH AIRPORT (INACTIVE DRONE BASE)**
Arba Minch, Ethiopia

㉓ **CAMP GILBERT**
Dire Dawa, Ethiopia

㉔ **NAKASONGOLA AIRPORT**
Nakasongola, Uganda

㉕ **UGANDA ARMY AIR BASE**
Entebbe, Uganda

㉖ **CAMP SINGO**
Singo, Uganda

㉗ **BUJUMBURA OUTPOST**
Bujumbura, Burundi

㉘ **LEOPARD VALLEY BASE**
Windhoek, Namibia

㉙ **GABRONE AIRBASE**
Gabrone, Botswana

㉚ **LUSAKA OUTPOST**
Lusaka, Zambia

㉛ **US NAVAL MEDICAL RESEARCH UNIT NO. 3**
Cairo, Egypt

㉜ **GARISSA MILITARY CAMP**
Garissa, Kenya

㉝ **MOMBASA AIRPORT / SEAPORT**
Mombasa, Kenya

㉞ **NAVAL SUPPORT FACILITY DIEGO GARCIA**
Diego Garcia, British Indian Ocean Territory (UK)

African states in which the US has conducted military staging, exercises, or operations since October 2008 (AFRICOM activation)

Note: "Other bases" refer to a variety of facilities. The range includes fuel depots and larger posts from which forces can be deployed. As with most of the drone bases, these bases belong to ally states with which the US has agreements to use their facilities.

Map created by Aarón Martel and Khury Petersen-Smith, based on 2017 data, for this volume.

The Birth of AFRICOM

The big picture remains the Pentagon's Africom spreading its militarized tentacles against the lure of Chinese soft power in Africa, which goes something like this: in exchange for oil and minerals, we build anything you want, and we don't try to sell you "democracy for dummies." The Bush administration woke up to this threat a bit too late—at Africom's birth in 2008. Under the Obama administration, the mood is total panic. For Petraeus, the only thing that matters is "the long war" on steroids—from boots on the ground to armies of drones; and who are the Pentagon, the White House and the State Department to disagree?

—Pepe Escobar[65]

Since the closing years of the twentieth century, economic and strategic goals have driven a new militarization in Africa and the dominance of the "war on terror" framework for imperial aims on the continent. As in the Middle East, promoting "democracy" has provided a useful pretext for military intervention. As former US Vice President Dick Cheney once observed at an oil industry conference, "the good Lord didn't see fit to put oil and gas reserves where there are democratic governments."[66] From the perspective of political stability, key regions of the continent present challenges and contradictions for the United States in the recent scramble for African resources. In the broadest terms, US officials fear instability could threaten strategic control over the region's oil and minerals. As Africa began to draw heightened attention and interest at the turn of the millennium, State Department officials, the Pentagon, and industry heads likewise sought a coherent policy balancing investment opportunities and "security risks."[67]

As elsewhere in the world, the "war on terror" provided a key ideological framework for US ruling-class strategy in confronting these obstacles, while Africa's proximity to the Middle East and large Muslim populations made that project all the more critical. Having launched wars in Iraq and Afghanistan, the administration of President George W. Bush came to view the African landscape as an opportunity to secure greater "energy security" beyond the Middle East and to challenge China's rising influence on the continent. Asserting this role for the United States was not without its complications; for one, ongoing insurgency in places like Nigeria, as well as protracted civil wars in the Horn of Africa and the Great Lakes region, presented challenges in terms of political stability. Nonetheless, a bulked-up US military force could now be deployed in Africa to play a critical role under the new rubric of a global war on terror.

The Clinton administration first designated a "terror" target in Africa, dropping bombs on the Sudanese Al-Shifa pharmaceutical factory in Khartoum in 1998 to underscore the point. The following year, Secretary of State Madeleine Albright stated, "Africa is a major battleground in the global fight against terror, crime, drugs, illicit arms-trafficking, and disease"[68]— echoing the narrative of "failed states" and their supposed proliferation in Africa. Yet it was under Bush that this agenda for Africa was more fully elaborated, with a number of anti-terrorism initiatives, such as the Eastern Africa Counter-Terrorism initiative, launched in 2005, focused on Kenya, Ethiopia, Uganda, Tanzania, Eritrea, and Djibouti, and the 2002 Pan-Sahel Initiative— later to become the Trans-Sahara Counterterrorism Initiative—for Mali, Mauritania, Chad, and Niger. The impact of these initiatives soon made themselves felt: historian David Gutelius argued that Bush administration "mismanagement of the war on terror has deeply undermined stability across Africa in the past year. In its African incarnation, that war has managed to produce almost exactly the opposite of what was intended. US foreign policy in Africa has inspired radicalism, discredited moderate African Muslims, and fomented political instability in key nations."[69]

The early years of the new millennium marked a pivotal turn for US foreign policy and military strategy for Africa, and spending on military operations on the continent doubled in the four years after September 11 compared to the four years preceding it.[70] Accompanying this revised assessment of Africa's strategic importance and risks came new exhortations for African states to "do their part," where a neoliberalized militarism took the form of a call for "partnership" in the war on terror. In fact, as described by the Council on Foreign Affairs, "partnership peacekeeping has become the norm."[71] Secretary of Defense Paul Wolfowitz declared in 2004, "I believe that strengthening institutions in Africa has got to be the key to moving forward" because of the imperative for African states to join the fight "against the scourge of global terrorism."[72] Or, as Giles Mohan and Tunde Zack-Williams have described, this imperial posture becomes one of "giving back ownership of conflict resolution."[73] Notwithstanding the embrace of "agency" on the part of African states, "peacekeeping" forces were funded and deployed to protect and extend US interests.

A key strategic advance for the Bush administration was the launching of the Africa Command, known as AFRICOM, in 2007. Although based in Stuttgart, Germany, the inauguration of the command reflected a decisive attempt to project imperial interests onto the continent by more coherently extending strategic and tactical military initiatives while heightening opportunities for military flexibility. As Nunu Kidane describes, "If you're thinking traditional bases with thousands of military personnel, think again. General Kip Ward has said it is not about 'bases' and 'garrisons' but rather a network of sophisticated military operations strategically placed throughout the continent which can be moved around and utilized for any purpose."[74] At an AFRICOM conference held in early 2008 at Fort McNair, Vice Admiral Robert T. Moeller, the head of AFRICOM, declared, "Protecting the free flow of natural resources from Africa to the global market is one of AFRICOM's guiding principles," and cited "oil disruption," "terrorism," and China's rise as a major competitor to the United States in Africa.[75] A number of African nations refused to consider an AFRICOM base on their soil. However, in 2003, the same year as the US invasion and occupation of Iraq, the US military built a base in the strategic location of Djibouti, a tiny country next to Somalia and across the Red Sea from Yemen. As Rear Admiral Richard Hunt, the commander of the Combined Joint Task Force–Horn of Africa at Djibouti's Camp Lemonnier—the site of a former French Foreign Legion base—ominously declared: "Africa is the new frontier that we need to engage now, or we are going to end up doing it later in a very negative way."[76]

US policy under Bush had a concerted focus on the Horn of Africa region, elevating Ethiopia, in particular, as a crucial partner in counterterrorism. The Horn of Africa has been characterized by a Council on Foreign Relations publication as the "hottest conflict zone" in the world.[77] The December 2006 invasion of Somalia by Ethiopia and the toppling of the Islamic Court–led government marked a critical advance on the part of the United States in attempting to assert control in the region. The United States used Camp Lemonnier to train Ethiopian forces in the lead-up to the brutal invasion and conducted periodic air strikes against so-called terrorist camps.[78] The US offensive against the Islamic Courts Union government, according to John Pendergast and Colin Thomas-Jensen, also included "funding . . . warlords to pursue terrorists on its behalf."[79]

In contrast, the United States denied Somalia the humanitarian assistance it extended to other countries in the region.[80] The immediate impact of the invasion and the toppling of the Islamic Courts was horrific. Pendergast and Thomas-Jensen continue: "The Courts had brought [relative] peace and stability, and their defeat . . . returned Mogadishu to the warlords . . . of the past two decades."[81] According to Amnesty International, "some 6,000 civilians were reportedly killed in fighting in the capital Mogadishu and across southern and central Somalia in 2007, and over 600,000 Somali civilians were internally displaced from and around Mogadishu. In addition, an estimated 335,000 Somali refugees fled Somalia in 2007."[82] In the long term, the invasion injected a higher degree of instability into the Somalia-Ethiopia-Kenya region that would reverberate throughout the decade to follow.

"Unofficial" military forces also rose to prominence in Africa under the auspices of the Bush administration, including well-connected military contractors providing training and paramilitary and logistical "support" to African militaries.[83] At the military base in Djibouti, the United States arguably is modeling another role in the "war on terror" through the implementation of public works projects—what Nicholas Kristof of the *New York Times* has called a "softer touch" utilizing "aid workers with guns," in which US troops pitch in during natural disasters, dig wells, and build hospitals.[84] This supposed "soft" approach is but one strand in the web of political, economic, and military relations drawing US policymakers closer to their African allies and designed to ease the interjection of military power. Via this approach, AFRICOM officials were able to build a wide ring of US military bases operating across the continent, trained on counterterror, "instability," and "insurgency"—that is, forces perceived as threats to capital accumulation and the forging of crucial alliances. Properly understood, for imperial rulers and those they represent, those threats are not only those posed by the widening war on terror, but also the struggles and aspirations of struggles from below.

Secret Bases and Drone Warfare: Obama in Africa

Part of having a credible American leader again who is unimplicated with the war in Iraq who is very attractive to people around the world, is to somehow use that early wind at his back to try to extract commitments to patrol the commons, to actually deal with these broken people and broken places.

—Samantha Power, then US Ambassador to the United Nations[85]

George W. Bush's launch of AFRICOM represented a critical advance of US power into Africa. The Obama administration extended, and deepened, that military involvement still further. Intensified imperial competition with China in Africa, and other powers such as Russia, fueled higher levels of US military deployment on the continent. A vast network of military bases, covert operations, and thousands of Western-funded troops pointed to the unavoidable conclusion that the Obama years produced, in essence, a US war in Africa.

The scale of military intervention made a decisive jump during Obama's tenure, with a 200 percent increase in military missions[86] as well as a widening presence of Defense Department staff into State Department realms. For example, Camp Lemonnier became host to 2,000 military personnel, while US Department of Defense staff were assigned to US embassies across Africa.[87] This widening presence reflected an enlarged scope of anti-terror activities. As Daniel Volman writes:

> The continuity with Bush administration policy is especially evident in several key regions. In Somalia, for example, the Obama administration has provided some US$20 million worth of arms to the Transitional Federal Government.... Furthermore, President Obama has continued the program initiated by the Bush administration to assassinate alleged al-Qaeda leaders in Somalia and, in August 2009, he authorized an attack by US Special Forces units that killed Saleh Ali Saleh Nabhan, who was accused of being involved in the bombing of the US embassies in Kenya and Tanzania by al-Qaeda in August 1998. In the Sahel, the Obama administration has also sought increased funding for the Trans-Saharan Counter-Terrorism Program (US$20 million in 2010) and begun a special security assistance program for Mali to provide the country with some US$5 million of all-terrain vehicles and communications equipment. Administration officials have justified this escalating military involvement in the Trans-Saharan region by arguing that the increasing involvement of al-Qaeda in the Islamic Maghreb in criminal activity (including kidnapping for ransom and drug-trafficking) constitutes a growing threat to US interests in this resource-rich area.[88]

Alex Kane makes a similar point, commenting: "The intensification of the global 'war on terror' has continued apace during Obama's second term. One front the administration has focused on more intently is Africa, specifically the northern region and what is known as the Sahel—the narrow strip of land that stretches across countries such as Mali, Algeria, Niger and Chad."[89]

Emphasizing programmatic continuity with Bush administration policy, the Obama administration pivoted global imperial strategy away from "boots on the ground" and toward so-called "alliance-building"—that is, cementing US indispensability to African political stability in areas critical to its geostrategic interests. A Pentagon document in 2012 heralded "working with allies and partners to establish control over ungoverned territories."[90] However, intrinsic to this approach is the understanding that the United States can use wide flexibility to operationalize this aim, with an increasingly active and direct military role under the rubric of "partnership." As Obama's commander for US Army Africa, David R. Hogg, characterized the approach: "We are here to enable, where wanted, the African forces to figure out and solve their own problems."[91]

In this period, increased global support for the State Department and programs such as USAID was paired with higher levels of defense spending, even as Obama declared that he would completely withdraw US troops from Iraq and Afghanistan—a promise broken well before the end of his tenure.

The United States relies on key allies to further its aims as proxies on the ground. Ugandan President Yoweri Museveni, for example, established even greater importance for himself during the course of the Obama administration as a lynchpin to the US strategy for stability in the East Africa and Great Lakes region. Several dynamics underscore the importance of this relationship: for one, oil discoveries—proven but not yet procured—in East Africa and the Great Lakes region elevate their strategic value to imperial interests. As we have seen, oil discoveries have markedly heightened competition in these areas and placed increased value on tamping down insurgency. But Uganda also plays a crucial role as a proxy force and base of operations for the United States further afield. Chiefly, Uganda has played an important role in US designs for regional stability, meaning establishing a network of pro-US client states and a predictable status quo. An important example of this relationship is Uganda's intervention in Somalia under the auspices of African Union troops deployed to back up the US-supported Somali government. As Mamdani has commented: "Somalia is Uganda's claim that we have a solution for your security concerns in the region. It fits very nicely with the American claim that the primary problem of Africa is not development, nor democracy, nor even the lack of human rights, but security."[92] Likewise, as Angelo Izama describes,

> Museveni epitomizes a generic formulation within Western foreign policy making in Africa dating back to the cold war, where strong (pro-western) leaders are supported as anchorage for a wide range of interests centered on security and stability. . . . Kampala is the political equivalent of a brokerage firm for rebels, rebellions and peace missions. It has more troops abroad than any other country aside from the United States itself. The head of that firm is Mr. Museveni. The West is his biggest client with a resource hungry China waiting anxiously outside.[93]

The hunt for the insurgent Lords' Resistance Army (LRA) leader Joseph Kony served as the auspices under which a small number of US troops, along with US-trained regional forces, have inserted themselves militarily in the region. The LRA was founded in 1988 among the oppressed Acholi people in northern Uganda and southern Sudan in response to occupation and subjugation by Museveni's army. As David Whitehouse describes, "in response to . . . the LRA insurgency, Museveni intensified repressive measures against civilians. In the mid-1990s, the . . . [National Resistance Army] forcibly relocated most rural Acholis to concentration camps amid allegations of summary executions and the destruction of entire villages."[94] The LRA, in turn, has been responsible for the displacement of thousands and the recruitment of child soldiers in the course of its insurgency against the Ugandan government.

The Kony 2012 campaign, driven by the US-based—and right-wing funded—Invisible Children, put out a dramatic call for a "grassroots" movement to bring Kony to justice and compel the West to save Africans from themselves.[95] Their infamous "Kony 2012" video—which went viral, with over 100 million views—brought global media attention to the LRA. However, revelations of Invisible Children's and founder Jason Russell's right-wing backers threw the human rights focus of the campaign into question. Worse, by resurrecting a "white man's burden" in modern form, it became a humanitarian cover for the Obama administration to intervene in support of a critical regional ally.

Citing the 2005 arrest warrant issued for Kony by the International Criminal Court for war crimes and crimes against humanity, in 2011 Obama announced he would send 100 troops to Uganda to "remove" Kony "from the battlefield."[96] But this announcement of a mere 100 troops papered over widening military operations in East Africa in the form of a $45 million military aid package that year alone, including four drones.[97] The following year, the African Union announced it was moving a 5,000-strong force into the region, with backing from the European Union. Yet US declarations notwithstanding, prior to intervening militarily, the LRA had been routed from Uganda and reduced from 10,000 at its height to a small force of several hundred moving between the Central African Republic, the Congo, and South Sudan, and posed little threat to the Ugandan government.[98]

Joseph Kony's human rights record has undoubtedly been a long and sordid one.[99] Yet the record of the chief US partner, Museveni, is arguably much worse. Not unlike the beneficiaries of US partnership elsewhere in Africa and globally, criticisms of the Museveni government record have been largely muted on the part of Western leaders. A *Guardian* profile characterized the Museveni regime as "a constitutional dictatorship, with a rubber stamp parliament, powerless judiciary, censored media and heavily militarized civil institutions" marked by "the harassment of Museveni's political opponents, detention without trial, torture, extrajudicial killings, suppression of protests and homophobic witch-hunts."[100] Museveni rose to power in the wake of a brutal civil war that followed the overthrow of dictator Idi Amin, a war that lasted from 1979 to 1986, during which 500,000 people were killed. Amin himself was ushered in with the support of foreign powers in his coup in 1971 against President Milton Obote, who had drawn hostility from imperial governments for his nationalization of British companies after independence. Pat Hutton and Jonathan Bloch write:

> The Israelis had clearly been cultivating Amin for some time through their military presence in a manner consistent with their role as US proxies. These times were the heyday of the CIA's worldwide efforts to subvert radical regimes and in Africa to assert the predominance of the United States as far as possible. Active in Kenya, Ghana, Mozambique, Tanzania, and Nigeria, the United States was also seeking to gain influence in Uganda, especially by means of intelligence officers of the navy and air force based in Kampala, together with the CIA agents working under the cover of USAID.[101]

It has been estimated that Idi Amin's terror was responsible for the loss of life of 100,000 Ugandans.

Museveni's regime has been a long-standing recipient of US military assistance, of which the suppression of the LRA is but one component. Museveni's war against the people of Northern Uganda has been brutal, driving nearly 2 million into what were essentially concentration camps in the mid-1990s;[102] according to the World Health Organization, a thousand people a week perished in these conditions.[103] In 2008, in a dress rehearsal for Obama's later campaign, AFRICOM allocated $1 million for "Operation Lightning Thunder," a multinational pursuit of the LRA on the part of Ugandan, Congolese, and South Sudanese forces into the Democratic Republic of Congo, where the LRA was based at the time. The results were disastrous for ordinary people in the region: over 1,000 people were killed and up to 200,000 displaced, with documentation of widespread use of rape, torture, and looting of natural resources.[104]

As part of the hunt for Kony, the United States has also partnered with "unsavory" forces from a base in the northern Central African Republic—as characterized by journalist Craig Whitlock, "working closely with Muslim rebels—known as Seleka—who toppled the central government two years ago and triggered a still-raging sectarian war with a campaign of mass rapes and executions."[105] The Kony campaign provided a humanitarian veneer for wider intervention in the region, embraced not only by Western officials but also some organizations that likewise provided a liberal cover to the operation. Human Rights Watch, for example, supported heightened involvement in the region, citing rising LRA attacks, and "called on the US advisers to develop concrete measures to protect civilians from retaliatory attacks by the LRA as part of the joint military planning."[106] Yet this cover provides a toehold that further strengthens imperial projection into the region more broadly via proxy forces. Thus, not only has the United States created the conditions in which Uganda served as willing supplier of African Union troops in support of the US-backed Somali government, but it provides further momentum for growing amounts of military aid to other major allies such as Kenya and Ethiopia, which host military outposts and drone bases.[107] The United States also armed and trained forces in Kenya on Somalia's border, facilitating Kenya's ability to launch incursions against the Somali insurgency al-Shabab and fueling a destabilizing refugee on the border, with half a million Somali refugees at the al-Daadab camp alone. The self-serving ends, and the price tag in human terms, of US imperial policy are difficult to avoid. As Antoine Roger Lokongo asked shortly after Obama's launch of the Kony campaign,

> Why now, when in the Congo the worst atrocities occur daily, committed by militias far more brutal than the LRA, which were created and sustained by Uganda's Museveni and Rwanda's Kagame? These two US-backed dictators have been able to siphon billions of dollars of Congo's wealth by sponsoring mayhem—massacres, mass rapes and mutilations—in the vast country through their allied militias. . . . Several UN reports have used the word "genocide" in Congo. Why is Obama not lifting a finger to punish those responsible for crimes against humanity in Congo? Isn't it because he is shielding Museveni and Kagame from accountability?[108]

Beyond a heightened reliance on proxy warfare under Obama, the shift in strategy meant that aerial campaigns, proxy warfare, and indirect support became increasingly crucial. The Libya bombing campaign by NATO, for example, became a potential model for future interventions and regime change in Africa, as well as an opportunity to gain strategic advantage over its rivals (in this case, China). In Libya, China controlled a sizeable portion of oil contracts before Muammar Gaddafi's fall, but the terrain transformed dramatically after NATO intervention. As David Axe of *Wired*, a frequent writer on security in Africa, has commented, this is "the US military's 'offshore balancing' strategy, . . . an approach meant to minimize long-term deployments of large ground armies by emphasizing air and naval forces working in conjunction with local and regional 'proxy' armies. . . . Full-scale interventions like Afghanistan are probably a thing of the past. Somalia-style, 'hands-off' campaigns are the future."[109]

As part of this process, Obama made a tactical turn toward heavier reliance on drone warfare and Special Ops. As Jeremy Scahill has described in *Dirty Wars: The World Is a Battlefield* (2013), Obama's defense strategy worldwide spawned a vast infrastructure of clandestine operations, along with an array of new government agencies tasked with carrying the torch in the war on terror's secret machinations.[110] Investigative reporting by Scahill also uncovered a secret US campaign in Somalia against so-called Islamic terrorists al-Shabab, complete with interrogation chambers, CIA surveillance, drone attacks, and Special Forces.[111] Whitlock has likewise documented the rapidly expanding military footprint in Africa, with its vast network of surveillance operations, outposts, and bases and an increasing reliance on Special Operations forces during Obama's tenure. Writing in 2012, he characterized this expansion as "part of a growing shadow war against al-Qaeda affiliates and other militant groups. The surveillance is overseen by US Special Operations forces but relies heavily on private military contractors and support from African troops."[112]

Clandestine as they may be, the size and reach of these projects has been immense. Journalist Nick Turse has amassed a vast array of documentation on the scope of this "pivot to Africa" and its key operations, such as the NATO war on Libya, expanded drone operations, and a US Navy flotilla in the Indian Ocean. Other "regional enemies" include al-Qaeda in the Islamic Maghreb and Boko Haram, based in Nigeria. Turse has engaged in determined efforts to establish exactly the scale of this involvement, concluding that in fiscal year 2014 the United States

> carried out a total of 674 military missions across Africa, nearly two per day, up from 546 the year before. Those 674 missions amounted to an almost 300% jump in the number of annual operations, exercises, and military-to-military trainings since US Africa Command was established in 2008. These missions form the backbone of US military engagement on the continent. "The command's operations, exercises, and security cooperation assistance programs support US Government foreign policy and do so primarily through military-to-military activities and assistance programs," according to AFRICOM. "These activities build strong, enduring partnerships with African nations, regional and international organizations, and other states that are committed to improving security in Africa." Very little is known about most of these missions due to AFRICOM's secretive nature.[113]

Yet lurking behind these secretive interventions is a growing infrastructure of counterterrorism operations across the region. As Turse describes in *Tomorrow's Battlefield: US Proxy Wars and Secret Ops in Africa* (2015), while the military may decry any permanence to its operations, in reality they have built a vast network of outposts, drone facilities, and aircraft landing support; Obama's Africa policy has been one of vastly increased military spending and an expanded footprint encompassing virtually every African nation.[114] An array of military personnel and contractors provide logistics, equipment, and "training support" for African troops, and civilian infrastructure has been upgraded for military uses. These expanded operations provide the basis for a number of "shadow wars." Turse reveals that from 2009 to 2012, US agencies spent $390 million on construction, from barracks to training centers,[115] with an expanded infrastructure that has translated into heightened military "surge capacity." In a West Point speech in 2013, Obama signaled this tactical shift, announcing, "The war on terror is over. We must define our effort not as a boundless 'Global War on Terror,' but rather as a series of persistent, targeted efforts to dismantle specific networks of violent extremists that threaten America."[116]

But with this continuous military presence has come a widening blowback, and the scale of terrorism on African soil has only increased in response to US activities. Describing how "the United States has facilitated a terror diaspora, imperiling nations and endangering people across Africa,"[117] Turse points out that one new area with such a designation is the West African Gulf of Guinea, where piracy has jumped immensely. Faced with heightened security concerns in the Gulf, the United States poured millions into "maritime security activities" and "counter-piracy training."[118] Yet despite these initiatives, from 2010 to 2013 the Gulf saw an 80 percent rise in piracy, from oil theft to kidnapping, making it the "most insecure and violent waterway in entire world."[119]

Finally, an important element of US imperial strategy has been selective efforts at nation-building, or the "repair" of "broken places," as Samantha Power described it. The secession of South Sudan, with ample backing by the United States, stands out as a leading example of the period. Sudan had been the site of protracted civil wars for several decades, with two major civil wars since the 1980s. The Sudan People's Liberation Movement, led by John Garang, and its army led the South Sudanese war for independence that resulted in a 2011 referendum establishing Africa's newest nation. "It was George Bush and the Christian fundamentalists who heard the cry of South Sudan," wrote University of Juba literature professor Taban Lo Liyong the day after independence. "Today is Barack Obama's day. We don't know what he is going to do."[120] The two civil wars alone brought 2.5 million deaths and an additional 4 million displaced. Turse writes:

> The South Sudanese suffered, bled and died for their independence, but they didn't win it alone. As John Kerry, then-chair of the Senate Foreign Relations Committee, put it in 2012, the United States "helped midwife the birth" of South Sudan. From the mid-1980s onward, a bipartisan coalition in Washington and beyond championed the rebels and, in 1996, the US began

funneling military equipment to them through nearby Ethiopia, Eritrea and Uganda. As the new nation broke away from Sudan, the US poured in billions of dollars in aid, including hundreds of millions of dollars of military and security assistance. It also sent military instructors to train the country's armed forces and advisors to mentor government officials. On independence day, President Barack Obama hailed the moment as a "time of hope" and pledged US partnership to the new land, emphasizing security and development.[121]

Secession was enthusiastically championed by US business interests, who saw in South Sudan hopes for previously thwarted access to Sudanese oil and one of the few visible successes of the administration's policy in Africa.[122] As Whitehouse described at the time of the referendum:

> The US supported the Southern rebels in the late phases of the civil war, as the regime in Khartoum, the Sudanese capital, became a vocal opponent of US policy in the Muslim world. At the same time, US sanctions against Sudan—in particular, the inclusion of Sudan on the list of "state sponsors of terrorism" —prohibited US companies from cashing in on Sudan's growing oil business. Capital from China, along with Malaysia and India, filled the investment vacuum. China has spent more than $8 billion to get Sudan's oil flowing, including the construction of the key pipeline.[123]

South Sudan is thought to have Africa's third-largest oil reserves, after Angola and Nigeria. Oil revenues account for 98 percent of South Sudan's budget, making it arguably one of the most oil-dependent nations in the world. Disputes over access to oil helped drive the two-decade civil war in the formerly united nation, since most of the oil lies in South Sudan, but the refineries and pipelines to transport it out of the landlocked country flow through Sudan.[124]

In late 2013, these contradictions emerged in a new civil war in South Sudan that erupted between supporters of President Riek Machar and his ousted Vice President Salva Kiir. As the think tank Stratfor wrote at the time, "Cooperation in the oil sector is the only sustainable option for both [South Sudan and Sudan] to guarantee meaningful and ongoing revenues . . . In the past, [Sudanese President Omar al] Bashir has accused South Sudan of supporting Sudanese rebel groups, leading to a dispute over oil exports. At the time, there was some speculation that Machar and others had in fact been supporting the rebel groups to undermine Kiir's authority as well as his ability to placate Bashir and get oil production back online. Continued competition between these separate factions in South Sudan could lead to a repeat of these events."[125] Intermittent civil war in South Sudan continued for some years, threatening to further destabilize the wider Horn of Africa region. The United States thus faces a challenge in the region, as Nii Akuetteh has noted:

"The US would love to get rid of Bashir and get some more compliant person in Khartoum, and . . . they definitely would like it if they were the big recipient of the oil instead of the Chinese. The other thing that is important to the US is to build up South Sudan as a strong, self-reliant, rich country because it has a lot of oil."[126]

Despite their initial interest in South Sudanese "nation-building," the US government in fairly short order walked back its commitments to the new nation, despite widespread evidence of humanitarian disaster. At the time of the 2013 outbreak in fighting, South Sudanese had already experienced widespread poverty, with more than 50 percent of the country living below the poverty line. In the state of Unity, the leading oil producer among the country's ten states, almost half of children were malnourished, and just 2 percent of the households had water on the premises. When the fighting began, crisis conditions deepened even further, with tens of thousands forced into refugee camps without access to shelter or clean drinking water.[127] As fifty-one-year-old Nuer refugee Peter Bey described at the time, "We see from history that the UN has left people behind before in Rwanda. They put their own people on helicopters and left the people who died."[128] Nick Turse echoes this comparison, writing upon a visit how he tried "to understand how a new nation only years before 'midwifed' by my own country and hailed as a great hope for Africa could be laid so low that people were starting to whisper 'Rwanda' and talk about South Sudan as a possible next epicenter of genocide."[129] When Obama visited a refugee camp in Juba, South Sudan's capital, journalist Turse—encountering the president walking through the camp—described the devastation:

> This is the legacy of America's nation-building project in Africa, and of the policies of a president born of an African father, a president whose name was once synonymous with hopes for the future. Over the course of the Obama presidency, American efforts on the continent have become ever more militarized in terms of troops and bases, missions and money. And yet from Libya to the Gulf of Guinea, Mali to this camp in South Sudan, the results have been dismal. Countless military exercises, counterterrorism operations, humanitarian projects, and training missions, backed by billions of dollars of taxpayer money, have all evaporated in the face of coups, civil wars, human rights' abuses, terror attacks and poorly coordinated aid efforts. The human toll is incalculable. And there appears to be no end in sight.[130]

China's Expanding Military Footprint

As Lenin and others in the classical Marxist tradition have described, capitalists and their nation-states increasingly enter a competitive collision course in a race to secure strategic interests. As we have seen, intensified competition in the present era has driven a new militarization on the part of both the United States and China. In 2015, the Council on Foreign Relations, an influential think tank, issued a report entitled "Revising US Grand Strategy Toward China," arguing that tensions were heightening between the two powers. Laurence Shoup comments that the report's

> perspective is one of US global hegemony, and the prevention of the rise of any potential future global competitor. They call this "primacy": "preserving US primacy in the global system ought to remain the central objective of US grand strategy in the twenty-first century." This imperialist and hegemonic worldview is seen as consistent with US history as a whole: "Since its founding, the United States has consistently pursued a grand strategy focused on acquiring and maintaining preeminent power over various rivals, first on the North American continent, then in the Western Hemisphere, and finally globally." Now the United States must fundamentally change its policy to aggressively balance China's rise, since China is the only world power that could threaten US "primacy . . . the US position at the apex of the global hierarchy."[131]

The US Department of Defense has reported that China's People's Liberation Army (PLA) is steadily growing. China's military budget, they outline, averaged a 9.8 percent growth rate from 2006 through 2015.[132] These developments undoubtedly pose a strategic challenge to the United States:

> PLA modernization and development trends over the last decade reflect an expansion in the PLA's capabilities to address regional and global security objectives. PLA ground, air, naval, and missile forces are increasingly able to project power during peacetime and to contest US military superiority in the event of a regional conflict. The PLA's growing ability to project power also augments China's globally oriented objectives to be viewed as a stakeholder in ensuring stability and a regional power.[133]

As part of this unfolding dynamic, the United States has bolstered bases in Asia and built up their presence in the surrounding waters. In 2012, then US Secretary of Defense Leon Panetta announced that, by 2020, 60 percent of American warships would be stationed in Asia along with other "investments" so that the United States could "rapidly project military power if needed to meet our security commitments."[134] These imperial tensions have also begun to spill onto the African continent. The Chinese military has begun to engage in unprecedented naval exercises in the Indian Ocean. In the decade before 2014, China's official military budget grew an average of 9.5 percent per year.[135] Concomitant with the US "pivot to Asia" as a means of containing Chinese imperialism, China has looked to Africa as the site of massive infrastructure investment—partly to extend its economic interests, as we have seen, and also as a precursor to a military footprint on the continent. These designs took more tangible form when, as reported by the *New York Times*,

> China announced [in late 2015] that it would establish its first overseas military outpost and unveiled a sweeping plan to reorganize its military into a more agile force capable of projecting power abroad. The outpost, in the East African nation of Djibouti, breaks with Beijing's longstanding policy against emulating the United States in building military facilities abroad. The Foreign Ministry refrained from describing the new installation as a military base, saying it would be used to resupply Chinese Navy ships that have been participating in United Nations antipiracy missions. Yet by establishing an outpost in the Horn of Africa—more than 4,800 miles away from Beijing and near some of the world's most volatile regions—President Xi Jinping is leading the military beyond its historical focus on protecting the nation's borders.[136]

The foundation for this decisive turn was laid in the preceding decade, with smaller-scale operations marking China's widening military presence. Francis Njubi Nesbitt outlines this recent history, writing:

> China has also participated in peacekeeping operations, anti-piracy campaigns, and post-war reconstruction efforts around the continent. There are currently an estimated 1,600 Chinese peacekeepers participating in eight UN peacekeeping missions around the continent. . . . Beijing has long sold arms to African allies. Most recently arms deals with countries such as Sudan, Zimbabwe, and Nigeria have drawn criticism. In some cases, these shipments have included military aircraft. In 2008, [it was] estimated that China controls about 15 percent of Africa's small arms market. It is the third-largest exporter of conventional and small arms to Africa after Germany and Russia. China also provides training for military officers and maintains military-military exchanges with a reported twenty-five African countries."[137]

More recently, according to *Foreign Policy*, China has directly intervened in the South Sudanese civil war, arming President Salva Kiir's forces in the war against former Vice President Riek Machar while also "secur[ing] a deal that will put the UN's famed blue helmets to work protecting workers in South Sudan's oil installations, where China has invested billions of dollars."[138] China imports approximately three-quarters of South Sudanese oil.

The Gulf of Aden off the Horn of Africa, in particular, has developed into a region of intensified conflict and competition. A crucial shipping lane to the Suez Canal, the area is now the site of US, Chinese, Indian, and Japanese naval patrols, all seeking to protect their investments from Somali pirates. With the US-backed Saudi war in Yemen, the Gulf states have drawn several Horn of Africa nations into their mobilization; Sudan has provided some ground troops, while Eritrea, Somalia, and Djibouti have played a logistical role.[139] China's priorities are reflected both by immediate concerns over investments, but also by a wider interest in its own preeminence. As J. Peter Pham of the Africa Center at the Atlantic Council has argued, "US global leadership is predicated heavily on the US role in protecting and to an extent controlling sea lanes of communication. If China establishes itself as a fellow protector of the global commons, then it certainly increases its stature."[140] The rise of China in Africa has driven the heightened interest in militarization on the US part as well, and military involvement jumped during the same period. For example, "for the 2010 financial year, the Obama administration proposed significant increases in funding for US arms sales and military training programs for African countries. . . . The 2010 budget proposed to increase foreign military funding spending for Africa by more than 300 per cent."[141] As the United States has bolstered military forces alongside of China's, during Obama's tenure the United States has also deepened its financial support for UN "peacekeeping" operations in Africa, as the Council on Foreign Relations has documented.[142]

Ebola and the Militarization of Social Crisis[143]

Faced with this outbreak, the world is looking to the United States and it is a responsibility we are prepared to embrace. We are prepared to take leadership on this. This is an epidemic that is not just a threat to regional security; it's a potential threat to global security if these countries break down, if their economies break down and people panic.

—President Barack Obama[144]

In 2014, an Ebola epidemic in West Africa that the World Health Organization called "unparalleled in modern times" provided another context for increased US military presence on the continent under the guise of humanitarian intervention.[145] The United Nations likewise characterized the Ebola outbreak, centered in Liberia, Guinea, and Sierra Leone, as "a threat to international peace and security."[146] WHO head Margaret Chan declared that the crisis was "likely the greatest peacetime challenge that the United Nations and its agencies have ever faced."[147]

Public health officials clamored for a rapid mobilization of a medical response. The Obama administration possessed the technological and logistical resources to aggressively mount such a response and contain the outbreak in Africa, but opted instead for a militarized approach, deploying thousands of troops in the countries hardest hit by the epidemic. As in other instances of so-called humanitarian intervention, the deployment was intended to facilitate Washington's ability to project its imperial presence on the continent.

The outbreak was by far the worst since the virus was discovered in 1976, with a projected fatality rate of 70 percent.[148] By the end of the crisis, according to the WHO, close to 29,000 cases had been reported, including over 11,000 deaths.[149] The crisis was profoundly worsened by the devastated conditions of West African health care systems, already among the poorest in the world:[150] a severe shortage of trained health care professionals as well as basic supplies for disease containment and treatment exacerbated the epidemic. The Nigerian state was able to gather sufficient resources to halt an outbreak of the scale seen in neighboring countries.[151] Guinea, on the other hand, ranked last in a 2011 World Bank study of hospital beds per capita, while the health care systems of both Liberia and Sierra Leone had borne the brunt of almost two decades of uninterrupted civil war.[152]

Neoliberal austerity measures dramatically undermined the ability of nations to build adequate health care infrastructure able to cope with infectious outbreaks. Public health expert Lawrence Gostin reported that the nations currently most impacted are "ranked lowest in global development and do not have the basic infrastructure to contain the Ebola epidemic. . . . More than 20 Ebola outbreaks have erupted in sub-Saharan Africa, yet the world was unprepared for the current tragedy, with no licensed vaccines or treatments."[153] Meanwhile, over the two years prior to the outbreak, the WHO had reduced its budget by 12 percent and cut more than 300 jobs. The 2014–2015 budget reflected a more than 50 percent reduction in the WHO's outbreak and crisis response. A news account at the time captured the scale of the crisis:

> Sierra Leone's President Koroma admitted on national television that his country does not have trained nurses and doctors to deal with the outbreaks because its public health system is badly broken. He further shocked the viewers by pleading for basic necessities such as gloves and masks, a devastating story of the chronic failure by the government to deliver basic services to its people, half a century after independence, and almost 15 years after peace was brokered. Sierra Leone is among the top 10 diamond-producing nations, with estimates ranging between $250 million and $300 million per annum.[154]

Poverty and the legacy of underfunded health care were heavily implicated in the disease's spread. Paul Farmer of Partners in Health described how the crisis was "a reflection of long-standing and growing inequalities of access to basic systems of health care delivery, and that includes the staff, the stuff and systems. . . . How are we building local capacity to do that so these epidemics don't spread—as they would never spread in the United States, by the way?"[155] The scale of inequality in access to resources for ordinary West Africans prompted the WHO to allow the use of experimental drugs, but the most promising treatments, such as ZMapp, were limited to Western patients.[156]

Obama and the US government initially faced criticism for the slowness of their response. When the mobilization got underway, the president insisted that the Pentagon would "have to get US military assets just to set up, for example, isolation units and equipment there to provide security for public health workers."[157] His plan rested on the deployment of up to 3,000 military personnel to the hardest-hit countries, to be drawn from the 4,800-member Africa Command.[158] Obama claimed that the US military would coordinate with civilian organizations to distribute supplies and construct up to seventeen treatment centers. Yet the US government plan failed to mobilize or recruit sufficient numbers of medical personnel to actually treat victims of Ebola, and its field hospital was constructed to be used for foreign health workers only.[159] As Gostin wrote, people in affected countries were also victimized by the militarization and policing by local forces:

> Countries have erected cordons sanitaires (guarded lines preventing anyone from leaving), but are using ancient methods to enforce the quarantine. In West African hot spots, armed troops have established blockades, closed roads, and banned travel beyond the guarded perimeter. As a result, the populace is finding it hard to obtain food and other basic necessities . . . Transmission hot zones can't be ignored, but neither can the needs and human rights of communities.[160]

Protests erupted against the repressive approach to treating the disease, such as in the Liberian capital of Monrovia, where the West Point neighborhood of 70,000 poor residents rose up against the military and government.[161]

The announcement of US military intervention was met with ambivalence from some. Doctors Without Borders, for example, while initially rejecting calls for troops and heightened security, ultimately provided lukewarm support for Obama's plan.[162] Other organizations rejected military involvement on the part of the United States, but chiefly on the grounds that US military personnel were not equipped for humanitarian work, rather than as a critique of the premise of a militarized response. In contrast, US military officials established a definitive statement on the dangers posed to regional stability. "At the end of the day," declared Mike Hryshchyshyn, chief of humanitarian and health activities at AFRICOM, "we see a pandemic or other disaster as a potential security risk. If it occurs on a large-scale magnitude, it has the possibility of eroding basic security institutions and systems. In a worst-case scenario, chaos can break loose."[163]

Narcisse Jean Alcide Nana outlines the long and sordid history of militarizing epidemics in Africa, and the need, instead, for a public health solution:

> The international system has long become inured to the relentless hiccup of African insecurity malaise. Major clichés and few strong allegories conjure up the spasms of this ongoing malaise to the point of oversimplifying the field of African security. A cascade of crises encapsulated by patterns of sociopolitical "fragility", "failure", and "vulnerabilities" has been plying the continent's security environment with regards to the HIV/AIDS pandemic, the Ebola outbreak in West and Central Africa, as well as the hydra

of terrorism and bout of violent conflicts. . . . To be sure, demilitarizing epidemic diseases in West Africa will divert resources to building roads that lead to good hospitals and schools of medicine to train public health personnel for the continent.[164]

Competition and Conflict

By the end of the Obama era, it might seem as if the military strategy for Africa had failed on its own terms. Terror attacks rose markedly in African nations such as Mali, Nigeria, Kenya, Burkina Faso, and Ivory Coast. Protracted crises in Somalia and South Sudan remain unresolved after years of US "involvement." The scramble for resources, markets, and investments has rapidly spilled over into a frightening militarization across the continent, creating and fueling the conditions for further instability. As a result of this scramble, the twenty-first century has witnessed expansion not only of US and Chinese forces in Africa, but a renewed presence of European imperialism as a persistent rival of the global superpowers. Notably, France intervened in Mali beginning in 2013; again, "counterterrorism" was deployed as a device to project their own power in North Africa. Then French President François Hollande, as Whitehouse has written, "like Nicolas Sarkozy before him, [was] positioning France as West Africa's 'indispensable power,' the one that can arbitrate disputes and determine political outcomes. France has already played kingmaker in Mali's neighbor, Côte D'Ivoire—another former French colony. French troops based in the country intervened with force repeatedly through the last decade."[165]

Thus, the Marxist theory of imperialism as a systemic tendency toward competition and conflict is borne out in Africa today. Just as in the period of "classical imperialism" a century ago, the world's major powers are embroiled in tensions placing them on a collision course in different pockets of the globe. This return of former colonial powers to Africa alongside the new great powers can only intensify competition and militarization on the continent.

This conflict—which heightens instability for millions of ordinary Africans—has raised new challenges for resistance. For some on the African left, the necessary counter to AFRICOM is a military command under regional auspices, such as the African Union.[166] Jean Nanga, however, characterizes the African Union as the creation of a would-be enlightened fraction of the African neoliberal elite, preoccupied with the 'African Renaissance'. . . . [where] the African Union is supposed to conclude a project of continental integration, from the Mediterranean to the Indian Ocean. However, at the same time, the founding states are pursuing xenophobic policies, making immigrants from other sub-Saharan countries scapegoats for the failure of their neoliberal social policies . . . not to mention wars between neighbor states.[167]

Much of the African Union's backing comes from major powers, such as the United States, and likewise tends to reflect their priorities—such as intervention in Somalia—or those of the neoliberal elite Nanga describes, including support for dictators who have repressed social movements and democratic rights.[168] In December 2015, African Union troops, encouraged by close US ally Rwanda, were deployed to Burundi against the will of its president, Pierre Nkurunziza, marking the first time African Union forces had been used against a member nation without its consent.[169] As elsewhere across the globe, imperial militarization and its local partners will be trained on insurgencies and, potentially, mass struggles for justice from below. The historical record of resistance across Africa is a very long one, and in the face of intensifying economic, social, and ecological crisis, the likelihood and the urgency of that resistance only increases as well, but in the current period, now faces a vastly more militarized continent. For, as Bruce Dixon described at the dawn of the new era of AFRICOM,

local Africans are demanding respect and a share in what is after all, their oil. They are now routinely, viciously suppressed in eastern Nigeria, in Equatorial Guinea and elsewhere, by African troops trained and equipped with American tax dollars. When resistance continues, as it certainly will, America is preparing to up the ante with more American equipment, with military and civilian advisers, with bombs, bullets and if need be, with American bodies. That's what AFRICOM is about, and what it will be doing in the new century.[170]

Chapter Eight

Class Struggle
and Permanent Revolution

At every point in the fossil fuel production chain where your members "add value" and make profit, ordinary people, workers and their environments are assaulted and impoverished. Where oil is drilled, pumped, processed and used, in Africa as elsewhere, ecological systems have been trashed, peoples' livelihoods have been destroyed and their democratic aspirations and their rights and cultures trampled. . . . Your energy future . . . threatens the global environment, imposing on all of us the chaos and uncertainty of climate change and the violence and destruction of war. Another energy future is necessary: yours has failed!

—Petition to the World Petroleum Congress[1]

Africa has a long tradition of struggle. Mass movements in the anticolonial period, supported by millions of workers and peasants, shattered the political control of European powers on the continent. These newly emerging African economies, however, were not able to fulfill the aspirations of their populations after the era of liberation. As we have seen, hobbled with weak infrastructures inherited from the colonial regimes and insufficient capital to technologically advance, these economies fell increasingly behind. The new nationalist elites, meanwhile, were forced into the mold of all ruling classes: exploiters of workers and peasants, driven by the logic of international competition.

But the fight for self-determination did not end with colonialism's demise, and African workers and the poor waged a new round of strikes and protest movements decades later against new African ruling classes; over three dozen dictatorial regimes were toppled by struggles from below in the 1990s alone.[2] Revolts against neoliberal structural adjustment policies began in the 1980s; so-called IMF riots and class struggle exploded in the 1990s. These included strikes against wage cuts, antipoverty activism, mobilizations for AIDS treatment, struggles against the privatization of water and electricity, and movements for debt relief. Many of these struggles have laid the basis for alliances and longer-term battles over basic needs and human rights for workers and the poor today.

Two important books have compiled and chronicled the legacies of struggle in the anticolonial and postcolonial periods: Leo Zeilig's edited volume *Class Struggle and Resistance in Africa* (2009) and Peter Dwyer and Leo Zeilig's *African Struggles Today: Social Movements Since Independence* (2012). Both books not only highlight important chapters from the struggles from below across the continent, but also draw out key conclusions of the challenges faced by workers, students, peasants, and the poor in these movements. As these authors argue, some on the left have dismissed the liberatory potential of the African working class as a so-called "labor aristocracy"—that is, a section of the working class solely focused on its own advancement. In this distorted view, these workers have been too enmeshed in narrow economic demands, both before and after independence, to unite with the continent's peasants and the urban poor to embrace a broader emancipatory vision for social change. Dwyer and Zeilig describe the problem in the following way:

> Why did a wider politics beyond "independence" not emerge? . . . The emergent African working-class engaging in anti-colonial struggles was relatively small, without a developed, independent, and clearly articulated ideological position. It emerged into a political context dominated by both nationalism and a Stalinist form of communism that saw political progress in distinct stages, with the question of "socialism" entirely postponed until after the transition to "democracy" was complete.[3]

However, they point out,

> This unfortunately dovetailed with the . . . accusation that organised workers represented, in an African context, a "labour aristocracy" whose selfish defense of its privileges was at the expense of other, particularly rural, sections of society.[4]

More recently others, such as Mike Davis in *Planet of Slums*, have argued that liberalization and privatization have decimated the working class, leaving massive slums of urban poor delinked from the formal economy and power-less to resist. Davis's account is a fundamentally pessimistic one. This bleak view lends itself to one-sided conclusions about prospects for resistance: namely, that much as workers' power brought down colonialism, workers, so-cialists, and other activists have struggled since then to challenge single-party regimes and build alternatives to state-run trade unions.

The question of resistance from below is tied up with the historical dy-namics of class formation. David Seddon points out that the historical creation of an African working class evolved from the process of colonial exploitation itself. He writes:

> Despite the efforts of the colonial authorities to constrain the emergence of either an African capitalist class or a proletariat, the increasing demands of the colonial state for revenues to support . . . capital investment meant that the local population was subject to a variety of taxes and levies. These, in turn, obliged rural producers either to increase sales of farm produce for the market, or to seek wage employment.[5]

The colonial project likewise relied on this labor for the extraction of profit from Africa through its direct exploitation in the mines, on the rubber plan-tations, and in the fields.

For one, both the colonial and the new national states meted out harsh forms of repression in the face of resistance. Frantz Fanon's *Wretched of the Earth* (1961)[6] conveys the brutality of the colonial period and the violence inflicted on those rebelling against its rule. In the era of independence, the suppression of struggle from below took several forms, including the role played by authoritarian rulers, leaders likely as not to be supported by former colonial powers as well as the United States. The "disciplining" of the African working class also took the form, as we have seen, of the tyranny of the inter-national financial institutions and their harsh structural adjustment programs. A core element of structural adjustment's "liberalization" was a direct assault on workers' wages and social spending, an economic violence that continued the violence of previous eras in a new form.

As Dwyer, Zeilig, and others have also described, African working classes and social movements faced other challenges in the postcolonial period. The building of independent trade unions and social movements was hampered by the dominance of state-run formations and the imposition of rule by a new national bourgeoisie. The weakness of the nationalist left in Africa was

expressed in a two-stage theory of revolution, where national leaders typically asserted that anticolonial and anti-apartheid struggles would precede
a much-deferred socialist revolution. These politics reflected the mixed-
class composition of nationalist forces and the will of bourgeois and petty-
bourgeois African leaders to subsume workers' demands to those of national
independence. For example, South Africa's left, notes Dwyer, "relied on trade
unions to build a working-class movement, while not forming an independent socialist organization that could have united the political struggles in
the trade unions and townships."[7] For Mandela's African National Congress
(ANC), "the potential they generated was used to gain strategic access to existing institutionalized political and economic power."[8]

Despite these obstacles and limitations, powerful movements have risen
up, shaking African regimes to their roots. Dwyer and Zeilig write that to see
only the impact of neoliberalism would be a mistake: "The last thirty years, as
well as being a record of capitalist destruction across the continent, have also
been an astonishing record of anticapitalist protest and revolt."[9] The early
1990s saw multiparty elections held for the first time in a generation. Above
all, apartheid's defeat by South African workers in 1994—workers with their
hands on some of the most valuable minerals in the world—showed how
working-class struggle, concentrated at key points, can unify the resistance of
many oppressed groups, from ethnic minorities to the unemployed.

An edited volume by Firoze Manji and Sokari Ekine, *African Awakening:
The Emerging Revolutions* (2011), charts the uprisings of 2011 and the context of
the "Arab Spring."[10] As its contributors describe, the large revolts in Tunisia
and Egypt were accompanied by protests across sub-Saharan Africa, including Ethiopia, Gabon, Kenya, Morocco, Swaziland, and elsewhere, compelled
by the same forces of austerity and repression that drove working classes
across North Africa and the Middle East to take to the streets. As Manji has
described,

> over the last 30 years, you've seen massive unemployment, dispossession of
> their land, dispossession of their jobs, a decline in living standards, but also
> a political dispossession, so that people feel that their governments are more
> accountable to the banks and to the international multinational corporations
> than they are to their citizens. . . . There's a growing discontent that people
> feel that they have no means for determining their own destinies. And so
> self-determination has become a real vital dynamic within the continent.[11]

During that period, for example, a jump by one-third in food prices in
Uganda brought people into the streets denouncing President Museveni as

"the Hosni Mubarak of sub-Saharan Africa." That same month, a strike by tens of thousands of public-sector workers in Botswana—the world's second-largest diamond producer—took on a government that had been in power forty-five years, held up as one of the models of economic growth and "good governance." In Zambia, thirteen workers at a Chinese-owned mine were shot by security guards in 2010, driving unions fed up with barbaric conditions to go out on strike early the following year.[12]

In a 2012 article, Patrick Bond, Ashwin Desai, and Trevor Ngwane raise important questions about the challenges faced by social movements and the left in South Africa, writing:

> In the face of the government's embrace of neoliberal social policies since shortly after the fall of Apartheid, what are often called "service delivery protests" occurring many thousands of times a year according to police statistics, are at once the site of poor people's demands for greater responsiveness to human needs in general, but are also intensely localized and self-limited in their politics. The upsurge of protest since the late 1990s invariably invokes images of the anti-Apartheid struggle and thus focuses analysis on continuities and breaks between the old anti-Apartheid mass action and the new mass action in post-apartheid society. And yet, the majority of community protesters operate in close interconnection with parts of the Tripartite Alliance, composed of the . . . ANC, the trade union movement represented by the Congress of South African Trades Unions . . . and the South African Communist Party . . . , and so the line between insurgencies and governing organizations is not always clear. . . . "Uneven and combined Marxism" implies a way of considering the difficulties of constructing independent left politics in the conjuncture of a long-term capitalist stagnation in a 21st century South Africa in which some sectors of the economy—construction, finance and commerce—have been booming while many other former labor-intensive sectors of manufacturing have shrunk (or shifted from general production for a local mass market to niche production for a global upper-class market, such as luxury autos and garments), and in which large sections of society are still peripheral—aside from serving as a reserve army of unneeded surplus labor—to the interests of capital, domestic and global.[13]

It is these conditions that lead some on the left to draw the conclusion that Africa's high levels of unemployment, large concentration of peasantry, and the dominance of slums in the cities have undermined the possibility for working-class resistance as Marxists understand it: a class with the social weight to act collectively based on their relationship to the means of production. Davis's *Planet of Slums* is a well-known example of this argument—a description, as he puts it, of "urbanisation without industrialization," even deindustrialization, and thus a class, in his view, dislodged from its emancipatory potential.[14] Others have argued that the working class is too hopelessly divided by religion, ethnicity, oppositions between urban and rural communities, and other oppressions.

As Dwyer and Zeilig suggest, "In this respect Mike Davis's thesis in *Planet of Slums* is correct. Many of the urban unemployed created over the past 30 years cannot be counted as members of a reserve army, because they have never had a wage job and cannot expect ever to have one."[15] However, they continue, the lesson from South Africa is of the clear potential for the working class as a unifying and leading force, both through its members' power in strategic industries and the role they play in forging links with social movements. Despite high levels of unemployment, the working class is in fact integrated into the neighborhoods and lives of the unemployed, those taking to the streets at service delivery protests. For example, research in response to Davis by Zeilig and Claire Ceruti shows that "the jobless and formally employed are not hermetically sealed off from each other, in terms of either the household or neighbourhood. Nor are they clustered in the 'informal' slum settlements of Soweto. . . . The South African township and slum might be viewed as a meeting point for trade unionists, university students, graduates, the unemployed and informal traders. Though the spectre of unemployment affects all layers of society, these groups are not permanently cut off from each other and can be found in the same household supporting each other."[16]

Baba Aye argues that the informalization of the African working class in

> countries like Nigeria, extend[s] back to the period of colonialism which came to an end barely 50 years back, [while] neoliberal "structural adjustment" has led to a qualitatively different form of the informalization of work and labor relations. This phenomenon, borne out of the labor market deregulation and flexibilization regime, has led to a situation where, according to the ILO . . . two thirds of all workers globally are employed in the informal economy."[17]

Given these conditions, the mass struggles in Africa of the 2010s will be best advanced by workers there playing a central role, as the class best able to contend politically with the challenges posed by the diversity and unevenness across African societies as a whole. The insights of Russian revolutionary Leon Trotsky, explored below, are a useful way to frame this question.

Permanent Revolution

The unevenness within the African working class indicates a central characteristic of working classes everywhere: the unique role played by workers given their key place in the productive process. The ability of workers' struggles—as a liberatory class—to link together the interests of diverse groups creates the potential to unify the exploited and oppressed across an "uneven" landscape. Trotsky theorized the possibilities for international revolution under the conditions of what he described as the nature of combined and uneven development under capitalism and the potential for "permanent revolution." For Trotsky, combined and uneven social and economic conditions are a key feature of capitalist society, where the totality of relations indicate the potential for more "advanced" sections of capitalism to bind with and liberate noncapitalist or "developing" relations in order to revolutionize society as a whole. This dynamic unfolds as permanent revolution, by which Trotsky meant "permanent" in a double sense: its spread across society and across national borders, and its cementing of a socialist revolution—in other words, establishing the revolution for socialism as "permanent." In Trotsky's words, it is "a revolution which . . . goes over to socialist measures and to war against reaction from without; that is, a revolution whose every successive stage is rooted in the preceding one and which can end only in the complete liquidation of class society."[18]

The relationship between democratic movements and other struggles, the unbroken relationship between national and international revolution, make the case for permanent revolution, Trotsky argues, "regardless of whether it is a backward country that is involved, which only yesterday accomplished its democratic revolution, or an old capitalist country which already has behind it a long epoch of democracy and parliamentarism."[19] Yet some debate exists regarding the relevance of the framework of permanent revolution for class struggle today. Neil Davidson, for example, has suggested that the theory is now a "historical concept."

Davidson's assertion that this theory no longer applies to today's world rests on three ideas. First, permanent revolution was never applicable to all so-called "backward" nations. Permanent revolution, in Davidson's view, was only meant to explain a *particular* set of conditions under which revolution could advance—that is, a certain balance of combined and uneven development, *not* all cases. But Trotsky never saw those exceptions as refuting the concept in its entirety. As Paul D'Amato writes:

> Precisely because international capitalism's unevenness created different "forms and methods" of bourgeois rule, [Trotsky] argued, "it follows that the dictatorship of the proletariat also will have a highly varied character in terms of the social basis, the political forms, the immediate tasks, and the tempo of work in the various capitalist countries." It is necessary, therefore,

to study each country, its class relations, and its place in international world capitalism in its specificity. One size doesn't fit all.[20]

Second, Davidson writes, "Trotsky saw permanent revolution as a strategy which would enable the less developed countries to decisively break with feudal, tributary or colonial rule under working-class leadership and move directly to socialism as components of an international revolutionary movement."[21] Yet, he argues, because capitalism is the dominant mode of production in every country in the world, the concept of an unbroken fusion of bourgeois and socialist revolution no longer is relevant. Finally, according to Davidson, because capitalism now dominates the globe, strategic questions about the relationship of a small working-class movement to other revolutionary forces no longer carry as much significance; where the working class remains the minority today, any alliances forged with other classes do not constitute "permanent revolution" but simply the revolutionary process in a broader sense. Yet Davidson is incorrect here as well, since Trotsky's understanding of the role of the working class within a revolutionary movement was not simply about its numeric size or weight, but about its political *leadership* in a struggle for all of the poor and the oppressed.

Examined through the wider lens of a global system, the "totality" that Trotsky describes—the possibility for permanent revolution through an interlinked working class, tied to capitalist relations of production—remains crucial. The struggles against international capitalism today are tied up with those for social justice and liberation more inextricably than ever. The continuing relevance of the theory of permanent revolution today also rests on the interweaving, or combination, of workers' struggles with those for democracy and socialism that arise out of the uneven and combined nature of capitalism itself. Because of the interdependence of these dynamics, uneven and combined conditions create the opportunity, through their instability and volatility, for revolution. This explosiveness only intensifies as the internal contradictions and drive to compete on a world scale likewise grow.

The fundamental instability produced by capitalism is described well by Davidson when he appears to make the case for the ongoing relevance of the theory:

> Uneven and combined development is therefore likely to be an ongoing process, which will only be resolved by either revolution or disintegration. But in the meantime, China and other states like India and Brazil where growth has been less dramatic remain both inherently unstable in their internal social relations and expansive in their external search for markets, raw materials and investment opportunities.[22]

For, he continues elsewhere, "It is in this inherent instability that the possibilities for permanent revolution lie . . . combination is not 'the world revolutionary cataclysm,' it is the objective enabling condition for it to take place."[23]

Geoff Bailey writes that Davidson's arguments for the limitations of permanent revolution as a strategy rest on its *specificity* for a given historical moment—a moment when links are forged between the working class and the revolutionary peasantry. Bailey writes, "Davidson would likely argue that in ignoring the historical specificity of permanent revolution, this simply folds the theory into the broader work of Marxists on the relation of the working class to other exploited classes in the process of revolution. However, we should be able to recognize the historic specificity of Trotsky's writings, while also recognizing that they advance and rise to a higher level in earlier scattered and incomplete lines of thinking within the classical tradition."[24] In other words, the general insights remain important, particularly given worldwide unevenness and the necessity for linkages between the working class and other forces within and between the Global South and the developed world. As Paul LeBlanc describes, "permanent revolution has application in the capitalist heartland, not simply in the periphery. . . . Rather than arguing that permanent revolution is irrelevant, then, one could argue that the dynamics underlying Trotsky's theory are more generally relevant today than ever before."[25]

Critically, the theory of permanent revolution maintains the primacy of workers' self-activity. Trotsky's *Results and Prospects* (1906), his first extended discussion of the idea, asserts the centrality of independent working-class action and socialism from below, concluding that "the worst illusion the working class has suffered is the reliance on others."[26] Struggles of the African working class for self-determination and fundamental change underscore the point via the uprisings against colonialism and the challenges in building movements against neoliberalism—both African and international—imposed from above.

The Point of Extraction and Beyond

As African economic development has been marked by uneven development, resistance can be seen in centers of working-class opposition across the continent, including important sites of extraction such as South Africa and Nigeria, where a concentration of workers provides the *potential* social weight to bind together the struggles of whole regions and overcome ethnic barriers. Most crucially, the example of apartheid's defeat at the hands of South African workers—with their hands on some of the most valuable minerals in the world—shows how working-class struggle, concentrated at key points, can unify the resistance of many oppressed groups, from ethnic minorities to the unemployed in a region. Although the revolutions of the twentieth century have clearly demonstrated the potential for winning national liberation under the leadership of other forces besides the working class, history has also shown that winning true equality and liberation for the majority is impossible without a mass working-class movement. The legacy of those twentieth-century struggles—in China, Cuba, and the "African socialist" regimes like Tanzania and Ghana—has proven decisively that the notion of "socialism in one country" is a myth, and the enduring relevance of the idea of permanent revolution as a vision of internationalism.

With the new scramble for wealth in Africa and the role workers play in producing it, Africa's workers are crucially positioned to battle exploitation because of their close ties to international capital, as well as to develop the potential, in a larger sense, for global resistance linking the "developed" and the "developing" world. In other words, despite the unevenness of the concentration of workers in African society, it's fundamentally a *political* question, and not an objective one, of their potential to mount a resistance. And as these economies lurch into crisis—with the crash of commodities' prices and government-imposed austerity and mass layoffs—their struggles play a critical role.

In Nigeria, for example, a groundswell of strikes against nonpayment of wages emerged in 2015 in the wake of crashing commodities prices, as wages collapsed to very low levels.[27] Nigeria has witnessed nine general strikes since 1999.[28] The oil unions, according to Aye, are strong and have an important history of militancy, winning the right to organize contract workers in 2005, who come mainly from the communities where oil extraction is taking place. This was a major victory for a large section of the workforce in the face of oil industry employers recalcitrant to allow unionization industry-wide.[29] The weight of workers in the oil sector is one indication of the unifying potential and power of the Nigerian working class as a whole, for although the extractive industries, as we have seen, are highly capital intensive, they both centralize workers in industries key to the economy as well as create a wide range of secondary industries in which other workers are employed.[30] As Andy Wynne has described,

Like many countries in Africa, especially South Africa, there has been a mass strike wave in Nigeria for the last decade or so. There are nearly seven million trade union members in Nigeria out of a total population of around 175 million, but when they take action they are actively supported by the majority of poor Nigerians. Thus the trade union movement carries significant political weight although attempts to build a Labour Party to directly represent this movement have yet to be successful.[31]

The revolution in Burkina Faso of 2014–2015 marked a crucial point in working-class struggle and an important example of the critical ties between those struggles and wider upheavals across society as a whole. State repression, inequality, and the impact of structural adjustment "reform" laid the groundwork for the massive uprising. President Blaise Compaoré's decision in 2014 to run for a fifth term was met with massive upheavals and protest both in the streets and at workplaces. As Aye has written, "by 2011, the dress rehearsal of what would be the 2014 revolution played itself out. A massive wave of strikes in the mining sector engulfed the country, poor farmers joined the fray, demonstrating against poor prices for their produce and mutinies rocked the army including within the ranks of the elite [Regiment of Presidential Security] . . . over unpaid wages."[32] The "insurrection populaire" rose up again in 2014, and Compaoré was forced from power.

The revolutionary wave continued after his ouster. Strikes in gold and manganese mines erupted once again, alongside those of transport and other workers across the country. Protesters in the tens of thousands took to the streets in the capital, Ouagadougou, and other cities. In response to the upheaval, sections of the ruling class attempted to resolve the crisis from above, launching a coup against the transitional government in September 2014. Again the movement from below rose up, launching a ten-day general strike across the country. Zeilig describes how the "resistance was also marked by the militancy of the young, many unemployed, who had built the barricades and defended neighbourhoods in the capital from the RSP and supporters of the old regime. The picture was the same across the country."[33] In the face of this second uprising within one year, the coup was effectively defeated. Aye continues:

The triumph of the revolutionary moment last year was however not just a Burkinabé moment. It represented the contradictory currents of struggle on the continent. These as a whole cannot be separated from the global era of crises and revolts, where "the old is dying and the new cannot be born". . . . The moment we are in presently, which the events in Burkina

Faso demonstrate, is one where not only governments are being defeated but working-class people are demanding new regimens of politics.[34]

Irvin Jim, socialist leader of the National Union of Metal Workers of South Africa (NUMSA), has similarly pointed to the political questions and challenges posed by the struggles of workers in the extractive industries. For Jim, key questions include not only "who owns and controls" the mines, but who holds decision-making power over the use and distribution of their products. In a 2016 speech, he described the need to "take that social surplus." "Our struggle is about changing the social relations of production," he said. "We need to talk about beneficiation and diversification of economy."[35] NUMSA, as Jim describes, is struggling to cohere the working-class movement behind these political questions: "Africa is rich, the primary beneficiaries of those resources should be us, our own minerals must benefit us, [where] the state could take ownership of the steel, take ownership in downstream activities."[36] Elsewhere, he outlines how this perspective must be integrated into a program of class struggle:

> There is more to be fought for in 2016, including advancing the demand for localization, for government procurement policies and practices to be geared toward local content and local products, and to expand the range of goods and services which must be produced locally. . . . In 2016, we shall fight and demand that government must move swiftly to nationalize not just the steel industry but the entire steel value chain. Only this way can the government protect genuine local industries and advance the cause for value add local manufacturing and protect jobs.[37]

In other words, possible constraints of workers' struggles in capital-intensive extractive industries are not foregone conclusions, and working-class movement leaders are putting forward perspectives for a wider vision of redistribution and reconstruction of society itself. Of necessity for working-class liberation, such a vision must extend beyond national borders, forging ties of solidarity across the continent and beyond.

The Marikana massacre in South Africa: Interview with Rehad Desai and Jim Nichol of *Miners Shot Down*[38]

The massacre at the Lonmin platinum mine in Marikana on August 16, 2012, was a watershed moment in South African history. Thirty-four workers were gunned down and many more injured in a brutal assault by the South African police. Just days earlier, 3,000 rock-drill operators had waged a wildcat strike for higher wages over the opposition of the leadership of the National Union of Mineworkers (NUM), who urged "patience" despite the desperate poverty of their members. This wildcat action was first met by violence from both company security forces and the NUM before the police murdered the strikers. For their part, the strikers were affiliated to a break-away union, the more militant Association of Mineworkers and Construction Union (AMCU), led by Joseph Mathunjwa.[39]

Twenty years after the overthrow of apartheid, the massacre encapsulates many of the key contradictions of the so-called "non-racial" neoliberal order ushered in by Nelson Mandela and the ANC. Amidst blatant and growing inequality, a new Black ruling class is driving accumulation through its Black Economic Empowerment initiatives with the long-standing complicity of the ANC-aligned union federation, COSATU, and the South African Communist Party (SACP) in pushing its neoliberal agenda. Meanwhile, international capital and the front-men of the new Black Economic Empowerment elite leverage the vast powers of the state, ensuring that the fruits of neoliberalism remain in the hands of a tiny (now multiracial) minority. All of this was expressed, on a world stage, in Marikana.

A boom in the price of commodities, including raw materials like platinum, since the end of the global recession of 2008 has made huge profits for companies in extractive industries. The struggle in Marikana is part of a South African strike wave in the mines owned by Lonmin, Impala, Amplats, and others. In fact, the massacre at Lonmin led to a successful strike at the platinum mines in 2014, which in turn ushered in major wage increases and a further es-trangement of the workers' movement from the ANC alliance. Yet with the subsequent collapse in global commodity prices, the spec-ter of mass layoffs haunts South Africa: in 2015, Anglo American an-nounced their intention to lay off 85,000 workers worldwide, many of them in South Africa.[40]

But there is a specific South African historical resonance to this conjuncture that gave rise to the Marikana tragedy. Mass worker movements, like those in the mining sectors, and the burgeoning student movement for fee strikes—often framed as a struggle against the colonial settler legacy of South Africa—both won key victories.[41] These harken back to the heights of the anti-apartheid movements of the late 1980s and early 1990s. As much as the ANC and its allies would like to claim ownership of the legacy of that his-tory, it grew and developed—in important ways—independent of the ANC and SACP in exile. And its return—after more than two decades of disillusionment with the new, nonracial neoliberal order, cannot be a surprise to any who truly appreciate the decades of struggle and long-standing aspirations of the country's Black work-ing class.

Activists now have a vital tool for the struggles ahead: the award-winning film *Miners Shot Down* (2014), directed by Rehad Desai.[42] The film—a depiction of the events leading up to the Marikana massacre and its aftermath—powerfully captures the contradictions of capitalism in South Africa today in all of its bru-tality. It also provides substantial footage of the strike's leaders, participants, and supporters, human faces of not only the victims of murder—some captured on film—but also active fighters in the working-class struggle that overthrew apartheid twenty years ear-lier and continues to this day. Desai, along with Jim Nichol, attorney for the miners and their families, conducted the following interview with Aaron Amaral and Lee Wengraf while touring the United States with the film in 2015 to build support for the campaign.

What is the importance to the state of the extractive industry, es-pecially the value of the platinum industry, and how much does that aspect factor into the Marikana situation?

Jim: Whenever there's a strike, we see the government's sup-port of the employers against the strikers. That's a sort of given, really. Here was an international company that was at the back end of a recession, and it wasn't doing very well. It had done well until 2008, and it kept all the money and sent a lot of it overseas. They were desperate not to settle the strike, absolutely desperate. And they knew that a previous miner's strike at Impala Platinum in Rustenburg earlier that year had been successful after nine weeks of struggle despite people being killed. The question facing the company was how they could win the dispute. So they had a real reason for wanting to break the miners.

Then you have the government itself. It already knew Impala had won their strike. It was terrified that throughout South Africa people would be demanding these extraordinary wage increases. Secondly, what would the extraordinary wage increases and the strikes do to international investor confidence in the extractive industries in particular? Then you have the third element, which was the National Union of Mineworkers, the biggest single union that had supported the ANC, through thick and thin, that was now losing membership in the platinum industry like there was no tomorrow to the new union on the block, AMCU. So when all three of those factors come together like that, the strength of what they wanted makes a fist, which is much stronger than fingers. So there was a lot at stake for all of them. So that's why they went for it.

The people that get away with murder, by the way, are Lonmin. One day they may prosecute some middle-ranking policeman for something, but as for Lonmin? They have gotten away with murder. The tragic events of Marikana would not have occurred had it not been for the intransigence of Lonmin in protecting its profits and financial stability against the interest of poor miners and refusing to negotiate with them. They took this stance knowing that guns would be used by police officers in order to quell the strike and to arrest strikers.

Rehad: And who was the face of that? Cyril Ramaphosa! It's the attempt to legitimize a very rapacious capitalist system which is characterized by racial hierarchy in the labor force, and the ownership seeks to "deracialize." Supposedly you do it through the Black Economic Empowerment policy. But it is very clear after a while that ordinary people can say, "He is doing well, it's my turn next." But when your turn doesn't come, people start getting very impatient. That is what started happening around the end of 2010, 2011, with the rise of unofficial strikes and the real pressure of wages because of rising unemployment and food inflation. And I think even now the richest people in the country are getting worried about the credibility of the African National Congress given the rampant levels of corruption and the fact that there are a handful of Black people who are super rich. For instance, in 2007, 72 percent of the three hundred Black empowerment deals that were concluded—worth tens of billions of rand—were in the hands of four people, four Black people, the so-called Fab Four: Ramaphosa, Tokyo Sexwale,[43] Saki Macozoma,[44] and Patrice Motsepe.[45] These people are rentiers, completely unproductive. Due to their political connections, they got their hands on discounted shares, held on to them for a year or two, and then began selling them off for a massive profit.

Today there is a lot of anxiety because of the volatility of the commodities market. These corporations are pretty shaken up right now.

Rehad: This is one of the most interesting things. Julius Malema[46] called for nationalization in 2010, 2011. He's got some closeness to Tokyo Sexwale. Some claim his call for nationalization is to bail out Black financial leaders who got into trouble because of the downward spiral of commodities prices. But because the dividends would be a lot less than what they're paying now, nationalization would serve their interests. It's a bailout for the tycoons. This is part of the problem. That is why NUMSA and SACP have refused to support the demands for nationalization. The question we must ask is: if you nationalize, who will actually take control?

Jim: If you go to a place like Lonmin or Impala, they have twenty or thirty thousand workers and the company says, "We are going to retrench, we need redundancy. We are going to close this current shaft with 20,000, 30,000 workers in it." We should be saying, "No, you don't. We nationalize all the shafts. They don't get to choose the shafts to close."

I am for nationalization. Without a shadow of a doubt, I am for nationalization. But to win people to it, you have to be clear on what nationalization means, from our perspective. Now of course, we'd like to say nationalization means workers controlling power in the workplace, at the point of production, as part of a revolutionary process. We are for democratic control. We say we are for the seven-hour day. We also say that no miner can work in the mine for more than twenty years of their life because after that you probably have acquired serious health problems. We say that you can only work three weeks in four. We call for health care. We say that you get retraining after your twenty-year stint.

Rehad: Most importantly, the call for nationalization has to be without compensation for the mine owners. There will be a fight over that. The big challenge will be to bring the big battalions to fight tooth and nail. It poses the argument for workers' control, but it begins to gain some traction because you need mass struggle.

And what of Joseph Mathunjwa, the head of the new union, AMCU? What does he say?

Rehad: It's very important he didn't sign this latest deal. The government, NUM, and the industry said, "Let's commit to dialogue and working together to save the mining industries," and then tens of thousands of retrenchments [firings] come. And the bosses turn around and say, "Well, the NUM signed a deal." NUM may claim to have never discussed retrenchments. But they had signed a memorandum of understanding.

Jim: For the miners themselves the AMCU is a union that fights, even though it puts down the left at times. But what's also important is that there is now a substantial union of probably 160,000 or 170,000 miners, out of 500,000 miners working in total in the country. And AMCU is the majority of miners in platinum–that's important to understand. This is a union that is a beacon to South African workers, blue-collar, white-collar workers–they both look to it. Mathunjwa claims to be apolitical, which drives me to distraction, but there is a strength to that approach because people will say, "He isn't part of the old order, he refuses to be a part of the old order."

AMCU is a beacon. Then you take the Marikana events. It propelled the split in COSATU to the left by NUMSA. Life is never going to be the same again in South Africa. Never going to be the same again.

How much has Marikana and the rising combativeness within the workers' movement between 2012 and 2014 contributed to the general radicalization? How did the Marikana workers and the movement building of the family members impact the campaign and workers' struggles overall?

Jim: The confidence of the families! I can tell you, they are wonderful to watch. They came to the commission and they were isolated, depressed, and they cried. But then you look at what happened over this period, and they changed, they became stronger people, and they took the jobs of their husbands and the like. And they do great campaigning.

Rehad: Of the widows and the family members, and the injured and arrested, it's been critical that they remain in the forefront. What we have been doing for the last three years has been acting on their mandate, and trying not to make any big move without them.

What has been the international reception to the film?

Rehad: The film has been likened to *Salt of the Earth* and *Harlan County USA*, and there have been only a handful of documentaries that have been able to do that. I think that for many people, the inequality in South Africa sits uncomfortably. It's not just the varying degrees of poverty or whatever. It is highly unequal and people see it every day. They see the huge wealth. Forty-five percent of the population, the working population, are living on the poverty line, are working poor, earning under $300 a month. You have two people owning as much as the poorest 50 percent of the population. Working-class people aren't stupid. This is a general phenomenon. It is happening everywhere. We are seeing rising mass unemployment in large parts of Europe, and a rising opposition. It is clear for many people. The rising inequality is due to the rising power of the corporations, the hold of the corporations over our lives.

And so the film is a bit of a hit because people know—they know this story. They know this story of a working-class hero like Cyril Ramaphosa, who has turned his back on his people, joined the big corporation, and gotten super rich, and that is what we see in many countries, the way people see it. But we also thought that the days where the state would come together with corporations and politicians and mow people down in a brute arrogant fashion was something we left behind us.

After the Sharpeville massacre of 1960, millions upon millions of people became involved in the anti-apartheid campaign internationally over the years. And so to see what happened at Marikana, this is shocking for people. People have wanted to do something. People want to stop the rot. They want to use the film in some way to change what is happening in South Africa, but also as a way to start a wider conversation of what is happening in the world.

The Left's Challenges

Revolts against neoliberal structural adjustment policies first emerged in the 1980s, and so-called IMF riots and class struggle exploded in the 1990s.[47] Yet despite the mobilization of the working class, the leftist politics of students and the intelligentsia dominated this later era of protest for democratic reforms. Thus, the weakness of working-class organization and political leadership created a resilience on the part of national elites, who were able to mobilize nationalism and facilitate the expansion of neoliberal policy on the African continent in this context.[48] The resistance to neoliberalism continues to this day, and the battle against the new scramble for Africa's resources has put the oil and other extractive industries in the crosshairs. African social movements and the working class are building new movements to take on some of the worst exploitation on the globe, with the left's clear task to build leadership independent of the politics of Stalinism, national development, guerilla warfare, or neoliberalism.

With the onset of a new era of austerity in Africa and the end of the "African boom," workers will be challenged not only to build resistance on the job, but against government retrenchment as well. As Patrick Bond wrote at the start of the commodities crash, "poor families face double-digit inflation this year thanks to food, electricity and transport hikes. . . . They will struggle to find more holes in their frayed belts to tighten them up, given that 63% of South Africans—mostly women—already live below the poverty line."[49] Yet the examples of mass struggles from below, such as in Burkina Faso, Nigeria, South Africa, Ivory Coast, Zimbabwe, and elsewhere, show conclusively the power of working classes on the continent. This evidence conclusively puts to rest the notion of a "planet of slums" in Africa, where ordinary people lack agency to bring about social change.

A new front of privatization and assault on ordinary peoples' living conditions has taken shape in the face of massive land grabs on the part of multinational agribusinesses at the behest of local governments, a front that is likely to intensify as the search for arable land and agricultural commodities heightens. In Mozambique, for example, 80 percent of the population are small farmers. Justiça Ambiental has been organizing for the rights of farmers and communities in the face of land grabs and to stop the construction of the Mphanda Nkuwa dam on the Zambezi River. Anabel Lemos of Justiça Ambiental commented: "The government invites in both economically developed and developing countries, like Brazil and China, as well as international corporations, saying that there's plenty of free land. But there is no free land in Mozambique. Land belongs to communities."[50]

Forced resettlement and other human rights abuses against Anuak farmers have grown exponentially in Ethiopia, a major site of African land grabs, particularly in the lowland regions such as the Gambella. A repressive government campaign against the struggle has created a new group of political prisoners held in Addis Ababa, such as Pastor Omot Agwa, whose campaign has garnered international attention. As Tom Burgis has described, "A faultline of history—or, perhaps, of modernity—has opened up in Gambella. The forces of global markets have smashed up against the instinct to preserve a homeland. . . . If a global land rush is at hand, Gambella's rift will not be the last."[51] The dynamics of accumulation in Africa—and attempts to manage its accompanying crises—will continue to create new cracks in society as ordinary Africans resist this "new scramble" in its many forms.

It is not difficult to anticipate how some of these rifts will widen. Recent chapters in movement history in Africa indicate the possibilities, as Africans defend their jobs and livelihoods in the face of cutbacks. Following on a decades-long working-class struggle, in January 2012—less than a year after the start of the Arab Spring—the Nigerian government announced it was slashing its fuel subsidy as a budget-cutting measure, forcing an overnight doubling of fuel prices. Mass protests and a national strike broke out, and then President Goodluck Jonathan conceded to a partial reduction in gas prices. Inspired by both the Arab Spring and Occupy Wall Street, protesters referred to the uprising as "Occupy Nigeria." As described by Kwei Quartey, Nigerians are "expressing the same sentiment behind much of the worldwide protests of 2011: people are sick and tired and are not going to take it anymore."[52]

This partial victory points to the potential for mass mobilization, but also the as yet-unmet challenges and urgency of building sustained, independent workers' organization, all the more so as crisis and retrenchment deepen. In the context of austerity, a vacuum of organization from below creates space for the tightening of a political hold from above. Kunle Wizeman Ajayi draws out those very dangers in the retreat of the unions after the gas price hike, a move that fell far short both economically and politically:

Since the paltry 10 naira reduction in the gas price by the federal government, which was massively rejected, the unions have had less engagement.
So the political engagements with the neoliberal policies of the government
have been weak. Privatization and other anti-poor policies of the government
are having negative effects on the mass of poor people. The environment
becomes quite ripe for what is popularly termed "stomach infrastructure,"
where the big parties churn out cash and sachets of rice and kerosene to poor
people in exchange for votes. The army of the unemployed, which continues
to grow *en masse*, becomes a reputable resource for thugs and brigands who
are used to foment violence during elections.[53]

Class polarization has intensified the dynamics of struggle against austerity in South Africa as well. South Africa arguably leads the globe in the level
of strikes and demonstrations—with the rest of sub-Saharan Africa not far
behind, both driven forward by massive waves of privatization and neoliberal
policies. In recent years, millions of public-sector workers have gone out on
strike with demands that included pay and housing allowance increases. The
ANC government has also been a frequent target of service delivery protests
over horrific conditions in communities and the need for social programs,
such as the "No Land, No House, No Vote" campaign by the group Abahlali
baseMjondolo, the largest poor people's organization in the country. The
Landless Peasant Movement—an organization of shack-dwellers—issued the
following statement at the height of a wave of protests in 2010:

> It is clear to all the organisations . . . that there is no democracy in South
> Africa. Every time that there is an election, the poor are promised land,
> housing, water, electricity, toilets, education and jobs. After the elections we
> are denied these things. If we ask for the promises that have been made to us
> to be kept we are beaten, arrested and jailed. If we occupy land and appro-
> priate water and electricity we are beaten, arrested and jailed. Sometimes we
> are tortured. Sometimes we are even killed.[54]

Challenging Capitalism

For many on the African left today, the challenge is finding a way to fuse the
unfinished struggles from the pre-liberation period with a systemic challenge
to capitalism as a whole. Trevor Ngwame, himself a socialist expelled from
the South African Communist Party, describes the pressing need for that independent left:

> The struggle is about alternatives—fighting to put in power a government
> that consistently puts the interests of the working class first—a workers'

government. The solidity and breadth of the public-sector strike indicates that the seeds of something better, albeit scattered in the isolated different working-class outbursts, are beginning to grow. The social weight of organized, mobilized workers is beginning to consolidate. It is not just about the ANC-SACP-COSATU Alliance, nor is it about the government, the state, the capitalists, the leadership or the left. It is about what millions of ordinary working-class people are thinking and feeling—and beginning to do.[55]

This challenge has a long history and is one that has confronted the left from the colonial period down to the present day. Writing in 1982, Eddie Madunagu outlined the challenges of building an independent Nigerian working-class movement capable of contending with the repressive state, one free from the constraints of an apparatus that forces workers' demands through its "bureaucratic machine."[56] Some decades later, Aye offers a similar perspective from Nigeria on the need for a broad, revitalized, nonsectarian left, writing:

Working class parties can . . . not simply be electoral machines like the parties of the bosses in Nigeria. They must be the political fighting organs of the working class. When small sects partake as parties in elections, eulogising themselves over a few thousands or tens of thousands of votes they win, it is not bad in itself. But it erodes confidence in the Left as anything but marginal parties.[57]

As retrenchment across the continent continues to unfold in the second decade of the twenty-first century, the class solidarity and linkages will be highlighted all the more sharply. NUMSA, for example, pledged its solidarity with students striking against fee hikes in 2015, recognizing the shared victimization of neoliberal policy that produced cuts both to education and employment—as it described, "the neoliberal economic policies being championed by the ANC government on behalf of the big corporations of the Minerals Energy Complex."[58] The battle lines of which section of South African society will be compelled to pay for the next round of crisis will only become an increasingly important political question. The question of workers' power reverberates not only within the centers of accumulation on the continent as a whole, such as South Africa and Nigeria, but across the working class continent-wide.

For the left in the "Global North," those reverberations of workers' resistance in Africa of necessity must be embraced in an internationalist vision of solidarity and struggle from below. The chains of extraction and exploitation link workers in Africa to those elsewhere through—as Marxists understand it—the "combined" nature of capitalism and the ever-increasing internationalization of our labor. From the anticolonial struggles of the 1960s and 1970s to the global anti-apartheid movement, the identification and solidarity with the African left and working class has a long history. Traces of those fault lines are taking form today, from opposition to the horrors of drone warfare, AFRICOM, and covert operations to the rampages of Shell, Exxon, and many more for corporate domination over Africa's natural resources.

Solidarity with workers from Tunis to Cairo to Marikana and beyond also point to a path forward. The violence of imperialism and capitalism in Africa will only be brought to a halt by resistance from below. As Azwell Banda writes, "workers and the poor people of Africa must break their chains of oppression. Among the first solid steps toward this must surely be to study and appreciate the central role that the workers' movement has played, and continues to play, in the continent's struggles for social change."[59] The working classes of Africa hold the potential to build alliances with wider sections of society and thus lead in those struggles for change facing all of the oppressed on the continent, from the urban slums to the rural poor—the strikes by Kenyan workers, for example, in opposition to displacement by the LAPSSET pipeline, or the solidarity of South African mine workers with service delivery protests and student strikes. When workers move into action, they carry the potential to play a revolutionary role for all those in society struggling against oppression. The prospects of austerity, tuition hikes, militarization, land grabs, and environmental devastation on the continent underscore the urgency of workers playing this leading role.

As this book was going to press in 2017, a crisis of immense proportions faced millions in Africa with the specter of famine produced by war and climate change. Michael Klare writes:

> Not since World War II have more human beings been at risk from disease and starvation than at this very moment. On March 10th, Stephen O'Brien, under secretary-general of the United Nations for humanitarian affairs, informed the Security Council that 20 million people in three African countries—Nigeria, Somalia, and South Sudan—as well as in Yemen were likely to die if not provided with emergency food and medical aid. "We are at a critical point in history," he declared. "Already at the beginning of the year we are facing the largest humanitarian crisis since the creation of the U.N. . . . There can be no doubt that pervasive water scarcity and prolonged drought (expected consequences of global warming) are contributing significantly to the disastrous conditions."[60]

The unfolding devastation—fueled by capitalist competition and environmental crisis, and in which extractive industries play no small part—urgently demands movements for social justice to compel an end to this horror. But it also demands a different kind of society altogether, one built on human need and equality. For socialists, that vision of another world is inextricably bound up with a strategy for workers' power that is *international*. A globally interconnected system of capitalism can only be replaced by a struggle from below, one likewise interconnected across workplaces, communities, and nations. For the left, the struggle to uproot capitalism in Africa can only advance the fight for its alternative everywhere.

Selected Bibliography

Books, Papers, and Speeches

Adu Boahen, A. *African Perspectives on Colonialism*. Baltimore and London: The Johns Hopkins University Press, 1989.

Amin, Samir. *Accumulation on a World Scale*. New York: Monthly Review Press, 1974.

Bacevich, Andrew J. *The Limits of Power: The End of American Exceptionalism*. New York: Henry Holt Books, 2008.

Bassey, Nnimmo. *To Cook a Continent: Destructive Extraction and the Climate Crisis in Africa*. Nairobi and Oxford: Fahamu Books & Pambazuka Press, 2012.

Blum, William. *Killing Hope: US Military and CIA Interventions since World War II*. Monroe, ME: Common Courage Press, 1995.

Bond, Patrick and Ana Garcia. *BRICS: An Anti-Capitalist Critique*. Chicago: Haymarket Books, 2015.

Bond, Patrick, Horman Chitonge, and Arndt Hopfmann, eds. *The Accumulation of Capital in Southern Africa: Rosa Luxemburg's Contemporary Relevance*. In Proceedings of the 2006 Rosa Luxemburg Seminar and the University of KwaZulu-Natal Centre for Civil Society's Colloquium on Economy, Society and Nature. Johannesburg: Rosa Luxemburg Foundation, 2007.

Bond, Patrick. *Looting Africa: The Economics of Exploitation*. London: Zed Books, 2006.

Boyce, James K., and Léonce Ndikumana. *Africa's Debt: Who Owes Whom?* Amherst, MA: Political Economy Research Institute, Working Paper Series Number 48, 2002.

Brautigam, Deborah. *The Dragon's Gift: The Real Story of China in Africa*. Oxford and New York: Oxford University Press, 2009.

Brewer, Anthony. *Marxist Theories of Imperialism: A Critical Survey*. London and Boston: Routledge & Kegan Paul, 1980.

Bukharin, Nikolai. *Imperialism and World Economy*. New York: International Publishers, 1929. www.marxists.org/archive/bukharin/works/1917/imperial/index.htm.

Burgis, Tom. *The Looting Machine: Warlords, Oligarchs, Corporations, Smugglers, and the Theft of Africa's Wealth*. New York: Public Affairs, 2015.

Calderisi, Robert. *The Trouble with Africa: Why Foreign Aid Isn't Working*. New York:

Palgrave Macmillan, 2006.

Callinicos, Alex. *Imperialism and Global Political Economy.* Cambridge: Polity Press, 2009.

Cartey, Wilfred, and Martin Kilson, eds. *The Africa Reader: Independent Africa.* New York: Vintage Books, 1970.

Chamberlain, M. E. *The Scramble for Africa.* 3rd ed. Abingdon and New York: Routledge, 2014.

Chung, Clairmont, ed. *Walter Rodney: A Promise of Revolution.* New York: Monthly Review Press, 2012.

Collier, Paul. *The Bottom Billion: Why the Poorest Countries Are Failing and What Can Be Done about It.* Oxford: Oxford University Press, 2008.

Cooper, Frederick. *Africa Since 1940.* New York: Columbia University Press, 2002.

Davis, Mike. *Planet of Slums.* London: Verso, 2006.

Day, Richard B., and Daniel Gaido, *Discovering Imperialism: Social Democracy to World War I.* Chicago: Haymarket Books (Historical Materialism Books), 2011.

Dwyer, Peter, and Leo Zeilig. *African Struggles Today: Social Movements Since Independence.* Chicago: Haymarket Books, 2012.

Fanon, Frantz. *The Wretched of the Earth.* New York: Grove Press, 1963.

Fitch, Bob, and Mary Oppenheimer. *Ghana: The End of an Illusion.* New York and London: Monthly Review Press, 1966.

Frank, Andre Gunder. *Capitalism and Underdevelopment in Latin America: Historical Studies of Chile and Brazil.* New York: Monthly Review Press, 1967.

French, Howard. *China's Second Continent: How a Million Migrants Are Building a New Empire in Africa.* New York: Vintage, 2014.

Ghazvinian, John. *Untapped: The Scramble for Africa's Oil.* New York: Harcourt Books, 2007.

Gourevitch, Philip. *We Wish to Inform You That Tomorrow We Will Be Killed with Our Families: Stories From Rwanda.* New York: Farrar, Straus, and Giroux, 1998.

Harman, Chris. *A People's History of the World: From the Stone Age to the New Millennium.* London: Bookmarks, 2008.

Harris, Nigel. *The End of the Third World.* New York: The Meredith Press, 1986.

Harvey, David. *A Brief History of Neoliberalism.* Oxford: Oxford University Press, 2005.

Harvey, David. *The New Imperialism.* Oxford: Oxford University Press, 2005.

Hicks, Celeste. *Africa's New Oil: Power, Pipelines and Future Fortunes.* London: Zed Books, 2015.

Hilferding, Rudolf. *Finance Capital. A Study of the Latest Phase of Capitalist Development.* Edited by Tom Bottomore. London: Routledge & Kegan Paul, 1981. www.marxists.org /archive/hilferding/1910/finkap/index.htm.

Hobsbawm, Eric. *The Age of Empire: 1875-1914.* New York: Vintage Books, 1989.

Hochschild, Adam. *King Leopold's Ghost: A Story of Greed, Terror, and Heroism in Colonial Africa.* New York: Houghton Mifflin, 1999.

Humphreys, Macartan, Jeffrey D. Sachs, and Joseph E. Stiglitz, eds. *Escaping the Resource Curse.* New York Columbia University Press, 2007.

Kashi, Ed, photog., and Michael Watts, ed. *Curse of the Black Gold: 50 Years of Oil in the Niger Delta*. Brooklyn, NY: Powerhouse Books, 2010.

Klare, Michael T. *The Race for What's Left: The Global Scramble for the World's Last Resources*. New York: Picador, 2012.

Lenin, V. I. "Imperialism: The Highest Stage of Capitalism." In *Lenin's Selected Works*. Vol. 1. Moscow: Progress Publishers, 1963, 667-766. www.marxists.org /archive/lenin/works/1916/imp-hsc/.

Lens, Sidney. *The Forging of the American Empire. From the Revolution to Vietnam: A History of US Imperialism*. London: Pluto Books; Chicago: Haymarket Books, 2003.

Lewis, Rupert. *Walter Rodney's Intellectual and Political Thought*. Detroit: Wayne State University Press, 1998.

Lindqvist, Sven. *"Exterminate All the Brutes": One Man's Odyssey into the Heart of Darkness and the Origins of European Genocide*. New York: The New Press, 2007.

Liska, George. *Imperial America: The International Politics of Primacy*. Baltimore: Johns Hopkins University Press, 1967.

Lumumba, Patrice. *The Truth about a Monstrous Crime of the Colonialists*, 44–47. Moscow: Foreign Languages Publishing House, 1961, www.marxists.org/subject /africa/lumumba/1960/06/independence.htm.

Luxemburg, Rosa. *The Accumulation of Capital*. Edited by W. Stark. London: Routledge and Kegan Paul, 1951. www.marxists.org/archive/luxemburg/1913 /accumulation-capital/index.htm.

Madunagu, Eddie. *Problems of Socialism: The Nigerian Challenge*. London: Zed Books, 1982.

Mamdani, Mahmood. *Citizen and Subject: Contemporary Africa and the Legacy of Late Colonialism*. Princeton, NJ: Princeton University Press, Princeton Series in Culture/Power/History, 1996.

Mamdani, Mahmood. *Saviors and Survivors: Darfur, Politics, and the War on Terror*. New York and London: Doubleday, 2009.

Manji, Firoze, and Sokari Ekine, eds. *African Awakening: The Emerging Revolutions*. Cape Town, Dakar, Nairobi, and Oxford: Pambazuka Press/Fahamu Books, 2011.

Manji, Firoze, and Stephen Marks. *African Perspectives on China in Africa*. Cape Town, Dakar, Nairobi, and Oxford: Pambazuka Press/Fahamu Books, 2007.

Marx, Karl and Frederick Engels, "Manifesto of the Communist Party," in *Marx/Engels Selected Works, Vol. One*. Moscow: Progress Publishers, 1969, 98-137. www.marxists.org/archive/marx/works/1848/communist-manifesto/index.htm

Marx, Karl. *Capital: A Critique of Political Economy*. Vol. 1. Moscow: Progress Publishers, 1887. www.marxists.org/archive/marx/works/1867-c1/ch31.htm.

Mkandawire, Thandika, and Charles C. Soludo. *Our Continent, Our Future: African Perspectives on Structural Adjustment*. Dakar: Council for the Development of Social Science Research in Africa, 1998.

Mott, William H. *United States Military Assistance: An Empirical Perspective*. Westport, CT: Greenwood Press, 2002.

Nkurunziza, Janvier D. *Capital Flight and Poverty Reduction in Africa*. Amherst, MA:

Political Economy Research Institute, Working Paper Series Number 365, 2014.

Okonta, Ike. *When Citizens Revolt: Nigerian Elites, Big Oil, and the Ogoni Struggle for Self-Determination*. Trenton, NJ: Africa World Press, 2008.

Okonta, Ike, and Oronto Douglas. *Where Vultures Feast: Shell, Human Rights, and Oil in the Niger Delta*. London: Verso, 2003.

Onimode, Bade, ed. *The IMF, the World Bank and the African Debt: The Economic Impact*. London: Zed Books, 1989.

Panitch, Leo, and Sam Gindin. *The Making of Global Capitalism: The Political Economy of American Empire*. London: Verso, 2012.

Renton, David, David Seddon, and Leo Zeilig. *The Congo: Plunder and Resistance*. London and New York: Zed Books, 2007.

Robinson, William. *A Theory of Global Capitalism: Production, Class, and State in a Transnational World*. Baltimore and London: Johns Hopkins University Press, 2004.

Rodney, Walter. *How Europe Underdeveloped Africa*. Nairobi and Washington, DC: East African Educational Publishers and Howard University Press, 1972.

Roy, Arundhati. *Capitalism: A Ghost Story*. Chicago: Haymarket Books, 2014.

Scahill, Jeremy. *Dirty Wars: The World Is a Battlefield*. New York: Nation Books, 2013.

Scholvin, Sören, ed. *A New Scramble for Africa? The Rush for Energy Resources in Sub-Saharan Africa*. Abingdon and New York: Routledge, 2016.

Shah, Sonia. *Crude: The Story of Oil*. New York: Seven Stories Press, 2004.

Southall, Roger, and Henning Melber, eds. *A New Scramble for Africa? Imperialism, Investment and Development*. Scottsville, South Africa: University of KwaZulu-Natal Press, 2009.

Toussaint, Eric. *Your Money or Your Life: The Tyranny of Global Finance*. Chicago: Haymarket Books, 2005.

Trotsky, Leon. "The Program of the International Revolution or a Program of Socialism in One Country?" *The Third International After Lenin*. New York: The Militant, 1929. www.marxists.org/archive/trotsky/1928/3rd/

Trotsky, Leon. *Results and Prospects*. Marxists' Internet Archive, 1906. www.marxists.org/archive/trotsky/1931/tpr/rp-index.htm.

Trotsky, Leon. *The Permanent Revolution*. Marxists' Internet Archive, 1929. www.marxists.org/archive/trotsky/1931/tpr/prre.htm.

Turse, Nick. *Next Time They'll Come to Count the Dead: War and Survival in South Sudan*. Chicago: Haymarket Books, 2016.

Turse, Nick. *Tomorrow's Battlefield: US Proxy Wars and Secret Ops in Africa*. Chicago: Haymarket Books, 2015.

Williams, Eric. *Capitalism and Slavery*. Chapel Hill: University of North Carolina Press, 1944, 1994.

Wolf, Eric R. *Europe and the People Without History*, 2nd edition. Berkeley: University of California Press, 2010.

Zack-Williams, Tunde, ed. *When the State Fails: Studies on Intervention in the Sierra Leone Civil War*. London: Pluto Press, 2012.

Zeilig, Leo, ed. *Class Struggle and Resistance in Africa*. Chicago: Haymarket Books, 2009.

Documentaries

Concerning Violence. 2014. Director: Göran Olsson.

Drilling and Killing: Chevron and Nigeria's Oil Dictatorship. 2003. *Democracy Now!* radio documentary. Directors: Amy Goodman and Jeremy Scahill.

Miners Shot Down. 2014. Director: Rehad Desai.

Poison Fire. 2008. Director: Lars Johansson.

Quel Souvenir: The Chad-Cameroon Pipeline. 2009. Director: Danya Abt.

Sweet Crude. 2007. Director: Sandy Cioffi.

Notes

Chapter One

1. Karl Marx, *Capital: A Critique of Political Economy.* vol. 1 (Moscow: Progress Publishers, 1887).

2. Patrick Bond, *Looting Africa: The Economics of Exploitation* (London: Zed Books, 2006), 2.

3. Cited in Sokari Ekine, "Women's responses to state violence in the Niger Delta," *Pambazuka News,* February 18, 2009, https://www.pambazuka.org/gender-minorities/women%E2%80%99s-responses-state-violence-niger-delta.

4. Sokari Ekine, "Women's responses to state violence in the Niger Delta," *Pambazuka News,* February 18, 2009, https://www.pambazuka.org/gender-minorities/women%E2%80%99s-responses-state-violence-niger-delta.

5. Chido Okafor Warri, "Protesters invade Chevron's facility, demand better deal," *Guardian* (Nigeria), August 11, 2016, https://guardian.ng/news/protesters-invade-chevrons-facility-demand-better-deal/.

6. Walter Rodney, *How Europe Underdeveloped Africa* (Nairobi and Washington, DC: East African Educational Publishers and Howard University Press, 1972), 27.

7. Cf. Leo Zeilig, ed. *Class Struggle and Resistance in Africa* (Chicago: Haymarket Books, 2008).

8. A note on terminology: throughout the book, I use the term "Third World" when discussing the period prior to the collapse of the Soviet Union and the end of the Cold War in 1991. This term was commonly used at the time to distinguish the so-called "First World" of North America, Western Europe, and Japan, the "Second World" of the Communist and Eastern bloc nations, and the "Third World" of the "developing" nations of Africa, Asia, and Latin America. When referring to the post-1991 period, I use the term "Global South," as this description is now standard, particularly for those writing from the left.

9. Howard French, *China's Second Continent: How a Million Migrants Are Building a New Empire in Africa* (New York: Vintage, 2014).

10. Deborah Brautigam, *The Dragon's Gift: The Real Story of China in Africa* (Oxford and New York: Oxford University Press, 2009).

11. United States Department of Defense, *Sustaining US Global Leadership: Priorities for 21st Century Defense*, 4. http://archive.defense.gov/news/Defense_Strategic _Guidance.pdf.

12. Nick Turse, "America's War-Fighting Footprint in Africa: Secret US Military Documents Reveal a Constellation of American Military Bases Across That Continent," *TomDispatch*, April 27, 2017, http://www.tomdispatch.com /post/176272/tomgram%3 A_nick_turse%2 C_the_u.s._military_moves _deeper_into_africa/#more.

13. Thandika Mkandawire and Charles C. Soludo, *Our Continent, Our Future: African Perspectives on Structural Adjustment* (Dakar: Council for the Development of Social Science Research in Africa, 1998), 22.

14. Ibid., 24.

15. Cited in John Pilger, "Iran may be the greatest crisis of modern times," *International Socialist Review* 53 (2007), http://www.isreview.org/issues/53/pilger.shtml.

16. Michael Watts, "Oil, Development, and the Politics of the Bottom Billion," *Macalester International* 24 (2009): 79–80.

17. Mahmood Mamdani, *Saviors and Survivors: Darfur, Politics, and the War on Terror* (New York and London: Doubleday, 2009), 19.

18. Karl Marx and Frederick Engels, "Manifesto of the Communist Party," in *Marx/Engels Selected Works*, vol. 1 (Moscow: Progress Publishers, 1969), 98–137.

19. Cf. V. I. Lenin, "Imperialism: The Highest Stage of Capitalism," in *Lenin's Selected Works*, vol. 1 (Moscow: Progress Publishers, 1963), 667–766.

20. Rosa Luxemburg, *The Accumulation of Capital*, ed. W. Stark (London: Routledge and Kegan Paul, 1951).

21. Cf. Nikolai Bukharin, *Imperialism and World Economy* (New York: International Publishers, 1929).

22. Cf. Rudolf Hilferding, *Finance Capital. A Study of the Latest Phase of Capitalist Development*, ed. Tom Bottomore (London: Routledge & Kegan Paul, 1981).

23. Luxemburg, *The Accumulation of Capital*.

24. David Harvey, *The New Imperialism* (Oxford and New York: Oxford University Press, 2005), 137.

25. Alex Callinicos makes this observation in his *Imperialism and Global Political Economy* (Cambridge: Polity Press, 2009), 42.

26. Patrick Bond, Horman Chitonge, and Arndt Hopfmann, eds., "The Accumulation of Capital in Southern Africa: Rosa Luxemburg's Contemporary Relevance," in *Proceedings of the Rosa Luxemburg Seminar 2006 and the University of KwaZulu-Natal Centre for Civil Society's Colloquium on Economy, Society and Nature* (Johannesburg: Rosa Luxemburg Foundation, 2007).

27. Lenin, "Imperialism: The Highest Stage of Capitalism," 667–766.

28. Ibid.

29. Richard B. Day and Daniel Gaido, *Discovering Imperialism: Social Democracy to World War I* (Chicago: Haymarket Books, 2011), 86.

30. Others, such as Bukharin and Hilferding, shared much of Lenin's approach, and Lenin's pamphlet "Imperialism" built on the contributions of both. All shared a similar general starting point. As Brewer puts it: "Today, the term imperialism is

generally taken to refer to the dominance of more developed over less developed countries. For the classical Marxists it meant, primarily, rivalry between advanced capitalist countries, rivalry expressed in conflict over territory, taking political and military as well as economic forms, and tending, ultimately, to inter-imperialist war." See Anthony Brewer, *Marxist Theories of Imperialism: A Critical Survey* (London and Boston: Routledge & Kegan Paul, 1980), 79–80.

Hilferding's view stressed particularly the growing role played by finance capital and the use of protectionism and tariffs in ushering in an intense period of rivalries. For Hilferding, finance capital was bound up with the state. As he put it, "The old free-traders saw in free trade not only the most just economic policy, but also the basis for an era of peace. Finance capital . . . does not believe in the harmony of capitalist interests, but knows that the competitive struggle becomes more and more a political struggle. . . . The ideal is to insure for one's own nation the domination of the world." See Hilferding, *Finance Capital. A Study of the Latest Phase of Capitalist Development*, ed. Tom Bottomore (London: Routledge & Kegan Paul, 1981), https://www.marxists.org/archive/hilferding/1910/finkap/index.htm.

Bukharin's work probably represents the most developed of the classical Marxist theories. He extended Lenin's and Hilderding's analysis on the tendencies toward concentration and centralization, concluding that massive monopolies increasingly fused with national states, resulting in pressures toward both nationalization and internationalization of capital. As he puts it, "It is much easier to overcome competition on a 'national' scale than on a world scale. The contradiction between these two opposed tendencies drives the system into war and breakdown." He termed this fusing of state and capital "state capitalist trusts," meant to mitigate internal conflict, but as Brewer puts it, "in Bukharin's vision, the anarchy of capitalist competition is entirely suppressed at the national level, only to re-emerge in an even more disruptive form at the world level" (Brewer, *Marxist Theories of Imperialism*, 107).

Likewise, we can identify a weakness in Hilferding and Bukharin's approach borne out by historical events—namely, their argument that capitalism becomes fused with the state to such an extent that it takes control over the actual process of accumulation. As Callinicos points out, "on the eve of the Great Depression, Bukharin claimed that the system was escaping the danger of economic crises, writing 'From the point of view of the economic analysis of present-day world economy, war is the *central problem of the present day*" (Alex Callinicos, *Imperialism and Global Political Economy* [Cambridge: Polity Press, 2009], 57). The theoretical tendency to *overstate* the ability of the state to disconnect from and transcend economic crisis has been proven incorrect through history.

31. Lenin, "Imperialism: The Highest Stage of Capitalism," 667–766.
32. Leon Trotsky, "The Program of the International Revolution or a Program of Socialism in One Country?" *The Third International After Lenin* (New York: The Militant, 1929), https://www.marxists.org/archive/trotsky/1928/3rd/ti01.htm.

33. Horace Campbell, "Walter Rodney, the Prophet of Self Emancipation," *Pambazuka News,* May 12, 2005, https://www.pambazuka.org/governance/walter-rodney-prophet-self-emancipation. Cf. Clairmont Chung, ed., *Walter Rodney: A Promise of Revolution* (New York: Monthly Review Press, 2012). The Chung volume includes contributions from Shivji, Thomas, and others on Rodney's legacy.

34. Cited in Rupert Lewis, *Walter Rodney's Intellectual and Political Thought* (Detroit: Wayne State University Press, 1998), xvii.

35. Rodney, *How Europe Underdeveloped Africa*, 206.

36. Ibid., 10.

37. Ibid., 96.

38. Ibid., 100.

39. Ibid., 105–07.

40. Cf. Eric Hobsbawm, *The Age of Empire: 1875–1914* (New York: Vintage Books, 1989).

41. Chris Harman, *A People's History of the World: From the Stone Age to the New Millennium* (London: Bookmarks, 2008), 394.

42. Eric R. Wolf, *Europe and the People Without History,* 2nd ed. (Berkeley: University of California Press, 2010).

43. Rodney, *How Europe Underdeveloped Africa*, 229–30.

44. Cited in M. E. Chamberlain, *The Scramble for Africa*, 3rd ed. (Abingdon and New York: Routledge, 2014), 4.

45. A. Adu Boahen, *African Perspectives on Colonialism* (Baltimore and London: Johns Hopkins University Press, 1989), 1.

46. Ibid., 55.

47. Harman, *A People's History of the World*, 395.

48. Adam Hochschild, *King Leopold's Ghost: A Story of Greed, Terror, and Heroism in Colonial Africa* (New York: Houghton Mifflin, 1999).

49. Cited in Sven Lindqvist. *"Exterminate All the Brutes": One Man's Odyssey into the Heart of Darkness and the Origins of European Genocide* (New York: The New Press, 2007).

50. Luxemburg, *The Accumulation of Capital.*

51. Rodney, *How Europe Underdeveloped Africa*, 152.

52. Ibid., 142.

53. Ibid., 26.

54. Ibid., 174

55. Ibid., 180.

56. Ibid., 84.

57. Ibid., 165.

58. Ibid., 25.

59. Ibid., 212.

60. Ibid., 261.

61. Ibid., 216.

62. Ibid., 262.

63. Ibid., 279–80.
64. Ibid., 199–200.

Chapter Two

1. Frantz Fanon, *The Wretched of the Earth* (New York: Grove Press, 1963), 27.
2. Eric Toussaint, *Your Money or Your Life: The Tyranny of Global Finance* (Chicago: Haymarket Books, 2005).
3. Office of the Press Secretary, The White House, "Remarks by the President to the Ghanaian Parliament," 2009, https://obamawhitehouse.archives.gov /the-press-office/remarks-president-ghanaian-parliament.
4. Christine Lagarde, International Monetary Fund, speech to the Nigerian National Assembly, "Nigeria—Act with Resolve, Build Resilience, and Exercise Restraint," 2016, https://www.imf.org/external/np/speeches/2016/010616.htm.
5. Jubilee USA Network, *Unmasking the IMF: The Post-Financial Crisis Imperative for Reform* (Washington, DC: Jubilee USA Network, 2010), http://www.jubileeusa .org/fileadmin/user_upload/Resources/IMF_Report.pdf.
6. Cf. Matina Stevis, "Angola to Seek IMF Aid to Cope with Looming Financial Crisis," *Wall Street Journal*, April 6, 2016, https://www.wsj.com/articles/angola -to-seek-imf-aid-to-cope-with-looming-financial-crisis-1459957868; Matina Stevis, "IMF's African Push Reopens Old Wounds," *Wall Street Journal*, February 20, 2016, https://www.wsj.com/articles/imfs-african-push-reopens-old -wounds-1456050601.
7. Pete Binns, "Revolution and state capitalism in the third world," *International Socialism* 2, no. 25 (1984): 37–68, https://www.marxists.org/history/etol/writers /binns/1984/xx/3world.htm. Binns notes that at the time, the United States had more than 50 percent of world manufacturing and finance at its disposal.
8. Africa Action, "Akwaaba! . . . Ghana Should Meet Obama With Cautious Optimism," press release (2009), https://www.commondreams.org/newswire /2009/07/06/akwaaba-ghana-should-meet-obama-cautious-optimism.
9. Catherine Blampied, "African Governments Must Take Responsibility on Poverty," *Financial Times* (2014), https://www.ft.com/content/e84d07dc-6fc7- 3a6a-a427 -50d9bc00ae0c.
10. Carey L. Biron, "Africa 'Net Creditor' to Rest of World, New Data Shows," *Inter Press Service* (2013), http://www.ipsnews.net/2013/05/africa-net-creditor-to -rest-of-world-new-data-shows/.
11. Patrick Bond, "Is Africa Still Being Looted? World Bank Dodges Its Own Research," *Links International Journal of Socialist Renewal* (2010), http://links.org.au /node/1843.
12. World Health Organization, *World Health Statistics 2015* (Geneva: WHO Press, 2015), http://apps.who.int/iris/bitstream/10665/170250/1/9789240694439 _eng.pdf, 52, 74, 122.
13. Ibid., 23.

14. UNICEF and World Health Organization, *Progress on Sanitation and Drinking Water—2015 update and MDG assessment* (Geneva: WHO Press, 2015), http://apps.who.int/iris/bitstream/10665/177752/1/9789241509145_eng.pdf?ua=1, 13.

15. World Bank Africa Region. *Africa Development Indicators 2007: Spreading and Sustaining Growth in Africa* (Washington, DC: World Bank, 2008), http://elibrary.worldbank.org/doi/pdf/10.1596/978-0-8213-7283-8.

16. African Development Bank, Organisation for Economic Co-operation and Development, United Nations Development Programme, *African Economic Outlook 2014: Global Value Chains and Africa's Industrialisation* (2014), http://www.africaneconomicoutlook.org/en/telechargements, 158.

17. Jennifer Abrahamson, "Meet the buppies," *Salon*, April 29, 2004, http://www.salon.com/2004/04/29/buppies/.

18. John Ghazvinian, *Untapped: The Scramble for Africa's Oil* (New York: Harcourt Books, 2007), 68.

19. Ibid., 19.

20. Mike Davis, *Planet of Slums* (London: Verso, 2006), 164.

21. Charlie Kimber, "Aid, governance and exploitation," *International Socialism* 107 (2005), http://isj.org.uk/aid-governance-and-exploitation/.

22. Gavin Capps, "Redesigning the Debt Trap," *International Socialism* 107 (2005): http://isj.org.uk/web-update-the-new-debt-trap-finalised/.

23. Cf. Andre Gunder Frank, *Capitalism and Underdevelopment in Latin America: Historical Studies of Chile and Brazil* (New York: Monthly Review Press, 1967).

24. Cf. Samir Amin, *Accumulation on a World Scale* (New York: Monthly Review Press, 1974).

25. Cf. David Harvey, *A Brief History of Neoliberalism* (Oxford: Oxford University Press, 2005); Harvey, *The New Imperialism.*

26. Cf. Bond, *Looting Africa.*

27. Mahmood Mamdani, *Citizen and Subject: Contemporary Africa and the Legacy of Late Colonialism* (Princeton, NJ: Princeton University Press, Princeton Series in Culture/Power/History, 1996), 74–77.

28. Peter Dwyer and Leo Zeilig, *African Struggles Today: Social Movements Since Independence* (Chicago: Haymarket Books, 2012), 74.

29. Ibid.

30. Cf. Mamdani, *Citizen and Subject.*

31. Vishwas Satgar, "Global Capitalism and Neo-Liberalisation of Africa," in *A New Scramble for Africa?: Imperialism, Investment and Development,* ed. Roger Southall and Henning Melber (Scottsville, South Africa: University of KwaZulu-Natal Press, 2009), 41.

32. Nigel Harris, *The End of the Third World* (New York: The Meredith Press, 1986), 168.

33. David Seddon, "Historical Overview of Struggle in Africa," in *Class Struggle and Resistance in Africa,* ed. Leo Zeilig (Chicago: Haymarket Books, 2009), 81.

34. Fanon, *The Wretched of the Earth,* 12.

35. Ekuru Aukot, "Northern Kenya: A Legal-Political Scar," *Pambazuka News* 401 (2008), http://pambazuka.org/en/category/comment/51035.

36. Munyonzwe Hamalengwa, "No Land, No Freedom," *Pambazuka News* 726 (2015), http://pambazuka.org/en/category/comment/94717. Cf. Tom Burgis, "Ethiopia: The billionaire's farm," *Financial Times,* March 1, 2016, https://ig.ft.com /sites/land-rush-investment/ethiopia/.

37. Seddon, "Historical Overview of Struggle in Africa," 78.

38. Kwame Nkrumah, "Neocolonialism in Africa," in *The Africa Reader: Independent Africa,* ed. Wilfred Cartey and Martin Kilson (New York: Vintage Books, 1970), 217–18.

39. Bob Fitch and Mary Oppenheimer, *Ghana: The End of an Illusion* (New York and London: Monthly Review Press, 1966).

40. Mamdani, *Citizen and Subject,* 25.

41. Ibid., 22–23.

42. Rodney, *How Europe Underdeveloped Africa,* 262.

43. Ibid., 25.

44. Frederick Cooper, *Africa Since 1940* (New York: Columbia University Press, 2002), 16.

45. Chris Harman, "The End of Poverty?" *Socialist Review* 297 (2005), http:// socialistreview.org.uk/297/end-poverty.

46. United Nations Economic Commission for Africa, *Survey of economic conditions in Africa, 1970* (Addis Ababa: United Nations Economic Commission for Africa, 1971), http://repository.uneca.org/pdfpreview/bitstream/handle /123456789/16796/Bib-59150-Summ.pdf?sequence=1, 13.

47. Ibid., 3.

48. UNICEF, "The 1960s: Decade of development," http://www.unicef.org /sowc96/1960s.htm.

49. Frederick Cooper, "Modernizing Bureaucrats, Backward Africans, and the Development Concept," *International Development and the Social Sciences: Essays on the History and Politics of Knowledge,* ed. Frederick Cooper and Randall M. Packard (Berkeley, CA: University of California Press, 1997), 64–92.

50. Fitch and Oppenheimer, *Ghana,* 45.

51. Ibid., 70.

52. Ibid., 47.

53. Elise Huillery, "The Black Man's Burden: The Cost of Colonization of French West Africa," *The Journal of Economic History* 74 (2012): 5, http://econ.sciences -po.fr/sites/default/files/file/elise/Black_Man_Burden_20june2012.pdf.

54. Ibid.

55. Rodney, *How Europe Underdeveloped Africa,* 245.

56. Ibid., 206.

57. Senate Committee on Foreign Relations, *Study Mission to Africa, November-December 1960: Report* (Washington, DC: US Government. Printing Office, 1961), 22.

58. Rodney, *How Europe Underdeveloped Africa,* 205.

59. Mamdani, *Citizen and Subject,* 104.

60. Sidney Lens, *The Forging of the American Empire. From the Revolution to Vietnam: A History of US Imperialism* (London: Pluto Books; Chicago: Haymarket Books, 2003), 349.

61. Fanon, *The Wretched of the Earth*, 35.

62. Lens, *The Forging of the American Empire*, 350–1.

63. Robert McNamara interview, *The Banker* (1969).

64. One example is the preparations by Belgian capital for the end of colonialism in the Congo. Cf. David Renton, David Seddon, and Leo Zeilig, *The Congo: Plunder and Resistance* (London and New York: Zed Books, 2007), 127.

65. Cited in Alemayehu G. Mariam, "Financing for (Under)development in Africa? How the West Underdeveloped Africa and Is Now Trying to 'Finance Develop' It," *Pambazuka News* (2015), https://www.pambazuka.org/governance/financing-underdevelopment-africa.

66. "Eurafrica" was an orientation of the European Economic Community (EEC) that sought close economic collaboration and shared development projects between Europe and African nations. These goals were reiterated in agreements such as the Yaoundé Convention held in Yaoundé, Cameroon, in 1963 and several subsequent gatherings.

67. Oginga Odinga, "Not Yet Uhuru," in *The Africa Reader: Independent Africa*, ed. Wilfred Cartey and Martin Kilson (New York: Vintage Books, 1970), 229.

68. Kwame Nkrumah, "Neocolonialism in Africa," in *The Africa Reader: Independent Africa*, ed. Wilfred Cartey and Martin Kilson (New York: Vintage Books, 1970), 217.

69. Fanon, *The Wretched of the Earth*, 54.

70. Senate Committee on Foreign Relations, *Study Mission to Africa, November–December 1960*, 2.

71. W.W. Rostow, "US Policy in a Changing World," *Department of State Bulletin* (1964), 642.

72. Senate Committee on Foreign Relations, *Study Mission to Africa, November–December 1960*, 3.

73. Ibid., 43.

74. Fitch and Oppenheimer, *Ghana*, 12.

75. Cited in Fitch and Oppenheimer, *Ghana*, 12–13.

76. Senate Committee on Foreign Relations, *Study Mission to Africa, November–December 1960*, 32–33.

77. *Survey of Current Business*, August 1963, October 1968, and 1971.

78. Dick Clark, United States Senate, *US Corporate Interests in South Africa: Report to the Committee on Foreign Relations.* (Washington, DC: US Government Printing Office, 1978), 5.

79. Ibid., 8.

80. Ibid., 10.

81. William F. Komer, Special Assistant for National Security Affairs, speaking in 1966, cited in Charles Quist-Adade, "The Coup That Set Ghana and Africa 50 Years Back," *Pambazuka News* (2016), http://www.pambazuka.net/en/category.php/features/96756.

82. Fitch and Oppenheimer, *Ghana.*

83. Yao Graham, "Nkrumah: Model Challenge for Ghana's Rulers," *Pambazuka News* (2009), http://www.pambazuka.net/en/category.php/features/57083/.

84. Lawrence A. Marinelli, "Liberia's Open-Door Policy," *Journal of Modern African Studies* 2, no. 1 (1964): 91–98.

85. US Bureau of the Census, *Economic Assistance over the Period 1962–1971, Statistical Abstract of the US: 1972,* 93rd ed. (Washington, DC: 1972), 774–75.

86. Renton, Seddon, and Zeilig, *The Congo*, 85.

87. Patrice Lumumba, *The Truth about a Monstrous Crime of the Colonialists* (Moscow: Foreign Languages Publishing House, 1961), 44–47, https://www.marxists.org/subject/africa/lumumba/1960/06/independence.htm

88. Renton, Seddon, and Zeilig, *The Congo*, 95.

89. Abayomi Azikiwe, "The Re-Emerging African Debt Crisis: Renewed IMF 'Economic Medicine,'" *Pan African News* (2015), http://panafricannews.blogspot.com/search?q=The+Re-emerging+African+Debt+Crisis%22+Azikiwe.

90. Cf. William Blum, *Killing Hope: US Military and CIA Interventions Since World War II* (Monroe, ME: Common Courage Press, 1995).

91. Harris, *The End of the Third World*, 13–14.

92. Leo Zeilig and David Seddon, "Marxism, Class, and Resistance in Africa," in *Class Struggle and Resistance in Africa,* ed. Zeilig (Chicago: Haymarket Books, 2008), 27.

93. Pete Binns, "Revolution and State Capitalism in the Third World," *International Socialism* 25 (1984): 37–68.

94. Leo Zeilig, "Tony Cliff: Deflected permanent revolution in Africa," *International Socialism* 126 (2010), http://www.isj.org.uk/?id=641.

95. Harris, *The End of the Third World*, 118.

96. Roger Southall, "Scrambling for Africa? Continuities and Discontinuities with Formal Imperialism," in *A New Scramble for Africa?,* ed. Roger Southall and Henning Melber (Scottsville, South Africa: University of KwaZulu-Natal Press, 2009), 10.

97. Pete Binns, "Revolution and State Capitalism in the Third World," *International Socialism* 25 (1984): 37–68, https://www.marxists.org/history/etol/writers/binns/1984/xx/3world.htm.

98. Harris, *The End of the Third World*, 160. Along similar lines, Fanon wrote in *The Wretched of the Earth:* "The national bourgeoisie has the psychology of a politician, not an industrialist." Cf. Mireille Fanon-Mendès-France, "Frantz Fanon and the Current Multiple Crises," *Pambazuka News* (2011). http://pambazuka.org/en/category/features/78515.

99. Harris, *The End of the Third World*, 163.

100. Pete Binns, "Revolution and State Capitalism in the Third World," *International Socialism* 25 (1984): 37–68, https://www.marxists.org/history/etol/writers/binns/1984/xx/3world.htm.

101. Ibid.

102. Harris, *The End of the Third World*, 143.

103. Ibid., 23.

104. Ibid., 117.

105. Toussaint, *Your Money or Your Life*, 251.

106. Zeilig, *Class Struggle and Resistance in Africa*.

107. Harris, *The End of the Third World*, 201.

108. Pete Binns, "Revolution and State Capitalism in the Third World," *International Socialism* 25 (1984): 37–68, https://www.marxists.org/history/etol/writers/binns/1984/xx/3world.htm.

109. Zeilig and Seddon, "Marxism, Class, and Resistance in Africa," 46–50.

110. Binns, "Revolution and State Capitalism in the Third World."

111. Ibid., 186.

Chapter Three

1. *The Conference Board Review*, "Questioning Authority: Interview with Robert Calderisi," (2006).

2. Development economist Paul Collier is a well-known advocate of this designation. See *Wall Street Journal*, "What's Holding Back Africa? Jackson Hole's Sleeper Hit," (2006), http://blogs.wsj.com/washwire/2006/08/26/jackson-holes-sleeper-hit/.

3. Other theorists of transnational capitalism have offered more compelling explanations. William Robinson, for one, rejects claims of a stateless world, writing, "by the early twenty-first century the vast majority of the world's peoples had been integrated into the capitalist market and brought into capitalist production relations" (*A Theory of Global Capitalism: Production, Class, and State in a Transnational World* [Baltimore and London: Johns Hopkins University Press, 2004, 6]). For Robinson, the rise of transnational capital allows it to "go global," and "the obstacles to moving capital around the world have decreased dramatically. . . . In the process, national production systems have become fragmented and integrated externally into new globalized circuits of accumulation" (ibid., 9–10). Yet despite these outward pulls, "this worldwide decentralization and fragmentation of the production process has taken place together with the centralization of command and control of the global economy in transnational capital" (ibid., 15). Based on those processes, he posits the rise of "transnational state" formations, which have emerged to "function as the collective authority for a global ruling class," and within which nation-states are being absorbed, namely the United Nations, the World Trade Organization, and the IMF and World Bank (ibid., 88).

   However, while such frameworks correctly identify important features in today's world system, this approach tends to overstate its centralizing role both with regard to transnational bodies and the global economy. Paradoxically, in the twenty-first century, these global integration strategies may in fact have compelled the need to sharpen the role of the company's home country, all the more so in the face of economic crisis. Issues of tariffs and protectionism, for instance, have by no means fallen to the wayside, and ruling classes rely on national states to enforce their interests as against their competitors, whether through trade agreements or outright military conflict.

4. Abayomi Azikiwe, "The Re-Emerging African Debt Crisis: Renewed IMF 'Economic Medicine,'" *Pan African News* (2015), http://panafricannews.blogspot .com/search?q=The+Re-emerging+African+Debt+Crisis percent22+Azikiwe.

5. Graham, "Nkrumah: Model Challenge for Ghana's rulers."

6. Azikiwe, "The Re-Emerging African Debt Crisis: Renewed IMF 'Economic Medicine."

7. Cited in Toussaint, *Your Money or Your Life*, 203.

8. Ibid., 206.

9. Cited in Biodun Olamosu and Andy Wynne, "Africa rising? The Economic History of Sub-Saharan Africa," *International Socialism* 146 (2015), http://isj.org .uk/africa-rising/.

10. Bade Onimode, "Introduction," in *The IMF, the World Bank and the African Debt: The Economic Impact*, ed. Bade Onimode (London: Zed Books, 1989), 2.

11. Harvey, *A Brief History of Neoliberalism*, 12.

12. Joel Geier, "International Monetary Fund: Debt Cop," *International Socialist Review* 11 (2000), http://www.isreview.org/issues/11/debt_cop.shtml.

13. Toussaint, *Your Money or Your Life*, 142.

14. Cited in Olamosu and Wynne, "Africa rising?"

15. Harvey, *A Brief History of Neoliberalism*, 29.

16. Eric Toussaint, Daniel Munevar, Pierre Gottiniaux, and Antonio Sanabria, "World Debt Figures 2015," Committee for the Abolition of Illegitimate Debt (2015), http://www.cadtm.org/The-World-Bank-and-the-IMF.

17. Joseph Stiglitz, *Globalization and Its Discontents* (London: Penguin Books, 2002), 12.

18. Harvey, *A Brief History of Neoliberalism*, 15.

19. Bade Onimode, "IMF and World Bank Programmes in Africa," in *The IMF, the World Bank and the African Debt: The Economic Impact*, ed. Bade Onimode (London: Zed Books, 1989), 25.

20. Bond, *Looting Africa*, 14–15.

21. Ibid., 15.

22. Olamosu and Wynne, "Africa rising?" Onimode also describes declining terms of trade and a fall in export earnings, with a loss of $19 billion in export earnings in 1985 and 1986 alone. Bade Onimode, "IMF and World Bank Programmes in Africa," 27.

23. Roger Southall, "Scrambling for Africa?" 31.

24. Cited in John J. Saul and Colin Leys, "Sub-Saharan Africa in Global Capitalism," *Monthly Review* 51, no. 3 (1999): https://monthlyreview.org/1999 /07/01/sub-saharan-africa-in-global-capitalism/.

25. Capps, "Redesigning the Debt Trap."

26. Jean Nanga, "New Capitalist Domination and Imperialism in Africa," Committee for the Abolition of Illegitimate Debt (2015), http://cadtm.org/ New-capitalist-domination-and-nb1.

27. Michael Watts, "Empire of Oil: Capitalist Dispossession and the Scramble for Africa," *Monthly Review* (2006), https://monthlyreview.org/2006/09/01/empire-of-oil-capitalist-dispossession-and-the-scramble-for-africa/.

28. Peter Lawrence and Yao Graham, "Structural Transformation and Economic Development in Africa," *Review of African Political Economy* (2015), http://roape.net/2015/12/18/structural-transformation-and-economic-development-in-africa/.

29. Capps, "Redesigning the Debt Trap."

30. Peter Dwyer, "South Africa Under the ANC: Still Bound to the Chains of Exploitation," in *Class Struggle and Resistance in Africa*, ed. Zeilig (Chicago: Haymarket Books, 2008), 193.

31. "Interview with Trevor Ngwane," in *Class Struggle and Resistance in Africa*, ed. Zeilig (Chicago: Haymarket Books, 2008), 217.

32. Henning Melber, "The New Scramble for Africa's Resources," *Pambazuka News* (2007), https://www.pambazuka.org/governance/new-scramble-africa percentE2 percent80 percent99s-resources.

33. Tax Justice Network Africa, *Tax Us If You Can: Why Africa Should Stand Up for Tax Justice* (Nairobi, Kenya, 2011), http://www.taxjusticeafrica.net/wp-content/uploads/2015/11/Tax-Us-If-You-Can-Why-Africa-should-Stand-up-for-Tax-Justice.pdf.

34. The full declaration can be found at http://www.ifg.org/wssd/acsnepad_decl.htm.

35. Ashwin Desai, "Mandela's Legacy," *International Socialist Review* 35 (2004), http://www.isreview.org/issues/35/mandelaslegacy.shtml.

36. Data cited in John J. Saul and Colin Leys, "Sub-Saharan Africa in Global Capitalism," *Monthly Review* 51, no. 3 (1999), https://monthlyreview.org/1999/07/01/sub-saharan-africa-in-global-capitalism/). Despite the falling *rate* of investment at this time, as Saul and Leys point out, the *return* of investment in Africa was "the highest of any region in the world (25.3 percent in 1997)."

37. James K. Boyce and Léonce Ndikumana, *Africa's Debt: Who Owes Whom?* (Amherst, MA: Political Economy Research Institute, Working Paper Series Number 48, 2002), 1.

38. Stiglitz, *Globalization and Its Discontents*, 8.

39. Xan Rice, "Biwater Fails in Tanzanian Damages Claim," *Guardian* (2008), http://www.theguardian.com/business/2008/jul/28/utilities.tanzania.

40. Jubilee Debt Campaign, *The New Debt Trap: How the Response to the Last Global Financial Crisis Has Laid the Ground for the Next* (2015), http://jubileedebt.org.uk/wp-content/uploads/2015/07/The-new-debt-trap-report.pdf.

41. Capps, "Redesigning the Debt Trap."

42. Jubilee Debt Campaign, *The New Debt Trap*.

43. Michael Thomson, Alexander Kentikelenis, and Thomas Stubbs, "Structural Adjustment Programmes Adversely Affect Vulnerable Populations: A Systematic-Narrative Review of Their Effect on Child and Maternal Health," *Public Health Reviews* 38 (2017), https://publichealthreviews.biomedcentral.com/track/pdf/10.1186/s40985-017-0059-2?site=publichealthreviews.biomedcentral.com.

44. Jubilee USA, "President Obama Visits Africa as Corporate Tax Avoidance and Debt Crisis Trap Millions of Africans in Poverty," press release, June 28, 2013, https://officeofpublicwitness.blogspot.com/?m=0.

45. Lee Wengraf, "Washington Fuels Africa's crisis," *Socialist Worker* (2009), http://socialistworker.org/2009/08/17/washington-fuels-crisis-in-africa.

46. Bond, *Looting Africa*, 58.

47. Toussaint, *Your Money or Your Life*, 279.

48. Cited in ibid., 278.

49. David Cronin, "African Countries Fight EU for Survival," *Inter Press Service* (2007), http://www.ipsnews.net/2007/05/trade-african-countries-fight-eu-for-survival/.

50. Emily Jones, *Signing Away the Future: How Trade and Investment Agreements Between Rich and Poor Countries Undermine Development* (Oxfam International, 2007), http://policy-practice.oxfam.org.uk/publications/signing-away-the-future -how-trade-and-investment-agreements-between-rich-and-po-114595.

51. Davis, *Planet of Slums*, 23.

52. ActionAid International, *Trade Invaders: The WTO and Developing Countries' "Right to Protect"* (2005), https://www.actionaid.org.uk/sites/default/files /doc_lib/6_3_trade_invaders.pdf.

53. Cited in Capps, "Redesigning the Debt Trap."

54. Bond, *Looting Africa*, 99.

55. Olamosu and Wynne, "Africa rising? The Economic History of Sub-Saharan Africa."

56. Dani Rodrik, "Premature Deindustrialization" (Cambridge, MA: Harvard University Press, 2015): http://drodrik.scholar.harvard.edu/files/dani-rodrik/files /premature_deindustrialization_revised2.pdf.

57. Toussaint, *Your Money or Your Life*, 18.

58. Cited in Bond, *Looting Africa*, 57.

59. Davis, *Planet of Slums*, 156.

60. World Bank, *Africa Development Indicators, 2007* (Washington, DC: 2008).

61. Toussaint, *Your Money or Your Life*, 195.

62. Leo Zeilig and David Seddon, "Marxism, Class, and Resistance in Africa," in *Class Struggle and Resistance in Africa,* ed. Zeilig (Chicago: Haymarket Books, 2008), 51.

63. Toussaint, *Your Money or Your Life*, 27.

64. Ibid., 281.

65. Mohamed Sultan and Stephen Yeboah, "Guest Post—Why Tackling Illicit Financial Flows Offers Energy and Climate Opportunities for Africa," *Africa in Perspective* (2015), https://africainperspective.com/2015/07/06/guest-post-why-tackling -illicit-financial-flows-offers-energy-and-climate-opportunities-for-africa/.

66. Bond, *Looting Africa*, 51.

67. Global Financial Integrity, *Illicit Financial Flows from Africa: Hidden Resource for Development* (2008), http://www.gfintegrity.org/storage/gfip/documents /reports/gfi_africareport_web.pdf.

68. Léonce Ndikumana, "Savings, Capital Flight, and African Development, Part 1," *Triple Crisis: Global Perspectives on Finance, Development and Environment* (2014), http://triplecrisis.com/savings-capital-flight-and-african-development-part-1/.
69. Léonce Ndikumana, "Savings, Capital Flight, and African Development, Part 1."
70. James K. Boyce and Léonce Ndikumana, *Africa's Debt: Who Owes Whom?* (Amherst, MA: Political Economy Research Institute, Working Paper Series Number 48, 2002), 3.
71. Tim Jones, "UK Government Response to Debt Trap Campaign," *Jubilee Debt Campaign* (2016), http://jubileedebt.org.uk/blog/uk-government-response-on -debt-trap-campaign.
72. Capps, "Redesigning the Debt Trap."
73. Africa Action press release, 2001, cited in Capps, "Redesigning the Debt Trap."
74. Salaheddine Lemaizi, "Poverty in Africa, the unvoiced failures of the World Bank," *Committee for the Abolition of Illegitimate Debt* (2016), http://cadtm.org /Poverty-in-Africa-the-unvoiced.
75. Thandika Mkandawire, "Maladjusted African Economies and Globalization," *Africa Development* 30, nos. 1, 2 (2005), 1–33.
76. Carey L. Biron, "Africa 'Net Creditor' to Rest of World, New Data Shows," *Inter Press Service*, (2013), http://www.ipsnews.net/2013/05/africa-net-creditor-to -rest-of-world-new-data-shows/.
77. Bond, *Looting Africa*, 50.
78. Tax Justice Network Africa, *Walking the Talk on Illicit Financial Flows: The G20's Responsibility in Combating Illicit Capital Flight: A Policy Brief for South Africa* (Nairobi, Kenya, 2015), http://www.taxjusticeafrica.net/wp-content /uploads/2015/11/Policy-Brief-Illicit-Flows-Tax-Evasion-SA-G20.pdf.
79. Ibid.
80. Tax Justice Network Africa, *Tax Us If You Can.*
81. Ibid.
82. Ibid.
83. Francesca Carnibella, "The Movement to End Tax Havens Is Already 100,000 Strong and Growing," *Oxfam International* (2016), https://blogs.oxfam.org/en /blogs/16-01-25-movement-end-tax-havens-already-100000-strong-and -growing.
84. Janvier D. Nkurunziza, *Capital Flight and Poverty Reduction in Africa* (Amherst, MA: Political Economy Research Institute Working Paper Series Number 365, 2014), http://www.academia.edu/3219040/Capital_Flight_and_Human _Development_in_Africa.
85. Fanon, *The Wretched of the Earth*, 59.
86. Robert Calderisi, *The Trouble with Africa: Why Foreign Aid Isn't Working* (New York: Palgrave Macmillan, 2006), 7.
87. *The Conference Board Review*, "Questioning Authority: Interview with Robert Calderisi," (2006).
88. Catherine Blampied, "African Governments Must Take Responsibility on Poverty," *Financial Times* (2014), https://www.ft.com/content/e84d07dc-6fc7-

3a6a-a427
-50d9bc00ae0c.

89. Calderisi, *The Trouble with Africa*, 9.

90. Oxfam International, "Oxfam Reaction to the Publication of New OECD Aid Figures" (2015), https://www.oxfam.org/en/pressroom/reactions/oxfam -reaction-publication-new-oecd-aid-figures.

91. Organisation for Economic Co-operation and Development "The 0.7 Percent ODA/GNI Target—A History" (2016), http://www.oecd.org/dac/stats /the07odagnitarget-ahistory.htm. The European Union nations in 2004 were France, Germany, Austria, Finland, Sweden, Cyprus, the Czech Republic, Estonia, Hungary, Latvia, Lithuania, Malta, Poland, Slovakia, and Slovenia.

92. Share the World's Resources, "Financing the Global Sharing Economy, Part Three (5): Increase International Aid" (2012), http://www.stwr.org/information -centre/reports/financing-global-sharing-economy-part-three-5-increase -international.

93. Hugh Williamson, "Annan Chides G8 on Aid to Africa," *Financial Times* (2007), https://www.ft.com/content/5cfa0396-f27b-11db-a454-000b5df10621.

94. Dorota Sienkiewicz, "2015 EU Aid Statistics Heavily Inflated by In-Donor Refugee Costs," *CONCORD* (2016), https://www.concordeurope.net/hubs/hub2 /announcements/concord_press_release_2015_eu_aid_statistics_heavily _inflated_by_in_.

95. The ONE Campaign, *The 2015 Data Report: Putting the Poorest First* (2015), https://s3.amazonaws.com/one.org/pdfs/DATA_Report_2015_EN.pdf.

96. Share the World's Resources, "Financing the Global Sharing Economy, Part Three (5): Increase International Aid" (2012), http://www.stwr.org/information -centre/reports/financing-global-sharing-economy-part-three-5-increase -international.

97. The ONE Campaign, *The 2015 Data Report: Putting the Poorest First*.

98. Ibid.

99. Oxfam International, "Oxfam Reaction to the Publication of New OECD Aid Figures."

100. Oxfam International, *Paying the Price: Why Rich Countries Must Invest Now in a War on Poverty* (Oxford: Oxfam Publishing, 2005), 5.

101. Bond, *Looting Africa*, 35.

102. Nanga, "New Capitalist Domination and Imperialism in Africa."

103. ActionAid International, *Real Aid: An Agenda for Making Aid Work* (Johannesburg South Africa, 2005), http://www.actionaid.org/sites/files/actionaid/real_aid .pdf, 30. ActionAid classified a full 86 percent of aid from the United States as "phantom."

104. Jubilee Debt Campaign, *The New Debt Trap*.

105. ActionAid International, *Real Aid: An Agenda for Making Aid Work* (Johannesburg South Africa, 2005), http://www.actionaid.org/sites/files/actionaid/real_aid.pdf.

106. David Roodman, *Straightening the Measuring Stick: A 14-Point Plan for Reforming the Definition of Official Development Assistance (ODA)* (Washington, DC, Center for

Global Development Policy Paper 044, 2014), https://www.oecd.org/dac /financing-sustainable-development/ROODMAN percent20straightening -measuring-stick-redefining-oda.pdf.

107. Jubilee Debt Campaign, "£139 Million of 'Made-Up Money' to Count as UK Aid," (2016), http://jubileedebt.org.uk/press-release/139-million-of-made-up -money-to-count-as-uk-aid.

108. Oxfam International, "Paddling Against the Tide: How the Changes in the OECD's Definition of Aid Continue to Undermine Global Efforts Against Poverty. A Statement by African Civil Society" (2016), https://blogs.oxfam.org/en /blogs/16-02-29-paddling-against-tide.

109. Cited in Toussaint, *Your Money or Your Life*, 29.

110. Bond, *Looting Africa*, 41. The Committee For The Abolition Of Illegitimate Debt (CADTM) has likewise characterized the HIPC as a "fiasco." Cf. Salaheddine Lemaizi, "Poverty in Africa, the Unvoiced Failures of the World Bank," *Committee For The Abolition Of Illegitimate Debt* (2016), http://cadtm.org/Poverty-in -Africa-the-unvoiced.

111. See James K. Boyce and Léonce Ndikumana, *Africa's Debt: Who Owes Whom?* (Amherst, MA: Political Economy Research Institute, Working Paper Series Number 48, 2002), 6. As the authors point out, "at the end of the 19th century, the United States government repudiated the external debt owed by Cuba after seizing the island in the Spanish-American war. The US authorities did so on the grounds that Cuba's debt had not been incurred for the benefit of the Cuban people, that it had been contracted without their consent, and that the loans had helped to finance their oppression by the Spanish colonial government. For similar reasons, much of the debt of SSA can today be termed 'odious.'"

112. Africa Action, "Debt Cancellation Urgently Needed in Face of Global Financial Crisis," *Common Dreams* (2009), http://www.commondreams.org/newswire /2009/04/01/debt-cancellation-urgently needed-face-global-financial-crisis.

113. Tax Justice Network Africa, *Tax Us If You Can*.

114. Toussaint, *Your Money or Your Life*, 28.

115. The ONE Campaign, *The 2015 Data Report: Putting the Poorest First*.

116. Claire Ngozo, "Programme of Action Adopted for World's Poorest Nations," *Inter Press Service* (2011), http://www.ipsnews.net/2011/05/development -programme-of-action-adopted-for-worlds-poorest-nations/.

117. United Nations, *The Millennium Development Goals Report 2015*, http://www.un.org/millenniumgoals/2015_MDG_Report/pdf/MDG percent202015 percent20revpercent20(July percent201).pdf.

118. Organisation for Economic Co-operation and Development, "Development Aid Stable in 2014 but Flows to Poorest Countries Still Falling," (2014), http://www. oecd.org/dac/stats/development-aid-stable-in-2014-but-flows-to-poorest -countries-still-falling.htm.

119. Oxfam International, "Hunger Threatens Millions Due to Massive Funding Gap for South Sudan," (2015), https://www.oxfam.org/en/pressroom

/pressreleases/2015-06-16/hunger-threatens-millions-due-massive-funding-gap-south-sudan.

120. Jeffrey, James, "Ethiopian Camps Swell with Internal Migrants as Most Aid Goes Elsewhere," *Irish Times* (2017), https://www.irishtimes.com/news/world/africa/ethiopian-camps-swell-with-internal-migrants-as-most-aid-goes-elsewhere-1.3176853.

121. Joint United Nations Programme on HIV/AIDS (UNAIDS), *The Gap Report* (New York: UNAIDS, 2014), http://www.unaids.org/sites/default/files/media_asset/UNAIDS_Gap_report_en.pdf.

122. Ibid.

123. The Henry J. Kaiser Family Foundation, "The US and the Global Fund to Fight AIDS, Tuberculosis and Malaria" (2016), http://kff.org/global-health-policy/fact-sheet/the-u-s-the-global-fund-to-fight-aids-tuberculosis-and-malaria/.

124. Mukoma Wa Ngugi, "Africa Does Not Need More Western Philanthropy," *ZNet* (2007), http://www.africafiles.org/article.asp?ID=15229.

125. Ibid.

126. *Socialist Worker,* "Mass Protests Send a Message to the G8," (2005), http://socialistworker.org/2005-2/550/550_02_G8.shtml. The article reports that "some in the global justice movement, including South African activists Dennis Brutus, Patrick Bond and Virginia Setshedi, have criticized the mainstream Make Poverty History campaign for failing to take on the G8 and dropping the demand to completely abolish Third World debt."

127. *Socialist Worker,* "Mass Protests Send a Message to the G8."

128. Capps, "Redesigning the Debt Trap."

129. Cf. Bond, *Looting Africa,* 44.

130. Capps, "Redesigning the Debt Trap."

131. Walden Bello, "A Brief History of the G-8," *Pambazuka News* (2008): http://www.pambazuka.org/governance/brief-history-g-8.

132. Oxfam International: "Press Release: Make Poverty History, and G8 promises—Was It All Really Worth It?" (2013), http://www.oxfam.org.uk/media-centre/press-releases/2013/05/make-poverty-history-and-g8-promises-was-it-all-really-worth-it.

133. ActionAid International, *Real Aid: An Agenda for Making Aid Work* (Johannesburg South Africa, 2005), http://www.actionaid.org/sites/files/actionaid/real_aid.pdf, 30.

134. *Washington Post,* transcript, "Bush Addresses Focus of Final G8 Summit," (2008), http://www.washingtonpost.com/wp-dyn/content/article/2008/07/02/AR2008070201312.html.

135. Daniel Ooko, "Africa Urges G8 Leaders Not to Backtrack on Promises to Africa," *China View* (2008), http://news.xinhuanet.com/english/2008-07/05/content_8496387.htm.

136. Yash Tandon, "G8 and Africa: Some Give, Plenty of Take," *Pambazuka News* (2009), http://www.pambazuka.org/governance/g8-and-africa-some-give-plenty-take.

137. Oxfam International, "Oxfam's Verdict on the G8 Summit: Cooking the Books and Cooking the Planet," (2009), https://www.oxfam.org/en/pressroom

/pressreleases/2009-07-10/oxfams-verdict-g8-summit-cooking-books-and -cooking-planet.

138. Oxfam International, "Aid Still at 1993 Level Despite Increase," (2009), www.oxfam.org/en/pressroom/pressrelease/2009-03-30/aid-still-1993-level -despite-increase.

139. Africa Progress Panel, *Africa's Development: Promises and Prospects Report of the Africa Progress Panel 2008* (2008), https://www.essex.ac.uk/armedcon/story_id /africaprospectspromises.pdf; cf. Dorothy Kweyu, "Africa: Pressure Mounts On G8 to Honour Pledges," *Daily Nation* (2008).

140. Adam Forrest, "Did Live 8 Work? 10 Years On, the Debt Burden Returns," *Forbes* (2015), http://www.forbes.com/sites/adamforrest/2015/07/13/did-live -8-work-10-years-on-the-debt-burden-returns/#77fc64437147.

141. Alex Perry, "Come Back, Colonialism, All Is Forgiven," *Time* (2008), http://content.time.com/time/world/article/0,8599,1713275,00.html.

142. Patrick Bond, "Africa's Ridiculous 'Rising' and Overdue Uprising," *Pambazuka News* (2012), https://www.pambazuka.org/governance/africa percentE2 per- cent80 percent99s-ridiculous-percentE2 percent80 percent98rising percentE2 percent80 percent99-and-overdue-uprising.

143. Jeffrey Gettleman, "Africa's Dirty Wars," review of *Warfare in Independent Africa* by William Reno, *New York Review of Books*, March 8, 2012, http://www.nybooks .com/articles/2012/03/08/africas-dirty-wars.

144. Avery Wear and David Whitehouse, "Save Darfur from US Intervention," *International Socialist Review* 50 (2006), http://isreview.org/issues/50/Darfur.shtml.

145. Satgar, "Global Capitalism and Neo-Liberalisation of Africa," 43.

146. Renton, Seddon, and Zeilig, *The Congo* (London and New York: Zed Books, 2007), 174.

147. Philip Gourevitch, *We Wish to Inform You That Tomorrow We Will Be Killed with Our Families: Stories from Rwanda* (New York: Farrar, Straus, and Giroux, 1998), 56.

148. Renton, Seddon, and Zeilig, *The Congo*, 86.

149. Stiglitz, *Globalization and Its Discontents*, 244.

150. Bond, *Looting Africa*, 129.

151. Ibid., 40.

152. Mahmood Mamdani, "The New Humanitarian Order," *The Nation* (2008), http://www.thenation.com/article/new-humanitarian-order/?page=0,0.

153. Frida Berrigan, "The New Military Frontier: Africa," *Foreign Policy in Focus*, September 18, 2007, http://fpif.org/the_new_military_frontier_africa/.

154. Cited in Emily Jones, *Signing Away the Future: How Trade and Investment Agreements between Rich and Poor Countries Undermine Development* (Oxfam International, 2007), http://policy-practice.oxfam.org.uk/publications/signing-away-the -future-how-trade-and-investment-agreements-between-rich-and-po-114595.

155. Mahmood Mamdani, "The State, Private Sector and Market Failures: A Response to Prof Joseph Stiglitz," *Pambazuka News* 595 (2012), https://www. pambazuka.org/global-south/state-private-sector-and-market-failures.

156. Bade Onimode, "IMF and World Bank Programmes in Africa," in *The IMF, the World Bank and the African Debt: The Economic Impact*, ed. Bade Onimode (London: Zed Books, 1989), 30.

Chapter Four

1. Joanna Chung, "Sub-Saharan Africa Confident It Can Attract Investment," *Financial Times* (2007), https://www.ft.com/content/ef8208b2-f816-11db-baa1 -000b5df10621.
2. Katrina Manson, "US Pension Funds Embrace Private Equity in Africa," *Financial Times* (2015), http://www.ft.com/intl/cms/s/0/e6eb9bcc-5e2f-11e5-a28b -50226830d644.html.
3. James Kynge, "Africa Set to Turbo-Charge Growth of Middle Class," *Financial Times* (2014), The author anticipates that the number of middle-class households in those nations would increase to 22 million by 2030.
4. Ashley Smith, "China, Inc.: The Rise of a New Power," *International Socialist Review* 42 (2005), http://isreview.org/issues/43/china.shtml. By the turn of the millennium, foreign enterprises made up 15 percent of its gross industrial output and a remarkable 45 percent of its global exports.
5. *Economist*, "The Hopeful Continent: Africa Rising," (2011), http://www. economist.com/node/21541015. From 2000 to 2008, a full 25 percent of the growth in Africa was attributable to natural resources.
6. Cited in Olamosu and Wynne, "Africa rising?"
7. Mariam, "Financing for (Under)Development in Africa?"
8. Henning Melber, "Global Trade Regimes and Multi-Polarity: the US and Chinese Scramble for African Resources and Markets," in *A New Scramble for Africa?*, ed. Southall and Melber, 56–82.
9. Based on OECD figures. Cited in Ron Nixon, "Just When Africa's Luck Was Changing," *New York Times* (2009), http://www.nytimes.com/2009/08/02 /business/02africa.html.
10. Based on African Economic Outlook 2011 data. Cited in Miriam Gathigah, "Africa Begins to Rise Above Aid," *Inter Press Service* (2012), http://www.ipsnews .net/2012/01/africa-begins-to-rise-above-aid/.
11. EY, *EY's Attractiveness Survey Africa 2015: Making Choices*, 11.
12. Cited in Mariam, "Financing for (Under)Development in Africa?"
13. Ibid.
14. Patrick Bond, "Is Africa Still Being Looted?" *Counterpunch* (2010), http://www .counterpunch.org/2010/08/17/is-africa-still-being-looted/.
15. Miria Pigato and Wenxia Tang, *China and Africa: Expanding Economic Ties in an Evolving Global Context* (Washington, DC: World Bank Group, 2015), http:// documents.worldbank.org/curated/en/241321468024314010/China-and -Africa-expanding-economic-ties-in-an-evolving-global-context, 9.

16. United Nations Economic Commission on Africa, *Industrializing through Trade: Economic Report on Africa* (2015), http://www.uneca.org/sites/default/files/PublicationFiles/era2015_eng_fin.pdf, 40.

17. Ron Nixon, "Just When Africa's Luck Was Changing," *New York Times* (2009), http://www.nytimes.com/2009/08/02/business/02africa.html.

18. Rodney, *How Europe Underdeveloped Africa*, 27.

19. International Trade Administration, "Summary of AGOA I" (Department of Commerce, 2000), http://trade.gov/agoa/legislation/index.asp.

20. Cf. Andrew Mizner, "The US and Africa: Building Bridges," *African Law and Business* (2015), https://www.africanlawbusiness.com/news/5757-the-us-and-africa-building-bridges.

21. International Trade Administration, "AGOA Frequently Asked Questions" (Department of Commerce, 2000), http://trade.gov/agoa/faq.asp#11.

22. Satgar, "Global Capitalism and Neo-Liberalisation of Africa," 50–51.

23. Melber, "Global Trade Regimes and Multi-Polarity," 19.

24. Cited in Patrick Bond, "Africa Crashing," *Counterpunch* (2013), http://www.counterpunch.org/2013/07/01/africa-crashing/.

25. AFL-CIO Solidarity Center, *Building a Strategy for Workers' Rights and Inclusive Growth—A New Vision for the African Growth and Opportunity Act* (2014), 2–3.

26. Ibid.

27. Ibid.

28. Melber, "Global Trade Regimes and Multi-Polarity," 19.

29. AFL-CIO Solidarity Center, *Building a Strategy for Workers' Rights and Inclusive Growth*. Their analysis is based on African Development Bank figures.

30. Roger Southall and Alex Comninos, "The Scramble for Africa and the Marginalisation of African Capitalism," in *A New Scramble for Africa?*, ed. Southall and Melber, 367.

31. Margaret C. Lee, "Trade Relations between the European Union and Sub-Saharan Africa under the Cotonou Agreement: Repartitioning and Economically Recolonising the Continent?" in *A New Scramble for Africa?*, ed. Southall and Melber, 96.

32. Tunde Oyateru, "The Scramble for Africa: A Continuing Narrative," *Pambazuka News* (2015), http://www.pambazuka.net/en/category.php/comment/93946. Trade between Africa and the EU reached over $200 billion by 2013.

33. Nanga, "New Capitalist Domination and Imperialism in Africa."

34. Cited in ibid.

35. David Cronin, "African Countries Fight EU for Survival," *Inter Press Service* (2007), http://www.ipsnews.net/2007/05/trade-african-countries-fight-eu-for-survival/.

36. David Cronin, "African Countries Fight EU for Survival."

37. Lee, "Trade Relations between the European Union and Sub-Saharan Africa under the Cotonou Agreement," 96.

38. Ibid., 86.

39. Specifically for the period 2003–2012. Cited in Nanga, "New Capitalist Domination and Imperialism in Africa." After the UK, the leading five nations for M&A deals in Africa were France, China, India, and then the United States in fifth place.

40. Nanga, "New Capitalist Domination and Imperialism in Africa."

41. NEPAD was later institutionally incorporated as the "development" arm of the African Union (AU).

42. National Intelligence Council, *Mapping Sub-Saharan Africa's Future: Conference Summary* (2005), http://www.au.af.mil/au/awc/awcgate/nic/africa_future.pdf, 9.

43. EY, *EY's Attractiveness Survey Africa 2015: Making Choices* (2015), http://www.ey .com/Publication/vwLUAssets/EY-africa-attractiveness-survey-2015-making -choices/$FILE/EY-africa-attractiveness-survey-2015-making-choices.pdf, 27. The initiative reportedly secured $7.4 billion in commitments, estimated to create approximately 33,000 jobs.

44. Friends of the Earth International, *Who Benefits from GM Crops? The Expansion of Agribusiness Interests in Africa through Biosafety Policy* (Amsterdam, the Netherlands, 2015), http://www.foei.org/wp-content/uploads/2015/02/Who-benefits -2015.pdf, 12. These initiatives were carried out through the African Biosafety Network of Expertise, an advisory committee of NEPAD. Friends of the Earth International also reports that the Gates Foundation funded an agency to consult on the African Biosafety Network of Expertise setup, and that "the same agency teamed up with Monsanto in the Philippines to play the part of 'honest broker' in a bid to strengthen Monsanto's market there," http://www.foei.org /wp-content/uploads/2015/02/Who-benefits-2015.pdf, 18.

45. Cf. Bond, *Looting Africa.*

46. Statement issued by Council for Development and Social Science Research in Africa (CODESRIA) and the Third World Network Africa, cited in Bond, *Looting Africa*, 127–128.

47. CBONDS, "Renaissance Capital Led $300 Million Equity Offering by Nigeria's United Bank For Africa," (2007), http://cbonds.com/news/item/367407.

48. Chung, "Sub-Saharan Africa Confident It Can Attract Investment."

49. *Economist*, "The Hopeful Continent: Africa Rising" (2011), http://www. economist.com/node/21541015.

50. International Monetary Fund, *World Economic Outlook: Spillovers and Cycles in the Global Economy* (Washington, DC: 2007).

51. African Arguments, "Foreign Investment Isn't Necessarily Good for Africa, but Here's How It Can Be" (2015), http://africanarguments.org/2015/08/20/ foreign-investment-isnt-necessarily-good-for-africa-but-heres-how-it-can-be/. This dramatic growth took place over the period of 1990–2013.

52. EY, *EY's Attractiveness Survey Africa 2015*, 4. Reflects the rate of increase for 2014, for a total of $128 billion. This number reflects an enormous investment. However, these figures still pale in comparison to the world's largest companies. For example, the market capitalization of Apple exceeds $600 billion.

53. Oyateru, "The Scramble for Africa."

54. African Arguments, "Foreign Investment Isn't Necessarily Good for Africa, but Here's How It Can Be."

55. EY, *EY's Attractiveness Survey Africa 2015*, 5, 18.

56. Javier Blas, "Buyout Group Helios Raises Record $1bn Africa Fund," *Financial Times* (2015), https://www.ft.com/content/bec321e6-974d-11e4-9636 -00144feabdc0.

57. EY, *EY's Attractiveness Survey Africa 2014: Executing Growth* (2014), 13, http://www .ey.com/Publication/vwLUAssets/EY-attractiveness-africa-2014/$FILE/EY -attractiveness-africa-2014.pdf.

58. Oxfam International, *An Economy for the 1%: Oxfam Briefing Paper: How Privilege and Power in the Economy Drive Extreme Inequality and How This Can Be Stopped* (Oxford: Oxfam Publishing, 2016), https://www.oxfam.org/sites/www.oxfam.org/files /file_attachments/bp210-economy-one-percent-tax-havens-180116-en_0.pdf, 8.

59. William Wallis, Andrew England, and Katrina Manson, "Africa: Ripe for Reappraisal," *Financial Times* (2011), http://www.ft.com/intl/cms/s/0/2ab8b334 -817c-11e0-9c83-00144feabdc0.html.

60. Ron Nixon, "Just When Africa's Luck Was Changing," *New York Times* (2009), http://www.nytimes.com/2009/08/02/business/02africa.html.

61. William Wallis, Andrew England, and Katrina Manson, "Africa: Ripe for Reappraisal."

62. Katrina Manson, "US Pension Funds Embrace Private Equity in Africa," *Financial Times* (2015), http://www.ft.com/intl/cms/s/0/e6eb9bcc-5e2f-11e5-a28b -50226830d644.html.

63. Joseph Cotterill, "Africa Private Equity Group Raises $1.4bn to Invest in Continent," *Financial Times* (2015), http://www.ft.com/intl/cms/s/0/0259f7e0-4801 -11e5-b3b2-1672f710807b.html.

64. Elaine Moore, "Oil Price Crash and US Dollar Spike Cause Africa Pain," *Financial Times* (2015), https://www.ft.com/content/e7d509ba-5e2f-11e5-a28b -50226830d644.

65. Ron Nixon, "Just When Africa's Luck Was Changing."

66. David Humphrey, "A Wall of Money Awaits Africa Power Projects," *Financial Times* (2015), https://www.ft.com/content/d803ae06-e91d-3596-9256 -cd03487e868c.

67. Patrick Bond, "BRICS: 'Anti-Imperialist' or 'Sub-Imperialist'?" *Links International Journal of Socialist Renewal* (2013), http://links.org.au/node/3265.

68. EY, *EY's Attractiveness Survey Africa 2015*, 50.

69. Tom Burgis, *The Looting Machine: Warlords, Oligarchs, Corporations, Smugglers, and the Theft of Africa's Wealth* (New York: PublicAffairs, 2015), 136.

70. Ben Leo, Vijaya Ramachandran, and Robert Morello, "Shedding New Light on the Off-Grid Debate in Power Africa Countries," *Center for Global Development* (2014), https://www.cgdev.org/blog/shedding-new-light-grid-debate-power -africa-countries.

71. David Humphrey, "A Wall of Money Awaits Africa Power Projects."

72. Dominic Omondi, "Kenya Turns into a Battlefield for World's Top Corporate Firms," *KTN Kenya* (2015), https://www.standardmedia.co.ke/business/article /2000175411/kenya-turns-into-a-battlefield-for-world-s-top-corporate-firms.

73. *PRNewswire,* "ContourGlobal Closes Innovative Financing with OPIC and IFC for Cap des Biches Power Project and Announces 32 MW Extension" (2015), http://www.prnewswire.com/news-releases/contourglobal-closes-innovative -financing-with-opic-and-ifc-for-cap-des-biches-power-project-and -announces-32-mw-extension-300194696.html.

74. Office of the Secretary of Defense, *Annual Report to Congress: Military and Security Developments Involving the People's Republic of China 2016* (2016), https://www .defense.gov/Portals/1/Documents/pubs/2016%20 China%20 Military% 20 Power%20 Report.pdf, ii–iii.

75. Robert D. Blackwill and Ashley J. Tellis, *Revising US Grand Strategy toward China* (New York: Council on Foreign Relations Special Report No. 72, 2015), http://www.cfr.org/china/revising-us-grand-strategy-toward-china/p36371, 4.

76. Ashley Smith, "US Imperialism's Pivot to Asia," *International Socialist Review* 88 (2013), http://isreview.org/issue/88/us-imperialisms-pivot-asia.

77. Leo Panitch and Sam Gindin, *Global Capitalism and American Empire* (London: Merlin Press, 2004), 18.

78. Leo Panitch and Sam Gindin, "Superintending Global Capital," *New Left Review* 35 (2005), https://newleftreview.org/II/35/leo-panitch-sam-gindin -superintending-global-capital.

79. Cf. Geoff Bailey, "Accumulation by Dispossession: A Critical Assessment," *International Socialist Review* 95 (2014), http://isreview.org/issue/95/accumulation -dispossession. Bailey has offered an important critique of the ways Harvey's account of the "forcible" means of accumulation are conflated with a wide range of other processes that, properly understood, constitute the fundamental dynamics of capitalist expansion, as identified by Marx himself. As Bailey describes: "What is crucial is the distinction between the workings of the capitalist economy in its quest for profit and the numerous ways in which the state uses extra-economic compulsion to augment and accelerate that process. We should be careful to not blur the two even if both are often at work." Confusion on the distinction between these processes, and the extent to which they may lie "inside" or "outside" of the system, has important implications for how we understand the nature of capitalism and how we mobilize resistance to it.

80. Harvey, *The New Imperialism,* 75–81.

81. Ashley Smith, "The Class Politics of Neoliberalism," review of *A Brief History of Neoliberalism* by David Harvey, *International Socialist Review* 65 (2009), http:// isreview.org/issue/65/class-politics-neoliberalism.

82. United States Africa Command, *2016 Posture Statement. US Africa Command's Formal Report to the US House and Senate Armed Services Committees* (2016), http://www .africom.mil/media-room/document/28035/2016-posture-statement.

83. Patrick Bond and Ana Garcia, *BRICS: An Anti-Capitalist Critique* (Chicago: Haymarket Books, 2015).

84. Johanna Mendelson Forman, "The New Atlanticism or a Wider Atlantic?" *Center for Security Studies (CSS), ETH Zurich* (2015), https://www.files.ethz.ch /isn/193549/ISN_192688_en.pdf.

85. Confederation of Indian Industry (CII) and World Trade Organization (WTO), *India-Africa: South-South Trade and Investment for Development* (2013), https://www .wto.org/english/tratop_e/devel_e/a4t_e/global_review13prog_e/india_africa _report.pdf.

86. UNCTAD, "South-South Cooperation Offers New Opportunities for Transforming African Economies, Report Says," June 17, 2010, http://unctad.org/en /pages/PressReleaseArchive.aspx?ReferenceDocId=13160; Cf. United Nations, *Economic Development in Africa Report 2010 - South-South Cooperation: Africa and the New Forms of Development Partnership* (New York and Geneva, 2010): http:// unctad.org/en/Docs/aldcafrica2010_en.pdf, 30–32.

87. African Development Bank, Organisation for Economic Co-operation and Development, United Nations Development Programme, *African Economic Outlook 2014: Global Value Chains and Africa's Industrialisation* (2014), http://www .africaneconomicoutlook.org/en/telechargements, 74.

88. Michael Wines, "China's Influence in Africa Arouses Some Resistance," *New York Times,* February 10, 2007, www.nytimes.com/2007/02/10/world /africa/10assess.html.

89. William Wallis and Geoff Dyer, "Wen Calls for More Access for Africa," *Financial Times,* May 16, 2007, https://www.ft.com/content/34e52c64-0365 -11dc-a023-000b5df10621.

90. *Economist,* "The Chinese in Africa: Trying to Pull Together," April 20, 2011, http://www.economist.com/node/18586448.

91. UNCTAD figures cited in Pigato and Tang, *China and Africa,* 1.

92. Pigato and Tang, *China and Africa,* 15.

93. Olamosu and Wynne, "Africa Rising?" See also United Nations Conference on Trade and Development, *World Investment Report 2016* (2016), http://unctad.org /en/PublicationsLibrary/wir2016_en.pdf, 38.

94. Aubrey Hruby and Jake Bright, "Why China's Role in Africa Isn't as Dominant as You Think," *Washington Post,* December 4, 2015, https://www.washingtonpost .com/news/monkey-cage/wp/2015/12/04/why-chinas-role-in-africa-isnt-as -important-as-you-think/?utm_term=.53700d8efcdd.

95. Amadou Sy, Amy Copley, and Fenohasina Maret Rakotondrazaka, "Africa in Focus: The US-Africa Leaders Summit: A Focus on Foreign Direct Investment," *Brookings* (2014), https://www.brookings.edu/blog/africa-in-focus/2014/07/11 /the-u-s-africa-leaders-summit-a-focus-on-foreign-direct-investment/#cancel. Based on UNCTAD data covering 2002–2012, with an increase of investment from $27.2 billion to about $132.8 billion. See African Development Bank, the OECD Development Centre, and the United Nations Development Programme, *African Economic Outlook 2015: Regional Development and Spatial Inclusion* (Paris: OECD Publishing, 2015) for country-by-country inbound FDI.

96. Pigato and Tang, *China and Africa*, 3. The authors write, "FDI flows from China to SSA rose from next to nothing a decade ago to US$3.1 billion in 2013."
97. EY, *EY's Attractiveness Survey Africa 2015*, 20.
98. Pigato and Tang, *China and Africa*, 3.
99. EY, *EY's Attractiveness Survey Africa 2015*, 20.
100. Cited in David Pilling, "Africa Ties with China Are About More Than Raw Materials," *Financial Times*, October 5, 2015, https://www.ft.com/content/e6b692ec-5e2f-11e5-a28b-50226830d644.
101. Burgis, *The Looting Machine*, 137.
102. Pigato and Tang, *China and Africa*, 8.
103. Organisation for Economic Co-operation and Development (OECD), *Mapping Support for Africa's Infrastructure Investment* (2012), http://www.oecd.org/daf/inv/investment-policy/MappingReportWeb.pdf , 48; Burgis, *The Looting Machine*, 137.
104. Pigato and Tang, *China and Africa*, 15.
105. Thuso Khumalo, "China Announces $60 Billion for Africa," *AFP, Reuters*, April 12, 2015, http://www.dw.com/en/china-announces-60-billion-for-africa/a-18892967?maca=en-rss_en_nr_home-7347-xml-mrss.
106. Jeremy Frost, "China Inks $6.5bn Worth of Deals with South Africa," *International Business Times,* December 4, 2015, http://www.ibtimes.com.au/china-inks-65bn-worth-deals-south-africa-1489611.
107. *Al Jazeera*, "China Pledges $60 Billion to African Development," December 4, 2015, http://www.aljazeera.com/news/2015/12/china-pledges-60-billion-african-development-151204204624495.html. The report cites South African economist Xhanti Payi on this shortfall.
108. Valentina Romei, "China and Africa: Trade Relationship Evolves," *Financial Times*, December 3, 2015, https://www.ft.com/content/c53e7f68-9844-11e5-9228-87e603d47bdc.
109. Keith Bradsher and Adam Nossiter, "In Nigeria, Chinese Investment Comes with a Downside," *New York Times*, December 5, 2015, https://www.nytimes.com/2015/12/06/business/international/in-nigeria-chinese-investment-comes-with-a-downside.html.
110. Ibid.
111. Oyateru, "The Scramble for Africa: A Continuing Narrative." Trade between China and Africa expanded from $166 billion to $210 billion over the past decade.
112. Jendayi Frazer, "Investing in Africa: How the US Can Play Catch-Up," *Fortune*, August 12, 2014, http://fortune.com/2014/08/12/investing-in-africa-how-the-u-s-can-play-catch-up/.
113. Wallis and Dyer, "Wen Calls for More Access for Africa."
114. Pigato and Tang, *China and Africa*, 1.
115. Office of the Secretary of Defense, *Annual Report to Congress*, 48. China's top crude suppliers in 2014 were (in 1,000 barrels/day): Saudi Arabia 1,012 (15% of total); Russia 850 (13%); and Angola 775 (12%).

116. African Development Bank, the OECD Development Centre, and the United Nations Development Programme, *African Economic Outlook 2015: Regional Development and Spatial Inclusion* (Paris: OECD Publishing, 2015), x.

117. Pigato and Tang, *China and Africa*, 4.

118. The other exception is trade between the United States and Africa, which began a slow but steady decline starting in 2011, when US shale oil production started to take off and oil imports took a nosedive; the changes in US consumption of African oil will be discussed further in the next chapter.

119. African Development Bank, the OECD Development Centre and the United Nations Development Programme, *African Economic Outlook 2015: Regional Development and Spatial Inclusion*, iv. This report is a joint research project of the African Development Bank Group, the OECD, the United Nations Development Project, and the European Union.

120. Smith, "China, Inc.: The Rise of a New Power."

121. Office of the Secretary of Defense, *Annual Report to Congress*, 95.

122. Cited in Patrick Bond, "Africa Crashing," *Counterpunch* (2013), http://www.counterpunch.org/2013/07/01/africa-crashing/.

123. *Economist,* "Africa and China: Rumble in the Jungle," April 20, 2011, www.economist.com/node/18586678.

124. Alan Beattie and Eoin Callan, "China Loans Create 'New Wave of Africa Debt,'" *Financial Times*, December 7, 2006, https://www.ft.com/content/640a5986-863a-11db-86d5-0000779e2340.

125. Wallis and Dyer, "Wen Calls for More Access for Africa."

126. At the same time, China has sought an expanded role within the international financial institutions themselves. See Robert D. Blackwill and Ashley J. Tellis, *Revising US Grand Strategy toward China* (New York: Council on Foreign Relations, 2015), http://cfr.org , 4.

127. Wallis and Dyer, "Wen Calls for More Access for Africa."

128. F. William Engdahl, "Darfur? It's the Oil, Stupid . . . China and USA in New Cold War over Africa's Oil Riches," May 20, 2007, *Geopolitics-Geoeconomics:* http://www.oilgeopolitics.net/Geopolitics___Eurasia/Oil_in_Africa/oil_in_africa.html.

129. *Financial Times*, "Chinese Model is No Panacea for Africa," February 6, 2007, http://www.ft.com/cms/s/0/c1a221ca-b586-11db-a5a5-0000779e2340.html?ft_site=falcon&desktop=true#axzz4flQweHMn.

130. Cited in Patrick Bond, "Washington in Africa, 2012: Who will Obama 'Whack' next?" Address to the Muslim Youth Movement 40th Anniversary Conference, University of KwaZulu-Natal, Durban, *Links International Journal of Socialist Renewal* (2012), http://links.org.au/node/3043.

131. Jim Yardley, "China Defends Sudan Policy and Criticizes Olympics Tie-In," *New York Times*, March 8, 2008, www.nytimes.com/2008/03/08/world/asia/08darfur.html.

132. US House of Representatives Committee on Foreign Affairs, "Press Release: Lantos, House Colleagues Send Strong Message to Chinese President, Demand

Action on Darfur" (2007), https://democrats-foreignaffairs.house.gov/news
/press-releases/lantos-house-colleagues-send-strong-message-chinese
-president-demand-action.

133. Robert D. Blackwill and Ashley J. Tellis, *Revising US Grand Strategy toward China*
(New York: Council on Foreign Relations, 2015), http://cfr.org, 15–16.

134. Cited in Ali Noor, "Development or Fraud? Another Coastal Paradise to Die for
Big Oil," *Pambazuka News* (2014), https://www.pambazuka.org/governance
/development-or-fraud-another-coastal-paradise-die-big-oil.

135. Ibid.

136. Zahra Moloo, "Kenya's New Port: The End of Lamu's Cultural Heritage?" *Pambazuka News* (2010), https://www.pambazuka.org/arts/kenya%E2%80%99s
-new-port-end-lamus-cultural-heritage.

137. David Malingha Doya, "Kenya, US Firms in Talks on Mega $26 Billion Lamu
Port Southern Sudan-Ethiopia Deal," *Mail and Guardian Africa*, July 26, 2015,
http://mgafrica.com/article/2015-07-26-kenya-us-firms-in-talks-on-mega-26-
billion-lamu-port-southern-sudan-ethiopia-deal.

138. NEPAD, "Lamu Port Southern Sudan-Ethiopia Transport Corridor," http://
www.nepad.org/content/lamu-port-southern-sudan-ethiopia-transport
-corridor, retrieved April 28, 2016.

139. Andrew Teyie, "Kenya: Sh1.2 Trillion Deal Struck but Not All Are Winners
After US President Visit," *Daily Nation*, August 2, 2015, allafrica.com/stories
/201508030436.html.

140. Bernard Namunane, "President Kenyatta Woos US Firms to Invest in Lamu
Port," *Daily Nation*, September 29, 2015, http://www.nation.co.ke/news/Uhuru
-woos-US-firms-to-invest-in-Lamu-port/1056-2890938-v487n4z/index.html.

141. Cited in *Daily Nation*, "President Uhuru Kenyatta Invites US Firms to Invest in
Lapsset Project," September 29, 2015, http://www.nation.co.ke/business/Uhuru
-invites-American-firms-to-invest-in-Lapsset-project/996-2890858-133qtv7
/index.html. According to the Corporate Council for Africa website, "CCA is
the premier American organization devoted to US-Africa business relations
and includes as members more than 180 companies, which represent nearly 85
percent of total US private sector investments in Africa." See http://www
.africacncl.org/.

142. Cited in Moses Michira, "American Firms Could Edge Out Chinese from Lapsset Project," *The Standard*, July 26, 2015.

143. Save Lamu website, https://www.savelamu.org.

144. Dominic Omondi, "Kenya Turns into a Battlefield for World's Top Corporate
Firms," *KTN Kenya*, September 6, 2015, https://www.standardmedia.co.ke
/business/article/2000175411/kenya-turns-into-a-battlefield-for-world-s-top
-corporate-firms.

145. Deloitte, *Competitiveness: Catching the Next Wave—Africa* (2015), https://www2
.deloitte.com/content/dam/Deloitte/global/Documents/About-Deloitte/gx
-gbc-africa-competitiveness-report.pdf, 29.

146. Lilian Ochieng, "Kenya to Construct Its Pipeline as Uganda Deal Fails," *Daily Nation,* April 23, 2016, http://www.nation.co.ke/news/Kenya-to-construct-its -pipeline-as-Uganda-deal-fails/1056-3173246-laf6a2z/index.html.

147. Deloitte, *Competitiveness: Catching the Next Wave,* 29.

148. Omondi, "Kenya Turns into a Battlefield for World's Top Corporate Firms."

149. Ochieng, "Kenya to Construct Its Pipeline as Uganda Deal Fails."

150. Adow Mohamed, "Addis-Djibouti Pipeline Threatens the Lapsset," *The Star,* October 2, 2015, http://www.the-star.co.ke/news/2015/10/02/addis-djibouti -pipeline-threatens-the-lapsset_c1216234.

151. Paul Wafula, "Ethiopia Enters Sh160b Pipeline Deal That Could Challenge Lapsset," *The Standard,* October 2, 2015, https://www.standardmedia.co.ke/ business/article/2000178262/ethiopia-enters-sh160b-pipeline-deal-that-could -challenge-lapsset.

152. Deloitte, *Competitiveness: Catching the Next Wave,* 28.

153. Ministry of Defence, Kenya, "President Obama Reaffirms US Government Commitment to Helping Kenya in the Fight Against Terrorism (2015), http://www.mod.go.ke/?p=5095.

154. John O. Kakonge, "Environmental Impact Assessment: Why It Fails in Kenya," *Pambazuka News* (2015), https://www.pambazuka.org/land-environment /environmental-impact-assessment-why-it-fails-kenya.

155. Cited in Noor, "Development or fraud?"

156. Ibid.

157. Save Lamu website, https://www.savelamu.org.

158. LAPSSET Corridor Program official website, http://www.lapsset.go.ke /investment/#1441873920660-a173daba-0456462a-966b.

159. Kalume Kazungu, "Lands Commission Says 'No' to Demands for More Money in Lapsset Deals," *Daily Nation,* May 2, 2016, http://www.nation.co.ke/counties /lamu/Lands-Commission-says-no-to-demands-for-more-money/3444912 -3186692-11ycddx/index.html.

160. *Daily Nation,* "Lapsset Fuelling Border Wars in Meru and Isiolo, Say MPs," November 1, 2015, http://www.nation.co.ke/news/Lapsset-fuelling-border-wars -in-Meru-and-Isiolo/1056-2937732-2i7peuz/index.html.

161. *PGI Intelligence,* "Kenya: Financing and Security Concerns Threaten to Delay Lapsset Infrastructure Projects" (2015), https://pgi-intelligence.com/news /getNewsItem/Kenya-Financing-and-security-concerns-threaten-to-delay -LAPSSET-infrastructure-projects/564; *Business Daily,* "Demand for higher wages hits standard gauge rail project," February 17, 2015, http://www .businessdailyafrica.com/Demand-for-higher-wages-hits-SGR/-/539546 /2625708/-/j96akl/-/index.html.

162. *RFI,* "Kenya, Ethiopia Sign 'Historic' Trade Deal," December 8, 2015, http://en.rfi. fr/africa/20151208-historic-trade-deal-signed-between-kenya-and-ethiopia.

163. EY, *EY's Attractiveness Survey Africa 2015,* 5.

164. EY press release, "Africa Is the Top Investment Destination for UK Businesses," June 27, 2014.

165. EY, *EY's Attractiveness Survey Africa 2015*, 11.

166. Tunde Oyateru, "Africa: The Scramble for Africa—A Continuing Narrative," *AllAfrica*, February 12, 2015.

167. *African Arguments*, "Foreign Investment Isn't Necessarily Good for Africa, but Here's How It Can Be."

168. Lawrence and Graham, "Structural Transformation and Economic Development in Africa."

169. EY, *EY's Attractiveness Survey Africa 2015*, 4.

170. Mike Casey, "Guest Post: Framing Africa's Private Equity Landscape in a Pan-Emerging Markets Context," *Financial Times*, November 12, 2014, http://blogs.ft.com/beyond-brics/2014/11/12/guest-post-framing-africas-private-equity-landscape-in-a-pan-emerging-markets-context/.

171. Olamosu and Wynne, "Africa Rising? The Economic History of Sub-Saharan Africa."

172. Melber, "Global Trade Regimes and Multi-Polarity," 61. Melber cites World Bank data showing that OECD nations spent $311 billion in agricultural subsidies alone, costing farmers in the "developing world" at least $30 billion per year. Arundhati Roy has written frequently of the devastating impact of corporate globalization on Indian farmers, an estimated 250,000 of whom have committed suicide when compelled, and unable to, produce crops for a market economy. See Roy's *Capitalism: A Ghost Story* (Chicago: Haymarket Books, 2014), 8.

173. Dani Rodrik, "Premature Deindustrialization" (Cambridge, MA: Harvard University, 2015), http://drodrik.scholar.harvard.edu/files/dani-rodrik/files/premature_deindustrialization_revised2.pdf, 23.

174. Tony Hawkins, "Zimbabwe Ponders the Struggle to Industrialize," *Financial Times*, November 3, 2014, https://www.ft.com/content/b948e415-e847-3eb0-a6f6-ad30db83ca9d.

175. Lawrence and Graham, "Structural Transformation and Economic Development in Africa."

176. Matina Stevis, "Africa Bruised by Investor Exodus," *Wall Street Journal*, February 25, 2016, https://www.wsj.com/articles/africa-bruised-by-investor-exodus-1456050601.

177. Cited in Ron Nixon, "Just When Africa's Luck Was Changing," *New York Times* (2009), http://www.nytimes.com/2009/08/02/business/02africa.html.

178. Pigato and Tang, *China and Africa*, 6.

179. Ibid., 4.

180. Ibid., 3–4.

181. Norimitsu Onishi, "China's Slowdown Tarnishes Economic Boom in Copper-Rich Zambia, *New York Times*, December 2, 2015, https://www.nytimes.com/2015/12/03/world/africa/zambia-china-economic-slowdown.html.

182. Lawrence and Graham, "Structural Transformation and Economic Development in Africa."

183. Cited in Alemayehu G. Mariam, "The World Bank and Ethiopia's 'Growth and Transformation,'" *ECADF Ethiopian News and Views,* February 2, 2015, http://ecadforum.com/2015/02/02/the-world-bank-and-ethiopia/.

184. Alemayehu G. Mariam, "The World Bank and Ethiopia's 'Growth and Transformation,'" *ECADF Ethiopian News and Views,* February 2, 2015, http://ecadforum .com/2015/02/02/the-world-bank-and-ethiopia/. Mariam also points out the concerns raised about human rights abuses, saying that serious doubts were raised in a 2014 World Bank internal report on the "village-ization" program of the Anuak people in western Ethiopia, which "documented incompetence, indifference and borderline criminal negligence on the part of the World Bank's managers in Ethiopia. Their professional conduct in the implementation and administration . . . in Gambella evinced depraved indifference to the welfare of Anuak communities." See International Monetary Fund, *IMF Country Report No. 13/308, The Federal Democratic Republic of Ethiopia* (Washington, DC: International Monetary Fund Publication Services, 2013), https://www.imf.org/external /pubs/ft/scr/2013/cr13308.pdf.

185. Oxfam International, "Ethiopia," https://www.oxfam.org/en/countries/ethiopia.

186. Patrick Bond, "Africa's Ridiculous 'Rising' and Overdue Uprising," *Pambazuka News* (2012), https://www.pambazuka.org/governance/africa%E2%80%99s -ridiculous-%E2%80%98rising%E2%80%99-and-overdue-uprising.

187. Patrick Bond, "Africa's Ridiculous 'Rising' and Overdue Uprising," *Pambazuka News* (2012), https://www.pambazuka.org/governance/africa%E2%80%99s -ridiculous-%E2%80%98rising%E2%80%99-and-overdue-uprising.

188. Patrick Bond, "Latest Fibs from World Financiers: Are 'African Lions' Really Roaring?" *Links International Journal of Socialist Renewal* (2011): http://links.org.au /node/2302.

189. EY, *EY's Attractiveness Survey Africa 2015,* 10. Only Asia-Pacific received a higher proportion of global FDI than Africa in this period.

190. African Development Bank and Africa Progress Panel reports cited in William Wallis, Andrew England, and Katrina Manson, "Africa: Ripe for Reappraisal," *Financial Times* (2011), http://www.ft.com/intl/cms/s/0/2ab8b334 -817c-11e0-9c83-00144feabdc0.html.

191. Olamosu and Wynne, "Africa Rising?"

192. *Economist,* "The Chinese in Africa: Trying to Pull Together," April 20, 2011, http://www.economist.com/node/18586448.

193. Keith Bradsher and Adam Nossiter, "In Nigeria, Chinese Investment Comes with a Downside," *New York Times,* December 5, 2015, https://www .nytimes.com/2015/12/06/business/international/in-nigeria-chinese -investment-comes-with-a-downside.html.

194. Andrew England, "Reality Check in Africa as Boom Time Ends," *Financial Times,* October 5, 2015, https://www.ft.com/content/e81d0b70-5e2f-11e5-a28b -50226830d644.

195. Wallis, England, and Manson, "Africa."

196. Patrick Bond, "South Africa's Development Goals Won't Be Met," *Links International Journal of Socialist Renewal* (2010): http://links.org.au/node/1917.

197. Bond, "Latest Fibs from World Financiers."

198. "Less Poverty in Africa but Numbers Remain Stubbornly High," *AFP*, October 16, 2015, http://www.straitstimes.com/world/africa/less-poverty-in -africa-but-numbers-remain-stubbornly high.

199. Michael Roberts, The Next Recession blog, https://thenextrecession.wordpress .com/2015/10/13/weve-never-had-it-so-good/.

200. Salaheddine Lemaizi, "Poverty in Africa, the Unvoiced Failures of the World Bank," *Committee For The Abolition Of Illegitimate Debt* (2016), http://cadtm.org /Poverty-in-Africa-the-unvoiced.

201. Cited in Mariam, "Financing for (Under)Development in Africa?"

202. Council on Foreign Relations, "The Unfinished Health Agenda in Sub-Saharan Africa: Statement before the Senate Foreign Relations Subcommittee on Africa and Global Health Policy, March 19, 2015," (2015), http://www.cfr.org/health /unfinished-health-agenda-sub-saharan-africa/p36297.

203. Mariam, "Financing for (Under)Development in Africa?"

204. The ONE Campaign, *The 2015 Data Report: Putting the Poorest First.*

205. Sungu Oyoo, "Africa Rising: Myth or Reality?" *Pambazuka News* (2015), https://www.pambazuka.org/governance/africa-rising-myth-or-reality.

206. Shawn Donnan, "Poverty: Vulnerable to Change," *Financial Times*, September 23, 2015, https://www.ft.com/content/f599b75c-6042-11e5-a28b-50226830d644.

207. Lawrence and Graham, "Structural Transformation and Economic Development in Africa."

208. Salaheddine Lemaizi, "Poverty in Africa, the Unvoiced Failures of the World Bank," *Committee for the Abolition of Illegitimate Debt* (2016), http://cadtm.org /Poverty-in-Africa-the-unvoiced.

209. Omar Mohammed, "Tough Times Ahead," *Quartz Africa*, January 22, 2016, https://qz.com/600693/this-is-another-bad-sign-for-africas-economies/.

210. Norimitsu Onishi, "African Economies, and Hopes for New Era, Are Shaken by China," *New York Times* January 26, 2016, https://www.nytimes.com /2016/01/26/world/africa/african-economies-and-hopes-for-new-era-are -shaken-by-china.html.

211. Ibid. See also International Monetary Fund, 2015, *Regional Economic Outlook: Sub-Saharan Africa: Navigating Headwinds* (2015), https://www.imf.org/external /pubs/ft/reo/2015/afr/eng/pdf/sreo0415.pdf.

212. World Bank Group Office of the Chief Economist for the Africa Region, *Africa's Pulse: An Analysis of Issues Shaping Africa's Economic Future*, vol. 15 (Washington, DC: World Bank, 2017), 10.

213. Ibid., 18.

214. Abayomi Azikiwe, "The Re-Emerging African Debt Crisis: Renewed IMF 'Economic Medicine,'" *Pan African News* (2015), http://panafricannews.blogspot .com/search?q=The+Re-emerging+African+Debt+Crisis%22+Azikiwe.

215. Ibid.

216. Lawrence and Graham, "Structural Transformation and Economic Development in Africa."

Chapter Five

1. Cyril I. Obi, "Scrambling for Oil in West Africa," in *A New Scramble for Africa?* ed. Southall and Melber, 197.

2. Based on 2007 UNCTAD data, cited in Jana Honke, "Extractive Orders: Transnational Mining Companies in the Nineteenth and Twenty-First Centuries in the Central African Copperbelt," in *A New Scramble for Africa?* ed. Southall and Melber, 277.

3. Obi, "Scrambling for Oil in West Africa," in *A New Scramble for Africa?* 194.

4. Southall and Comninos, "The Scramble for Africa and the Marginalisation of African Capital," 358–59.

5. Based on World Bank data, cited in Wilson Pritchard, "The Mining Boom in Sub-Saharan Africa: Continuity, Change and Policy Implications," in *A New Scramble for Africa?* ed. Southall and Melber, 242.

6. Nnimmo Bassey, *To Cook a Continent: Destructive Extraction and the Climate Crisis in Africa* (Nairobi and Oxford: Fahamu Books & Pambazuka Press, 2012), 49–50.

7. Pritchard, "The Mining Boom in Sub-Saharan Africa," 245.

8. US Energy Information Administration, Total Oil Supply (Thousand Barrels Per Day), 1980–2014, https://www.eia.gov/.

9. International Energy Agency (IEA) figures, cited in Celeste Hicks, *Africa's New Oil: Power, Pipelines and Future Fortunes* (London: Zed Books, 2015), 3.

10. Ghazvinian, *Untapped*, 3.

11. US Bureau of Economic Analysis. Balance of Payments and Direct Investment Position Data: US Direct Investment Abroad. Accessed September 11, 2015, https://www.bea.gov. The fifteen-year trajectory was, in US dollars (millions):

1999	2000	2001	2002	2003	2004	2005	2006	2007
8,111	7,204	10,720	11,208	12,163	9,376	10,096	14,502	14,668

2008	2009	2010	2011	2012	2013	2014
19,484	25,077	30,243	32,723	33,538	36,384	41,217

12. Bassey, *To Cook a Continent*, 25.

13. Ibid., 30.

14. Yao Graham, "Minerals Dependence, Jobs and Transformation," presentation to International Trade Union Confederation/Third World Network Africa/Review of African Political Economy Workshop on Employment, Structural Transformation and Economic Development, July 20, 2015, http://twnafrica.org/MINERALS%20 DEPENDENCE,%20 JOBS%20 AND%20 TRANSFORMATION.pdf. Emphasis added.

15. Burgis, *The Looting Machine*, 8.

16. *Economist*, "Wish You Were Mine: Resource Nationalism in Africa," February 11, 2012, http://www.economist.com/node/21547285.

17. Burgis, *The Looting Machine*.

18. United Nations Economic Commission on Africa. 2016. *African Governance Report IV. Measuring corruption in Africa: The international dimension matters*, http://www.uneca.org/publications/african-governance-report-iv, 10.

19. Paul Burkhardt, "Africa Oil Boom Fades as $50 Crude Shuts Door on High-Cost Deals," *Bloomberg*, November 20, 2015, https://www.bloomberg.com/news/articles/2015-11-20/africa-oil-boom-fades-as-50-crude-shuts-door-on-high-cost-deals.

20. *The Oil Daily*, "Majors Turn to Africa for Growth, but Face Mounting Competition," November 10, 2005; Dino Mahtani, "The New Scramble for Africa's Resources," *Financial Times*, January 28, 2008, http://www.ft.com/cms/s/0/56dd8e0a-cd41-11dc-9b2b-000077b07658.html?ft_site=falcon&desktop=true#axzz4fmXYXTyW.

21. Stefan Andreasson, "US fracking boom puts West African oil economies at risk," *The Conversation*, August 6, 2014, https://theconversation.com/us-fracking-boom-puts-west-african-oil-economies-at-risk-29289. http://theconversation.com/us-fracking-boom-puts-west-african-oil-economies-at-risk-29289.

22. Michael T. Klare, *The Race for What's Left: The Global Scramble for the World's Last Resources* (New York: Picador, 2012), 61.

23. US Energy Information Administration, accessed August 5, 2017, https://www.eia.gov/beta/international/rankings/#?prodact=53-1&cy=2017. Nigeria and Angola's daily output was 453,000 and 415,000 barrels of oil per day, as compared to Ghana's 40,000.

24. Bassey, *To Cook a Continent*, 29.

25. Jad Mouawad, "Angola, One of the Poorest Places on Earth, is an Oil Industry Darling," *New York Times*, March 19, 2007, http://www.nytimes.com/2007/03/19/business/worldbusiness/19iht-angola.4961071.html.

26. Andrew England, "Angola Pledges Tighter Bank Regulation in Face of Dollar Drought," *Financial Times*, February 2, 2016, https://www.ft.com/content/82be18d2-c671-11e5-808f-8231cd71622e.

27. Matina Stevis, "Angola to Seek IMF Aid to Cope with Looming Financial Crisis," *Wall Street Journal*, April 6, 2016, https://www.wsj.com/articles/angola-to-seek-imf-aid-to-cope-with-looming-financial-crisis-1459957868.

28. Cited in Kenneth Agutamba, "East Africa: Weak Global Economy Dampens EAC Oil Hopes," *New Times* (Rwanda), http://www.newtimes.co.rw/section/article/2015-01-25/185297/.

29. Deloitte, *The Deloitte Guide to Oil and Gas in East Africa: Where Potential Lies* (2013), https://www2.deloitte.com/content/dam/Deloitte/global/Documents/Energy-and-Resources/dttl-er-deloitte-guide-oil-gas-east-africa%20-08082013.pdf, 2.

30. Hicks, *Africa's New Oil*, 156.

31. Oilprice.com, "Tanzania's Crackdown on Mining Companies Intensifies" (2017), http://oilprice.com/Metals/Commodities/Tanzanias-Crackdown -On-Mining-Companies-Intensifies.html.

32. Marta Tveit, "The Oil Giants Are Coming to Tanzania," *Africa Is a Country,* May 22, 2015, http://africasacountry.com/2015/05/the-oil-giants-are-coming-to -tanzania/.

33. Artur Colom-Jaén and Eduardo Bidaurratzaga-Aurre, "The Resource Curse Debate after Mozambique's Emergence as an Energy Exporter," in *A New Scramble for Africa? The Rush for Energy Resources in Sub-Saharan Africa,* ed. Sören Scholvin (Abingdon and New York: Routledge, 2016), 111–130.

34. Katie Nguyen, "Indonesia, Kuwait Eye Somali Oil Firm," *Reuters,* August 7, 2007, http://uk.reuters.com/article/somalia-oil-idUKL0787786220070807; Ka-trina Manson "Somalia: Oil Thrown on the Fire, "*Financial Times,* May 13, 2013, https://www.ft.com/content/538e9550-b3e1-11e2-ace9-00144feabdc0.

35. Dominik Balthasar, *Oil in Somalia Adding Fuel to the Fire?* (Mogadishu: Heritage Institute for Policy Studies, 2014), http://www.heritageinstitute.org/wp-content /uploads/2014/06/HIPS-Oil_in_Somalia-ENGLISH.pdf, 2.

36. Alex Dick-Godfrey, "Somalia: The Next Oil Superpower?" *The National Interest,* January 15, 2015, http://nationalinterest.org/blog/the-buzz/somalia-the -next-oil-superpower-12041.

37. Dominik Balthasar, *Oil in Somalia Adding Fuel to the Fire?,* 8.

38. Burgis, *The Looting Machine,* 132.

39. Hicks, *Africa's New Oil,* 111.

40. Brookings updated their original 2011 research to show a continuation of the same trends. Cf. Homi Kharas, *The Unprecedented Expansion of the Global Middle Class: An Update,* Brookings Global Economy and Development, Working Paper Number 100, February 2017, https://www.brookings.edu/wp-content/uploads /2017/02/global_20170228_global-middle-class.pdf.

41. ExxonMobil press release, "ExxonMobil's Outlook for Energy Sees Global Increase in Future Demand," December 9, 2014, http://news.exxonmobil.com /press-release/exxonmobils-outlook-energy-sees-global-increase-future -demand. Full report, *The Outlook for Energy: A View to 2040,* February 2015, https://www.ief.org/_resources/files/events/exxonmobils-outlook-for-energy -a-view-to-2040/2015-exxonmobil-energy-outllook-presentation-february.pdf.

42. Howard French, *China's Second Continent: How a Million Migrants Are Building a New Empire in Africa* (New York: Vintage, 2014), 6.

43. Burgis, *The Looting Machine,* 81.

44. Padraig Carmody, *The New Scramble for Africa* (Cambridge and Malden, MA: Polity, 2011), 66.

45. French, *China's Second Continent,* 42.

46. International Energy Agency. *World Energy Outlook 2015 Factsheet: Global Energy Trends to 2040,* www.worldenergyoutlook.org.

47. Obi, "Scrambling for Oil in West Africa," 192.

48. Ibid.

49. French, *China's Second Continent*, 4.
50. Carmody, *The New Scramble for Africa*, 75.
51. Khadija Sharife, "All Roads Lead Back to China," *Pambazuka News* (2011), http://www.pambazuka.org/global-south/all-roads-lead-back-china.
52. Cited in David Pilling, "Africa: Between Hope and Despair," *Financial Times*, April 24, 2016, https://www.ft.com/content/4da8bd90-0894-11e6-b6d3-746f8e9cdd33.
53. Sharife, "All Roads Lead Back to China."
54. Hicks, *Africa's New Oil*, 82.
55. Carmody, *The New Scramble for Africa*, 86.
56. Cited in French, *China's Second Continent*, 12.
57. Clifford Krauss, "Stock Prices Sink in a Rising Ocean of Oil," *New York Times*, January 15, 2016, https://www.nytimes.com/2016/01/16/business/energy-environment/oil-prices-one-million-barrel-glut.html.
58. Carola Hoyos, "The New Seven Sisters: Oil and Gas Giants Dwarf Western Rivals," *Financial Times*, March 12, 2007, https://www.ft.com/content/471ae1b8-d001-11db-94cb-000b5df10621.
59. US Energy Information Administration (EIA) 2007 Figures, https://www.eia.gov/beta/international/rankings/#?prodact=5-2&cy=2007&pid=5&aid=2&tl_id=2-A&tl_type=a. The US share of world oil production fell over the following decade and stood at 20 percent of total oil consumption in 2015: https://www.eia.gov/beta/international/rankings/#?prodact=5-2&cy=2015&pid=5&aid=2&tl_id=2-A&tl_type=a.
60. Hoyos, "The New Seven Sisters."
61. Ashley Smith, "US Imperialism's Pivot to Asia," *International Socialist Review* 88 (2013), http://isreview.org/issue/88/us-imperialisms-pivot-asia.
62. Nick Turse, *Tomorrow's Battlefield: US Proxy Wars and Secret Ops in Africa* (Chicago: Haymarket Books, 2015), 22.
63. Ghazvinian, *Untapped*, 12.
64. Burgis, *The Looting Machine*, 2.
65. Ryan Olson, "Guest Post: Sub-Saharan Africa's Sovereign Wealth Funds Struggle in Era of Low Oil," *Financial Times*, February 24, 2015, http://blogs.ft.com/beyond-brics/2015/02/25/guest-post-sub-saharan-africas-sovereign-wealth-funds-struggle-in-era-of-low-oil/.
66. Burgis, *The Looting Machine*, 3.
67. World Bank, *Global Economic Prospects Weak Investment in Uncertain Times* (Washington, DC: World Bank, 2017), http://pubdocs.worldbank.org/en/712231481727549643/Global-Economic-Prospects-January-2017-Weak-investment-uncertain-times.pdf.
68. Based on figures from the International Monetary Fund's World Economic Outlook database, http://www.imf.org/external/pubs/ft/weo/2015/01/weodata/download.aspx.
69. David Pilling, "Africa: Between Hope and Despair," *Financial Times*, April 24, 2016, https://www.ft.com/content/4da8bd90-0894-11e6-b6d3-746f8e9cdd33.

70. Dino Mahtani, "The New Scramble for Africa's Resources," *Financial Times*, January 28, 2008, http://www.ft.com/cms/s/0/56dd8e0a-cd41-11dc-9b2b -000077b07658.html?ft_site=falcon&desktop=true#axzz4gR1 Er1 Af.

71. Carmody, *The New Scramble for Africa*, 97.

72. Yao Graham, "Minerals Dependence, Jobs and Transformation," presentation to International Trade Union Confederation/Third World Network Africa/ Review of African Political Economy Workshop on Employment, Structural Transformation and Economic Development, July 20, 2015, http://twnafrica .org/MINERALS%20 DEPENDENCE,%20 JOBS%20 AND% 20 TRANSFORMATION.pdf. Graham cites the World Bank's 1992 Strategy for African Mining as follows: "The recovery of the mining sector in Africa will require a shift in government objectives toward a primary objective of maximizing tax revenues from mining over the long term, rather than pursuing other economic or political objectives such as control of resources or enhancement of employment. This objective will be best achieved by a new policy emphasis whereby governments focus on industry regulation and promotion and private companies take the lead in operating, managing and owning mineral enterprises."

73. Alun Thomas and Juan P. Treviño, *IMF Working Paper: Resource Dependence and Fiscal Effort in Sub-Saharan Africa* (Washington, DC: International Monetary Fund, 2013, https://www.imf.org/external/pubs/ft/wp/2013/wp13188.pdf, 4.

74. Burgis, *The Looting Machine*, 112.

75. Michael Watts, "Nigeria and the Politics of Price," *The Mark,* January 25, 2012.

76. Tax Justice Network Africa, *Tax Us If You Can*, 7.

77. Graham, "Minerals Dependence, Jobs and Transformation."

78. Hicks, *Africa's New Oil*, 137. Figures cited are from 2014.

79. Ibid., 70.

80. Graham, "Minerals Dependence, Jobs and Transformation."

81. Ibid.

82. ExxonMobil press release, "ExxonMobil's Outlook for Energy Sees Global Increase in Future Demand," December 9, 2014, http://news.exxonmobil.com /press-release/exxonmobils-outlook-energy-sees-global-increase-future -demand.

83. Michael Watts, "Crude Politics: Life and Death on the Nigerian Oil Fields," *Niger Delta Economies of Violence,* Working Paper No. 18 (2009), http://geog.berkeley .edu/ProjectsResources/ND%20 Website/NigerDelta/WP/Watts_25.pdf.

84. Anthony Dipaola and Jonathan Ferro, "Eni Sees Biggest Mediterranean Gas Find Boosting Cash Flow," *Bloomberg,* August 31, 2015, http://www.bloomberg .com/news/articles/2015-08-31/eni-ceo-sees-biggest-mediterranean-gas-find -boosting-cash-flow.

85. Ghazvinian, *Untapped: The Scramble for Africa's Oil*, 11.

86. Carmody, *The New Scramble for Africa*, 18.

87. Ibid. 18, 28.

88. Pritchard, "The Mining Boom in Sub-Saharan Africa: Continuity, Change and Policy Implications," 261.

89. Deloitte, *The Deloitte Guide to Oil and Gas in East Africa: Uniquely Structured* (2014), 11.

90. Nicholas Shaxson, *Poisoned Wells: The Dirty Politics of African Oil* (New York and Basingstoke: Palgrave Macmillan, 2008).

91. Ibid.

92. Michael Watts, "Nigeria and the Politics of Price," *The Mark*, January 25, 2012.

93. Grieve Chelwa, "What Happened to 'Africa Rising'?" *Africa Is a Country*, March 20, 2016.

94. See the section about Agenda 2063 on the African Union website at https://au.int/en/agenda2063.

95. Graham, "Minerals Dependence, Jobs and Transformation."

96. Hicks, *Africa's New Oil*, 3.

97. Bassey, *To Cook a Continent*, 31.

98. Graham, "Minerals Dependence, Jobs and Transformation."

99. Ghazvinian, *Untapped: The Scramble for Africa's Oil*, 12.

100. Burgis, *The Looting Machine*, 129.

101. Ibid., 150.

102. Shaxson. *Poisoned Wells: The Dirty Politics of African Oil*. Elsewhere, Shaxson has indicated "a trend in actual events that has eroded the basis of arguments that imperialist oil companies are exploiting Africans: along with the rise of OPEC in the 1970s, the bigger oil producers in Africa (notably Nigeria and Angola) began wresting a greater share of revenue from the oil companies, and now these countries receive, on average, more than 50 per cent of the value of their oil as state revenue. Once costs—especially large in Angola's case, because of the number of expensive deep-water projects—are removed from the equation, that figure exceeds 80 per cent. Nobody in Angola's oil industry would dispute that today it is the Angolan state oil company Sonangol, not ExxonMobil or BP or Sinopec, that calls the shots." See "Oil, Corruption and the Resource Curse," *International Affairs* 83, no. 6 (2007): 1125.

103. Hicks, *Africa's New Oil*, 126.

104. Paul Burkhardt, "Africa Oil Boom Fades as $50 Crude Shuts Door on High-Cost Deals," *Bloomberg*, November 20, 2015, https://www.bloomberg.com/news/articles/2015-11-20/africa-oil-boom-fades-as-50-crude-shuts-door-on-high-cost-deals.

105. Obi, "Scrambling for Oil in West Africa," 206.

106. EY Mining & Metals. *Resource Nationalism Update*, October 2013, http://www.ey.com/Publication/vwLUAssets/EY-M-and-M-Resource-nationalism-update-October-2013/$FILE/EY-M-and-M-Resource-nationalism-update-October-2013.pdf.

107. *Economist*, "Wish You Were Mine," February 11, 2012, http://www.economist.com/node/21547285.

108. Ibid.

109. Obi, "Scrambling for Oil in West Africa," 202–203.

110. Sharife, "All Roads Lead Back to China."

111. Pritchard, "The Mining Boom in Sub-Saharan Africa: Continuity, Change and Policy Implications," 252.

112. Melber, "Global Trade Regimes and Multi-Polarity," 50.

113. Dominik Balthasar, *Oil in Somalia Adding Fuel to the Fire?* (Mogadishu: Heritage Institute for Policy Studies, 2014), http://www.heritageinstitute.org/wp-content/uploads/2014/06/HIPS-Oil_in_Somalia-ENGLISH.pdf , 10.

114. Emily Greenspan, "Free, Prior, and Informed Consent in Africa: An Emerging Standard for Extractive Industry Projects," *Oxfam America Research Backgrounder series* (2014), www.oxfamamerica.org/publications/fpic-in-africa, 6.

115. Ibid., 33.

116. I. Niang, O. C. Ruppel, M. A. Abdrabo, A. Essel, C. Lennard, J. Padgham, and P. Urquhart, "Africa," in *Climate Change 2014: Impacts, Adaptation, and Vulnerability. Part B: Regional Aspects. Contribution of Working Group II to the Fifth Assessment Report of the Intergovernmental Panel on Climate Change*, ed. V. R. Barros, C. B. Field, D. J. Dokken, M. D. Mastrandrea, K. J. Mach, T. E. Bilir, M. Chatterjee, K. L. Ebi, Y. O. Estrada, R. C. Genova, B. Girma, E. S. Kissel, A. N. Levy, S. MacCracken, P. R. Mastrandrea, and L. L. White (Cambridge and New York: Cambridge University Press, 2014), 1199-1265, https://www.ipcc.ch/pdf/assessment-report/ar5/wg2/WGIIAR5-Chap22_FINAL.pdf.

117. Bassey, *To Cook a Continent*, 42.

118. Hicks, *Africa's New Oil*, 167.

119. Ibid., 172–73.

120. Alice Klein, "Uganda's Fledgling Oil Industry Could Undermine Development Progress," *Guardian*, December 12, 2011, https://www.theguardian.com/global-development/2011/dec/12/uganda-oil-industry-threatens-development.

121. See Friends of Lake Turkana, https://www.facebook.com/FoLTurkana.

122. Hicks, *Africa's New Oil*, 187.

123. *Economist*, "The Chinese in Africa: Trying to Pull Together," April 20, 2011, http://www.economist.com/node/18586448.

124. Cited in Barry Bearak, "Zambia Uneasily Balances Chinese Investment and Workers' Resentment," *New York Times*, November 20, 2010, http://www.nytimes.com/2010/11/21/world/africa/21zambia.html.

125. Ibid.

126. Burgis, *The Looting Machine*, 30.

127. Ibid., 45.

128. Ibid., 53.

129. Bassey, *To Cook a Continent*, 73.

130. Burgis, *The Looting Machine*, 46.

131. Patrick Bond, "Is Africa Still Being Looted? World Bank Dodges Its Own Research."

132. Tax Justice Network Africa, *Tax Us If You Can*, 7.

133. *Reuters*, "Special Report: Areva and Niger's Uranium Fight," February 5, 2014, http://www.reuters.com/article/us-niger-areva-specialreport-idUSBREA140AA20140205.

134. Cited in Carmody, *The New Scramble for Africa*, 128.
135. Cited in Baher Kamal, "Climate: Africa's Human Existence Is at Severe Risk," *InterPress Service*, April 21, 2016, http://www.ipsnews.net/2016/04/climate -africas-human-existence-is-at-severe-risk/.
136. Ibid.
137. Burgis, *The Looting Machine*, 64.
138. Ukoha Ukiwo, "Empire of Commodities," in *Curse of the Black Gold: 50 Years of Oil in the Niger Delta*, photog. Ed Kashi; ed. Michael Watts (Brooklyn, NY: Powerhouse Books, 2010), 70.
139. G. Ugo Nwokeji in *Curse of the Black Gold: 50 Years of Oil in the Niger Delta*, ed. Ed Kashi and Michael Watts (Brooklyn, NY: Powerhouse Books, 2010), 63
140. Cited in Sonia Shah, *Crude: The Story of Oil* (New York: Seven Stories Press, 2004), 92.
141. Bruce Dixon, "Africa—Where the Next US Oil Wars Will Be," *Black Agenda Report* (2007), https://blackagendareport.com/content/africa-%E2%80%93 -where-next-us-oil-wars-will-be.
142. Bassey, *To Cook a Continent*, 2.
143. Ken Henshaw, "Ken Saro-Wiwa and the Power of Resistance," *Red Pepper* (2015), http://www.redpepper.org.uk/ken-saro-wiwa-and-the-power-of-resistance/.
144. Cited in Nnamdi Ikeagu, "Shell Pays for Oil Spill in Bodo," *Socialist Workers League* (Nigeria), May 20, 2015, http://socialistworkersleague.org/2015/05 /shell-pays-for-oil-spill-in-bodo/.
145. Amy Goodman and Jeremy Scahill, *Drilling and Killing: Chevron and Nigeria's Oil Dictatorship*, radio documentary (2003), https://www.democracynow .org/1998/9/30/drilling_and_killing_chevron_and_nigerias.
146. In *Curse of the Black Gold: 50 Years of Oil in the Niger Delta*, photog. Ed Kashi, ed. Michael Watts (Brooklyn, NY: Powerhouse Books, 2010), 90.
147. Sabella Ogbobode Abidde, "State and Politics: Nigeria's Policy Towards the Ijaw," *Pambazuka News* (2009), http://www.pambazuka.org/governance /state-and-politics-nigeria%E2%80%99s-policy-towards-ijaw.
148. Michael Watts, "Crude Politics: Life and Death on the Nigerian Oil Fields," *Niger Delta Economies of Violence*, Working Paper No. 18 (2009), http://geog.berkeley .edu/ProjectsResources/ND%20 Website/NigerDelta/WP/Watts_25.pdf.
149. Ike Okonta, "Nigeria—Danger Signs on Democracy Road," *Pambazuka News* (2007), http://www.pambazuka.org/governance/state-and-politics-nigeria %E2%80%99s-policy-towards-ijaw.
150. Nanga, "New Capitalist Domination and Imperialism in Africa."
151. Described by Sola Omole, Chevron's general manager of public affairs, in a statement given in Amy Goodman and Jeremy Scahill. *Drilling and Killing: Chevron and Nigeria's Oil Dictatorship*, radio documentary (2003), https://www .democracynow.org/1998/9/30/drilling_and_killing_chevron_and_nigerias. Environmentalist Oronto Douglas is quoted saying, "It is very clear that Chevron, just like Shell, uses the military to protect its oil activities. They drill and they kill."

152. Quoted in Goodman and Scahill. *Drilling and Killing: Chevron and Nigeria's Oil Dictatorship*. Ubani was tragically killed in a car accident in 2005 at the age of 43, along with Tunji Oyeleru. Baba Aye wrote in a moving tribute on the ten-year anniversary of his death: "Chima Ubani stood for the unity of organized labor and the civil society movement. . . . All his conscious life, Chima waged a struggle to change the system, playing leading roles in different ways, at different times. He was convinced that a better Nigeria, indeed a better world, is possible and can be won only through the working people's ceaseless struggle." The full statement is available at http://saharareporters.com/2015/09/22/chima-ubani-tunji-oyeleru-10-years-after-civil-society-and-quest-system-change.

153. Ike Okonta, "Behind the Mask: Explaining the Emergence of the MEND Militia in Nigeria's Oil-Bearing Niger Delta," *Niger Delta Economies of Violence Project*, Working Paper No. 11 (Berkeley: University of California–Berkeley 2006), http://geog.berkeley.edu/ProjectsResources/ND%20 Website/NigerDelta/WP/11-Okonta.pdf.

154. Anna Zalik and Michael Watts, "Imperial Oil: Petroleum Politics in the Nigerian Delta and the New Scramble for Africa," *Socialist Review* 305 (2006), http://socialistreview.org.uk/305/imperial-oil-petroleum-politics-nigerian-delta-and-new-scramble-africa.

155. Carmody, *The New Scramble for Africa*, 115.

156. Julian Lee, "Forget the Saudis, Nigeria's the Big Oil Worry," *Bloomberg* (2016), https://www.bloomberg.com/gadfly/articles/2016-05-15/nigeria-s-a-bigger-worry-for-oil-than-saudi-arabia.

157. Ukoha Ukiwo, "Empire of Commodities," in *Curse of the Black Gold: 50 Years of Oil in the Niger Delta*, photog. Ed Kashi, ed. Michael Watts (Brooklyn, NY: Powerhouse Books, 2010), 73.

158. Bassey, *To Cook a Continent*, 117.

159. Cf. Andy Wynne, "Mass Strikes in Nigeria: Is Austerity Taking Its Toll?" *Pambazuka News* (2017), https://www.pambazuka.org/taxonomy/term/9219.

160. Baba Aye, "War and Elections in Nigeria," *Socialist Worker*, March 26, 2015, http://socialistworker.org/2015/03/26/war-and-elections-nigeria.

161. Quoted in Goodman and Scahill, *Drilling and Killing: Chevron and Nigeria's Oil Dictatorship*.

162. Bruce Dixon, "Africa—Where the Next Us Oil Wars Will Be," *Black Agenda Report* (2007), https://blackagendareport.com/content/africa-%E2%80%93-where-next-us-oil-wars-will-be.

163. Secretary of State Hillary Rodham Clinton, "Remarks with Nigerian Foreign Minister Ojo Maduekwe" (2009), https://2009-2017.state.gov/secretary/20092013clinton/rm/2009a/08/127823.htm.

164. Bruce Dixon, "Africa—Where the Next Us Oil Wars Will Be," *Black Agenda Report* (2007), https://blackagendareport.com/content/africa-%E2%80%93-where-next-us-oil-wars-will-be.

165. Rodney, *How Europe Underdeveloped Africa*, 76.

Chapter Six

1. Cited in Steve Johnson, "African GDP Growth Sliding Towards 17-Year Low," *Financial Times*, April 7, 2016.

2. International Energy Agency, *World Energy Outlook 2015: Executive Summary* (Paris: International Energy Agency, 2015), https://www.iea.org/Textbase/npsum /WEO2015 SUM.pdf, 2.

3. Neil Gough, "As China's Growth Slows, Banks Feel the Strain of Bad Debt," *New York Times*, April 15, 2016, https://www.nytimes.com/2016/04/16 /business/dealbook/china-economy-bad-loans.html. For example, as noted in the report, "the Bank of Tianjin . . . said that nonperforming corporate loans— or loans that had gone sour—rose 46 percent between the end of 2014 and September of 2015, the most recent data available. It cited the Chinese economy and problems in the steel industry. . . . For China's banking system, the coming months are almost certain to bring more defaults, bankruptcies and other debt problems, according to economists."

4. Analysis by Dorian Bon, based on US Energy Information Administration figures; see https://www.eia.gov/tools/faqs/faq.cfm?id=32&t=6. During this period, US production rose from 1,954.2 million barrels in 2009 to 3,176.6 million barrels in 2014. With the absolute decrease in oil imports to the United States beginning in 2009, the proportion of total US imports drawn from particular countries has shifted. For example, the United States has increased oil imports from Canada, the country's largest foreign oil provider, even as total oil imports to the United States have dropped. In 2009, the United States imported 21 percent of its oil from Canada, while in 2014, it obtained 37 percent from this source. Likewise with Saudi Arabia: in 2009, Saudi oil accounted for 7.8 percent of US imports, while in 2014 this figure reached 12.6 percent. See https://www .eia.gov/dnav/pet/pet_crd_crpdn_adc_mbbl_a.htm.

5. Analysis by Dorian Bon, based on US Energy Information Administration figures; https://www.eia.gov/tools/faqs/faq.cfm?id=32&t=6.

6. Grieve Chelwa, "Nigeria's Economy Is Doing Like This. It's Blinking, Shaking," *Africa Is a Country*, April 18, 2016, http://africasacountry.com/2016/04/nigerias -economy-is-doing-like-this-its-blinking-shaking.

7. World Bank commodity prices, http://pubdocs.worldbank.org/en /790991501702837052/CMO-Pink-Sheet-August-2017.pdf. Accessed August 2, 2017.

8. Hadas Thier, *Peoples' Guide to Capitalism: An Introduction to Marxist Economics* (Chicago: Haymarket Books [forthcoming]).

9. Clifford Krauss, "Stock Prices Sink in a Rising Ocean of Oil," *New York Times*, January 15, 2016, https://www.nytimes.com/2016/01/16/business /energy-environment/oil-prices-one-million-barrel-glut.html.

10. Ibid.

11. Steve Johnson, "African GDP Growth Sliding Towards 17-Year Low."

12. Andrew England, "Reality Check in Africa as Boom Time Ends," *Financial Times*, October 5, 2015, https://www.ft.com/content/e81d0b70-5e2f-11e5-a28b -50226830d644.

13. Angelo Izama, "Year-Ender: Can Uganda Benefit from Low Oil Prices?" December 30, 2014, http://angeloizama.com/year-ender-can-uganda-benefit-from -low-oil-prices/.

14. Andrew England, "China Turbulence Casts Shadow on Africa," *Financial Times*, August 31, 2015, https://www.ft.com/content/40be88d6-4cc8-11e5-b558 -8a9722977189.

15. Ibid.

16. Analysis by Dorian Bon, based on US Energy Information Administration figures; see https://www.eia.gov/dnav/pet/pet_move_impcus_a2_nus_epc0 _im0_mbblpd_a.htm.

17. Javier Blas, "Victim of Shale Revolution, Nigeria Stops Exporting Oil to US," *Financial Times*, October 2, 2014, http://blogs.ft.com/beyond-brics/2014/10/02 /victim-of-shale-revolution-nigeria-stops-exporting-oil-to-us/.

18. Based on US Energy Information Administration historical data available at https://www.eia.gov/. By early 2017, US imports of Nigerian crude had recovered slightly, reaching 6.2 million barrels per month—still a dramatic fall from the peak a decade earlier.

19. Elaine Moore, "Oil Price Crash and Us Dollar Spike Cause Africa Pain," *Financial Times*, October 5, 2015, https://www.ft.com/content/e7d509ba-5e2f-11e5 -a28b-50226830d644.

20. David Pilling, "Africa Ties with China Are About More Than Raw Materials," *Financial Times*, October 5, 2015, https://www.ft.com/content/e6b692ec-5e2f -11e5-a28b-50226830d644.

21. Cited in ibid.

22. Rodney, *How Europe Underdeveloped Africa*, 82.

23. Ryan Olson, "Guest Post: Sub-Saharan Africa's Sovereign Wealth Funds Struggle in Era of Low Oil," *Financial Times*, February 24, 2015, http://blogs.ft.com /beyond-brics/2015/02/25/guest-post-sub-saharan-africas-sovereign-wealth -funds-struggle-in-era-of-low-oil.

24. Ibid.

25. Maggie Fick, "Nigeria Passes High-Spending Budget Despite Oil Price Woes," *Financial Times*, April 24, 2016, https://www.ft.com/content/15b7c63c-f10c -11e5-aff5-19b4e253664a.

26. England, "Angola Pledges Tighter Bank Regulation in Face of Dollar Drought."

27. Matina Stevis, "Angola to Seek IMF Aid to Cope with Looming Financial Crisis," *Wall Street Journal*, April 6, 2016, https://www.wsj.com/articles/angola -to-seek-imf-aid-to-cope-with-looming-financial-crisis-1459957868.

28. Matina Stevis, "IMF's African Push Reopens Old Wounds," *Wall Street Journal*, February 20, 2016, https://www.wsj.com/articles/imfs-african-push-reopens -old-wounds-1456050601.

29. Ibid.

30. Shawn Donnan, "World Bank Lending at Record Since Aftermath of Financial Crisis," *Financial Times*, April 10, 2016, https://www.ft.com/content/2fecc550-fed3-11e5-9cc4-27926f2b110c.

31. Cited in Shawn Donnan, "Oil: From Boom to Bailout," *Financial Times*, February 4, 2016, https://www.ft.com/content/7deea83e-ca78-11e5-be0b-b7ece4e953a0.

32. Stevis, "IMF's African Push Reopens Old Wounds."

33. Cited in Donnan, "Oil: From Boom to Bailout."

34. *Financial Times* Lexicon, http://lexicon.ft.com/Term?term=dutch-disease.

35. Burgis, *The Looting Machine*, 76.

36. Nicholas Shaxson, "Nigeria's Extractive Industries Transparency Initiative: Just a Glorious Audit? Chatham House report, November 2009, https://eiti.org/files/NEITI%20 Chatham%20house_0.pdf.

37. John Ghazvinian, *Untapped: The Scramble for Africa's Oil* (New York: Harcourt Books, 2007).

38. Nicholas Shaxson, *Poisoned Wells: The Dirty Politics of African Oil* (New York and Basingstoke: Palgrave Macmillan, 2008).

39. Celeste Hicks, *Africa's New Oil: Power, Pipelines and Future Fortunes* (London: Zed Books, 2015).

40. Southall and Comninos, "The Scramble for Africa and the Marginalisation of African Capital," 363.

41. Nicholas Shaxson, "Oil, Corruption and the Resource Curse," *International Affairs* 83, no. 6 (2007): 1125.

42. Burgis, *The Looting Machine*, 5.

43. Macartan Humphreys, Jeffrey D. Sachs, and Joseph E. Stiglitz, eds., *Escaping the Resource Curse* (New York, Columbia University Press, 2007), 10.

44. Humphreys, Sachs, Stiglitz, *Escaping the Resource Curse*, 4.

45. Carmody, *The New Scramble for Africa*, 95.

46. Humphreys, Sachs, Stiglitz, *Escaping the Resource Curse*, 14.

47. Paul Collier, *The Bottom Billion: Why the Poorest Countries Are Failing and What Can Be Done About It* (Oxford: Oxford University Press, 2008), 42-46.

48. Cited in Tax Justice Network Africa, *Tax Us If You Can*, 20.

49. Ibid., 18–19.

50. Carmody, *The New Scramble for Africa*, 24.

51. Shaxson, *Poisoned Wells*.

52. Michael Watts, "Crude Politics: Life and Death on the Nigerian Oil Fields," *Niger Delta Economies of Violence*, Working Paper No. 18, http://geog.berkeley.edu/ProjectsResources/ND%20 Website/NigerDelta/WP/Watts_25.pdf.

53. Michael Watts, "Oil, Development, and the Politics of the Bottom Billion," *Macalester International*, vol. 24 (Summer 2009).

54. Ibid.

55. Obi, "Scrambling for Oil in West Africa," 199.

56. Kairn A. Klieman, "US Oil Companies, the Nigerian Civil War, and the Origins of Opacity in the Nigerian Oil Industry, 1964–1971," *Journal of American History* 99 (2012): 155–65.

57. Bassey, *To Cook a Continent*, 12.
58. Simon Massey and Roy May, "Oil and War in Chad," in *A New Scramble for Africa?* ed. Southall and Melber, 222.
59. Ibid., 223.
60. Hicks, *Africa's New Oil* (London: Zed Books, 2015), 2.
61. Ibid., 20.
62. Anna Zalik and Michael Watts, "Imperial Oil: Petroleum Politics in the Nigerian Delta and the New Scramble for Africa," *Socialist Review* 305 (2006), http://socialistreview.org.uk/305/imperial-oil-petroleum-politics-nigerian -delta-and-new-scramble-africa.
63. Hicks, *Africa's New Oil*, 32.
64. Ibid.
65. Ibid., 17.
66. Ibid., 28.
67. Massey and May, "Oil and War in Chad," 225.
68. Ibid., 226.
69. Brendan Schwartz and Valéry Nodem, "A Humanitarian Disaster in the Making along the Chad-Cameroon Oil Pipeline—Who's Watching?" *AlterNet*, December 1, 2009, http://www.alternet.org/story/144303/a_humanitarian_disaster_in_ the_making_along_the_chad-cameroon_oil_pipeline_--_who%27s_watching.
70. Valéry Nodem, cited in *Africa Is a Country*, "An Interview with the Makers of 'Quel Souvenir,' A Film about an Oil Pipeline between Chad and Cameroon," February 23, 2012, http://africasacountry.com/2012/02/quelsouvenir.
71. Hicks, *Africa's New Oil*, 64.
72. Ibid., 35.
73. Ibid., 43.
74. Ibid., 61.
75. Ibid., 204, 207.
76. Nicholas Jackson, "A Failure but the Oil Keeps Flowing: The Chad-Cameroon Petroleum Development Project," *Pambazuka News* (2009), http://www. pambazuka.org/land-environment/failure-oil-keeps-flowing.
77. Patrick Bond, "Is Africa Still Being Looted? World Bank Dodges Its Own Research."
78. Human Rights Watch, https://www.hrw.org/news/2011/12/20/angola-explain -missing-government-funds.
79. Burgis, *The Looting Machine*, 19.
80. Magnus Taylor, "Paul Collier: Can Africa Harness Its Resources for Development?" *African Arguments* (2011), http://africanarguments.org/2011/11/01/paul -collier-can-africa-harness-its-resources-for-development.
81. Grieve Chelwa, "It's the Economy Stupid, N°2," *Africa Is a Country*, February 21, 2016, http://africasacountry.com/2016/02/its-the-economy-stupid-2.
82. Kairn A. Klieman, "US Oil Companies, the Nigerian Civil War, and the Origins of Opacity in the Nigerian Oil Industry, 1964–1971," *Journal of American History* 99 (2012): 155–65.

83. Shaxson, *Poisoned Wells.*

84. United Nations Economic Commission on Africa, *African Governance Report IV. Measuring Corruption in Africa: The International Dimension Matters* (2016), ix.

85. Ibid., 20.

86. Jeffrey D. Sachs, "Nigeria Hurtles into a Tense Crossroad," *New York Times,* January 10, 2012, http://www.nytimes.com/2012/01/11/opinion/nigeria -hurtles-into-a-tense-crossroad.html.

87. United Nations Economic Commission on Africa, *African Governance Report IV. Measuring Corruption in Africa: The International Dimension Matters,* 69.

88. Tax Justice Network Africa, *Tax Us If You Can,* 205.

89. Sharife, "All Roads Lead Back to China."

90. Charles Abugre, "Could Abolishing Tax Havens Solve Africa's Financing Needs?" *Pambazuka News,* Issue 579, March 29, 2012, https://www.pambazuka. org/governance/could-abolishing-tax-havens-solve-africas-financing-needs.

91. Tax Justice Network Africa, *Tax Us If You Can,* 41.

92. Ibid., 16–17.

93. Barack Obama, "Remarks by President Obama to the Kenyan People," speech, Nairobi, Kenya, July 26, 2015, https://www.whitehouse.gov/the-press-office /2015/07/26/remarks-president-obama-kenyan-people.

94. Carmody, *The New Scramble for Africa,* 79.

95. Ibid., 75–76.

96. *Financial Times,* "Chinese Model Is No Panacea for Africa," (2007), http://www .ft.com/cms/s/0/c1a221ca-b586-11db-a5a5-0000779e2340.html?ft_site =falcon&desktop=true#axzz4p1kooCIb.

97. *Financial Times,* "China: A New Force in Africa's Development" (2006), http:// www.ft.com/cms/s/0/6aac9124-a412-11da-83cc-0000779e2340.html?ft_site =falcon&desktop=true#axzz4p1kooCIb.

98. Andy Wynne, "Trying to Get Africa Right," review of *Africa: Why Economists Get It Wrong,* by Morten Jervis, *Socialist Worker,* November 11, 2015, https:// socialistworker.org/2015/11/11/trying-to-get-africa-right.

99. Ibid.

100. Tax Justice Network Africa, *Tax Us If You Can,* 8.

101. Burgis, *The Looting Machine,* 190.

102. Jason Hickel, "Saving Uganda from Its Oil," *Foreign Policy in Focus,* June 16, 2011, http://fpif.org/saving_uganda_from_its_oil/.

103. United Nations Economic Commission on Africa, *African Governance Report IV. Measuring Corruption in Africa,* 14.

104. Roger Southall and Henning Melber, "Conclusion: Towards a Response," in *A New Scramble for Africa?* ed. Southall and Melber, 411.

105. Grieve Chelwa, "Is Africa Really Rising? History and Facts Suggest It Isn't," *Africa Is a Country,* June 18, 2015, http://africasacountry.com/2015/06/is-afri-ca-really rising-history-and-facts-suggest-it-isnt/.

106. Grieve Chelwa, "It's the Economy Stupid, N°2," *Africa Is a Country,* February 21, 2016, http://africasacountry.com/2016/02/its-the-economy-stupid-2/.

107. Cf. Neelika Jayawardane, "Africa is Corrupt," *Africa Is a Country*, October 27, 2010, http://africasacountry.com/2010/10/africa-is-corrupt/.

108. Bassey, *To Cook a Continent*, 36.

109. Burgis, *The Looting Machine*, 163.

110. See Collier's charter at http://naturalresourcecharter.org/.

111. United Nations Economic Commission on Africa, *African Governance Report IV. Measuring Corruption in Africa: The International Dimension Matters* (2016), 10.

112. According to their website, "The Extractive Industries Transparency Initiative (EITI) is a global standard to promote the open and accountable management of oil, gas and mineral resources." Cf. www.eiti.org.

113. Humphreys, Sachs, Stiglitz, *Escaping the Resource Curse*, xiv.

114. Khadija Sharife, "'Transparency' Hides Zambia's Lost Billions," *Al Jazeera*, June 18, 2011, June 18, 2011, http://www.aljazeera.com/indepth/opinion/2011/06/20116188244589715.html.

115. Cited in Bassey, *To Cook a Continent*, 37.

116. Ibid., 39.

117. Jason Hickel, "Saving Uganda from Its Oil," *Foreign Policy in Focus,* June 16, 2011, http://fpif.org/saving_uganda_from_its_oil/.

118. Nicholas Shaxson, *Nigeria's Extractive Industries Transparency Initiative: Just a Glorious Audit?* (London: Chatham House, 2009), https://eiti.org/files/NEITI%20Chatham%20house_0.pdf.

119. Ibid.

120. Cf. Hicks, *Africa's New Oil*.

121. Khadija Sharife, "'Transparency' Hides Zambia's Lost Billions." Alternatively, she writes, a corporate country-by-country reporting method, created by Richard Murphy of the Tax Justice Network, would substantially improve the chances, over the EITI, of identifying corporate theft. However, given the major corporate support for schemes such as the EITI, the possibilities for implementing "transparency" reform are questionable.

122. Shaxson, *Poisoned Wells*.

123. Cited in Padraig Carmody, *The New Scramble for Africa*, 78.

124. Mark Taylor, "DRC: Conflict Minerals, Dodd-Frank and Due Diligence—Get on with It," *African Arguments*, September 2, 2011, http://africanarguments.org/2011/09/02/conflict-minerals-dodd-frank-and-due-diligence-get-on-with-it-by-mark-taylor/.

125. Burgis, *The Looting Machine*, 54.

126. Ibid., 58.

127. Ibid., 147.

128. United Nations Economic Commission on Africa, *African Governance Report IV. Measuring Corruption in Africa: The International Dimension Matters* (2016), 10–11.

129. Khadija Sharife and John Grobler, "Kimberley's Illicit Process," *World Policy Journal* (2013), http://www.worldpolicy.org/journal/winter2013/kimberleys-illicit-process.

130. Ibid.

131. Jolyon Ford, "The Kimberley Process and Diamond Demand," *African Arguments* (2011), http://africanarguments.org/2011/12/05/the-kimberley-process -and-diamond-demand-by-jolyon-ford-at-oxford-analytica/.

132. Patrick Bond, "Is Africa Still Being Looted? World Bank Dodges Its Own Research," *Links International Journal of Socialist Renewal* (2010), http://links.org.au /node/1843.

Chapter Seven

1. Secretary of State Hillary Rodham Clinton, "Remarks on Building Sustainable Partnerships in Africa," University of Cheikh Anta Diop, Dakar, Senegal, August 1, 2012, http://www.state.gov/secretary/20092013clinton /rm/2012/08/195944.htm.

2. Cited in Day and Gaido, *Discovering Imperialism,* 61.

3. Cited in ibid., 40–41.

4. Cited in ibid., 72.

5. Cited in ibid., 21.

6. V. I. Lenin, "Imperialism: The Highest Stage of Capitalism."

7. Not all critics of the United States's widening military presence in Africa have agreed that the United States and China are embroiled in an imperial struggle on the continent. Nick Turse, for example, leans toward an approach of "peaceful coexistence." See my review of Turse's *Tomorrow's Battlefield: US Proxy Wars and Secret Ops in Africa,* "The US War in Africa," *Socialist Worker,* August 11, 2015, https://socialistworker.org/2015/08/11/the-us-war-in-africa.

8. United States Department of Defense, *Sustaining US Global Leadership: Priorities for 21st Century Defense* (2012), http://archive.defense.gov/news/Defense _Strategic_Guidance.pdf, 4.

9. Paul D. Williams, "Enhancing US Support for Peace Operations in Africa," Council Special Report No. 73, Council on Foreign Relations (2015), 6.

10. Lance Selfa, "A New Colonial 'Age of Empire'"? *International Socialist Review* 23 (2002), http://www.isreview.org/issues/23/age_of_empire.shtml.

11. US Assistant Secretary of State Harlan Cleveland, "U.N. Operations in the Congo," *Hearings before Subcommittee on International Organizations and Movements,* House Committee on Foreign Affairs, April 13, 1961.

12. King stated that "the Congo civil war will not be resolved until all foreign elements are withdrawn. . . . [The Congo is reaping] the violent harvest of injustice, neglect and man's inhumanity to man across the years." Quoted in "Dr. King Proposes a Rights Alliance," *New York Times,* December 10, 1964, http:// www.nytimes.com/1964/12/10/dr-king-proposes-a-rights-alliange.html.

13. The United States also played an active role in support for the Portuguese government's repression of national liberation movements in its African colonies— Angola, Mozambique, and Guinea-Bissau. Under the fascist dictatorship of Portuguese prime minister António de Oliveira Salazar, the United States supplied Portugal with arms. One American eyewitness described how observers could, in

the early 1960s, observe "Portuguese planes bomb and strafe African villages, visit the charred remains of towns like Mbanza M'Pangu and M'Pangala, and copy the data from 750-point napalm casings from which the Portuguese had not removed the labels marked 'Property of US Air Force.'" Cited in Blum, *Killing Hope*, 250.

14. *Military Balance*, Issue 1 (1970): 47.

15. George Liska, *Imperial America: The International Politics of Primacy* (Baltimore: Johns Hopkins Press, 1967), 98.

16. Barry Cohen, "US Imperialism and Southern Africa," *Review of African Political Economy* 4, no. 9 (1977): 82–88.

17. William H. Mott, *United States Military Assistance: An Empirical Perspective* (Westport, CT: Greenwood Press, 2002), 267.

18. Cited in Vijay Prashad, "Bad Aid: Throw Your Arms around the World," *Pambazuka News* 476 (2010), http://www.pambazuka.org/human-security/bad -aid-throw-your-arms-around-world.

19. Blum, *Killing Hope*, 256.

20. David Barsamian, interview with Noam Chomsky, "War Crimes and Imperial Fantasies," *International Socialist Review* 37 (2004), http://www.isreview.org/issues /37/chomsky.shtml.

21. Harvey, *A Brief History of Neoliberalism*, 27.

22. Andrew J. Bacevich, *The Limits of Power: The End of American Exceptionalism* (New York: Henry Holt Books, 2008), 51. Cf. Lance Selfa, "Energy Imperialism," review of *The Limits of Power: The End of American Exceptionalism*, by Andrew J. Bacevich, and *Rising Powers, Shrinking Planet: The New Geopolitics of Energy*, by Michael Klare, *International Socialist Review* 62 (2008), http://isreview.org/issue/62 /energy-imperialism.

23. Charlie Kimber, "Interview: Mahmood Mamdani on Darfur," *Socialist Review* (2009), http://socialistreview.org.uk/337/interview-mahmood-mamdani-darfur.

24. Selfa, "A New Colonial 'Age of Empire.'"

25. Alex Gourevitch, "The Hutu's Willing Executioners?" *Lenin's Tomb* blog, August 13, 2009, http://www.leninology.co.uk/2009/08/.

26. Eric Schmitt, "US Is Considering a Base in Rwanda for Relief Teams," *New York Times*, July 28, 1994, http://www.nytimes.com/1994/07/28/world/us -is-considering-a-base-in-rwanda-for-relief-teams.html.

27. Ann Garrison, "Rwanda, the Enduring Lies: A Project Censored Interview with Professor Ed Herman," *San Francisco Bay View*, January 13, 2016, http://sfbayview .com/2016/01/rwanda-the-enduring-lies-a-project-censored-interview-with -professor-ed-herman/.

28. Matt Swagler, "The US Power Play in Africa," *Socialist Worker*, December 12, 2008, https://socialistworker.org/2008/12/12/us-power-play-in-africa.

29. Ashley Smith, "Humanitarian Imperialism and Its Apologists," *International Socialist Review* 67 (2009), http://isreview.org/issue/67/humanitarian-imperialism -and-its-apologists.

30. Mamdani, *Saviors and Survivors*, 45.

31. Ibid., 8.

32. Richard Seymour, "Sudan: A Young Imperialist's Guide to Darfur," *Third World Report* (Africa), 310 (2006).

33. Kimber, "Interview: Mahmood Mamdani on Darfur."

34. Avery Wear and David Whitehouse, "Save Darfur from US intervention," *International Socialist Review* 50 (2006), http://isreview.org/issues/50/Darfur.shtml.

35. *Associated Press*, "Obama: Countries Pledge 30,000-Plus Troops to UN Peace-Keeping in US Push to Modernize," September 28, 2015.

36. Zaya Yeebo, "Is the 'Global Coalition' Obstructing Africa's Progress?" *Pambazuka News* (2011), https://www.pambazuka.org/global-south/global-coalition-obstructing-africa%E2%80%99s-progress.

37. Tunde Zack-Williams, "Multilateral Intervention in Sierra Leone's Civil War. Some Structural Explanations," in *When the State Fails: Studies on Intervention in the Sierra Leone Civil War,* ed. Tunde Zack-Williams (London: Pluto Press, 2012), 14.

38. Ibid., 27.

39. Niels Hahn, "Celebrities and the Taylor Trial: Justice and False Consciousness," *Pambazuka News* (2010), https://www.pambazuka.org/governance/celebrities-and-taylor-trial-justice-and-false-consciousness.

40. Michael Kargbo, "International Peacebuilding in Sierra Leone: The Case of the United Kingdom," in *When the State Fails: Studies on Intervention in the Sierra Leone Civil War,* ed. Tunde Zack-Williams (London: Pluto Press, 2012), 87.

41. Jimmy D. Kandeh, "Intervention and Peacebuilding in Sierra Leone: A critical perspective," in *When the State Fails: Studies on Intervention in the Sierra Leone Civil War,* ed. Tunde Zack-Williams (London: Pluto Press, 2012), 112.

42. Mary Kaldor and James Vincent, *Evaluation of UN Assistance to Conflict-Affected Countries: Case study—Sierra Leone* (New York: United Nations Development Programme, 2006), 4, http://web.undp.org/evaluation/documents/thematic/conflict/SierraLeone.pdf.

43. Wear and Whitehouse, "Save Darfur from US Intervention."

44. Originally published as Lee Wengraf, "Making Somalia's Nightmare Worse: 'Operation Restore Hope,' 1992–1994," *International Socialist Review* 77 (2011), http://isreview.org/issue/77/making-somalias-nightmare-worse.

45. Cited in Mitchel Cohen, "Somalia and the Cynical Manipulation of Hunger," *Autonomedia,* January 7, 2002, http://dev.autonomedia.org/node/641.

46. Anna Simons, "Do We Know What We're Doing in Somalia?" *Africa News,* December 21, 1992–January 3, 1993, http://allafrica.com/stories/200101080503.html.

47. "'Buried in the Sands of the Ogaden': The Horn of Africa and SALT II, 1977–1979," Office of the Historian, US Department of State, https://history.state.gov/milestones/1977-1980/horn-of-africa.

48. Sophronia Scott Gregory, "How Somalia Crumbled: Clan Warfare and a Glut of Weapons Have Plunged the Country into Anarchy," *Time,* December 14, 1992, http://content.time.com/time/magazine/article/0,9171,977234,00.html.

49. Mark Fineman, "The Oil Stakes Factor in Somalia," *Los Angeles Times,* January 18, 1993, cited in Mitchel Cohen, "Somalia and the Cynical Manipulation of Hunger," *Autonomedia,* January 7, 2002, http://dev.autonomedia.org/node/641.

50. Rasna Warah, "Famine in Somalia," *Pambazuka News* (2011), http://www
.pambazuka.org/governance/famine-somalia.

51. Andy Pollack, "Somalia: Multi-National Capitalism's Latest Victim," *Modern
Times,* November 9, 1992, cited in Mitchel Cohen, "Somalia and the Cynical
Manipulation of Hunger," *Autonomedia,* January 7, 2002, http://dev.autonomedia
.org/node/641.

52. William D. Montalbano, "Food Output Fell in '91—Famine Threat Grows," *Los
Angeles Times,* December 21, 1991, http://articles.latimes.com/1991-12-21
/news/mn-610_1_food-security.

53. Laurence Binet, *Somalia 1991–1993: Civil War, Famine Alert and a UN "Military-
Humanitarian" Intervention* (Médicins San Frontières Speaking Out Report,
2013), http://www.speakingout.msf.org/en/somalia, 84.

54. Rakiya Omaar and Alex de Waal, "Somalia's Uninvited Saviors," *Washington Post,*
December 13, 1992, https://www.washingtonpost.com/archive/opinions
/1992/12/13/somalias-uninvited-saviors/260d715f-f4e6-4373-9108
-f0d66ebaa0c4/?utm_term=.021b3c711bd9.

55. Rakiya Omaar and Alex de Waal," Somalia: Saving Somalia without the Somalis," *Africa News,* December 21, 1992–January 3, 1993, http://allafrica.com
/stories/200101080506.html.

56. Stephen Zunes, "Somalia as a Military Target," *Foreign Policy in Focus,* January
11, 2002, http://fpif.org/somalia_as_a_military_target/.

57. Cited in Alex Cox, *Independent,* "Black Hawk Down: Shoot First, Don't Ask
Questions Afterwards," January 11, 2002, http://www.independent.co.uk/arts
-entertainment/films/features/black-hawk-down-shoot-first-dont-ask
-questions-afterwards-9204159.html.

58. Francis Elliott and Ruth Elkins, "UN Shame over Sex Scandal," *Independent,* January 7, 2007, http://www.independent.co.uk/news/world/politics/un-shame
-over-sex-scandal-431121.html; *CNN,* "Photos reveal Belgian paratroopers'
abuse in Somalia," April 17, 1997, http://edition.cnn.com/WORLD/9704/17
/belgium.somalia/.

59. Cohen, "Somalia and the Cynical Manipulation of Hunger."

60. Cited in Cohen, "Somalia and the Cynical Manipulation of Hunger."

61. Alex de Waal, "The UN's Brutal Peace Process," *Mail and Guardian,* November
7, 1997, https://mg.co.za/article/1997-11-07-the-uns-brutal-peace-process.

62. Lee Wengraf, "US Fingerprints on Somalia's Nightmare," *Socialist Worker,* February 9, 2009, https://socialistworker.org/2009/02/09/somalia-nightmare.

63. Nuruddin Farah, "Somalia Is No Hideout for Bin Laden," *New York Times,* January 9, 2002, http://www.nytimes.com/2002/01/09/opinion/somalia-is-no
-hideout-for-bin-laden.html.

64. Aarón Martel and Khury Petersen-Smith, original map (2017). Multiple
sources, including: AFRICOM official website: africom.mil; David Vine's Base
Nation website: basenation.us; Nick Turse: "Does Eleven Plus One Equal Sixty?
AFRICOM's New Math, the U.S. Base Bonanza, and 'Scarier' Times Ahead in

Africa," TomDispatch (2015): http://www.tomdispatch.com/blog/176070/tom-gram%3A_nick_turse%2C_america%27s_empire_of_african_bases

65. Pepe Escobar, "The US Power Grab in Africa, Oct. 21, 2011, " *Asia Times,* http://www.atimes.com/atimes/Global_Economy/MJ21 Dj03.html.

66. Cited in Brian Whitaker, "Fuelling the Status Quo," *Guardian,* April 5, 2004, https://www.theguardian.com/world/2004/apr/05/worlddispatch.oil.

67. See Institute for Advanced Strategic and Political Studies, "African Oil: A Priority for U.S. National Security and African Development," Washington, DC, May 2002.

68. Secretary of State Madeleine K. Albright, "Testimony before the Senate Foreign Relations Committee on Fiscal Year 2000 Budget," February 24, 1999, Washington, DC, as released by the Office of the Spokesman US Department of State.

69. Cited in Alex Kane, "America's Never-Ending War Intensifies in Africa: Will Blowback and Increased Violence Follow?" *AlterNet,* March 16, 2013, http://www.alternet.org/world/americas-never-ending-war-intensifies-africa-will-blowback-and-increased-violence-follow.

70. Sandra T. Barnes, "Global Flows: Terror, Oil and Strategic Philanthropy," *Review of African Political Economy* 32, no. 104/5 (2005): 235–52.

71. Paul D. Williams, "Enhancing US Support for Peace Operations in Africa," Council Special Report No. 73, Council on Foreign Relations (2015), 6.

72. Cited in Barnes, "Global Flows: Terror, Oil and Strategic Philanthropy," 235–52.

73. Giles Mohan and A. Zack-Williams, "Editorial: Imperialism in the Post-Cold War Era," *Review of African Political Economy* 22, no. 66 (1995): 481–84.

74. Nunu Kidane, "AFRICOM, Militarization, and Resource Control," *Pambazuka News* (2008).

75. Motsoko Pheko, "US Africa Command a Tool to Recolonise Continent," *Pambazuka News* (2011), https://www.pambazuka.org/resources/us-africa-command-tool-recolonise-continent.

76. Cited in Frida Berrigan, "The New Military Frontier: Africa," *Foreign Policy in Focus,* September 18, 2007, http://fpif.org/the_new_military_frontier_africa/.

77. John Pendergast and Colin Thomas-Jensen, "Blowing the Horn," *Foreign Affairs* (2007), https://www.foreignaffairs.com/articles/east-africa/2007-03-01/blowing-horn.

78. David Whitehouse, "Massacre in Somalia: Ethiopian Occupiers Carry out US Policy in the Horn of Africa," *International Socialist Review* 53 (2007), http://www.isreview.org/issues/53/somalia.shtml.

79. Pendergast and Thomas-Jensen, "Blowing the Horn."

80. Nick Dearden, "The War on Terror Hits Africa," *Counterpunch,* December 30, 2006, http://www.counterpunch.org/2006/12/30/the-war-on-terror-hits-africa/.

81. Pendergast and Thomas-Jensen, "Blowing the Horn."

82. Amnesty International, *Routinely Targeted: Attacks on Civilians in Somalia* (2008), https://www.amnesty.org/en/documents/AFR52/006/2008/en/, 1.

83. The list of companies operating in Africa at the time reads like a who's who of friends of the former Bush-Cheney administration, including Blackwater, DynCorp, KBR, and Barrick Gold; the last provided "intelligence" and security for operations in Congolese mines, playing a part in the bloody civil war of 1998–2003 with an estimated death toll of five million people. See *International Herald Tribune*, "US Hires Military Contractor to Support Peacekeeping Mission in Somalia," March 7, 2007.

84. Nicholas Kristof, "Aid Workers with Guns," *New York Times*, March 4, 2007, http://www.nytimes.com/2007/03/04/opinion/04kristof.html.

85. Cited in Edmund Berger, "Intervention Mentality and the Spectacle of Joseph Kony," *Dissident Voice*, April 14, 2012, http://dissidentvoice.org/2012/04/intervention-mentality-and-the-spectacle-of-joseph-kony/.

86. Turse, *Tomorrow's Battlefield*, 8.

87. Ibid., 12.

88. Daniel Volman, "Obama and US Military Engagement in Africa," *Pambazuka News* 478 (2010), http://www.pambazuka.org/governance/obama-and-us-military-engagement-africa.

89. Alex Kane, "America's Never-Ending War Intensifies in Africa: Will Blowback and Increased Violence Follow?" *AlterNet*, March 16, 2013, http://www.alternet.org/world/americas-never-ending-war-intensifies-africa-will-blowback-and-increased-violence-follow.

90. Cited in Spencer Ackerman, "Obama's New Defense Plan: Drones, Spec Ops and Cyber War," *Wired*, January 5, 2012, https://www.wired.com/2012/01/pentagon-asia-strategy/.

91. Max Lockie, "The US-Africa Relationship by the Numbers," *MSNBC*, September 13, 2013, http://www.msnbc.com/the-cycle/the-us-africa-relationship-the-numbers.

92. Mahmood Mamdani, "Somalia, Museveni and Militarising the Region," *Pambazuka News* 583 (2012), https://www.pambazuka.org/governance/somalia-museveni-and-militarising-region.

93. Angelo Zima, "The West's Man in Africa: Partner for Life," March 5, 2014, http://www.angeloizama.com/angelo-opi-aiya-izama/2014/03/04/the-wests-man-in-africa-partner-for-life.

94. David Whitehouse, "Where Did Kony Come From?" *Socialist Worker*, March 22, 2012, https://socialistworker.org/2012/03/22/where-did-kony-come.

95. Jason Russell of Invisible Children, who made the Kony 2012 video, was trained at a US military–sponsored information warfare center at the University of Southern California and has been affiliated with Liberty University, founded by Jerry Fallwell. The video's reliability was so dubious that even supporters of US foreign policy, such as the Council for Foreign Relations, said it was "manipulat[ing] facts for strategic purposes [and] exaggerating the scale of LRA abductions and murders." Cited in Horace Campbell, "Kony 2012: Militarization and Disinformation Blowback," *Pambazuka News*, March 22, 2012.

96. David Jackson, "Obama Dispatches 100 Troops to Africa," *USA TODAY* (2011), http://content.usatoday.com/communities/theoval/post/2011/10/obama-dispatches-100-troops-to-uganda/1#.WYm4tYjyvIV.

97. Steve Horn, "Has Obama Just Kicked Off Another Oil War—This Time in Africa?" *AlterNet*, November 8, 2011, http://www.alternet.org/story/152976/has_obama_just_kicked_off_another_oil_war_--_this_time_in_africa.

98. Antoine Roger, "The Congo Conundrum: Truth Catches up with Obama," *Pambazuka News* (2012), http://www.pambazuka.org/governance/congo-conundrum-truth-catches-obama.

99. Cf. Paul Mutter, "Great Game in the Horn of Africa," *Foreign Policy In Focus*, October 19, 2011, http://fpif.org/great_game_in_the_horn_of_africa/.

100. Peter Tatchell, "Uganda's Tyrant," *Guardian*, November 22, 2007, https://www.theguardian.com/commentisfree/2007/nov/22/ugandastyrant.

101. Pat Hutton and Jonathan Bloch, "Uganda: How the West Brought Idi Amin to Power," *Links International Journal of Socialist Renewal* (2012), http://links.org.au/node/2784.

102. Whitehouse, "Where Did Kony Come From?"

103. Matthew Kavanagh, "Why Kony 2012 Fails," *Foreign Policy in Focus*, March 20, 2012, http://fpif.org/why_kony_2012_fails/.

104. Gary K. Busch, "The United States and the Lord's Resistance Army," *Pambazuka News*, October 26, 2011, https://www.pambazuka.org/governance/united-states-and-lord%E2%80%99s-resistance-army.

105. Craig Whitlock and Thomas Gibbons-Neff, "US Troops Have Turned to Some Unsavory Partners to Help Find Warlord Joseph Kony," *Washington Post*, September 29, 2015, https://www.washingtonpost.com/world/national-security/us-military-opens-a-new-front-in-the-hunt-for-african-warlord-joseph-kony/2015/09/29/73ffef96-66a9-11e5-9223-70cb36460919_story.html?utm_term=.6530ca7cc822.

106. Human Rights Watch, "Central African Republic: LRA Attacks Escalate," April 20, 2012, https://www.hrw.org/news/2012/04/20/central-african-republic-lra-attacks-escalate. Horace Campbell has coined the term "humanitarian militarists" to describe such a posture by NGOs. See "Kony 2012: Militarization and Disinformation Blowback," *Pambazuka News*, March 22, 2012.

107. Turse, *Tomorrow's Battlefield*, 15. The contradictions between US military support for Ethiopia and the human rights abuses of the government were on public display during Obama's visit in July 2015, when Obama faced criticism for his silence regarding the blatant irregularities of the recently held parliamentary elections. See Alemayehu G. Mariam, "My Private Letter to President Obama," *Pambazuka News* (2015), https://www.pambazuka.org/global-south/my-private-letter-president-obama; Jacey Fortin, "Obama's Visit to Ethiopia Promises Little for Human Rights Activists," *New York Times*, July 26, 2015, https://www.nytimes.com/2015/07/27/world/africa/ethiopias-human-rights-activists-see-scant-hope-in-obamas-visit.html.

108. Antoine Roger Lokongo, "The Congo Conundrum: Truth Catches Up with Obama," *Pambazuka News* (2012), http://www.pambazuka.org/governance /congo-conundrum-truth-catches-obama.

109. David Axe, "Power Struggle Threatens Outsourced Somalia War," *Wired,* June 16, 2011, https://www.wired.com/2011/06/power-struggle-threatens-u-s-out-sourced-somalia-war/.

110. Jeremy Scahill, *Dirty Wars: The World Is a Battlefield* (New York: Nation Books, 2013). See Lee Wengraf, "War in the Shadows," review of *Dirty Wars*, by Jeremy Scahill, *International Socialist Review* 91 (2014), http://isreview.org/issue/91 /war-shadows.

111. Jeremy Scahill, "The CIA's Secret Sites in Somalia," *Nation*, December 10, 2014, https://www.thenation.com/article/cias-secret-sites-somalia/.

112. Craig Whitlock, "US Expands Secret Intelligence Operations in Africa," *Washington Post,* June 13, 2012, https://www.washingtonpost.com/world/nation-al-security/us-expands-secret-intelligence-operations-in-africa/2012/06/13/ gJQAHyvAbV_story.html?utm_term=.f7caaf9d725a.

113. Based on a March 2015 speech by AFRICOM head general David Rodriguez. Nick Turse, "The Numbers Racket: AFRICOM Clams up after Commander Peddles Contradictory Statements to Congress," *TomDispatch,* June 23, 2016, http://www.tomdispatch.com/blog/176156/tomgram%3 A_nick_turse%2 C _lies%2 C_damned_lies%2 C_and_statistics. . ._and_u.s._africa_command/. A fog of secrecy seems to surround AFRICOM's reporting of the number of operations, so assessing the scale of US military operations is challenging. Turse writes, for example: "A 2013 report by the Department of Defense's Inspector General on AFRICOM's Combined Joint Task Force–Horn of Africa found recordkeeping so abysmal that its officials 'did not have an effective system to manage or report community relations and low-cost activities.' A spreadsheet supposedly tracking such missions during 2012 and 2013 was, for example, so incomplete that 43 percent of such efforts went unmentioned. New definitions, poor recordkeeping, ineffective management, and incompetence aren't, however, the only possible explanations for the discrepancies. AFRICOM has a history of working to thwart efforts aimed at transparency and accountability and has long been criticized for its atmosphere of secrecy. Beyond spin, the highly selective release of information, the cherry-picking of reporters to cover a tiny fraction of its undertakings, and the issuing of news releases that tell a very limited story about the command, AFRICOM has taken steps to thwart press coverage of its footprint and missions."

114. Turse, *Tomorrow's Battlefield*, 40.

115. Ibid., 51.

116. Cited in Horace Campbell, "Is Obama Keen on Relations with Barons of Kenya or with the People?" *Pambazuka News* (2015), https://www.pambazuka.org /governance/obama-keen-relations-barons-kenya-or-people.

117. Turse, *Tomorrow's Battlefield*, 37.

118. Freedom C. Onuoha, "Piracy and Maritime Security in the Gulf of Guinea," *Al Jazeera*, June 12, 2012, http://studies.aljazeera.net/en/reports/2012 /06/2012612123210113333.html.
119. Turse, *Tomorrow's Battlefield*, 165.
120. Cited in ibid., 182.
121. Nick Turse, *Next Time They'll Come to Count the Dead: War and Survival in South Sudan* (Chicago: Haymarket Books, 2016), 34.
122. Lee Wengraf, "Obama's War in Africa," *Socialist Worker*, November 6, 2012, https://socialistworker.org/2012/11/06/obamas-war-in-africa.
123. David Whitehouse, "Africa's New Country," *Socialist Worker*, January 26, 2011, https://socialistworker.org/2011/01/26/new country-in-africa.
124. Lee Wengraf, "What's Behind the Violence in South Sudan?" *Socialist Worker*, January 6, 2014, https://socialistworker.org/2014/01/06/violence-in-south-sudan.
125. Stratfor, "In South Sudan, Tribal Frictions Persist," December 17, 2013, https://www.stratfor.com/analysis/south-sudan-tribal-frictions-persist.
126. Paul Jay, Real News Network, "Sudan's Bashir Threatens War against South Sudan: Interview with Nii Akuetteh," *Pambazuka News* (2012), http://www .pambazuka.org/human-security/sudans-bashir-threatens-war-against-south -sudan.
127. Reported by Médicins Sans Frontières, cited in *BBC*, "South Sudan Fighting continues ahead of Ethiopia Talks," January 2, 2014, http://www.bbc.com/news /world-africa-25573882.
128. Cited in Daniel Howden, "South Sudan: The State That Fell Apart in a Week," *Guardian*, December 23, 2013, https://www.theguardian.com/world/2013 /dec/23/south-sudan-state-that-fell-apart-in-a-week.
129. Turse, *Next Time They'll Come to Count the Dead*, 6.
130. Turse, *Tomorrow's Battlefield*, 184.
131. Laurence H. Shoup, "'Dangerous Circumstances': The Council on Foreign Relations Proposes a New Grand Strategy towards China," *Monthly Review* 67, no. 4 (2015), https://monthlyreview.org/2015/09/01/dangerous-circumstances/.
132. Office of the Secretary of Defense, *Annual Report to Congress*, ii.
133. Ibid., 66.
134. Cited in "The China Syndrome," *Economist*, June 9, 2012, http://www.economist .com/node/21556587.
135. Jane Perlez and Chris Buckley, "China Retools Its Military with a First Overseas Outpost in Djibouti," *New York Times*, November 26, 2015, https://www. nytimes.com/2015/11/27/world/asia/china-military-presence-djibouti -africa.html.
136. Ibid.
137. Francis Njubi Nesbitt, "America vs. China in Africa," *Foreign Policy in Focus*, December 1, 2011, http://fpif.org/america_vs_china_in_africa/.
138. Quoted in Turse, *Tomorrow's Battlefield*, 124.
139. International Crisis Group, "East Africa: Horn of Africa States Follow Gulf into the Yemen War," January 25, 2016, http://allafrica.com/stories/201601252174.html.

140. Cited in Kristina Wong, "China's Military Makes Move into Africa," *The Hill*, November 24, 2015, http://thehill.com/policy/defense/261153-chinas-military -makes-move-into-africa.

141. Daniel Volman, "Obama and US Military Engagement in Africa," *Pambazuka News* 478 (2010), http://www.pambazuka.org/governance/obama-and-us -military-engagement-africa.

142. Paul D. Williams, "Enhancing US Support for Peace Operations in Africa," Council Special Report No. 73, Council on Foreign Relations (2015), 17.

143. This excerpt originally published as Lee Wengraf, "Sending Soldiers to Save Lives?" *Socialist Worker*, October 2, 2014, https://socialistworker.org/2014/10/02 /sending-soldiers-to-save-lives.

144. Oriaifo E. Peter, "Obama Reveals Military Plan for Ebola Outbreak in Liberia," *Today's Nigeria*, September 16, 2014. At the time Obama delivered those words, the US Senate appropriations and health committees convened hearings on the crisis. Tennessee Senator Lamar Alexander marked the occasion by drama- tically comparing the dangers of the Ebola epidemic to that of Islamic extrem- ists, declaring: "We must take the deadly, dangerous threat of Ebola as seriously as we take ISIS. This is an instance where we should be running toward the burning flames with our fireproof suits on." Maggie Fox, "'A Global Threat': Obama Reveals Plan for Ebola Outbreak," *NBC News*, September 16, 2014, http://www.nbcnews.com/storyline/ebola-virus-outbreak/global-threat -obama-reveals-plan-ebola-outbreak-n204731.

145. Drew Hinshaw, Shirley Wang, and John W. Miller, "WHO Declares Ebola Virus Outbreak Public Health Emergency," *Wall Street Journal*, August 8, 2014, http://online.wsj.com/articles/ebola-virus-outbreak-is-public-health-emergency -worldhealth-organization-says-1407481875.

146. UN News Centre, "UN Announces Mission to Combat Ebola, Declares Out- break 'Threat to Peace and Security,'" September 18, 2014, http://www.un.org/ apps/news/story.asp?NewsID=48746#.V6 CECrgrLIU.

147. World Health Organization, "WHO Director-General Addresses UN Security Council on Ebola," September 18, 2014, http://www.who.int/dg/speeches /2014/security-council-ebola/en/.

148. WHO Ebola Response Team, "Ebola Virus Disease in West Africa—the First 9 Months of the Epidemic and Forward Projections," *New England Journal of Medicine* 371: 1481–1495.

149. World Health Organization, "Ebola Data and Statistics," http://apps.who.int/ gho/data/view.ebola-sitrep.ebola-summary-latest?lang=en.

150. Jeggan Grey-Johnson, "The Ebola Crisis Is More Than a Health Issue: It's about Governance," *Pambazuka News* (2014), http://www.pambazuka.org/food-health /ebola-crisis-more-health-issue-it%E2%80%99s-about-governance.

151. Donald G. McNeil Jr., "Nigeria's Actions Seem to Contain Ebola Outbreak," *New York Times*, September 30, 2014, https://www.nytimes.com /2014/10/01/health/ebola-outbreak-in-nigeria-appears-to-be-over.html.

152. Yohannes Woldemariam, "Musings on the Ebola Epidemic," *Pambazuka News*, September 4, 2014, https://www.pambazuka.org/food-health/musings-ebola -epidemic.

153. Lawrence Gostin, "Tackling the Ebola Epidemic," *JAMA Forum*, August 19, 2014.

154. Monica Mark, "Ebola Outbreak 'Moving Faster Than Efforts to Control It,' Says WHO Chief," *Guardian*, August 1, 2014, https://www.theguardian.com/society /2014/aug/01/ebola-outbreak-world-health-organisation-chief.

155. *Democracy Now!* "Dr. Paul Farmer on African Ebola Outbreak: Growing Inequality in Global Healthcare at Root of Crisis," August 22, 2014, https://www .democracynow.org/2014/8/22/dr_paul_farmer_on_african_ebola.

156. Rebekah Ward and Dora Curry, "An Epidemic Aided by Poverty," *Socialist Worker*, August 20, 2014, https://socialistworker.org/2014/08/20/epidemic-aided -by-poverty.

157. *Chicago Tribune*, "Obama: US Must Fight Ebola Now or Face Long-Term Risk," September 6, 2014, http://www.chicagotribune.com/news/nationworld /81293182-157.html.

158. Lena H. Sun and Juliet Eilperin, "US Military Will Lead $750 Million Fight against Ebola in West Africa," *Washington Post*, September 16, 2014, https:// www.washingtonpost.com/national/health-science/us-military-to-lead-ebola -fight/2014/09/15/69db3da0-3d32-11e4-b0ea-8141703bbf6f_story.html.

159. Joeva Rock, "Militarizing the Ebola Crisis," *Foreign Policy in Focus*, September 24, 2014, http://fpif.org/militarizing-ebola-crisis/.

160. Lawrence Gostin, "Tackling the Ebola Epidemic," August 19, 2014.

161. David Greene and Nurith Aizenman, "Liberia Blocks off Neighborhood in Ebola Quarantine, Sparking Riot," *NPR* (2014), http://www.npr.org/sections /goatsandsoda/2014/08/20/341883610/liberia-blocks-off-neighborhood-in -ebola-quarantine-sparking-riot.

162. Sun and Eilperin, "US Military Will Lead $750 Million Fight against Ebola in West Africa."

163. Donna Miles, "Africom Helps African Partners Prepare for Disaster Response," *American Forces Press Service*, December 18, 2013, http://archive.defense.gov /news/newsarticle.aspx?id=121363.

164. Narcisse Jean Alcide Nana, "Demilitarizing Epidemic Diseases in Africa," *Pambazuka News* (2014), https://www.pambazuka.org/governance/demilitarizing -epidemic-diseases-africa.

165. David Whitehouse, "The French plan for Mali," *Socialist Worker*, February 7, 2013, https://socialistworker.org/2013/02/07/the-french-plan-for-mali.

166. Cf. Ezekiel Pajibo and Emira Woods, "AFRICOM: Wrong for Liberia, Disastrous for Africa," *Foreign Policy in Focus*, July 26, 2007, http://fpif.org/africom_ wrong_for_liberia_disastrous_for_africa/.

167. Jean Nanga, "The Marginalization of Sub-Saharan Africa," *International Viewpoint*, December 18, 2003, http://www.internationalviewpoint.org/spip.php? article115.

168. Cf. Munyaradzi Gwisai, "Behind Mugabe's Landslide: Statement on Behalf of the International Socialist Organization–Zimbabwe," *Socialist Worker*, August 14, 2013, https://socialistworker.org/2013/08/14/behind-mugabes-landslide.

169. Real News Network, "Is the African Union a Western Front for Civil War in Burundi? Interview with Glen Ford," December 24, 2015, http://therealnews .com/t2/index.php?option=com_content&task=view&id=31&Itemid=74 &jumival=15342.

170. Bruce Dixon, "Africa—Where the Next Us Oil Wars Will Be," *Black Agenda Report*, February 28, 2007, https://blackagendareport.com/content/africa -%E2%80%93-where-next-us-oil-wars-will-be.

Chapter Eight

1.   Cited in Bond, *Looting Africa*, 76.

2.   Cf. Zeilig, *Class Struggle and Resistance in Africa*.

3.   Dwyer and Zeilig, *African Struggles Today*, 54.

4.   Ibid., 31.

5.   Seddon, "Historical Overview of Struggle in Africa."

6.   Göran Olsson's 2014 film *Concerning Violence*, based on Fanon's essay of the same name, elaborates on some of these themes, with a particular focus on the anticolonial struggles of the Portuguese colonies.

7.   Peter Dwyer, "South Africa under the ANC: Still Bound to the Chains of Exploitation," in *Class Struggle and Resistance in Africa*, ed. Zeilig.

8.   Ibid., 193.

9.   Peter Dwyer and Leo Zeilig, "Conclusion: 'Shinga Mushandi Shinga! Qina Msebenzi Qina!'" in *Class Struggle and Resistance in Africa*, ed. Zeilig, 262.

10. Firoze Manji and Sokari Ekine, eds., *African Awakening: The Emerging Revolutions* (Cape Town, Dakar, Nairobi, and Oxford: Pambazuka Press/Fahamu Books, 2011).

11. *Democracy Now!* "Tuareg Rebels in Mali Declare Independence: Part of an African Awakening for Self-Determination?" April 9, 2012, https://www.democracynow .org/2012/4/9/tuareg_rebels_in_mali_declare_independence.

12. Human Rights Watch, "'You'll Be Fired If You Refuse': Labor Abuses in Zambia's Chinese State-Owned Copper Mines" (2011), https://www.hrw.org /report/2011/11/04/youll-be-fired-if-you-refuse/labor-abuses-zambias -chinese-state-owned-copper-mines.

13. Patrick Bond, Ashwin Desai, and Trevor Ngwane, "'Uneven and Combined Marxism' within South Africa's Urban Social Movements," *Links International Journal of Socialist Renewal* (2012), http://links.org.au/node/2757.

14. Davis, *Planet of Slums*.

15. Dwyer and Zeilig, *African Struggles Today*, 48.

16. Leo Zeilig and Claire Ceruti, "Slums, Resistance and the African Working Class," *International Socialism* 117 (2007), http://isj.org.uk/slums-resistance-and -the-african-working-class/.

17. Baba Aye, "Combatting Precarious Work in the Nigerian Oil and Gas Industry: 'Nupengassan' and the Struggle for Transition from Informality to Formal Employment and Labour Relations" (Unpublished manuscript: n.d.).

18. Leon Trotsky, *The Permanent Revolution*, Marxists' Internet Archive, 1929, https://www.marxists.org/archive/trotsky/1931/tpr/prre.htm.

19. Ibid.

20. Paul D'Amato, "The Necessity of Permanent Revolution," *International Socialist Review* 48 (2006), http://www.isreview.org/issues/48/permrev-damato.shtml.

21. Neil Davidson, "From Deflected Permanent Revolution to the Law of Uneven and Combined Development," *International Socialism* 128 (2010), http://isj.org.uk/from-deflected-permanent-revolution-to-the-law-of uneven and-combined -development/.

22. Neil Davidson, "What Do We Mean by . . . Uneven and Combined Development?" *Revolutionary Socialism in the 21st Century* website, February 25, 2014, https://rs21.org.uk/2014/02/25/what-do-we-mean-by-uneven-and-combined -development/.

23. Davidson, "From Deflected Permanent Revolution to the Law of Uneven and Combined Development."

24. Geoff Bailey, "Revolution through the Ages," review of *We Cannot Escape History: Nations, States and Revolutions*," by Neil Davidson, *International Socialist Review* 100 (2016), http://isreview.org/issue/100/revolution-through-ages.

25. Paul Le Blanc, "Open Marxism and the Dilemmas of Coherence: Paul Le Blanc's Reflections on the Contributions of Michael Löwy," *Links International Journal of Socialist Renewal* (2013), http://links.org.au/node/3549.

26. Leon Trotsky, *Results and Prospects*, Marxists' Internet Archive, 1906, https://www.marxists.org/archive/trotsky/1931/tpr/rp-index.htm.

27. Author interview, Baba Aye, February 1, 2016.

28. Andy Wynne, author communication, January 5, 2017.

29. Author interview, Baba Aye, February 1, 2016.

30. Baba Aye, "Combatting Precarious Work in the Nigerian Oil and Gas Industry: 'Nupengassan' and the Struggle for Transition from Informality to Formal Employment and Labour Relations" (Unpublished manuscript: n.d.).

31. Andy Wynne, "Mass strikes in Nigeria: Is Austerity Taking Its Toll?" *Pambazuka News* (2017), https://www.pambazuka.org/taxonomy/term/9219.

32. Baba Aye, "Revolution and Counterrevolution in Burkina Faso," *Review of African Political Economy* (2015), http://roape.net/2015/11/25/revolution-and -counterrevolution-in-burkina-faso-lessons-problems-and-prospects-for -sub-saharan-africa/.

33. Leo Zeilig, "Burkina Faso's Second Uprising," *Review of African Political Economy* (2016), http://roape.net/2016/06/07/burkina-fasos-second-uprising-2015 -military-coup/.

34. Aye, "Revolution and Counterrevolution in Burkina Faso."

35. Amy Goodman, "New Waves of Resistance—An Interview with Irvin Jim," public forum, New York, NY, June 14, 2016.

36. Ibid.
37. Irvin Jim, "NUMSA Statement: United Front to Be Official Launched Early in 2016," January 1, 2016, http://www.politicsweb.co.za/politics/united-front-to-be-official-launched-early in-2016.
38. Excerpted from Aaron Amaral and Lee Wengraf, "The Marikana Massacre and the Contradictions of South Africa's 'Nonracial' Capitalism, Interview with Rehad Desai and Jim Nichol," *International Socialist Review* 101 (2016), http://isreview.org/issue/101/marikana-massacre-and-contradictions-south-africas-nonracial-capitalism.
39. Cf. Eric Ruder, "Massacre at a South African Mine," *Socialist Worker*, August 21, 2012, https://socialistworker.org/2012/08/21/massacre-at-a-south-african-mine.
40. Alanna Petroff, "Anglo-American to Shed 85,000 Jobs," *CNN Money*, December 8, 2015, http://money.cnn.com/2015/12/08/news/companies/anglo-american-85000-jobs/index.html?sr=fbmoney120815anglo-american-85000-jobs1247 PMStoryLink&linkId=19404471.
41. Simon Allison, "South African Students Score Tuition Fee Protest Victory," *Guardian*, October 23, 2015, https://www.theguardian.com/world/2015/oct/23/south-african-students-protest-pretoria-tuition-fees-rise.
42. The film's website is http://www.minersshotdown.co.za/.
43. Former ANC political prisoner, provincial premier, and government minister.
44. Former ANC political prisoner, member of parliament, and head of one of the largest national parastatals.
45. Mining magnate, known as "the Prince of Mines."
46. Julius Malema, former head of the ANC Youth League who became leader of the Economic Freedom Fighters, a left-populist political party.
47. Cf. Dwyer and Zeilig, *African Struggles Today*, 75–80.
48. Ibid., 50–91.
49. Patrick Bond, "Austerity Gathers Pace in Schizophrenic South Africa," *Counterpunch*, March 4, 2016, http://www.counterpunch.org/2016/03/04/austerity-gathers-pace-in-schizophrenic-south-africa/.
50. Interview with Anabela Lemos, conducted, edited, and condensed by Simone Adler, "Mozambique's Movement to End Land Grabs," *Other Worlds*, March 1, 2016, http://otherworldsarepossible.org/mozambiques-movement-end-land-grabs.
51. Burgis, "Ethiopia: The Billionaire's Farm."
52. Kwei Quartey, "Occupy Nigeria," *Foreign Policy in Focus*, January 19, 2012, http://fpif.org/occupy_nigeria/.
53. Kunle Wizeman Ajayi, "Class Matters in Nigeria's Elections," *Socialist Worker*, March 25, 2015, https://socialistworker.org/2015/03/25/class-matters-in-nigerias-election.
54. Landless People's Movement Press Statement, "The Attack on the Landless People's Movement Continues," June 4, 2010, http://abahlali.org/node/6964/.

55. Trevor Ngwane, "South Africa in 2010: A History That Must Happen," *Pamba-zuka News* (2010), https://www.pambazuka.org/governance/south-africa-2010 -history-must-happen.

56. Eddie Madunagu, *Problems of Socialism: The Nigerian Challenge* (London: Zed Books, 1982), 34.

57. Baba Aye, "Change and the Left in Nigeria: Problems and Prospects for the Labor Movement," *Socialist Workers' League*, August 31, 2015, http:// socialistworkersleague.org/2015/08/change-and-the-left-in-nigeria-problems -and-prospects-for-the-labour-movement/.

58. "Press Release: NUMSA Backs Students Demands for Free Education," October 21, 2015, http://www.numsa.org.za/article/numsa-backs-students-demands -for-free-education/.

59. Azwell Banda, "Foreword," in *Class Struggle and Resistance in Africa,* ed. Zeilig, xiv–xv.

60. Michael T. Klare, "Climate Change as Genocide: Inaction Equals Annihilation," *TomDispatch*, April 20, 2017, http://www.tomdispatch.com/post/176269 /tomgram%3 A_michael_klare%2 C_do_african_famines_presage_global _climate-change_catastrophe/#more.

Index

About Haymarket Books

Haymarket Books is a radical, independent, nonprofit book publisher based in Chicago.

Our mission is to publish books that contribute to struggles for social and economic justice. We strive to make our books a vibrant and organic part of social movements and the education and development of a critical, engaged, international left.

We take inspiration and courage from our namesakes, the Haymarket martyrs, who gave their lives fighting for a better world. Their 1886 struggle for the eight-hour day—which gave us May Day, the international workers' holiday—reminds workers around the world that ordinary people can organize and struggle for their own liberation. These struggles continue today across the globe—struggles against oppression, exploitation, poverty, and war.

Since our founding in 2001, Haymarket Books has published more than five hundred titles. Radically independent, we seek to drive a wedge into the risk-averse world of corporate book publishing. Our authors include Noam Chomsky, Arundhati Roy, Rebecca Solnit, Angela Y. Davis, Howard Zinn, Amy Goodman, Wallace Shawn, Mike Davis, Winona LaDuke, Ilan Pappé, Richard Wolff, Dave Zirin, Keeanga-Yamahtta Taylor, Nick Turse, Dahr Jamail, David Barsamian, Elizabeth Laird, Amira Hass, Mark Steel, Avi Lewis, Naomi Klein, and Neil Davidson. We are also the trade publishers of the acclaimed Historical Materialism Book Series and of Dispatch Books.

Also Available from Haymarket Books

African Struggles Today: Social Movements Since Independence
Peter Dwyer and Leo Zeilig

Apartheid Israel: The Politics of an Analogy
Edited by Sean Jacobs and Jon Soske, Foreword by Achille Mbembe

BRICS: An Anticapitalist Critique
Edited by Patrick Bond and Ana Garcia

Concerning Violence: Fanon, Film, and Liberation in Africa,
Selected Takes 1965–1987
Edited by Göran Olsson and Sophie Vukovic
Introduction by Gayatri Chakravorty Spivak

Next Time They'll Come to Count the Dead
War and Survival in South Sudan
Nick Turse

Poetry and Protest: A Dennis Brutus Reader
Edited by Lee Sustar

Reading Revolution: Shakespeare on Robben Island
Ashwin Desai

Tomorrow's Battlefield: US Proxy Wars and Secret Ops in Africa
Nick Turse

Urban Revolt: State Power and the Rise of People's Movements
in the Global South
Edited by Trevor Ngwane, Luke Sinwell, and Immanuel Ness

Voices of Liberation: Frantz Fanon
Leo Zeilig, Introduction by Mireille Fanon-Mendes France

About the Author

Photo by M. A. Bazante

Lee Wengraf is a writer and activist in New York City. Her articles have appeared in the *International Socialist Review, Socialist Worker, Review of African Political Economy, Pambazuka News, AllAfrica, Jacobin, Truthout, Green Left Weekly,* and the *Indypendent.*